RAIMON PANIKKAR

Opera Omnia (Vol. 1)

Mysticism and Spirituality

Part 2

Spirituality, The Way of Life

I left Europe (for India) as a Christian, Idiscovered I was a Hindu and returned as a Budhhist, without ever having ceased to be Christian.

RAIMON PANIKKAR

RAIMON PANIKKAR

Opera Omnia

(18 Books in 12 Volumes)

Edited by

MILENA CARRARA PAVAN

ISBN : 978-81-208-4225-0

1. Mysticism and Spirituality

1.1 : Mysticism, Fullness of Life

1.2 : Spiritualiy, the Way of Life

2. Religion and Religions

3. Christianity

3.1 : The Religion

3.2 : A Christophany

4. Hinduism

4.1 : The Vedic Experience : Mantramanjari

4.2 : The Dharma of India

5. Buddhism

6. Cultures and Religions in Dialogue

6.1 : Pluralism and Interculurality

6.2 : Interculural and Interreligious Dialogue

7. Hinduism and Christianity

8. Trinitatian and Cosmotheandric Vision

9. Mystery and Hermeneutics

9.1 : Myth, Symbol, and Ritual

9.2 : Faith, Hemencutics, and Word

10. Philosophy and Theology

10.1 : The Rhythm of Being

10.2 : Philosophical and Theological Throught

11. Sacred Secularity

12. Space, Time, and Science

RAIMON PANIKKAR

Opera Omnia (Vol. 1)

Mysticism and Spirituality

Part 2

Spirituality, The Way of Life

Edited by
MILENA CARRARA PAVAN

Forewords by
KAPILA VATSYAYAN
DR. KARAN SINGH

Motilal Banarsidass Publications

MOTILAL BANARSIDASS
PUBLICATIONS
4741/23, Ansari Road, Daryaganj, New Delhi - 110002 (India)
Email: *mlbd@mlbd.com* | *sales@mlbd.com* | *exports@mlbd.com*
Website: *www.mlbd.com*

Mysticism and Spirituality
Spirituality, TheWay of Life
by
Raimon Panikkar

First Indian Edition Published in 2023

Published in India by Motilal Banarsidass Publications

ISBN : 978-81-95055-32-6 (HB)
ISBN : 978-81-208-4225-0 (Set)

FOR SALE IN INDIA ONLY

Printed and bound in India

Series Foreword

All the writings it is my privilege and responsibility to present in this series are not the fruit of mere speculation but, rather, autobiographical— that is, they were first inspired by a life and praxis that have been only subsequently molded into writing.

This *Opera Omnia* ranges over a span of some seventy years, during which I dedicated myself to exploring further the meaning of a more justified and fulfilled human lifetime. I did not live for the sake of writing , but I wrote to live in a more conscious way so as to help my fellows with thoughts not only from my own mind but also springing from a superior Source, which may perhaps be called Spirit— although I do not claim that my writings are in any way inspired. However, I do not believe that we are isolated monads, but that each of us is a microcosm that mirrors and impacts the macrocosm of reality as a whole—as most cultures believed when they spoke of the Body of Âiva, the communion of the saints, the Mystical Body, *karman*, and so forth.

The decision to publish this collection of my writings has been somewhat trying, and more than once I have had to overcome the temptation to abandon the attempt, the reason being that, though I fully subscribe to the Latin saying *scripta manent*, I also firmly believe that what actually matters in the final analysis is to live out Life, as witnessed by the great masters who, as Thomas Aquinas remarks in the *Summa* about Pythagoras and Socrates (but not about Buddha, of whom he could not have known), did not write a single word.

In the twilight of life I found myself in a dark forest, for the straight path had been lost and I had shed all my certainties. It is undoubtedly to the merit of Sante Bagnoli, and of his publishing house Jaca Book, that I owe the initiative of bringing out this *Opera Omnia*, and all my gratitude goes to him. This work includes practically all that has appeared in book form, although some chapters have been inserted into different volumes as befitted their topics. Numerous articles have been added to present a more complete picture of my way of thinking , but occasional pieces and almost all my interviews have been left out.

I would like to make some practical comments which apply to all the volumes:

1. In quoting references, I have preferred to cite my previously published works following the general scheme of my publications.

2. Subject matter rather than chronolog y has been considered in the selection, and thus the style may sometimes appear uneven.
3. Even if each of these works aspires to be a self-sufficient whole, some ideas recur because they are functional to understanding the text, although the avoidance of unnecessary duplication has led to a number of omissions.
4. The publisher's preference for the *Opera Omnia* to be put into an organic whole by the author while still alive has many obvious positive features. Should the author outlive the printer's run, however, he will be hard put to help himself from introducing alterations, revisions, or merely adding to his original written works.

I thank my various translators, who have rendered the various languages I have happened to write in into the spirit of multiculturalism—which I believe is ever relevant in a world where cultures encounter each other in mutual enrichment, provided they do not mislay their specificity. I am particularly grateful to Milena Carrara Pavan, to whom I have entrusted the publication of all my written works, which she knows deeply, having been at my side in dedication and sensitivity during the last twenty years of my life.

R.P.

Dr. KARAN SINGH

3, NYAYA MARG
CHANAKYAPURI
NEW DELHI-110 021

Raimon Panikkar was one of the outstanding scholars of the 20th century. His work on Hindu texts, particularly his remarkable rendering of the Rig Veda in Mantramanjari stand as a monument to his scholarship. Equally at ease in Hinduism and Christianity, Panikkar was one of those rare scholars who was a bridge between the Indic and Abrahamic religion. He was a vibrant personality with whom I had many creative conversations on Hinduism and comparative religion.

Karan Singh
Dec. 20, 2018

TEL. : (011) 2611-5291, 2611-1744, FAX (91-11) 2687-3171, 2462-7102
Email : karansingh@karanshingh.com

Foreword

I am happy to respond to the request of Dr Milena Carrara Pavan, President, Fundacio Vivarium Raimon Panikkar, Tavertet Spain, to write a Foreword to the Opera Omnia, the Collected Works, of the great scholar and an extraordinary human being. Raimon Panikkar. It was a privilege to know Panikkar for many decades. The publication marks the centenary year of his birth.

The *Opera Omnia* ranges over a span of some seventy years of Raimon Panikkar's exploration and includes practically all that has appeared in book form. His reach is incomparable. The titles of the twelve volumes, being published in India by Motilal Banarsidas Publishers and mentioned below, make more explicit his depth and the razor-sharp intellect.

Mysticism and Spirituality
Religion and Religions
Christianity
Hinduism
Buddhism
Cultures and Religions in Dialogue
Hinduism and Christianity
Trinitarian and Cosmotheandric Vision
Mystery and Hermeneutics
Philosophy and Theology
Sacred Secularity
Space, Time and Science

It is no accident that Panikkar wanted to begin the publication of his *Opera Omnia* with the volume on *Mysticism and Spirituality, Fullness of Life*. He wrote:

"Actually, whenever I had an intuition I almost always started to write a new hook, or at least an article, with the aim of cheeking, clarifying, deepening and eventually formulating my experiences — although I then gave them a philosophical slant, which I believe is an indispensable form of expression".

He added:

> "I cannot recall when frst had the experience of advaita – which, together with the trinitarian experience, is perhaps my fundamental experience. They certainly go back to when I was very young, however, perhaps long before I had heard the name of advaita". (Raimon Panikkar and Milena Carrara, *A Pilgrimage to Kailash*, MLBD 2018, pp. 116 - 117.)

Each of Panikkar's writings can be considered a step of his long pilgrimage on earth, a physical step in time and space in human history, and a philosophical-spiritual step, by considering philosophy not as the 'love of knowledge' but as the 'knowledge of love,' and being aware – to use the last words of his philosophical testament. *The Rhythm of Being* – that more important than the tree of knowledge is the tree of Life.

To achieve fullness of life Panikkar always considered indispensable for him to be in dialogue with religions and cultures, expressions of man in his inexhaustible search for that harmony, which unites the earthly and the heavenly.

Simone Weil, in *Letter to a Priest*, sets as one of the conditions for embracing the Church the possibility of adopting without reserve the conviction that "Every time a man has, with a pure heart, called upon Osiris, Dionysius, Krishna, Buddha, the Tao, etc., the Son of God has answered him by sending the Holy Spirit".

This list of overlapping names and cultures seems to have been truly incarnated in the life and writings of Raimon Panikkar. With his heart set on a conversation between Hinduism. Buddhism and Christianity, the child of which would inherit the spiritual genetics of all the three while adding something new, he projected on the outer world, representing frst and foremost a complex interior knot, a personal challenge, as we can see more clearly in his diaries.

Once Panikkar said:

> "A book is a drop in the ocean of public opinion, a true prayer [is] a glass, but a book that is the fruit of contemplation can be a wholesome rain". What about the 12 volumes of his Opera Omnia? I will say, not the *wholesome* rain of one day but of a rich season and we are so grateful to him for them.

Panikkar consistently and all alone pursued a path of rigorous thinking, articulating a vision for the future of humanity. He covered all major issues of philosophy and theology, all areas of human life and has something to say that is prophetic and makes us think in a creative way. He was blessed with an inter-cultural and inter-religious background coupled with an intense commitment to academic pursuits, which brought together his whole life experience and bore fruit in his writings.

* * * *

On personal note, as I glanced through the contents of some of the volumes, my memory understandably made me travel through several decades of my friendship and communication with Raimon Panikkar. I had seen him as a researcher and scholar in the Banaras Hindu University where his sharp intellect was interacting with others. I had met him in conferences in India, Europe and the USA. Also. I visited him in his home in Travertet, Spam where he had fnally settled.

I shall never forget my walk with him in Travertet over the cliff with tin deep gorge below. This was to be my last meeting with him, As we walked in silence, there was communication beyond words. In Travertet he had set up his Vivarium Foundation, and devised an ecumenical gathering like a satsang with incense sticks burning, where people came and he read out to them ranging from Bible, Upanishads, and from the texts of all religions. I recall his having once said: "I left Europe (for India) as a Christian. I discovered I was a Hindu and returned as a Buddhist, without ever having ceased to be a Christian".

I also recall the three or four occasions where I was a listener - participant to his presentations and his mode of communication. I refer to his participation in two conferences on the 'Concepts of Space' and 'Concepts of Time' (organized by the Indira Gandhi National Centre for the Arts in Delhi in 1987/1990). In the frst conference on Space, his assertion that "there is no Outer without Inner Space" brought back the primacy of human consciousness. In the seminar on 'Concepts of Time', which had the privilege of having the presence of His Holiness the Dalai Lama, he said to the audience: "the experience of time is intrinsically connected with the awareness of life and of reality. It is pervious to any epistemological split between subject and object... and there is no possible phenomenology of time because its awareness cannot be encompassed in one single act of consciousness. Consciousness itself is temporal.... But Reality is not exhausted in time alone. And we moderns can only with diffculty accept a non-dualistic relation with an inseparable and yet distinct dimension of reality: Time and Timelessness".

I would like to recount two other occasions, one in Europe and one in India. 1 had gone to Switzerland to attend an international conference on the Dialogue of Religions under the auspices of Global Dialogue, where the Participants included Raimon Panikkar and Grevel Lindop, a renowned English poet. There was the opportunity of taking a trip with them on a ropeway. As we ascended, our conversation transcended the earthly to reach the spiritual. We shared the experience, yet we were making our own individual journeys. Panikkar refected on life. The going up and coming down was for him the levels of life in its ascension and descent. For Lindop it was poetry and painting. For me I was re-living the experience of the mountains, of the Himalayas.

I remember my visit with Raimon Panikkar, a Roman catholic priest, and Father Andrei Scrima, of the Greek Orthodox Church, to Paramacharya Sankaracharya, a most revered Hindu seer of the Kanchi Mutt, in the outskirts of Chennai in South India. It was like a reversal of roles, with the Paramacharya, sitting on a hay stack, giving a discourse on matters of philosophy and religions, to these two, seemed like his disciples, looking up and listening to the master. All the borders of religion and faith melted in a moment and just dissolved.

I might add here that the India International Centre organized an international conference in 2013 on Raimon Panikkar, participated by his contemporaries and some of his disciples and pupils, beside Madame Milena Carrara Pavan. The resultant publication, which I co-edited with Professor Côme Carpentier de Gourdon, was appropriately titled 'Raimundo Panikkar – A Pilgrim Across Worlds'.

The present generation and the future generations will be grateful to Dr. Milena Carrara Pavan and the Fundacio Vivarium Raimon Panikkar and the Motilal Banarsidas Publishers, for making available the writings of a most extraordinary human being of the twentieth century. Raimon Panikkar does not claim to be a reformer nor is he an iconoclast. He does not see any one side, regarding others as adversaries. He builds on the foundations of the past and nuances the traditional concepts and reinterprets them in the light of the contemporary situation he faces. He is a bridge-builder between cultures and religions.

KAPILA VATSYAYAN
Life Trustee and Past President, India International Centre,
and *Chairperson,* IIC-International Research Division.
Formerly: Secretary, Department of Culture, Government of India,
Academic Director, Indira Gandhi National Centre for the Arts,
Member of Parliament,
and Member, UNESCO Executive Board.

June 21, 2018

Contents

Part Two: The Christian Spiritual Journey

SECTION II: THE PATH OF THE MONK

Part One: Blessed Simplicity: The Challenge of Being a Monk

SECTION III: THE DWELLING PLACE OF WISDOM

Abbreviations

Hindū Scriptures

AB	*Aitareya-brāhmaṇa*
AV	*Atharva-veda*
BG	*Bhagavad-gītā*
BU	*Bṛhadāra ṇyaka-upaniṣad*
CU	*Chādogya-upaniṣad*
IsU	*Īśa-upaniṣad*
JabU	*Jābala-upaniṣad*
KaivU	*Kaivalya-upaniṣad*
KathU	*Kaṭha-upaniṣad*
KausU	*Kauṣitaki-upaniṣad*
KenU	*Kena-upaniṣad*
MahanarU	*Mānārāyaṇa-upaniṣad*
MaitU	*Maitrī-upaniṣad*
MandU	*Māṇḍūkja-upaniṣad*
Manu	*Mānava-dharmaśāstra*
MundU	*Muṇḍaka-upaniṣad*
PaingU	*Paiṅgala-upaniṣad*
RV	*Ṛg-veda*
SB	*Śatapatha-brāhmaṇa*
SU	*Śvetāśvatara-upaniṣad*
TB	*Taittirīya-brāhmaṇa*
TMB	*Tā ṇḍya-mahā-brāhmaṇa*
TU	*Taittirīya-upaniṣad*

Christian Scriptures

Ac	Acts
1 Co	First Letter to the Corinthians
2 Co	Second Letter to the Corinthians

1 Jn	First Letter of St. John
Col	Colossians
Dan	Daniel
Dt	Deuteronomy
Ex	Exodus
Gal	Galatians
Gn	Genesis
Heb	Letter to the Hebrews
Jas	James
Jb	Job
Jn	John
Lk	Luke
Mk	Mark
Mt	Matthew
Nb	Numbers
2 Pet	2 Peter
Pr	Proverbs
Ps	Psalms
Qo	Qohelet
Rev	Revelation
Rom	Letter to the Romans
Si	Sirach
Ws	Wisdom

Others

BC	Biblia catalana
BJ	Bible de Jérusalem
KJ	King James Version
Knox	Knox Bible
NácarColunga	Nácar-Colunga Bible
NEB	New English Bible
NRSV	New Revised Standard Version
PG	J.-P. Migne, *Patrologiae Cursus Completus*. Series Graeca, Paris, 1857–1866
PL	J.-P. Migne, *Patrologiae Cursus Completus*. Series Latina, Paris, 1844–1855
RV	Revised Version

Introduction

The first volume of this *Opera Omnia* has been divided into two books, one dedicated to *mysticism*, intended as the supreme experience of reality, and the second dedicated to *spirituality*, intended as the path toward such an experience. There are different paths, because they depend not only on tradition and worship but also on the different sensitivities of human beings and historical periods.

What kind of spirituality is appropriate to our times?

It is already a paradox to try to define what the spirituality for our times should be: the solution cannot be found in the answer, but in the question itself, that is, in the very formulation of the question and in feeling the need for this spirituality, although giving an answer is not possible. I will, however, present an outline, and I will begin by saying that this spirituality has to be integral: it must involve Man in his totality. Obviously we must then ask, "Who is Man?" and turn to anthropology for direction. Moreover, we must follow a discipline. . . . We must strive to achieve this spirituality as a whole without neglecting—as it often happens—the corporeal aspect.

The weakness (though mixed with much greatness) of the modern Western world derives from the second principle of the Cartesian method: "If you want to solve a problem, start by dissecting it," after which, however, the same thing happens as with the watchmaker's apprentice: when he puts the watch back together, some pieces are left over.

The fragmentation of reality is the weak point of Western culture.

When we say "Man" we think "individual"; to be more precise, we talk about the "body" and the "soul." Or, specifying even further, we talk of psychosomatics and we say that man is a set of *body*, *soul*, and *spirit*.

Avoiding esoterism, I will limit myself to a description of Man based on four words taken from the Greek tradition, of which the West and Christianity are heirs. Usually, we stop at the first two words, thus risking to fragment and alienate Man right from the start.

Man is the reality expressed by these four Greek words: *sôma—psychê—polis—kosmos*.

Man is (and not only "has") *sôma*: body. The body is not merely a support for the soul, as if it were a horse on which the soul rides when it is on earth. Man is body, so essentially so that, if there is no body, there is no Man; consequently, all bodily values belong to the essence of Man. Any spirituality making abstraction of the human body, undervaluing it or relegating it as secondary, would be lame. The body is a constitutive element of Man, integrating all the others. It would be interesting here to deal with the *śarira* of Indic* tradition; the gross body, the subtle and astral bodies, and so forth, and we could add all that gnostic and Sanskrit erudition has said on the subject. We know that the body is not just a set of proteins; it is something much more complex, more profound. There are different bodies. . . . Anyway, Man is *sôma*, body.

Man is also *psychê*: soul. He is thought, imagination, fantasy, will—that is to say, all that can be included in this very rich Greek word, *psychê*, that means "soul aware of itself."

Man is also *polis*: a word that can be translated as "tribe." Man is not an individual: he is society. The (lethal!) dichotomy between individuality and collectivity has been at the root of all kinds of tensions. It is a mistake to dialectically contrast the individual and society, liberalism and socialism. I think that this clash is the result of a defective anthropology, because Man is not an abstraction. Man is also tribe (polis), people, citizen, collectivity, society, church. . . . Man is family. There is no man who is not a son or daughter, or who is not part of a relationship (citizen, etc.). If we remove all the relationships that constitute Man, Man disappears. An anthropology that considers only the proteins, the nervous system, the conscious or unconscious psyche . . . , the personal attitudes, the right to property—that is, all that individualistic philosophy affirms—is a one-dimensional anthropology, and therefore incomplete.

The moment we enter into a relationship with others, if at the same time we are not this relationship, it means that we have alienated ourselves. Take, for example, the Gospel quotation, "Love your neighbor as yourself." This sentence is often interpreted almost as the opposite of what it means. It is in fact read as, "Love your neighbor as another self who has the same rights and duties as you, to whom you cannot deny a due demonstration of love, respect, and consideration." What those words actually mean is, however, "Love your neighbor as your self, as part of your being ," the "you" who is not "another," but your-self, your own "you."

---

* "Indic" refers to the culture of the Southeast Asiatic Subcontinent, as distinct from "Indian," which refers to India as a modern nation.

Man is not only tribe, society, community . . . but also *kosmos*: universe, world. That means that Man is not only the tribe of humans more or less separated from the rest: from animals, things, the earth, the planets; Man as "lord and master of nature," as Descartes calls him; as the king , the one using everything to his own advantage . . . to consider him only in this respect would prove, once again, an incomplete anthropology.

Man *is* world, and does not merely *have* (possess) the world. We are finally realizing that the earth reacts badly to human progress and the exploitation to which it has been subjected for centuries. Meanwhile, we carry on as before, but with a few precautions

. . . (rather like capitalism with the workers' trade unions). Now the earth also has its trade union! We have lost the awareness that the earth is not "the other," but is also a constitutive part of *Man*, who, as such, is also cosmos, earth. . . . Just as Man does not exist without a body, so Man cannot exist without *kosmos*.

The earth is often exploited as though Man could claim absolute rights over it, as though it belonged to him and he could do whatever he wanted with it. Yet we will pay dearly the consequences which can spring from such an attitude.

Man therefore *is* also earth, world, and *kosmos*.

How do we explain the fact that God (*theos*) does not appear in our discussions about Man? This is so because—deplorably—we have often made a caricature of the divine. The concept of transcendence without the intrinsic corrective of immanence is both unthinkable and contradictory, and therefore false. We should avoid linking Man to "another" reality (in this case, divine transcendence) and, afterward, place them in relation to each other. The reason being that the divine element is *immanent* as well as *transcendent*. Divine immanence signifies that the divine is found in the *sôma*, in the *psychê*, in the *polis*, and in the *kosmos*. And it is precisely this mysterious element, this inspiration, this transcendent and immanent presence that confers an identity on things, as well as on Man.

Therefore, it is not necessary to take God as a reference point in order to define Man, because for Man the divine is not "another" thing. Generally we say that there are animals, angels, the earth, men, plants, machines . . . and "(a) God." It is not like that! God is not other, *another*, no matter how great we can imagine Him. God is transcendent as well as immanent. The Divine can be found in the very *quaternitas* of the elements that define Man.

Even if we do not talk about God explicitly, that does not mean we have left Him aside. For example, if I say that God is the end of Man, there is a danger that, in defending theocentrism, we might convert God into a

"Supreme Being" and thus transform Him—without needing to cite Pascal—into the most insidious form of idolatry.

Before taking up the argument, we must keep in mind the following points:

1. I do not believe that *spirituality* should concentrate itself solely on the values of the spirit, separate from the rest of Man.

Neither do I believe in a *spirituality* that completely estranges Man from the world, as though this were the indispensable condition to attain human fullness (the a-cosmic ascetic).

Spirituality is like a "navigation chart" for the sea of Man's life: the sum total of the principles directing his dynamism toward "God," as some say, or toward a just society or overcoming suffering , as others say. We can, therefore, speak of Buddhist spirituality, even though Buddhists do not talk about God; or of Marxist spirituality, although Marxists are allergic to religious language. Such a conceptual broadness of the word "spirituality" expresses rather a quality of life, of action, of thought, and so on, that is not bound to any particular doctrine, confession, or religion, even though religious assumptions were easy to detect.

If I use the word "spirituality" it is because I cannot find another word that can embrace such diverse paths, whether they be related to the grace of God, to human effort, to the dynamism of history, to the destiny of creation, and so forth.

I would like to use the word "spirituality" in a way that makes it valid for all the different paths that lead Man to his destiny. While the word "religion" has been monopolized by some religions, the word "spirituality" has been to a certain extent protected from historical subordinations and rigid doctrines, even though it expresses different visions of reality and uses different languages.

2. We cannot remain in the world of abstraction, although I have always tried to work out a concept of Man that could be acceptable to all human traditions; this is why I have never used a language limited to any particular spirituality.

We are, undoubtedly, "fragmented" and we realize, especially in the West, that we find ourselves in a blind alley, and that we must find a way out. Depression is increasingly common, and joy increasingly rare; we are suffering an identity crisis.

I foresee *two ways* of getting out of this predicament.

The first one: to return to our roots and traditions, and listen to the message left by our mystical tradition. Without these roots, aimless superficiality will take over, leading nowhere. There is a great need for interiority, meditation, and stillness.

Many Westerners, dissatisfied with their own religion, go to the East, led by a sincere desire for spirituality, but often their involvement in a different spirituality remains superficial.

You cannot change your religion as casually as you change your clothes. These people have not yet appreciated their own ancestral traditions, yet they already want to embrace Eastern ones.

We must take up the path marked out by our ancestors. The West will not find its soul by forsaking , as rebellious teenagers do, twenty-five centuries of tradition.

The second way takes into account that in the West other religions have left their mark, and that the traditional path is no longer considered the only one.

Moreover, we should not forget, considering the present situation of humanity, that *no* religion, *no* civilization, *no* culture has sufficient strength or is able to give a satisfactory answer to Man: they all need each other.

From now on, we cannot expect the solution for the *whole* of humankind to come from a single source. We must benefit from what comes from the East, but most of all, we must strive for *cross-fertilization* of the various human traditions. They are all needed in order to face the present situation. We all are led toward the same destiny.

Then what should the spirituality for our time be?

There are no recipes or directives. I repeat that spirituality should be integral and cannot neglect any aspect of reality. Everything must be "purified by fire," everything must be transformed; it is the *apokatastasis* that St. Peter talks about (2 Pet 3:11). It is important to achieve a synthesis between interiority and exteriority. This will manifest the immediate and practical consequences of what was said earlier, that transcendence must not be separated from immanence.

Let us go back to the four elements I referred to above.

The four elements belong to my nature, to my reality; and the one of them not more than the other. I am not body more than soul, than people, than world. *Everything is a totality*. Recovering awareness of this unity is essential. Such *recovery*, or *new conquest*, cannot be effected by mere addition, nor can it be an optional choice, but must spring from a new awareness, in which I realize what I am, with all that I am. Then the inner life will stop being in dialectical opposition with the outer. This is expressed very well in a passage from the *Gospel of Thomas*: "The kingdom will come when the two are made one, when the inner is like the outer and the outer like the inner, and the upper like the lower, [. . .] then will you enter [the kingdom]."

Both things need to be done together. The effort that is required is symbolized by the *Incarnation*, in which the problems of the earth cannot be separated from the problems of heaven, since through the Incarnation the gap has been bridged.

The very fact of speaking of "a spirituality for our times" could be an obstacle, because it *cannot* be *a single* spirituality, as we said above, since sensibilities are different. In line with diverse traditions, however, what is needed is the "purification of the heart." In this lies the new innocence. The mystery of life is that evil exists, that tensions cannot be suppressed, that we must do what is possible, without being dominated by them and without ever believing that we have the absolute truth. We must accept the human condition, and understand that a certain form of doubt is not incompatible with faith; and that a sense of contingency is necessary in our lives. We must discover the meaning of life in its joys, its sorrows, and its passions. Instead of complaining about the hardships of life, and postponing the moment of *profound enjoyment* of life to some future time that will never come, we must find this meaning in *every moment*.

The book starts with two booklets in which some lines of argument, developed in the context of Christian religious retreats, were spelled out in the plain language of everyday speech.

The second section deals with a spirituality practised by monks, although not confined to institutional monasticism, but seen rather as a universal archetype to be found in every human being (the search for monos, union with the Divine). There follows a description of the ascetic tradition in India and, as an example of the encounter of western (Christian) spirituality with Indic spirituality, an article dedicated to my friend Henri Le Saux, who is an example of the fertile encounter between the two traditions.

The last section is dedicated to wisdom as the goal of a positive spirituality.

SECTION I

The Path of Faith

Part I

Icons of Mystery

Prologue

One needs a great deal of boldness, ingenuity, and innocence to publish a book today on the "experience of God," even without any notes. It grew out of a week of conferences that I gave a few years ago on this theme for the religion teachers at the Benedictine monastery of Silos. Since the audience was basically composed of Christians, the atmosphere of these pages and its language is Christian, although comprehensible, I believe, to those who do not belong to that religion.

When we try to speak of our supreme experience, the very word "God" is a biased one, although we cannot avoid employing one word or another. I hasten to note, moreover, that in spite of its ambiguity, the experience of God is an "impossibility." There is no possible experience of God, at least in the monotheistic sense of the word. We have too often imprisoned God—the academic expression would be "we have tried to comprehend Him"—within our contingency and our condition as creatures.

Neither is there an experience of God (subjective genitive) *in se*. There cannot be a genitive in God, for that would add nothing to what He is. Even the verb "to be" is inappropriate.

Nevertheless, the phrase keeps recurring in tradition. It has served as a conven- tional reference to designate the ultimate, the infinite, the mysterious, the unknown, the unseizable. But, once again, words only work in relationship to the code of a conventional myth. The issue is hence a paradox, a paradox we anyway preserve, since the only language possible in this case is the paradoxical and "oxymoric" language.[1] Thus both the

1 Here I will make a unique exception to the decision not to include notes in this book, in order to recall the meaning of the word *oxymôron*: the fact that the word is rarely used today is itself disturbing and significant. The neglect of this rhetorical figure reveals the influence of univocal thinking and the fear modern culture has of polysemy, on one hand, and of ambivalence, on the other. This forgetfulness shows that we are cut off from real thought, which is fundamentally comparative, since we need to place ourselves on the scale pointer in order to "weigh" things correctly.
The *oxymôron*, playing with the etymology of *oxys* (sharpened, pointed, penetrating) and *môros* (dulled, without point, hence inert, stupid, mad), would then be the sharpened-dulled, the penetrating foolishness, the piercing punch of stupidity, the point that

language and our very conception of the divine are relativized. But relativity does not mean relativism. It is to all this that this book makes allusion.

Tavertet, Epiphany 1998

---

penetrates the flabby. The *oxymôron* harmonizes two notions which, separately, are contraries. Paradox places two opinions (*doxai*) one beside (*para*) the other; the *oxymôron* makes one idea penetrate into another. Paradox confronts us with dualism, oxymoron with a-dualism, with *advaita*. Oxymoric thought cannot be reduced *ad unum*, to unicity or univocity; that would be a contradiction, and a contradiction cannot be thought. It resembles rather the normal vision that makes us see things in their three dimensions, even though we may not be able to copy them exactly on the two-dimensional plane of reason.

1
Speaking of God

The experience of humankind, expressed in innumerable traditions, both oral and written, has called by numerous names what we usually denominate "God." And, almost unanimously, it has named and understood God as a symbol, as a name, not as a concept.

The origin of the word "God" is Sanskrit: dyau (day, Latin dies), suggests bril- liance, the light, divinity (like theos in Greek). Light makes it possible to see and gives life. It is not at all by chance that the sun is universally accepted, including by Catholicism, as one of the divine symbols.

There is a politics of terminology; in our day, the mass media deeply influence the power of words. There exist numerous ways of understanding the word "God," and no one has a monopoly on its meaning. I have often asked myself if a moratorium on such a word would not be healthy. But, not having the power to do that, we will make use of that name, drawing from it the best possible advantage by levering the ancestral wisdom of humanity. This little book is nothing but a meditation on the meaning this frequently (and badly) used word can still have. If some readers are allergic to it, I would ask them to change it and try to see if, by chance, they are not referring to the same thing.

In the nine propositions that follow, we do not pretend to say anything about God, but simply to situate the point at which a discourse on the subject of God can have a meaning and be fruitful for those hoping to live a fuller and freer life. The question about God is not firstly the question about a Being, but the question about reality. If the "question about God" is no longer the central question of existence, then it is no longer the question about God, and is displaced in favor of the problem that has taken its place. We are not discussing the fact of knowing whether there exists a Someone or Something with such-and-such attributes. We are posing the question of the meaning of life, the destiny of the earth, whether or not there is a necessity for a foundation. We simply reflect on the ultimate question for each of us, or why such a question is not posed.

Here are the nine propositions.

1. *We cannot speak of God without a preliminary interior silence.*

Every discipline starts from some epistemological presuppositions that permit it to approach its own sphere. In the same way that, in order to detect an electron, one has need of sophisticated laboratories and complicated mathematics, the appropriate method for speaking about God calls for a purity of heart that enables us to listen to the voice of (divine) transcendence in (human) immanence.

Without purity of heart, not only is it not possible to "see" God, but it is equally impossible to have the least idea of what is involved. Without the silence of the intellect and the will, without the silence of the senses, without what some call "the third eye"—which is dealt with not only by the Tibetans but also by the medieval theologians of St. Victor—it is not possible to approach the sphere in which the word "God" can have a meaning. According to Richard of St. Victor, there are three eyes: the oculus carnis, the oculus rationis, and the oculus fidei (the eye of the body, the eye of reason, and the eye of faith). The so-called third eye is the organ of the faculty that distinguishes us from other living beings by giving us access to a reality that transcends, without denying, that which the intelligence and the senses catch.

2. *It is a sui generis discourse.*

The discourse about God is radically different from every other discourse on whatever "object," because God is not an object (nor is He any "subject matter," as the English tongue would put it). In which case, He would be nothing more than an idol.

The word "God" makes reference to a semantic field, to a field of research and teaching radically different from all others. Take physics, for example. The distinction does not consist in saying that God is mysterious and physics is not. The concepts of physics—energy, force, mass, number—are as mysterious as the word "God." But if, in physics, even while not knowing what it is, we dispose or can dispose of parameters that permit us to measure regularity or formulate possible laws in regard to the functioning of physical reality, such an operation is not possible in regard to God. There are no adequate parameters that would permit us to speak of the "functioning" of that reality we call "God."

The discourse about God is unique; therefore, it cannot be compared to any other human language. It is irreducible to any other discourse.

3. *It involves our whole being...*

... And not only feeling, reason, body, science, sociology, nor even academic philosophy or theology. No instrument can localize God. The discourse about God is not an elitist specialization of whatever type.

We do not need any mediation to open ourselves to the mystery of God. To speak, or feel, or be conscious of God, we certainly need the mediation of language, feeling, and consciousness. But we do not need a particular language, a predeter- mined feeling, a special content of consciousness. The only possible mediation is our own being, our naked existence, our very entity between God and nothingness.

The Book of the Twenty-Four Philosophers, so often cited and highly esteemed by Christian Scholastics, declares in proposition 14: Deus est oppositio ad nihil mediatione entis (God is the opposition to nothingness through the mediation of being). There is no other mediation except ourselves. We have no need of mediation, because this ultimate that we are, our being, is precisely mediation. "The creature is the mediation (the mediator) between God and nothingness," Thomas Aquinas has written. In brief, esse est co-esse (to be is to be-with). There is no absolute monism.

The human experience from all times has always tried to express a "mystery" that is found both at the origin and the end of all that we are, without excluding any of it. God, if He "is," cannot be found either on the right or on the left, neither on high nor below, no matter what meaning we give to those words. To claim to be able to situate God on our side, against others, is simply a blasphemy.

4. *It is not about any church, religion, or belief.*

God is not the monopoly of any human tradition: neither of the traditions that call themselves "theist" nor of those who are—wrongly—called "of faith," of believers. Neither is He the "object" of any kind of thought. A discourse that wanted to imprison Him in any kind of ideology would be sectarian.

In other terms, Christians can speak in the name of Christ, Buddhists can invoke Buddha, Marxists Marx, democrats Justice and Liberty, philosophers Truth, scien- tists Exactitude, Muslims Mohammed, and each of these human groups can believe themselves the interpreter of a conviction that comes from God or from reality itself—whether they call it faith, evidence, reason, common sense, or anything else.

But if the name of God is to play a part in all that, it must be as a symbol of another order, a symbol that serves to uproot the absolutism of every human activity, a symbol that clarifies the contingency of all human enterprises, and thus makes impossible every totalitarianism of whatever kind. "Not only is God not exterior to the world, but He is absolutely interior to it," Zubiri said. So interior to the world that we cannot separate Him from it metaphysically, nor divide Him politically, nor compartmentalize Him socially.

5. *It is a discourse always mediated by a belief.*

It is not possible to speak without the mediation of language, nor to utilize the latter without expressing some kind of belief, although discourse about God should never be identified with one particular belief. There is a "relationship of transcendence" between the God of whom we speak and what is said of Him. Western traditions have called it mystêrion, which does not mean "enigma" nor "unknown (quantity)." The names of God are not independent from God himself, and each denomination of the mystery represents an aspect of that mystery, of which we cannot say either that it is one or that it is multiple.

Each religion is a differentiated system of mediations. Every language is particular, and linked to a culture. Each language depends on a concrete context that gives it meaning, while at the same time limiting it. Here it is necessary to take into account the fundamental inadequacy of every expression. It is not a scandal if each religion defends its own formulations, on condition that it respect the others, and take into account that each mediation is, precisely, a mediation. This does not prevent the fact that we can, and should, argue about the greater or lesser adequation of the expressions employed, without forgetting, however, that the interpretation of every text requires the knowledge of its context and the intuition of its pre-text.

The "proofs of the existence of God" offered by Christian Scholasticism, for example, only tend to prove the nonirrationality of the divine existence to those who already believe in God. Otherwise, how would they be able to recognize that the proof "proves" what they are seeking ? It is obvious that what is proved depends on the probans—the one who proves—and that the probans is much more strong and powerful than what is proved.

6. *It regards a symbol, not a concept.*

God cannot be the object of a knowledge or of any belief whatsoever. The word "God" is a symbol that both reveals and veils itself in the very symbol of which we speak. Every symbol is such because it symbolizes, and not because it is interpreted into an objective eidetic content. There is no possible hermeneutic of the symbol, because its own hermeneutic lies intrinsically in itself. The symbol is symbol when it symbolizes, that is, when we recognize it as such. A symbol that does not speak immediately to the one who perceives it ceases to be a symbol. People can teach us to read symbols, but as long as we do not understand directly what we are reading, the symbol is a dead letter.

Unlike concepts, which tend to be univocal, symbols are polysemous. The symbol is eminently relative, not in the sense of relativism, but of relativity, of the relation between a subject and an object. It is something to be contemplated, nor does it pretend to be either universal or concrete. It is concrete and immediate, that is, without mediation between subject and object. It is at once objective and subjective; it constitutively implies relation. Therefore, the symbol symbolizes what is symbolized in it, not some "thing" else.

If language was only an instrument to designate objects or transmit a simple piece of information, a discourse about God would not be possible. People, however, do not speak only to transmit information, but also because they have a constitutive need to speak, that is, to live fully by participating—through the word—in a universe that is, in its turn, inseparable from the word, the logos.

7. *It is a polysemous discourse that cannot be an analogical one.*

The discourse about God has constitutively many meanings, and there cannot be a primum analogatum, since there cannot be a meta-culture on the basis of which such a discourse would be developed. There exist many concepts of God, but none of them "conceives" Him. A super-concept or a conceptual common denominator would not resolve the problem, precisely because it would eliminate from the scene the richest and most fruitful diversities, and turn God into an abstraction. God is not a mere formality.

We ought to accept the fact that several religious traditions exist, incommen- surable to one another, and that a—very questionable—common denominator of all religions would certainly not be the God of any real tradition. God is unique, hence incomparable, and the same is true of every experience of Him. There is no prior space, both neutral and common, that would permit us to establish compari- sons. To pretend to limit, define, or conceive of God is in itself a contradictory effort, since its achievement would be a creation of the mind, a creature. To wish to discover something more vast and more encompassing than God is a distortion of thought—although we are obviously able to compare different ideas of divinity.

8. *"God" is not the only symbol of the divine.*

Pluralism is inherent to the human condition and prevents us from speaking of God starting from a single perspective, or from a unique principle of intelligibility. The very word "God" is not necessary.

Every claim to reduce the symbol "God" to what we understand by it would not only destroy it but also cut our links with all those people and cultures that do not feel the necessity of that symbol. The pretension of offering a unified schema of intelligibility on the universal level is a perpetuation of cultural colonialism. To universalize our own perspective is an extrapolation that is not justified. The very idea of a "global perspective" is, to be sure, a contradiction in terms.

Philosophers and theologians certainly would be able to nuance the preceding two affirmations, but perhaps the solution would emerge more easily if we cut the Gordian knot of a universal theory about God and rediscovered the divine as a dimension and pluralism (not plurality) as an aspect of reality itself.

9. *It cannot but end in a new silence.*

A purely transcendent God would become a superfluous, even perverse, hypoth- esis—independently of the internal contradiction of all discourse about Him: how is one to speak of that which is purely transcendent? Such a hypothesis would obscure the divine immanence at the same time that it destroyed human transcendence. The divine mystery is ineffable, and no discourse can describe it.

It belongs to human experience to recognize itself as limited, not only as a linear segment limited by the future, but also in its essence, because of the very foundation that is given to it. Without love and without knowledge, without corporality and without temporality, this experience is not possible. "God" is the word, quite audible for some but less so for others, that gives us, in breaking the silence of Being, the opportunity to find it again. We are the ex-sistence of a sistence that permits us to spread out (in time) and extend (in space), to be consistent with the whole universe in which we insist on living, when we persist in our quest and resist the cowardice of frivolity, subsisting precisely in that mystery that many call God and others prefer not to name. Silence is the source of every authentic word. It is out of the primordial silence that the logos emerges, St. Irenaeus writes. Silence is the crossroads between time and eternity.

1
The Experience of God

The Silence of Life: The A Priori of Experience

The immediate character of what is *urgent* often distracts our attention from what is *important.* Fundamentally, it is a question of the tension between practice and theory. If the urgent is not important, we throw ourselves into a counterpro- ductive practice; in that case, the "urgent" can wait and is not worth the trouble. If the important is not urgent, we sink into an erroneous theory; the "important" then becomes nothing but a simple abstraction. I would define *prudence* as the harmonious union of the urgent (function of time) and the important (function of weight). The art of knowing how to combine the urgent and the important is a feature of wisdom, one of the conditions for living well.

If we were able to forget for a moment that we are professors, masons, clerks, and so on, if we were able to forget that we are Christians, and even human beings, we would thereby facilitate an openness to an awareness of reality for which we can be spokespersons. For this purpose we ought to divest ourselves, to relieve ourselves of the entire ensemble of attributes that—although structuring our own personality— limit us, when we identify ourselves exclusively with them, and often asphyxiate us.

The silence of Life is not the same as a life of silence, the silent life of the monks, of a hermitage. The life of silence is important and necessary to reach our goals, to plan our actions, or develop our relations, but it is not the silence of Life.

The silence of Life is the art of making silent the activities of life (that are not Life), in order to reach the pure experience of Life. We frequently identify Life with activities; we identify our being with our feelings, our desires, our will, with everything that we do and have. We instrumentalize our Life, while forgetting that it is an end in itself. Plunged into the activities of life, we lose the faculty of listening, and we alienate ourselves from our very source: Silence, Non-Being, God.

Silence appears at the moment when we position ourselves at the very source of Being. The source of Being is not Being, but *the source* of Being—Being is already on this side of the curtain. That prior place, the one that is earlier, the place of begin- ning, is the Silence of Life. To say this in Christian terms, "I have come in order that they may have life, life in abundance" (Jn 10:10). The entry into silence is not a flight from the world, a dichotomy between the essential and the relative; it is the discovery that the essential is essential uniquely because I speak starting from the relative; and the relative is relative only because I discover that a relation exists that permits me to be in silence when beginning with the essential.

It is not a matter of taking importance away from the activities of life. We certainly cannot live without eating, any more than without thinking, without feeling, without loving. We have spoken of the third eye, that third organ or faculty that opens us to a dimension of reality that transcends the knowledge that we would be able to acquire through the intellect and the senses. Without a silence of the intellect and the senses, this faculty remains atrophied, and as a consequence, Life, the experience of life, the Life anterior to its expression in different activities, life in its depths, escapes us. The link with the latent world remains hidden; participation in cosmic plenitude goes unnoticed. In this way our lives, deprived of their source, become impoverished, sad, and mediocre. To overcome this destitution, we have recourse to a multitude of things that sweeten it, enrich it, and give it meaning, importance, and dignity. And we identify ourselves with this multitude of things; we drown ourselves in this constant activity. Then we forget that the flower, the lily of the fields, the bird, do more "for the glory of God" (Mt 6:26–28) than all our efforts, impatience, and careers. We long for another life, and we do not live Life. Jesus said something about eternal life, which he promised us immediately. Simeon the New Theologian even says, "Who does not live eternal life here below, will not enjoy it later on."

Constituents of Experience

Experience includes four moments that can be distinguished, although not separated:

1. The *pure experience*, the instant we live in, that we feel immediately.
2. The memory of that moment, which permits us to speak of it, but which is already no longer pure experience, since it passes through the mediation of recollection. Memory cannot be separated from experience, but it should not be confused with it.
3. The interpretation that we develop of this, which leads us to describe it as painful, sensitive, spiritual, loving, the experience of Being, of God, of Beauty, and so on. The interpretation we give of experience is intimately linked to the experience itself, to memory, and obviously to our language.

4. Its reception in the cultural world that we have not created, which has been given to us, and which bestows on it a special resonance. Every experience is inscribed in a cultural environment outside of which it is not necessarily of further value.

This four-dimensional experience, which is always personal, can be communi- cated by "contagion" (resonance), love, assimilation, education, and other means including subjective participation—but never by a simple extrapolation of objective concepts, as if it were a question of a formal entity. In consequence, it is not possible to have a *mathesis universalis* (universal knowledge) of human experiences, and hence of interculturality.

The different cultures and the history of humankind have been forged by the great human experiences. Indisputably, the reception of an experience in the framework of a given tradition conditions the interpretation that is made of this experience. The great traditions generally emerge from extraordinary experiences that were most often received as revelations. Through memory, the interpretation of this experience survives and is transmitted: an interpretation that, in its turn, is conditioned by the culture in which it has been received.

Take, for example, the *experience* of Jesus. The *memory* of the impact that the experience of Jesus provoked among his contemporaries, and which was recorded in documents, has led to the interpretation that the first Christian communities grew out of this memory; the reception of all of that constitutes tradition. Its reception, conservation, transmission, deformation, and augmentation give form to religion and explain the richness of an experience that has created a whole civilization. The question is very complex, for it is not only a question of the experience of Jesus but of all those numerous other experiences (of Christ) that Christians have believed they have had afterward. In consequence, the living tradition is more than a simple exegesis of a past experience—a fact that a certain kind of theology seems to have forgotten. Theology is not archaeology.

There is no theology without language, and language is already culture. Religion gives to a specific culture its ultimate content, and culture gives religion its very language. Therefore, the relationship between religion and culture is constitutive for both, and consequently we ought to recognize that

- There is no religion without culture, and no culture without religion.
- The experience of God is not the monopoly of any religious system—however it may be called—nor of any church, nor, basically, of any culture.
- We need the mediation of language, and language is already a cultural phenomenon.

As a consequence, all our ideas about God, as well as our memory of it, our inter- pretation and our reception of that experience, need the mediation of a conception, a belief, or a religion. We cannot separate them, but surely we can distinguish between them. Some time ago I suggested a formula that might be useful to recall here:

$$E = e.m.i.r.$$

What we call experience (*E*) is a combination of personal experience, which is ineffable, unique each time, and foreign to repetition (*e*); conveyed by our memory (*m*); modeled by our interpretation (*i*); and conditioned by its reception (*r*) in the cultural context of our time.

I have used the word "combination" in the chemical sense—that is, *E* is not equal to $e + m + i + r$, for the identity of the separate constituents is distinct from its entity in the combination. Water is not H + O nor even H_2 + O but H_2O, in which the elements have lost their individual identity.

In consequence, we cannot, for example, affirm without further qualifications that the mystical experience (*e*) is the same in all religions, for we know *e* only through *E*. It is in this context that it is necessary to situate the problem of the encounter among religious traditions. It is necessary to arrive at what I have called an "ecumenical ecumenism." One of the most urgent tasks of the world today is the establishment of bridges between religions. That does not mean that, for the sake of tolerance and ecumenism, we should water down what constitutes the specificity of each religion, but that this specificity should be expressed in its complete integrity.

I have dealt with the issue, from a Christian standpoint, in a book with a crypti- cally ambiguous title, *The Unknown Christ of Hinduism*, who is not the Christ known to Christians and unknown to Hindūs. There are in fact other aspects of this same christic mystery that Christians do not know, and that Hindūs know under another name; Christians call it Christ, although it has aspects that are unknown to them. The formula of John, "Christ is the alpha and the omega," implies that Christ is alpha, beta, gamma, delta, all the way to omega—that is, all. Everything is in this Christ, who is prior to Abraham, and of whom Christians know a name, an aspect, but they do not know the totality of the mystery. The historic phenomenon of Jesus is an epiphenomenon of the mystery of Christ, which does not mean that he is neither real nor central. While for Western culture the historical fact is the fundamental character of reality, for most of Eastern culture it is only an epiphenomenon.

Faith, Act of Faith, and Belief

In order to explain the experience of God, which we are attempting to approach, it would be appropriate to distinguish between faith, the act of faith, and belief.

The word "faith" has many meanings. We have faith in something, we give testi- mony of our faith, and so on. And to increase its ambiguity, the action expressed by the substantive is spread out in at least three verbs: to trust, to have confidence, to believe. The title of this chapter must be understood in relation with the problem about God.

Faith is a constitutive element of Man. Every Man, by the very fact of being such, has faith, in the same way that every Man qua Man possesses a reason and feelings. One person may have a more obtuse and another a keener reason, one has a more lively sensibility and another is more dull; in the same way, every Man has faith, whether cultivated or neglected, whether or not he is conscious of it.

By faith the capacity of opening to "*beyondity*," to something *more*, to something *beyond*; a capacity which is not given to us either by the senses or the intelligence. This openness to "something beyond" could be called an openness to transcendence. Through faith, Man is capable of transcending himself, of growing, of being open to *beyondity*—capable of making a leap toward what is neither justified by his senses nor proved by his reason.

The seat of faith is in the heart, as the Latin word *credo*—from Greek *kardia*— indicates. The same thing occurs in Sanskrit with the word *śhraddhā* (to give the heart). Faith is the capacity, faculty, possibility of something *more* (that would be the simplest word), of *transcendence* (the most philosophical word), of *God* (the most theological word). The Scholastics called *capax Dei* this capacity for the infinite, for what has no limits.

The division between believers and nonbelievers does not resist the most elemen- tary logic; it is just a sweetened version of the insulting distinction between believers and infidels. This explains a logical misunderstanding. In fact, those who believe in A (that they call God) call themselves "believers," while calling "unbelievers" those who do not believe in A. This is a unilateral distinction, terming "unbelievers" those who do believe in B. This is merely a distinction of power. Why should A be the criterion of division, and not B?

Christian philosophy used to distinguish between *credere in Deum*, "to believe in God" (opening to the mystery), *credere Deo*, "to believe God" (to have confidence in what a supreme Being may have said), and *credere Deum*, "to believe that God is" (to believe in His existence). Faith, as such, has no object; objects belong to thought. If faith had an object, it would be an ideology, a fruit of thought. God is not an object, he is not a being, not even the supreme Being; He is not the chief, the one who commands. Divinity appears beyond the realm of thought. Without a mystic sense, therefore, we almost automatically deform, without intending to, a series of experiences; we deform that experience of a "more" that is found in every human being. I remind readers that we are speaking about God and not about Abrahamic monotheism, which would require a separate chapter.

The *act of faith* is that activity by which we put our faith in motion; it is the act that surges from the heart as symbol of the whole Man, and through which we make a leap to the third dimension, in which the human being is realized. The act of faith is a saving act—without going further now into what is salvation. The act of faith is not a conditioned reflex; it is a free act that does not cut us off from the human condition but which, indeed, allows it to attain its plenitude.

Belief, finally, is the formulation, the doctrinal articulation, generally made by a community, which has crystallized progressively during the course of time in propo- sitions, phrases, affirmations, and—in Christian terms—dogmas. Belief is the more or less coherent symbolic expression of faith, often formulated in conceptual terms.

Doctrinal articulation and conceptual expression presuppose institutionaliza- tion. The latter has often acquired a negative connotation, as an obstacle to the very experience it comes from. Religion is above all a constitutive dimension of Man; in consequence, the experience of God nourishes him in spite of the difficulties that institutions may cause. Besides, since Man is a social animal, institutions are necessary.

There can be reasons for indignation, even protest and rebellion, but not for scandal, in the face of certain forms of institutionalization and abuses of power. We must be aware that mistakes are part of the human condition, that we live in a world that the medieval writers called the *regnum dissimilitudinis*, which is not the kingdom of contradiction or necessarily of sin, but the kingdom of the differ- ence from the divine, of disharmony. We should interpret institutions not as a refuge that protects us and permits us experience, but as a stimulus to make that experience awaken, grow, and be nourished. This obviously requires a considerable degree of maturity.

We must be able to see institutionalization as a constantly open process. Only the conservative fossilization of some experiences ends in becoming an obstacle; of itself, institutionalization is a necessary human process. It is important to see this sociological dimension, and to try to realize that it is the crystallization or mani- festation of an experience that is not exhausted or fixed in such a structure; on the other hand, the structure is necessary to make it possible for others to have access to this experience. The purpose of the institution is to make the experience that establishes it transparent. But experience is incarnated in human beings who never stop shaping themselves: this is why the institution should adapt itself in order to be able to display an experience that is perpetually in progress.

Belief, in contrast to faith, can collapse; a particular formulation of it can be lost. *Actus fidei non terminatur ad enuntiabile, sed ad rem*, St. Thomas says (The act of faith does not find its end in what is declared but in its object). Dogmas are channels, instruments, through which we point to the mystery. If the constellation changes, or if we are no longer capable of capturing the mystery by means of those channels, it will be necessary to change them. The finger of

Buddha points to the moon, allowing us to discover it, Buddhist tradition says, but we should not remain amazed while looking at the finger—or at the *heavens*, like the "men of Galilee" after the Ascension. Prophets and angels are both necessary, but we must not adore them.

In sum, the experience of God generally occurs through the mediation of a belief, but should not be identified with it.

The Triple Horizon of Divinity

The divine has repeatedly burst into the human being, as history bears witness. But it is always a matter of human witness: that is why, instead of trying to describe these "descents" of the divine, we limit ourselves here to mentioning the various ascents of the human spirit to the mystery of divinity.

A reflection on the horizon of intelligibility within which we move seems indispensable for an understanding of our subject. Each culture provides us with this horizon, since it offers us the environment of intelligibility in which things and events take on meaning. That is why we define *culture* as the encompassing myth that reigns in a given time and space.

Phenomenologically speaking, the function of divinity seems to be to confer an ultimate sense of reference. We can situate this sense beyond the universe or in its center, in the depths of Man (intellect or heart), or, simply, nowhere. Cosmology, anthropology, and ontology offer us the three principal horizons in which the divine appears.

The Cosmological Horizon

Human beings, especially but not exclusively in antiquity, lived face to the world. The universe, as an animated habitat, constituted their center of interest. The eyes of Man were directed to the objects of heaven and earth. It was in that horizon that divinity appeared, not simply as one thing among others, but as its Lord, its Cause, its Origin or Principle. Its place is meta-cosmological.

Here the divine appears linked to the world; it is the divinity of the world, and in turn the world is interpreted as the world of divinity. The kind of function that is assigned to divinity, and the links that knot it to the world, are easy to spot in the different cosmologies. The divine is perceived as one pole of the world.

We would be able to say the same thing by making use of an essentially temporal metaphor. Divinity would be at the beginning, prior to the start of everything, even before the Big Bang, as the alpha point; or it would come at the end of the total evolution of the physical universe, as the omega point; or the divinity could indeed be the two points at once, alpha and omega, at both the beginning and the end of the universe.

The most widely used name for the divine is "God," expressed in some of His attributes: "Creator of heaven and earth" (Gn 14:19), "Varu...a, supreme Lord, master of the spheres (*RV* I.25.20), "He from whom all beings are truly born, through whom all live and to whom all return" (*TU* III.1.1), as well as the *Pantokratōr* of numerous traditions, both Eastern and Western. Even the *deus otiosus* belongs to this group. Divinity is a cosmological category, and its dominant trait is power. It is the supreme Architect, the all-powerful Engineer, and so on.

The Anthropological Horizon

At a specific moment of history, the principal interest of Man ceased to be nature and the surrounding world, and it centered on the human being itself. His glance concentrated on inner life: feelings, mind. The seat of the divine shifts toward the kingdom of the human, its place becomes anthropological.

Divinity is then perceived as the real symbol in which the end and perfection of the human being culminates. This notion of divinity is not so much the fruit of a reflection on the cosmos or an experience of its numinous nature, as rather the culminating summit of an anthropological self-consciousness. Divinity is the Plenitude of the human heart, the ultimate Destiny of humanity, the Guide of all peoples, the Beloved of mystics, the Lord of history, the complete fulfillment of what we really are. Divinity has no need to be anthropomorphic, although it can present some human traits. In this instance divinity is *ātman-brahman*, the completely divinized man, the Christ, Puru@a, or even the symbol of Justice, Peace, or Perfect Society. Here too it can be considered as immanent or transcendent, either identi- fied with Man or separate from him, but its functions are understood in relation with the human being. This is the living divinity, loving or threatening, who guides, is concerned, punishes, rewards, forgives. Every pilgrimage ends in this divinity, every distance disappears, every sin is annulled, every thought vanishes. Divinity is a meta-anthropological category.

The dominant trait of this horizon is freedom. Man experiences liberty, but in a limited and often painful form. Liberation, whether we understand it as salvation or in some other manner, is a human ideal. Divinity is in itself liberty, and therefore liberates Man from the slavery of sin or ignorance. Modern theologies of liberation belong in this framework. This is the divinity at work in history.

The Ontological Horizon

The apex of Man is the consciousness of transcendence. The power of reflection makes *Homo sapiens* the superior being we believe ourselves to be. The condition of divinity would here be that of a super-Being. Its place would be meta-ontological, beyond Being.

Human beings are proud of their capacity to recognize that they cannot under- stand everything.

Divinity is then perceived as not only beyond the physical world, but also beyond the confines of every natural domain, including the human world (intellect, desires, will), or whatever else. It will not even be called *natura naturans* (Averroès, Spinoza, et al.) or *ungenaturte Natur* (Eckhart), because it is not *natura.* The transcendence or otherness is so absolute that it transcends itself and cannot be called transcendent. Divinity *is* not; its *being* lies beyond Being. Its place is meta-ontologic. It *is* not even Non-Being. Here apophatism is absolute. Silence is our only attitude, not only because we cannot speak of it, but because its specificity consists in being silence. This silence neither hides nor reveals. Divinity is silence because it says nothing, because there is nothing to say. A possible name for this divinity is *nirvā...a* or "Neither-Being- Nor-Non-Being." Another name is the *mia pêge theotêtos* of the Fathers, adopted at the Sixth Council of Toledo (638), when they came together to call the Father *fons et origo totius divinitatis* (source and origin of all divinity). Divinity is perceived here as a meta-ontological reality. Every thought on its subject would be idolatry.

Here the dominant trait of divinity is the mutual relation between immanence and transcendence. A transcendence without its corresponding immanence would be contradictory and irrational. We cannot even mention a pure transcendence without destroying it. An immanence without transcendence would signify the inexpress- ible and unintelligible tautology of an identity that would not even be able to be one for itself. In fact, we could not even affirm "A" because with that affirmation, if it has to be intelligible, would be equivalent to "A = A"; that is to say, the copula projects the first A toward the second in order to affirm its identity. In other words, the true identity is an immanence that transcends itself. Divinity is precisely that immanence-transcendence that is inscribed in the heart of every being. I am divine insofar as I am what I *am*; and I am not divine insofar as I am *not* what I *am.* All this amounts to saying that an absolutely single Being does not exist. Being is relation. Even the One of Plotinus is not a Substance.

The three horizons do not exclude each other. Numerous thinkers in many traditions try to approach the mystery of divinity by encompassing all three levels. Thus, for example, *nirgu...a brahman* would correspond to the third type, *sagu...a- brahman* would practice the first function, and *Ù'svara* the second. On the other hand, Christian Scholasticism would combine the conception of God as Principle of motion (first function) with the personal God of believers (second function) and the God of mystics (third function). All that presents an accumulation of philosophical and theological problems that the various traditions try to resolve in different ways.

By means of these three ways, humankind, throughout its history, has expressed its intention of transcending itself and of recognizing the existence of a "mystery" that is beyond intelligibility and that, in a certain manner, is present in Man. We cannot understand the unintelligibility (that would be a contradiction!), but we can be conscious of it.

Fragments on the Experience of God

Everything that we would be able to say about the experience of God in a strictly rational manner would be idolatry. Indeed, there is something blasphemous about every theodicy and every form of apologetics. To try to justify God, to prove His existence or even defend Him, implies that we are presenting ourselves as the very foundation of God, transforming ontology into epistemology, and the latter into a logic that would be above the divine and the human. Ultimately, it is a question of the primacy of thought over being, which has characterized Western thought since Parmenides.

The experience of God cannot be monopolized by any religion or any system of thought. Inasmuch as it is ultimate experience, the experience of God is not only possible but even necessary for all human beings to arrive at the awareness of their own identity. Human beings reach their own human fullness only by experiencing their ultimate "foundation," what they really are.

The experience of God is not the experience of something or someone; it is not the experience of any object. The Christian tradition, from Denys the Areopagite to Thomas Merton, as well as the majority of the religious traditions, maintain that we can only know one thing about God: that we cannot know Him. "Blessed be the one who has arrived at infinite ignorance," says that great genius of the Christian world, Evagrius Ponticus. *Agnosia* is "learned ignorance," absolute nonknowledge. In the *Kena-upani@ad* (II, 3), we are sent back to the same experience. If we here call it "God," we do so in order not to break completely with those traditions that have utilized this word as symbol of mystery, but perhaps it would be preferable to dispense with it, as we suggested at the beginning.

The experience of God is not the experience of an object. There is no object "God" of which we can have the experience. It is the experience of nothingness; therefore, it is ineffable. It is the experience of discovering that one's own experience does not arrive at the depths of any reality. It is the experience of emptiness, of absence—the experience by which one becomes conscious that there exists "a something more," not in the quantitative order, not something that completes, but something that has no bottom, an emptiness, a Non-Being, a "something more," if you will, that precisely makes experience possible.

The experience of God is not a special, still less a specialized, experience. When we absolutely want to have the experience of God, when we "push" an experience of any kind, we inevitably deform it, and it escapes us. Without the links that unite us with all reality, we are unable to have the experience of God. In the experience of eating, drinking, loving, working, being with someone, giving him/her good advice, making a false move, and so on—*there* is where we perceive the experi- ence of God. Since it is not the experience of anything, the experience of God is pure experience. It is precisely the contingency of being-with, living-with, since it is not the experience of an "I am" but of a "we are." In Christian language, we call it Trinity.

The experience of God is the root of all experience. It is the experience in depth of all human experiences and of each of them: friendship, words, conversation. It is the experience beneath every human experience: pain, beauty, pleasure, goodness, anguish, coldness... beneath every experience insofar as it shows us a dimension of the infinite, of the unfinished, of the nonachieved; beneath every experience, therefore escaping complete expression in any idea whatever, or in any sensation or feeling.

The experience of God, in Christian terms, coincides paradoxically with the experience of contingency. The very root of that word suggests this: *cum tangere*, "to touch the tangent." It is in the recognition of tangentiality, when we touch our own limits, that our consciousness opens and we perceive a "beyond," "something" that escapes our own limits, that transcends every limitation. This experience is fundamentally so simple that, when we want to explain it, we complicate and deform it, and it is then that comparisons arise. But this experience eludes all comparisons.

I think that in this very context of contingency, and its recognition by Man, prayer finds its place. Etymologically, "prayer" (from the Latin verb *precor*) is related to precariousness. Prayer arises from an awareness of precariousness.

There are two types of prayer: there is the praise of one who adores, the thanks from one who finds him/herself saved, and there is the cry of human precariousness from all those who suffer injustice and pain. The two are necessary and inseparable: through the regeneration that develops in the person and is manifested in praise, this same person recognizes his/her precariousness. It was the perplexity of Luther, the intuition of the *simul iustus et peccator* (simultaneously a just man and a sinner). In recognizing this radical ambivalence of the human being, Luther had his greatest religious experience and came to recognize that the aporia finds its solution in Christ. *There* is our foundation; *this* is the human predicament.

To recognize this human condition as both precarious and glorious is to recognize that this experience overturns all our values. And it is precisely this rupture of our patterns that opens us to freedom and prevents us from clinging to nonentity, and judging on the basis of that very clinging. "Do not judge" (Mt 7:1; Lk 9:37): there is the beginning of freedom and the joy of living.

The experience of God that is beneath every experience and through which we become human gives us a consciousness of our contingency, making us humble and capable of understanding. Through this experience, we come to recognize that we are in the interior of something that encompasses everything; we become conscious of a double dimension of absence and presence, and aware of partici- pating in a "more" in which, in one way or another, we can have confidence. Some will call this "the experience of Being," which is actualized in the unselfish love of beings. On other occasions, I have called it "cosmotheandric confidence." Others may prefer to say that it is precisely the contact with contingency that brings us to discover the Other, Nothingness, Emptiness, and the Void. In order to understand that "all is vanity" (Qo 1:2), *vanitas*, *vacuum*, "emptiness," we ought already to have come to recognize that all is emptiness. "The infamy of vanity covers the absolute reality with its ego," says a verse of the *#ûfî* Mohammed Sherin Tabrizi Maghrebi; and the same fifteenth-century master adds, in his poem "Dīwān" that the support to the permanence of unity (monotheism) is found in the *kenôsis* (*fanâ*) of the ego.

Such is the experience of God, which, as we have already said, cannot be a specialized experience; it requires all our being and our whole being:

- All our being : intelligence, will, feelings, body, reason, love
- Our whole being, that is, nonfragmented

If we are not unified, if our experience goes in one direction and our body in another, if our thoughts push us toward the one side and our desires toward the other, our experience of God will be so fragmented that it will no longer be the simple experience of God. The indispensable condition for receiving the experience of God is for our whole being to be unified. Chinese wisdom tells us this in a simple metaphor: "When the gong is well forged, whatever be the place and the manner in which you strike it, it will always respond with a harmonious and well-distributed sound." When the person is unified, "well forged" like a gong, whatever blow one may receive, one will always transmit a harmonious vibration.

We have to be in harmony with ourselves and with the universe in order to speak properly of that which, precisely, is at the basis of every human experience. Every discourse and every theology from which this experience is absent is nothing but verbiage, the simple repetition of what we have been told, of what we have memo- rized, of what we do not know for ourselves.

The problem of divine revelation is shown here. The difficulty of revelation does not lie in the fact that God reveals, nor in what is said to us in revelation, but in what I am able to understand of what has been told me in revelation. *Quidquid recipitur ad modum recipientis recipitur* (Whatever is received, is received according to the mode of the one who receives it). Revelation is neither in the *revelans* (the one who reveals himself), nor in the *revelatum* (the content), but in the *revelanti* (the one who receives it), the receiver.

The experience of God is not an experience of "I." One of the most striking characteristics of the twentieth century is the process of "psychologization" of the most diverse domains of human life, and religious experience has not escaped the influence of this process. Psychoanalysis has structured the human *psychê* in three areas, in which the unconscious has acquired great importance.

In regard to what touches on the experience of God, many have begun to pose questions on the relationship between this experience and the experience of the deep ego, composed of something else than will and reason. The experience of God is evidently linked to that experience of the deep ego, but it cannot be reduced to it. To interpret it with categories referring to the experiences of the deep ego implies the overcoming of rationalism, in the sense of arriving at a very positive existential experience: life is not limited to the conscious, and I am not an individualized "ego," separate from all the rest. There is also in me an unconscious and a subconscious, and I participate in the archetypes of humanity, which open me to the mystery.

But the experience of God cannot be interpreted as a pure psychological phenom- enon that would not transcend the frontiers of the archetype and the deep ego. It is an ontic and ontological experience: it is an experience of beings and of Being in its most radical identity. It is an experience that surpasses me insofar as experience. Roles are exchanged: I am no longer its subject, but I place myself within the experience itself. Ultimately, this is the mystical experience, the experience of depth. I do not discover another object or other beings; I discover the dimension of depth, of the infinite, of liberty, which is found in everything and everyone. That is the reason why, almost automatically, the experience of God confers humility, on one hand, and on the other, freedom.

I get near God if I do not stop at myself—that is, if my deep ego turns, so to speak, into a "you" (we would even say the "you" of God). Otherwise, I can fall into a destructive spiritual narcissism. That is why spiritual life is dangerous, ambivalent, and constantly ambiguous. The experience of God liberates me from all fear, including the fear of losing my-self, of the negation of myself. "It is not I who lives, but Christ who lives in me" (Gal 2:20): by these words St. Paul expresses the profound aware- ness that what is deepest in me is Christ, not an *alter Christus* but *ipse Christus*. We must not be afraid of losing ourselves. The fear of the total negation of oneself is the evident proof that this fearful "oneself " is not the genuine and authentic "you." The you rests confidently in the ego.

On this relation between the experience of God and the experience of the psychological ego, two observations may be pertinent.

The first, regarding a phenomenological description of God, is intended especially for the new generations who do not seem very interested in these issues. *God is the one who breaks our isolation while respecting our solitude*: He breaks your isolation, enters into you, you are no longer isolated. And at the same time He respects your solitude and permits you to be yourself: yourself, and not what you are according to your identity papers, or the label of *sister*, *father*, *brother*, *friend*, *coreligionist*, or whatever. This is the *beata solitudo*, the blessed solitude in which I am truly myself, because God is not the being who closely examines me, but the one who permits me to be myself to the fullest. In other words, when I am genuinely alone, I encounter God—not as object but as *intimior intimo meo*, to speak as St. Augustine, "the most intimate aspect of myself," what is most interior to me, what I most truly am, and which then, precisely, opens me to others.

That is the reason why traditional counsels emphasize that without personal withdrawal, without *solitudo*, I am not myself, I do not reach the depths of myself, and ultimately I do not find neither myself, nor others, nor God. Only by removing the labels by which we so often define ourselves as an "I" will we be able to reach the heart of reality and be ourselves.

The second observation leads us to confront ourselves with the text in which YHWH asks Abraham to leave his land, his country, and the house of his father (Gn 12:1). To depart from his own land, his own home, requires that we are detached from ourselves, from our own individuality. The experience of God is risky, it over- throws our categories; we don't know where it leads us or where it will end up. It is nonsense to search for the experience of God while hoping that it will basically match what we previously expected.

Other religious traditions have also taken as a theme of reflection this relation between the experience of God and the experience of the ego. In the *vedānta*, for example, the experience of God is the experience of the I at which we arrive when we ask, "Who am I?"—*ko'ham*? In trying to answer that question, I begin to discover that I am a mystery, that I am not my body, which changes and fades; I am not my thought, this little psychological ego that undergoes a continuous transformation. I search for that "I," the ultimate subject of all things, about which I can say nothing without it ceasing to be subject and being transformed into a predicate. In arriving at the experience of "I am," *aham brahman*, I participate in the ultimate and unique experience of the one subject of every operation, which is obviously not my ego.

I would like to conclude these scattered reflections on the experience of God with a phrase that expresses the rupture such an experience provokes in any frame- work that is purely rational: God is "known by those who do not know Him, and unknown by those who know Him" (*KenU* II:3). This could be translated by citing Gregory of Nyssa in almost literal terms: "Those who [believe they] know God do not know Him, and those who do not know Him know Him." Recall also this *kōan* of Christ on the prayer of the publican and the Pharisee: the one who believes he is a righteous man is not forgiven, who considers himself a sinner obtains forgiveness (Lk 18:9ff.).

The phrase of the *Kena*, confirmed by the *Gītā* and numerous other texts from the most diverse traditions, lets us add a brief note: we who are so wise, and know that we do not know Him, are doubly unhappy. In fact, those who do not know Him know Him; and those who know Him believe they know Him, although they do not know Him, and are consequently in peace. But as for us intellectuals, who know that we do not know Him; there is no one who can save us. We need a new innocence.

The poets always know how to say it better. As John of the Cross reminds us:

> This knowing without knowing
> is of such great power
> that by no argument scholars
> will ever be vanquishing it;
> because their science cannot understand without understanding,
> by transcending all knowledge.

Of Initiation

After this sketch on the experience of God, there emerges the most proper and most typical question coming, although not only from that side, from the technocratic mentality: *How* to arrive at this experience? To affirm that we all have access to it, or that everyone possesses it though few realize it, only shifts the question: *How* does one come to the awareness of it? Or rather: Do we really have need of it? Perhaps no, for those who do not "know" it; perhaps yes, for those who are searching for it.

Whatever the case, one thing is certain. We do not arrive at this experience through will, as the *Kena* so apodictically affirms and St. Paul confirms. To desire *nirvāna* disqualifies one from attaining it. Everything belongs to another order, that of grace, as many schools would stress. Everything is linked to the whole: *sarvam sarvātmakam*, Âvaism affirms. But we cannot deal with everything, still less not all at one time.

We limit ourselves here to one remark. It concerns a feature that is present in the greater part of the traditions of humanity but relatively absent in modernity, for the latter finds itself mired in a metaphysical dualism as well as an anthropological individualism. I am referring to the sacramental or tantric vision of the universe—just liberating these two words from their superficial interpretations and superstitious degenerations.

I am referring to that worldview (*Weltanschauung*) that does not divide reality into matter and spirit, and does not sacrifice the first on the altar of the second (idealistic spiritualities of all kinds), nor the second on the altar of the first (empiricist materialisms of all kinds). In this tantric or sacramental vision, the word is effica- cious in the world of the spirit, thought exercises an influence on matter, the senses are spiritual, the divine is incarnated, and the human is impregnated with divinity.

But on this point we will mention again only one example in relation to the problems that occupy us. All traditions propose a preparation for the different states of life, whether it be an intellectual, social, or religious life. For example, the *vedānta* and the Church Fathers say that without faith it is not possible to do theology. Entry into the Platonic Academy required the knowledge of geometry; entry into the religious life calls for a novitiate; initiation into adult life begins with the use of reason, and the latter with the awakening of sexuality; acceptance by a guru requires a prior ceremony; the entry into certain communities requires circumcision; the practice of medicine requires a degree; and the priestly ministry, a consecration. All these traditions believe that reality is hierarchical, that is, that there are different levels in it, and that, at the same time, it is based on solidarity, because it is "solidly" assembled.

Solidarity and hierarchy are two presuppositions that give meaning to initiation. The latter consists in passing from one level to another (which may well be from one level of awareness to another) by virtue of an action "initiated" by a—generally human—agent, unanimously qualified for it. Initiation only has meaning in the framework of a hierarchical and interdependent world. Outside of it, it degenerates into superstition. To speak of initiation in a world ruled by a supposedly egalitarian and individualistic mentality would be nonsense, or an anachronism.

In the framework of solidarity, initiation is possible because it merely actualizes the *ontonomy* (not heteronomy, nor autonomy) of each individual. Initiation does not cause harm or alienation; it is a manifestation of the dynamism of being. The action of one being on another is possible because the very structure of reality is a solid, that is, a constitutive one: *pratītyasamutpāda*, *karma*, *corpus Christi mysticum*, *umma* are, respectively, fundamental concepts for four great religions. Of course, that does not prevent the fact that the abuse of power or other causes can introduce initiations that are contrary to nature and produce antihuman attitudes.

Within a hierarchical world—taking hierarchy in its etymological meaning (sacred order)—initiation is necessary because the leap from one state to another, from one degree to another, from one level to another, is not automatic; a collabo- ration is necessary between a hand that extends itself and arms that are raised to grasp that hand.

Initiation is a typical phenomenon of traditional societies that are conscious of the interdependent and hierarchical character of reality, and consider that the human path to perfection calls for a series of steps, for "progress" on the ladder of beings. That said, a well-defined initiation is the normal path to the experience of God. In extraordinary cases, even the fall from a horse, a voice that comes from on high, or a simple personal misfortune can work as initiatory factors. In any case, human life itself requires a continuous initiation. It is up to parents, teachers, elders, and, above all—in our time of family, pedagogical, and social crisis—it is up to genuine masters, who can initiate their fellow humans into the experience of God.

It is appropriate here to mention the personal responsibility of those to whom we have just alluded. To those who deplore the eclipse of God, especially among the young generation, we should ask what they have done to initiate their children, students, relatives, or simply neighbors into that ultimate wisdom of life we have called "the experience of God." It is true that many obstacles are put up by a desacral- ized and individualistic society, but unbelief and sarcasm are instilled into young people especially by the lack of clearness and light in those who are supposed to educate them.

We introduced the theme of initiation by raising the question of *how.* There is a reason for that, which goes as much against the dominant culture as what we have said before. Initiation is personal. There are no all-purpose recipes, no prefabricated remedies, just prescriptions that are valid case by case. That is why physicians have been called "doctors": not because they were experts in industrial pharmacopoeia, but because they knew how to recommend the right drug to the right person. I mean: How is it possible to guide anyone to the experience of God? "How can one communicate the flavor of the tea?" Eastern masters ask. Not with a great deal of quibbling or austerity, the *Upaniṣads* reply. "Come and see," said the Master of Nazareth. "Wayfarer, there is no road," says the poet Antonio Machado, echoing the teachings of Abhinavagupta, St. John of the Cross, and many others.

Initiation is personal, we have just said, and the experience of God, as we said at the beginning, is also personal. Each pilgrim has his or her own path. Maybe all roads lead to Rome, but there is no sure route that guides you to heaven. God's kingdom is a mysterious one—we have been told. In a word, there is no *how*, no recipe, no broad highway letting us attain an experience of God. This is precisely the task of the master and the function of initiation. Initiation is a personal process. A mother says one thing to her adolescent son and another to her unmarried daughter; the master takes us by the hand to help us discover our own personal paths, which are usually quite different from one another; the *mantra* is secret and personal (and it is not a magic formula, despite the danger it runs of becoming one); the water of baptism bathes the body of each child to be baptized even during a collective ceremony.

If the experience of God is such as we have suggested, it cannot be sold in any market, even if the market is called a temple. Someone got very angry, twenty centuries ago, in a case of that kind.

We say that it is up to each generation to initiate those who come after it in the experience of God, which is the experience of true Life, as we have just said. Neither the reading of a book, nor radio, television, or the Internet can be substituted for the personal factor. Sometimes a glance or an embrace can do more than a book, and a living and lived example more than a film, however edifying it may be.

Let me be permitted a brief excursus. Man—basically all traditions say—is the priest of nature, the mediator between heaven and earth. Man is neither a God nor a mere animal, neither divine nor earthly, neither angel nor beast, as Pascal said. He does not possess a specific nature, as things do, because he has to forge it himself, Pico de La Mirandola wrote; according to a certain Judeo-Christian exegesis, he is the king of creation (despite abuses); a "third world between God and nothingness," Scholasticism declared; neither just one more thing among things, nor their creator, as the Greeks, the Indians, and the Chinese perceived; neither divine nor natural, as the Africans teach; Man is not a ready-made being, philosophical reflection affirms.

Man belongs to solidarity, not to solitude. In order for him to fully realize his life—that is, in order to become truly Man—that does not simply mean a biological development; he has to be introduced into *such* a life by someone else. Nobody gives life to himself. That is where initiation is situated. No one initiates oneself.

This initiation has numerous degrees and levels. The first degree is the very fertilization of the human being; the second is birth. But these are just the starting steps, when the child is completely passive. There is not yet anything that can properly be called initiation. Initiation begins with the step from *bios* to *zoê*, from pure physical- chemical biology to humanly conscious life (without entering further into details).

Man, we said, is the priest of earth. This priesthood or mediation between the two worlds begins with the first initiation, which has as many names as there are different cultures. The first proper initiation transforms the child into a being who is reborn (as in Hinduism), into a mature member of the chosen people (Judaism), into a complete man as son of God, as Christ (Christianity), into a *sui iuris* member of the community (animism), and so on. It is then that human life, properly speaking, begins.

But initiations do not end there. Confirmation, marriage, ordination, and extreme unction are as many other initiations within the Christian tradition—in spite of trivialization, in many cases. We give this example because, until recently, studies on initiation have been limited to initiation rituals among so-called primitives or in secret societies. Varro in his *De re rustica* (III, 1:5) calls *initia* the "mysteries." And we know that the Greek word that is used (*teletê*) means "perfection, plenitude."

Without pursuing these arduous historical-religious paths any further, our proposal is the following. An animal cannot have the *experience* of *God* in the sense that we are giving these two words; in order for us to realize this experience, we have to achieve the fullness of our humanity (in its various degrees, which are not rigidly graded). The sentence, "It is not good for man to be alone," does not only mean that Man needs company to—literally—share bread (*cum-panis*); it also means that he belongs to a horizontal community with his fellows, and a vertical community in both directions, on the higher level with the divine, and on the lower with the chthonian. In different terms: the experience of God occurs in and with the totality of reality, directly in contact with the three worlds—a contact that many sages have called the mystical "touch."

Passive Attitude: *Yin*

We can, however, say more about the *how*, a strict corollary of what we have just presented. By saying that there is not a *how*, we are not defending some kind of anarchical individualism, where "each minor master has his own little treatise." In the first place, genuine masters have read many books, although they do not follow any of them blindly. Mothers do not learn to be mothers in hygiene classes or courses in child psychology (useful as this may be) but by giving birth to the child, feeding it, and living with it. And there is more than that.

We said, in fact, that initiation comes from the outside; it is an initiative of transcendence. This leads us to put the emphasis on our responsibility. The initiative of life comes from life. We cannot give it to ourselves. The initiative for all initiation comes from the Spirit. The initiative for initiation into the "experience of God" comes from God. *Pati divina*, the mystics say: to suffer the impact of the divine initiative. This leads us to reassert the value of the passive attitude in the face of our problem, although without falling into the opposite extreme or accepting degrading abuses.

So, our knowledge does not lead us to the goal, nor does our will open us to the experience of God. God cannot be the answer to any question—in which case, we would be making Him an idol, an object, a concept, an answer. If God is superior to us, the initiative has to come from Him. That is probably why Huang Po asserted, "Don't look for the truth. Your very search would destroy what you are looking for." He is telling us that the *yang* (masculine principle) would destroy the *yin* (feminine principle); God is not an *object* of research. As all the mystics know, the attitude before God is mainly passive—may I say feminine? It is truth that searches for us.

An endemic sin of humanity, which has millennial roots, is cultural patriarchy, the often despotic and mostly unilateral domination by one part of humanity. What we have here is something that definitely looks like a form of social "feminism." It is a matter, at this ultimate level, of Man forgetting the passive attitude (although not a quietist nor a "passivist" one) in the face of the mystery of reality. One example of this lies in the philosophical reductionism that identifies reality with what ontology reveals to us, and still worse, reduces ontology to a "word of being," to a purely rational interpretation of reality, since we think that we can dominate it through reason. This has led to the split between epistemology and ontology, and the reduc- tion of this new science of knowledge to what I have called "the epistemology of the hunter"—that is, to set out with reason as a weapon in order to reach the object, capture it, and fully grasp it. This masculine epistemology, which has eliminated the Spirit, is certainly incapable of being applied to God. This is the epistemology that makes us believe that we can know without loving.

There are passages in St. Luke, which I will merely cite, and resist the tempta- tion to comment on them (Lk 1:29, 34, 45; 2:19, 47–51), in which the evangelist lets us understand that Mary—like everybody else—had not grasped much of what had happened in Bethlehem, Jerusalem, and in the town of Judas, but she "kept all these things and pondered them in her heart" (Lk 2:19). Rational comprehension is not the only paradigm of intelligibility, nor the highest one. Keeping everything in one's heart is something more than reasoning.

To arrive at the experience of God, it is necessary to let oneself be fertilized, be surprised; it is necessary to reverse epistemology: "I know because I am known; I love because I am loved," say both John and Paul (1 Jn 4:10; Gal 2:20). This attitude of allowing oneself to be seized and known, of permitting the experience to take place in ourselves, is extremely widespread in humanity. Every experience, understood in its most profound sense, is always passive. It is neither projection nor objectivation; to desire it is of no great help and can even become counterproductive. It may take place or not, with or without meditation, by a sudden act or by a long process, or even a misfortune. We cannot reduce everything to our mental patterns.

In still other terms, the expression "experience of God" can be interpreted in the sense of a subjective and not an objective genitive. In fact, it is not *my* experience *about* God, but the experience *of* God—in me and through me—of which I am conscious. The meaning of the subjective genitive refers to the very experience of God, who, as much as He confers it on me or I participate in it, is what constitutes the deepest kernel of my being. That is to say, the experience of God is not my experience of Him, of which I am aware. "My experience" would be, to use the metaphor of the hunter, to aim at an object, a reality which is called God, and to try to experience it. But to pretend to make God fall into my experience seems even blasphemous to me. The experience of God in the sense of a subjective genitive would be a participation of myself in the experience of God. It implies my conscious response and my participa- tion in this experience, whose ultimate subject is precisely God. I understand my participation in that experience as a communion, a communion between God, who is the subject, and that experience of God which is mine insofar as I am aware of it.

To accept the experience of God in the sense of a subjective genitive implies understanding that the way leading there does not consist in searching but in letting Him meet us. We do not have the initiative. A brief story, taken from Huang Po, illustrates this well. A being thirsty for God, in search of the experience of God, goes off into the valley to do penance, to meditate. He goes there in order to prepare himself, to purify himself. But he achieves nothing, finds nothing. Then he cries, protests, claims. Then, he perceives a voice from the top of the mountain, and he climbs to the summit of the mountain in order to listen to it. But once there, he neither finds nor hears anything. He goes back into the valley with the feeling that he is being mocked, that he has been deceived; therefore, he cries out and protests again. And again he hears the voice. He climbs back to the summit of the mountain and finds nothing but silence. And he descends and climbs, climbs and descends— until he becomes silent, stops claiming, stops searching. He then understands that the voice that he had heard was nothing but his own echo.

3
Privileged Places for the Experience of God

We can encounter God everywhere. It is simply necessary to seek Him and hold ourselves ready for the encounter. This is a widely shared thesis. According to classical theology, God is immense, omnipresent. Another equally traditional thesis affirms that God is simple, although it is often forgotten that these attributes should be conjugated simultaneously. God is everywhere, is immense, yet does not have parts: He is simple. What this means is that we can meet Him completely in any place whatever. It happens too often that the concerns of life, especially modern life, prevent us from being conscious of this. The fish has a certain awareness of things but he does not perceive that he is surrounded by water, just as we do not perceive God; we do not go beyond our purely animal consciousness. The animal does not believe in God—he does not believe that he exists in water.

This metaphor permits us to go a little further. The fish does not get wet. It is only when he leaves the water that we become aware (because he dies) that he is drenched. It is the knowledge, which is always the knowledge of good and evil, that makes us aware that we are drenched (by God). And like the fish that dies, it is only by dying to ourselves, by abandoning the ego-latry, that we will discover ourselves drenched, surrounded by God—as it is described in a very beautiful way at the beginning of the *Īśa-upaniṣad*, among numerous other texts: "The Lord envelopes the totality of the world."

Nevertheless, some places exist in which the water that surrounds us is made more manifest than in others. We speak of "places" because of the poverty of our language and its incapacity to overcome spatiotemporal paradigms (categories). The metaphor of water can help us. Water (God), for the fish, exists in all places, although it is perhaps better seen in some places than others because in those places we more clearly perceive the water that drenches us. But the water that touches us is not seen; what we do see is the thing that is soaked. The experience of God is not the experi- ence of an object, not even of a special "object." It is the experience of the divinity of the thing, but not in the form of an accident "glued" to it. Here, however, the metaphor of water is no longer helpful to us. "God is that in comparison (with which) substance is an accident and the accident is nothing," says aphorism VI in *The Book of Hermetic Tradition of the XXIV Philosophers*, a text widely cited and appreciated by Christian Scholasticism. We have the experience of God in the thing, and God is not only inseparable from it, but also identical to the deepest reality of the thing itself—like in the Trinity, in whose bosom the "persons" are both equal and distinct.

After all we have said, it ought to be clear that these encounters with the divine are not always with a personal God as is commonly understood—without entering here into considerations on the misunderstanding that exists between East and West concerning the personality or nonpersonality of God. The first generations of Christians criticized the "heathens" because they personified the forces of nature by divinizing them. Recent post-Christian generations reproach Christians for having an anthropomorphic vision of God. In our time, we are perhaps in a position to see the misunderstandings of both. God is not reducible either to a super-*kosmos* or to a super-*anthrôpos*. Here is the root of the *cosmotheandric* intuition.

But then, it will be asked, what precisely is it that we encounter?

A response that would be too rapid, though not false, would say that we encounter Nothingness—that we encounter nothing. Haven't we been saying that God is not a thing?

Another response, that it would be necessary to examine at length, would say that we meet the *alter* and not the *aliud* of ourselves: the Other of ourselves, without which we would not exist. Let us not confuse the *alter* (symbol of that part of ourselves that is unknown to us) with the *aliud* (that part of ourselves that is distinct from us, which alienates us from ourselves). God is an *alter*, not an *aliud.*

A third reaction would consist in explaining that we meet the ātma*n*, the deepest aspect of ourselves.

Ultimately, the three answers end up saying the same thing : God is nothing other than this *alter* of myself, that is, the Self in its totality.

Perhaps we could say this in another way that would be more consistent with the mind of the West. The place where we experience God, by antonomasia, is Man, Man himself—as we have said, the Self. The "drama" of reality takes place between God and the Evil One in an arena that is Man himself, as it has been described in the very varied colors of world literature. Man is the meeting (and collision) point in which the dynamism of reality is played out. The privileged "place" is Man, certainly not the so-called rational animal, but the Man that includes Adam, Jacob, Gilgamesh, the Man that Dante did not dare to name, or Faust—these are only a few represen- tatives, among others... the Man who is perhaps too hidden in each one of us, and whom only poets, mystics, and a few philosophers are capable of describing for us.

History is the stage on which the battle between Gods and Asuras, God and Lucifer, is played out. The life of Jesus Christ offers us a paradigm in his constant struggle with the demons: this is the drama of redemption. The human vocation is sometimes too great for us. That is why we have belittled God. It is not by chance that Nietzsche, who was passionate about Christ, was so obsessed with Greek tragedy....

But our meditation was just trying to describe an experience, without having to linger over these—however fascinating—issues.

As we have already said, to communicate an experience is no minor affair. Let us remember that, according to several schools of Eastern spirituality, the master shows up only when the disciple is ready. The reading of a book that hopes to communi- cate something more than information requires the reader to receive the seed in a soil carefully prepared by manure. If the reader is not prepared, the writing will not penetrate into his/her heart. There exists a brief aphorism in the *Yoga-sūtra* (III.34): "It is in the heart that the knowledge that liberates lies" (*Hṛdaye cittasaμvit*). This insight is echoed in the *Gītā* (VIII.12) and is elaborated in the Sufist conception of heart (*qalb*). We would like to speak to the reader's heart.

But the responsibility of the text's author is still greater; he or she should not write about what he or she has not experienced. On the other hand, a certain modesty requires the author to adorn experience in poetry or present it in more or less philosophical prose. In both cases, the author utilizes words: words, moreover, that die as soon as they are written, like fish taken out of the water. Writing is not the natural element of the word. "The letter kills," St. Paul says (2 Co 3:6); the sheep "hear the voice of the shepherd," St. John reports (10:27). It is up to the reader not only to read but also to listen to the written and give it new life. Let this serve as an excuse for the fact that the pages that follow do not pretend to record experiences but to describe places to which the reader is invited.

Another important remark is necessary. This whole book is an endeavor to liberate God from both specialists and specializations. The experience of God is open to everyone. It is the Gospel, the "good news" accessible to children, the humble, the poor—to the people. It is not necessary to belong to a particular caste or to any religion, or to be a great scholar. But there is one indispensable condition, which is probably the hardest, since all the traditions of humanity tell us that those who are saved, who attain their realization, who will not be reincarnated but arrive at *nirvā...a*, those who reach Man's plenitude, will be few.... We meet God every- where, but not in just any way. We should never make the experience of God banal. Aesthetic ecstasy, erotic rapture, intellectual admiration, biological joy, suffering or enthusiasm about nature, none of these are experiences of the divine. They could be so, in extreme circumstances, but they would then have to be pure experiences. That is the condition: purity of heart.

I repeat: "Blessed are the pure of heart, for they will see God" (Mt 5:8), they will experience God. A pure heart is an empty heart, without ego, capable of reaching that depth at which the divine lives. The fact that the experience is simple does not mean that it is easy. A text of the *Upaniṣads*, on which we will comment later, after having told us that God is found in nourishment, in what is seen, what is heard and understood, adds that in any case the way passes through asceticism, effort, ardor, *tapas*—purification.

Among the innumerable "places" where God is to be found, we will briefly mention nine, without explaining precisely what is found in any of them. Don't we all admit that, ultimately, God is ineffable?

Love

There seems to be unanimity, both in the cultures of the North and of the South, in telling us that the most privileged place for the meeting of Man and God is the experience of love. "God is love," and those who encounter love encounter God. Up to this point, there is a great agreement of opinion. The difficulty appears with the dualism in the interior of love itself—basically, between the world and God.

The relegation of God to a sphere of transcendence and the absolute has created a virtually lethal split in the very being of Man. Love, as the *Vedas* say (*RV* X.129.4ff.), has existed from the Beginning; it is more sublime than all the Gods and is the first seed of the intellect. Humanity's most ancient monuments affirm something quite similar. There is no doubt that love is only another name for the dynamism of every being who tends to "that" which is not an *aliud* but an *alter*: such is the dynamism of love. We would not be able to experience the desire for God or the aspiration to the divine if "that" was absolutely foreign and unknown to us. This dynamism shows its validity in everything, from the Trinity to the last elementary particle of matter. How could it fail to be a place to meet God?

Whatever distinction it might be good or necessary to make, in the last instance there is *one and only one love*. In terms of medieval Scholasticism, whether Jewish, Christian, or Muslim, this ultimate love is God. To the degree that every being desires something, it desires God, as St. Thomas says explicitly.

Since the heart is the symbol of love, those who have a pure heart will see God. *Ubi caritas et amor, Deus ibi est,* as is prayed in a popular, paraliturgical Christian song.

The mysticism of every age and every continent has left us pearls of wisdom on the subject of love. "I am the religion of love," says a great mystic of Murcie in the twelfth to thirteenth centuries, and adds, "Where the camels of love are headed is where my religion and faith are found." The heart (*qalb*) is a fundamental idea in Sufism.

The heart, the nearly universal symbol of love, is a human organ, and this reaf- firms the unity of love. "It is through the heart that we know the truth," says another sacred text (*BU* III.9.23).

Love is one, we have said. This unity is an a-dualistic unity. There are not two loves, nor can divine and human love be separated, even though a distinction is needed. As soon as this distinction is transformed into a split, the rupture constitutes a sin.

It is difficult to enjoy the experience of God's love if one does not share human love. Similarly, it is difficult to persevere in human love if one doesn't discover in it a divine soul, so to speak. Genuine love is far more than a voluntarist projection or an example of simple sentimentality. It is not a matter of going beyond the love of creatures, of abandoning them in order to raise oneself to the divine love. God does not live only on the mountains of nothingness; he also has his dwelling place in the "woody valleys" of humanity. It is in human love itself that divinity resides. As the New Testament reminds us, a divine love that is not incarnated in the love of neighbor is nothing but a lie (1 Jn 4:20).

The You

The love of God and the love of things derive from the same dynamism of our being—what the Scholastics would call "appetite." These two loves are distinct but inseparable. In the love of neighbor this a-dualist relationship appears most clearly— in the love of *you*, the *you* of ourselves. The primacy accorded to the principle of noncontradiction, which is valid in logic but not necessarily in reality, has often led us to divide all of reality in terms of that principle: Christians/non-Christians, believers/nonbelievers, English/non-English, good/bad (in a moral sense), and so on. German idealism speaks of *Ich/Nicht Ich*, and European Cartesianism similarly starts out from the duality of body/soul, spirit/matter, in which one thing is defined by the fact of not being the other.

The you is neither the I nor the non-I. Nor is it a middle term that would then permit a synthesis. Its relation is *advaita*; there is no you without an I, and vice versa. The two are correlative.

In human loves, the love of the *you* dominates. This you is perhaps the most important and most universal place for the experience of God. In fact, to meet God in one's neighbor is part of the common cultural patrimony of humanity.

But we will restrict ourselves here to the experience of God as the experience of you. Let us recall that, in practice, the wisdom of every people teaches us how openness to the experience of God is able to emerge:

- By means of knowledge (*jñāna*), through the effort of the intelligence to transcend itself: God is experienced as an "I."
- By means of love (*bhakti*), through the heart's desire to seek what can fill it: God is seen as a "You."
- By means of deeds (*karma*), through the creativity of the creature who wishes to imitate the Creator by creating, that is, by doing : God is seen as a "He" (the model, the maker).

The different schools of spirituality that follow each of these three ways are well known. Inasmuch as they are ways, they lead with certainty to God. Our commentary, however, will not deal with the paths; it will look at the underlying experience of those who follow them.

The first way leads us to God as the ultimate and supreme I: YHWH, Aham, the ultimate Subject.... "How can we get to know the one who knows?" one *Upaniṣad* asks. He who knows—the I—as such cannot be known. In fact, if we knew the one who knows, we would transform him into a known object. Although we are able to say that the two are the same, our experience will turn on what is known, not on the one who knows. The latter, to the degree in which he is the one who knows, truly knows, but he is not known.

There is no possible experience of the I. The Son is the one who knows the Father; it is *Īśvara* who knows himself as *brahman*; the pure consciousness is pure consciousness and not the consciousness of anything (not even itself); the light remains invisible unless it illuminates something different from light itself. Our experience of the I is an experience of the *me*; it is my experience of "me," not of "I." The structure of experience cannot be monist: it would not have the polarity necessary for every experience. The very structure of experience is a-dualist. It implies a negation of duality, without falling into a monolithic monism. Strictly speaking, my I is a you-I; it is the I of a you. Only when I have the experience of me/myself as yours am I able to enter, as a you, into the experience of I.

In other words, God does not have the experience of "I-myself." He has it rather of "himself," which precisely implies a-duality, or the trinity. *Brahman* does not know that he is *brahman*, the *Vedānta* says. But *Īśvara* knows it; he knows himself as *brahman.* And it is this self-consciousness that makes *Īśvara* equal to *brahman.*

The way of love discovers God as a you. The majority of Abrahamic spiritualities see it in this way. God is the you to whom all prayers are addressed. Nevertheless, strictly speaking, we cannot say that we have the experience of God as a you. The experience is personal, and the you is you, it is not the I; whereas the subject of my experience is "I."

But I am able to experience God by experiencing myself as a you of God when I discover myself to be "His," that is to say, when I feel that I am yours, the you of the I. I discover God not when I discover Him as a you (to whom I address myself), but as an I who addresses himself to me, and for whom my "ego" is His "you." I am then a you of God.

The experience of God, therefore, is the experience of you, a you that God calls "you"—the experience that I am precisely "I," my true ego, the you, a you of God. The experience of God is so personal because each one of us is only that very experi- ence of God in me, in which I discover myself precisely as the "you" of that "I" who names me, and in naming me gives me being, as the texts of both Old and New Testament assert: "You are." This discovery is a revelation. God is disclosed in the form of you in me: "You are my son" (Mk 1:11; Lk 3:22); "I, today, have begotten you" (Ps 2:7; Ac 13:33). The initiative comes from me; my I is only a you, a you of God. And if I sense that God is saying to me, "you are," it is because in truth I am a you, and God is the unique I.

The word with which Jesus blesses Peter is very significant: "Who do people say that the Son of Man is?... But you, who do you say I am?" (Mt 16:13–15). And Peter answers, "You are the Christ, the Son of the living God" (Mt 16:16). Christ blesses Peter because he has pronounced the one word that reveals him: "you," "you are," before he adds, in the language and culture of the time, other predicates and adjectives (Messiah, Son) as additions to the discovery of the You.

I have defended elsewhere the thesis that the famous *mahāvākya*, the *upaniṣadic* affirmation, *tat tvam asi*, does not repeat, like others, "We are *brahman*," but that it adds, "You are that, Âvetaketu, a you" (that: you are).

We are identical with *brahman* without ceasing to be what we are, that is, the you of *brahman*: *sagu...a brahman*, identical with him, *nirgu...a brahman*.

But there is more. *Brahman* is everything, God is in all things. Consequently, this manner of discovering the divine you in everything, and especially in our neighbor, is the most common and human way of experiencing God. It is written: "Love your neighbor as yourself." Only when this "myself " is discovered as a divine you we will be able to love the other as a "myself." This means to discover God in one's neighbor, to discover him/her as a you of God, and hence divine.

There is not a dialectical relationship between the you and the I, but a dialogical, a-dualist one. The you is not the I, but neither is it the non-I. This is what Idealism forgot. Between the I and the non-I there is the you. The you is you because it is the you of the I, and we can affirm the same thing about the I. The I is always an I of a you. Not even God is a solitary Being, as we are reminded by both Prajāpati and the Trinity, though from two different standpoints. As for us, at the very moment when the I knows itself as you, as "yours," it is saved.

Whoever fails to arrive at the discovery of the "you"—which obviously cannot be done without thought, without love and without action—is cut off from the possibility of experiencing the divine. The experience of God is the experience of the "you," which leads us to the impossibility of the experience of the "I," because the "I" cannot experience itself without being "objectivized" into a "you." Therefore, "I" cannot be experienced, while "you" can. This is why, when one discovers oneself as the "you" of God, one experiences God by making the experience of "you." And, as everyone knows, it is only when we love that we discover the "you."

The "you" is also the poor man, the other, the friend, the partner, some will even say the enemy: the leap to transcendence, without breaking immanence. For only by starting from the immanence of a "you" that discovers itself as "yours" it is possible to experience God. In this way, we return to love, the point of arrival and departure—that love that the *Vedas* say is the first seed of the mind (*AV* XIX.52.1) and the first of the Gods (*AV* IX.2.19), and that Christian scripture declares (1 Jn 4:8, 16) is God himself.

"Were I to testify on my own behalf, my testimony would not be valid" (Jn 5:31). The I does not know itself. In this text Jesus does not say that his testimony would not be valid because it would be a lie; what he says is that the testimony of a you whom he calls his Father is genuine. I am not able to know myself, and therefore cannot bear a genuine witness of myself. This is up to a "you." Just, not any "you"; it is my you, that I recognize as such, and for that reason I know and recognize that he/she tells the truth.

The "know yourself " is therefore possible only if the myself is known by someone who is not just anyone, but my true *alter*, the you. I know to the degree to which I am known (1 Co 13:12). This knowledge is at once active and passive. I know inasmuch as I am known, but I also know that I am known. This you is intimately linked to the I inasmuch as they are neither two nor one: "Who can know the depths of a man, except the spirit of the man that is in him?" (1 Co 2:11). The true you is the spirit of the man that is in him. But the same is true of God (1 Co 2:12). And it is in this Spirit that we are able to experience God. But none of this can be understood without love.

Joy

Ultimately, all these "places" are linked together. Love is a source of joy, although it can be a source of suffering as well. But perhaps this is just a feature of our time, insofar as it "swings" between negative Manichean attitudes toward life and asphyxi- ating hedonist views of life itself.

Max Scheler, in his criticism of Kant and Protestant Puritanism, spoke of the "betrayal of joy" by Christianity. But this is not the only example of the absence of joy in religious manifestations. Catholics have been rightly criticized for their "Good Friday" spirituality, a piety that is far removed from life, a spirituality that is virtually the enemy of joy, which is considered as simply a concession to the old carnal Man.

We are not going to stop to recall the Scholastic thesis on happiness as the very purpose of our lives; neither are we going to comment on the *Upani@ ads* when they describe ānand*a*, or happiness, as the essential characteristic of *brahman*. We are tempted, however, to cite the *Taittirīya-upani@ad* (II.5.ff.) with its description of *brahman* and even ātma*n* as happiness.

What is clear is that in the current Western—and specifically Christian—mentality, joy is not generally seen as one of the places where the experience of God finds one of its purest expressions.

And we say "purest" because, in the experience of joy, reflection plays a minimal and only indirect role. A pure (moral) conscience is not enough to allow that kind of attenuation of (intellectual and reflective) consciousness that would permit the spontaneity and human joy that the presence of divine realities brings to light. Popular piety with its *gozos* (hymns of praise) to the Virgin may sometimes be more healthy.

"A saint who is sad is a bad saint," Léon Bloy said, and we are familiar with André Gide's criticism of the negative commandments. It hardly seems necessary to quote Albert Camus, Friedrich Nietzsche, and many others, including the verses of Rubén Darío, that make the same point—against Thomas à Kempis.

Many have commented in the same style on the usual absence of humor in theology and philosophy.

What we would want to underline here is not so much a negative criticism, or a theoretical defense of God as joy, as rather the fact that we do not sufficiently realize that joy is the privileged place for experiencing the divine. God is the God of the living, and life is *joy.*

Now, without stopping to give definitions of joy, or make subtle distinctions between happiness, cheerfulness, euphoria, satisfaction, felicity, pleasure, enjoy- ment, jubilation, and numerous other synonyms—what we are attempting to say is more simple.

The whole ensemble of synonyms could be reduced to sensation, feeling, the understanding of life's plenitude. The Christ said that he had come to give us life in abundance (Jn 10:10), and the fundamental text of his message bears the title "The Beatitudes."

It is the part of wisdom to discover true joy and the experience that it contains the very source of delight, which comes close to being a definition of God.

It is extremely significant that Christianity, which supposedly is the religion of joy, is so frequently considered a sad religion. The *alleluias* and cries of praise are the most frequent prayers in the Judeo-Christian tradition; sadness (*acedia*) was long considered a capital sin; the very word "grace," not only in Greek but also in English, connotes joy and jubilation; the *gaudium de veritate* is part and parcel of the most ancient Christian tradition; and the resurrection of the body holds a central place in the Christian message. Nevertheless, the equilibrium has often been lost. Numerous Christians enjoy life with a guilt complex, and a certain negative spirituality regarding life has invaded many circles, which have come to confuse perfection with what is least natural, yet has sometimes been christened as "supernatural."

Perhaps it is the responsibility of contemporary pedagogy to teach the true pleasures of life, those pleasures that are the most fundamental precisely because they are the most natural. We return again and again to the same point: only the innocent know complete joy and only a pure heart experiences joy—and with it, God.

Perhaps it is opportune here to mention again the text of the *Taittirīya-upaniṣad* (III.1.1ff.), when, speaking of *brahman* as happiness, it affirms the idea that the knowledge of *brahman* is an encounter with nourishment (food, *annam*), life (breath, *prā...a*), intellect (*manas*), and intelligence (*vijñāna*) and so on, that is, with an experience of human activity at its greatest depth.

Here, as everywhere, it is appropriate to maintain a middle way: "Nothing to excess" is an aphorism of the Presocratics, in addition to being a tautology.

Suffering

We ought to distinguish between pain, sorrow, and suffering. All three words are ambiguous and are too often used indiscriminately. Without pretending to define them, I would understand pain as basically a biological sensation. Animals do feel pain, and a number of authors speak of "soul pain," since animals have a soul. Sorrow would be chiefly a psychophysical pain. Sorrow is inflicted to and felt in the soul; sometimes the word is used to express something uniquely spiritual. We use the word "suffering" as the combination between the bodily, the psychic, and the spiritual. A certain suffering is not incompatible with joy. *Pati divina* is a traditional phrase of Latin mysticism, and it implies a great deal of ambivalence. If the experience of God in joy is ecstatic, then in suffering it may be called enstatic—to use the word Mircea Eliade has introduced, *enstasis.*

The cause of suffering may be pain, injustice, humiliation, the loss of a good, the anguish for an endangered or uncertain future.

It is not only the words that are ambivalent, but the very effects. Suffering is capable of bringing us closer to God, but it can also separate us from the divine. It can purify or degrade us, make us mature or bring us to despair.

We are not entering here into the area of voluntary sufferings, as practiced by a series of spiritualities of both East and West, which believe that voluntary suffering is capable of purifying us. It is a fact that this belief, shared by many *saμnyāsin*, monks, and even mystics, has produced positive results, however aberrant they appear to us. Our contemporary myth, however, rejects such negative asceticisms.

I would like to mention here the suffering that is not self-inflicted, but which is provoked by all kinds of causes, as well as that produced by an illness that affects us or someone else, all the way up to the physical and moral hardships due to unjust situations at the personal or the social level.

The passion for justice leads to suffering when one sees the forces of evil or the simple inertia of history offer resistance and defend themselves by attacking. The case of the persecutions against Christians in Latin America because they wanted to change an unjust *status quo* constitutes a clear illustration of this issue. The situation of Tibet and Africa, to cite only the most obvious examples, cannot leave us indifferent.

Personal suffering is also a meeting place with the divine, although it remains good advice, both psychological and religious, not to take pleasure in suffering as an end in itself. Nevertheless, suffering is a kind of existential awakening to a depth dimension in ourselves as well as in reality as a whole. According to popular wisdom, suffering brings us closer to God and to others, but we are requested no strange alchemical transformation, so that suffering can open us to Mystery rather than plunge us into despair.

Suffering is often so inexplicable that it brings us close to the divine mystery itself: it is the arena that reveals our freedom. "Learn to discern *brahman* by means of ascesis" (*Tapasā brahma vijijñāsasva*) is the refrain of the *Upaniṣad* already cited (*TU* III.2.1ff.).

Suffering is closely related to sensibility, both psychosomatic and cosmic, that is, to our participation in solidarity with the universe.

It is obvious that belief in a good and omnipotent God will give rise to blasphemy in us, rather than submission to what we cannot but consider as immoral—whether in not relieving evil when He was able to, or permitting it in view of a higher good, as if the end justified the means. We have here an example of an experience affected by a previous interpretation, but perhaps the very experience of suffering purifies the idea of God, too.

One fact, however, is empirically established: suffering, like joy, is a human situ- ation that can serve both as a vehicle for experiencing God as well as the complete opposite. Suffering confronts us with the irrational, with human wickedness, with evil, with the collapse of all our plans and security; it destabilizes and upsets us, it removes every impression we have of being self-sufficient, strips us of everything and places us before what is painful, incomprehensible, and makes us indignant, and against which we instinctively revolt. Think of the suffering of a man condemned to death or to life imprisonment, whether guilty or innocent. Think not just of a Job but of the millions of our brothers and sisters who suffer, together with the fact that we might theoretically be able to relieve most of their sufferings. Here the experience of God, before being a consolation, is a communion. We touch grace in the same way that we touch mystery.

The spirituality of the *bodhisattva* is an example that offers hope. The *bodhisattva* does not lose his joy but remains on earth, participating in the suffering of creatures in order thereby to help them liberate themselves.

We have said that suffering can be an awakening to transcendence and in this way be a meeting place with God. We have to complete this thought by saying that it can equally be a revelation of immanence—even in the very encounter with God.

The *bodhisattva*, the saint, and the wise one suffer not so much by reason of what does them harm individually, but perhaps even more for humankind, for all sensible beings, for the cosmos. That is the experience of *buddhakāya*, of *karman*, of the Mystical Body of Christ, of the universal fraternity—to give quite different examples of this experience of universal solidarity. The reason that makes those who are "fulfilled" more open to this participation in reality is simple. The *mahātma* (the magnanimous one, the great soul), the *jīvanmukta* (liberated soul), the *insan kamil* (perfect one), the *shen jen* (the holy one), the saint (*hagios*, *sanctus*, *kadosh*, etc.), the *edel Mensch* (the noble soul, according to Eckhart, commenting on Lk 19:12), to cite a great diversity of traditions—in a word, those who have reached human plenitude have broken the barriers of individualism and entered into communion with the entire cosmos. The wise person is the one who captures the hearts of all people, and Meister Eckhart, repeating a popular belief, affirms that "he who knows himself knows all creatures" (in his treatise, *The Noble Man*). This linking up of everything with everything else unites us to reality through contemplation, prayer, and glory, as well as by means of participation in the sufferings of creation, whether the agony of childbirth or of despair.

Here is another empirical constant: human beings seem to feel the link that unites them to all of reality when they are more conscious of the negative than the positive aspects—in the same way that we rarely think of our stomach when it functions normally.

In sum, suffering makes us feel our human condition and our creaturely state more profoundly, regardless of how it is interpreted. It is enough to listen to the text of any musical rendering of the *Stabat Mater* of Christian tradition (not necessarily the version by Palestrina) to understand what I mean. The participation through love in the pain of another—this awareness of being part of a whole opens us to the experience of God. It is well known that prisoners and victims of human cruelty collapse less readily if they keep alive their faith in something that transcends them and that at the same time lives within them.

Belief in the "satisfaction [of God's justice] by substitution [of us, made by Christ on the cross]" and in a certain usefulness of suffering can be a great consola- tion, but the pure experience of the divine mystery can assume more radical forms, which border on the terrible and the horrible. Faith is neither the rationalization of God nor of life. Christ's cry of despair on the cross is revealing—but so is his last exclamation: "Into your hands I commend my spirit" (Lk 23:46). In any case, we recognized that the experience of God is no trifling affair.

Evil

Religion includes what is best in the human being. It is from its inspiration that the greatest geniuses, the most refined cultures, the cathedrals, the most sublime temples, have emerged; the most heroic acts have been performed in its name. But it has also stirred up the worst and most wicked side of Man. Religion has not only been opium but poison as well; it has served as excuse for committing the greatest crimes and causing the worst aberrations at any level. Evil is an integral (though not necessarily constitutive) part of reality; and religion, precisely because it is real, participates in this ambivalence.

The problem of evil—without entering now into metaphysical discussions about its degree of reality—is definitely a fact, as well as an intrinsically religious question that has stimulated Man, throughout his entire history, to try to explain it according to the most diverse theories. From the conception of evil as being no more than an appearance to the recognition of its reality as equal to the principle of the good, we find a range of hypotheses that correspond to the various worldviews. It is interesting to note, too, that the great religions are never centered on Man but on the cosmos, in whose development evil plays an active role. Let us remember the numerous cosmogonies that show evil as the original sin, originating the actual condition of the cosmos.

Evil as evil is unintelligible. The *mysterium iniquitatis* is a mystery precisely because our reason cannot grasp it, because we find no explanation for it, because it has proved incomprehensible for us. If we did succeed in explaining evil, if—through Freud, Jung, Lacan, or whomever else—we found the key that permitted us to justify it, then evil would no longer exist. If we were indeed capable of explaining it, it would only be a bomb whose detonator has been turned off, thus deactivating it. Once the mystery was deactivated, evil would no longer exist.

Evil has no internal intelligibility; it has no ultimately rational *why*. There is no reason capable of explaining it, because it would then cease to be evil. In this case, in fact, it would be grounded in a sufficient reason, it would be reasonable. There cannot be evil for an omniscient being. In fact, absolute monotheisms will deny any metaphysical consistency to evil. To search for a cause of evil, in an attempt to explain it, leads back to an ultimate Cause that has then to be confronted with the Principle of the Good, as all cosmological dualisms well know. In the opposite case, Satan (as symbol of evil) cannot but be a faithful collaborator of God, as we so pathetically see in the book of Job. *Von Zeit zu Zeit, sen ich den Alten gern* (I like to go see the Old One from time to time), says Mephistopheles in *Faust*.

But the *mysterium iniquitatis* also constitutes a moral challenge to monotheism: How can evil have a place in a radical monotheism that believes in a good and all powerful God? The Jewish Kabbalah, which offers the hypothesis of a faraway God, would illustrate a fourth attempt at an explanation. Another example, drawn from Islamic theology—which perhaps represents the purest monotheism (and is not inclined to reduce evil to nothing but a pure appearance)—can serve to show how, in the ultimate instance, evil is in fact an integral part of the divine plan.

Let me summarize the moving and exciting story of the *Kitâb at-Tawâsîn*, attributed to the great mystic and martyr Al-Hallāj, which was translated into French by Louis Massignon. Iblîs (Lucifer), the most beautiful of the angels, the first and most glorious of the creatures that sprang forth from the hands of the Creator, clashes with Him when the latter lets him know that he will have to serve, and even adore, a mortal being composed of flesh, or mud (according to other texts): Man. Iblîs refuses, and says, "I am the one who knows you best of all; I am your most perfect creature. I have sworn fidelity and eternal love to you. How can you want me to turn my back on you who are the light and source of all, and go to serve—even by order of you—another creature who is distinct from you?" He adds that he knows that God intends to put into motion time and creation... and that he has decided to disobey, out of love and fidelity, while accepting the responsibility and punishment for his act. Iblîs is blinded by love and reacts like a rejected lover.

One day Moses and Iblîs meet, and Moses asks, "What prevented you from prostratingyourself ?" To which Iblîs responds that it is precisely his vision of God as the Only One to Be Adored that has prevented it, "while you have turned your back on Him by going to the mountain."

"Have you thereby transgressed a divine commandment?"

"It was not a commandment," Satan answers. "It was only a test."

"Are you sinless then?" Moses asks again.

And immediately Iblîs reiterates his love and fidelity to God, arguing that, if God had truly wanted, Iblîs would not have had any other option than to obey Him; but since he does not obey God, it means that God needs him in his plans.

"Then you still remember Him?"

"Oh, Moses," he responds. "Pure thought has no need of recollection.... His memory and mine will never be able to be separated.... And I serve Him with a greater purity, a more glorious recollection. Before, I served Him for my joy; now I serve Him for His."

God and Iblîs: theirs is the story of a fidelity that proves incomprehensible if we do not understand what love and fidelity are. The experience of evil cannot be separated from the existence of a living God, precisely because God is all of reality. The ultimate explanation would perhaps be this greater fidelity to what makes possible the bursting out of the mystery of time.

In a nonmonotheistic perspective, there is not such repugnance to integrating evil within the very bosom of divinity. Indra, for example, the great Vedic God, precisely as Lord of good and evil, assumes certain attitudes that, from an ethical viewpoint, are clearly immoral. Indra deceives, makes use of good and evil as it seems good to him, throws everything upside down. Unlike the Christian mentality, in which God is incapable of doing evil, here divinity is able to prompt evil, therefore letting us experience God in the very experience of evil.

But the theology of Indra goes even further. Indra is not only what is represented by his popular epithet, Indra Vṛtrahan, "he who defeats (kills) the demon Vṛtra" who provoked a deadly dryness by holding back the imprisoned waters. Indra is beyond good and evil and, as an *Upaniṣad* says regarding the "realized" Man, he never torments himself by asking whether he has done good or evil (*BU* IV.4.22; *TU* II.9.2). The great book of Indic wisdom, the *Mahābhārata* (XII.337–40), puts this counsel in the mouth of the perfect Man: "Renounce both good and evil [*tyaja dharmam adharmaµ ca*]; renounce both the truth and the lie [*ubhe satyānṛte tyaja*]; and, having renounced them, renounce [the consciousness of] that very renunciation." Bringing water to our mill (for we are unable to consider the whole problematic), we will say that the experience of God is not necessarily to be seen as the experience of the Good—unlike Plato.

Tell me what you see "beyond good and evil" (*anyatra dharmād anyatra adharmād*), Naciketas demands to Yama, the God of the other world (*KathU* I.2.14). Notice that the texts cited tell us clearly that we cannot be beyond good unless we are simultaneously beyond evil. If God is, at the very least, the epitome of all reality, then the experience of God does put us in contact with the highest heavens, but also with "the depths of Satan" (*Rv* 2.24; using a Christian phrase which the Vulgate ironically translates as *altitudines Satanae*).

We say that the experience of evil is intimately linked to the experience of God for two reasons. The first is that the experience of God transcends morality and ethics, without in any way denying them. Religion is not simply ethics, even though we cannot separate them. To say this in the language of tradition, the divine mystery is beyond good and evil. In saying that it transcends this dualism we are by no means absolutely affirming that this is a good—or an evil.

The second reason is even more delicate. We have said that evil is an uncontested fact, a reality that we cannot neither deny nor evade. We have also said that evil is unintelligible. All this leads us to discover the revelatory character of evil. Evil reveals to us is that there is something unintelligible, that reality does not have to mean rationality or intelligibility. And this opens up a radical metaphysical option. The alternative sounds as follows.

Evil would be incomprehensible to human intelligence, but not to divine omni- science. But, if God knows evil, evil stops being such. For God, there would be no evil: torture, hatred, injustice would not, strictly speaking, be evil; the fact is that we are myopic. If God permits it, there will have been a reason, we are in the habit of saying, and we console ourselves by saying that it is an enigma (that we will perhaps cope with in another life). Monotheism encourages such a solution.

We must point out here, however, a philosophical a priori: reality is intelligible. An omniscient God, in fact, is that being who knows everything, and by this very fact the Whole turns into the Knowable. The omniscient Being knows everything knowable, but not necessarily all of reality, unless we identify reality with the capacity of being known.

This brings us to the other option of the alternative. Evil is real, it is the obscure part of reality, its unintelligible side. In the adventure of the real, God would be co-implicated like ourselves who, in the words of St. Paul, are his co-operators, although the "like" does not signify equality, nor the same level. Here we could deal with the cosmotheandric experience, but that would require another essay.

Getting back to the point, we may conclude that the concern *about* the problem of evil belongs to our very experience of God. And perhaps this God teaches us, in the most practical way, without metaphysical encumbrances, to try to confront us with the problem of *malum* (evil) without any malice.

There is no way of eliminating evil by making use of a counterevil. *Reconcilia- tion* is the one effective way of overcoming evil. By itself, dialectical confrontation only leads to a truce until the vanquished take their revenge. Evil is impermeable to reason, and therefore to judgment. It is written that we must not judge (Mt 7:1), especially interiorly. Reason neither explains evil nor eliminates it. Against the Stoic *vivere secundum rationem*, Christian liturgy sets the *vivere secundum te*. Evil can be transformed *only* by the heart. Reason by itself can press us to perform evil acts *by* explaining (not justifying) that they are reasonable. A pure heart cannot do this, though this is just a qualified tautology—like all fruitful tautologies. Not victory over evil, but innocence—that forgotten beatitude (see Mt 5:5 in Greek), which is a literal translation of the Sanskrit *a-hiīsā*, *in-nocens*, and corresponds to Matthew's

Greek word *prays*—"will possess the earth." Creation must not be destroyed.

We have made this digression in order to disenchant those who imagine the experience of God as a bed of flowers for privileged souls who have never experienced evil. In spite of the romantic summaries found in the "lives of the saints," it is they themselves who tell us that they are great sinners. Leaving aside psychology, we say that the very experience of evil often stimulates and introduces us to the experience of God, or may indeed constitute part of the same experience. A real God—a God who is not a pure idea—cannot be ignorant of the existence of evil. Jesus Christ did clearly experience evil, and even abandonment by God. It is quite likely that reality has a dark side that the God of monotheism simply cannot invade. Here problems are terribly serious, and our technocratic superficiality is little accustomed to them, despite the multiple manifestations of evil in our time. "It is fearful to fall into the hands of the living God," St. Paul dares to exclaim: human existence is not a frivolous game for children. We will have, however, to leave the question there in order to proceed to a special example that is a little less tragic.

Transgression

One of the ways of opening ourselves to transcendence—that is, of going beyond our own limits, of catching a glimpse of the infinite and the unknown—is, precisely, *transgression.* When someone has contravened a norm that one considers obliga- tory, the anguish is so great, and the world into which one enters is so unknown and dangerous, that only pardon or despair presents itself as an alternative that does not cheapen the transgression. In fact, it is no longer possible to turn back. When we have transgressed, we have eliminated any possibility of going back, of piecing together what we have broken. In the necessity of overcoming this anguish, of moving beyond the evil that has been committed, Man can find an opening to transcendence—we are speaking of a conscious and responsible transgression. If we reduce it to an everyday matter, however, we are no longer dealing with transgression but rather a simple, trivial faux pas. Mary Magdalen loved deeply precisely because she had been greatly pardoned, and she was greatly pardoned because she loved so much. This is a vital circle, the circle of life. It is not a vicious circle, that of reason.

Transgression confronts us in our freedom, and therefore entails our responsibility. There is an initially disconcerting phrase of Jesus that has not been accepted as canonical and hence does not appear in the Vulgate, but is not apocryphal, since it can be found in numerous important Greek texts. The phrase conveys a judgment about the issue of the Sabbath. As he is passing through the Galilean countryside, Jesus "meets a man who is working on the Sabbath and says to him, O man, blessed are you [*Anthrōpe... makarios ei*], if you know what you are doing [in breaking the Sabbath and having the courage to do so. Blessed are you if you transgress while knowing that you transgress], but if you do not know this, then you are accursed and a law-breaker" (see Lk 6:4).

This is the exact opposite of the morality of the confessional, as can be clearly understood. In such a morality, a nonculpable ignorance frees Man from sin. Not so in the morality that results from this passage, one that can be linked, and rightly so, with Jesus's iconoclastic affirmation that the Sabbath is made for Man and not Man for the Sabbath. This text is certainly dangerous and destabilizing. Socrates was condemned on the pretext that he was corrupting the youth, al-Hallāj and many others because they uttered a blasphemy or defended a heresy, Jesus because he claimed to abolish the Law, or give it only a relative value, at least, and establish freedom. Not only the Sanhedrin but the Vatican, too—and many other institutions—have been and remain more "prudent." "The truth will make you free" (Jn 8:32); yes, but freedom is dangerous. Reason is often on the side of Torquemada, and anyway, to contradict it means risking the cross. But Man is not reason alone.

We are not saying, *Pecca fortiter*; it is not a matter of defending sin or anarchy. Let us restrict ourselves to our case. The experience of transgression, even simply on a psychological level, encourages an opening to *beyondity*; it leads to a change, to a novelty; it transforms Man. In the prototype of the perfect saint, who has never sinned, never fallen, never committed evil, this experience of "the fall," of fallibility, of contingency, is lacking; absent is that pain in his own flesh, that pain without which it gets very difficult to develop comprehension, acceptance of the human condition, communion, the encounter with the other; and without all this, of course, love is impossible. Unlike mercy and compassion, love is an equalizing, communitarian link. We cannot love from on high, we have to find ourselves on the same level. As a consequence, the one who loves is vulnerable. Without the *kenōsis* of Jesus Christ, his "redemption" by means of love remains incomprehensible. "God made the sinless one into sin" (2 Co 5:21) declares a bold text of Paul. *O felix culpa* (O happy fault), sings the liturgy.

Christian Scholasticism passionately discussed the following question: Would Christ have become incarnate had Man not sinned? Responding in the affirma- tive, Duns Scotus has always been more convincing to me than St. Thomas, who supported the negative. Christ is not just the one who comes to cure a wound or restore an order that had been disrupted by sin, but the one who leads creation to its divine fulfillment.

But all these suppositions are but wild imaginings, for in fact the situation of humanity and of the cosmos, such as it emerges from the creative or permissive hands of God, is one of disharmony—in traditional terms, one of original sin. If it is a flight from the real world to the empyrean heaven of a disembodied God, it cannot be an experience of the real God. It cannot be the Christian experience of the divine mystery, inseparable as it is from a divine incarnation, that is no way a docetist descent (like an *avatāra*, for example), but an event occurring in the very bosom of the Trinity and of History. We can therefore say that the Christian experience of God also includes the experience of evil; it is not the experience of an idea, but of that dimension of reality that we are accustomed to calling God, and which, according to Christian faith, became flesh at the heart of the cosmos itself. It will be useful to interpret what I am saying here by remembering my distinction between Christ and Jesus.

This meditation in depth on evil, which goes beyond disobedience, transgression, even the sense of sin, introduces us to a new aspect of the experience of God, since it is about one of the revelations of reality. The problem of evil breaks the schemas that we a priori had made about God, disrupts our categories and makes us understand that we don't have the answer for everything. It makes us humble, human, and more realistic, letting us realize that there is not only the community of saints but also the community of sinners. It makes us understand that the passion of Christ is also the passion of God—though not of the Father, as the "Patripassians" maintained.

Forgiveness

It is significant that the great majority of modern theological dictionaries omit the word "pardon." When some do speak of it, they almost never move beyond its juridical, moral, or liturgically sacramental aspect. We have fallen into the habit of interpreting it as a renunciation of the demand for "merited" punishment for a crime or an offense. As an act of generosity, it surely allows us to get closer to God, but we are referring here to something more fundamental.

Nor will we return to theological considerations of pardon as an act of "de-creation," that is, a human act that in fact cancels what it forgives. We will limit ourselves to the experience of meeting with God in and through the act of pardoning. By pardon we understand something more than the act of excusing a debt, of not demanding the practice of distributive justice, or being satisfied with a juridical reconciliation. Reconciliation is generally reciprocal, although it can lie on different levels. Pardon is something more: an active action that requires reciprocity—although it can provoke the latter by beginning with a unilateral initiative.

A passage in St. John (20:22–23) connects the reception of the Holy Spirit with the ability to pardon. In fact, those who are capable of pardoning feel that they are not doing so by virtue of a syllogism nor through the reasoning of common sense, which tells us that, without pardon, we are doing evil to ourselves as well as to another. The act of pardoning lies beyond the domain of will. I might be able to forgo the demand for satisfaction, to abandon the urge to punish, to no longer wish evil to the one who has offended me, and even forget the offense. But something would still be lacking : the Holy Spirit, a force that is given to me, something that does not come from my self and liberates me just as it liberates the "sinner." The Jews already realized that God and only God can forgive.

We insist: Pardon is neither a mutual reconciliation nor a nonaggression pact, nor a renunciation of vengeance; the experience of pardon belongs on another level. In the first place, we feel our powerlessness, for we would sometimes like to pardon but cannot do so. We will neither return evil for evil nor seek revenge; to pardon, however, belongs to an ontologically different level. It is something we experience as a grace, an act we feel ourselves incapable of, but which will one fine day become possible.

The absence of pardon is what overloads the negative *karman* in the history of mankind, which, while dreaming of a victory of good over evil, proceeds from vengeance to vengeance, from reparation to counterreparation, from war to war. If, for example, we do not pardon a Hitler, the evil that he represents will surface again in the dictators and monsters who succeed in obtaining supreme power, whether military, economic, or religious.

Someone who has been capable of forgiving has certainly encountered God. The experience of pardon shatters all our plans, both those of the intelligence and those of the will. It is impossible for the intelligence not to know that someone has done me an irreparable injury. It is impossible for the will not to want "justice" done and the debt to be settled. And if I pardon, it is neither because I believe my act will be useful (who knows if it will be beneficial?) nor because I want to pardon (in order to be good); when I genuinely pardon, I do so in a spontaneous and free way, without thinking of either motive or consequence.

From the very depth of my being, something or someone has given me the strength to pardon. The (divine) Spirit has acted in me and through me.

Crucial Moments

Time is not homogeneous, nor is life an indifferent succession of events. In the life of every human being there are some special moments as well as others that weigh heavily on one's life.

A birth, a death, an initiation, a marriage, an illness, a meeting, a love, the dazzling discovery of an aesthetic or intellectual experience, as well as many other events in human life, awaken us to a dimension that often seems to have been slumbering in the very depth of our being. We did not imagine that we were capable of living with such intensity and depth.

It is often a question of an experience of a religious type. At other times, what we experience does not seem in accord with what we call God nor with what we call religion. We tend to think that these experiences, apparently so different from what we ordinarily think of as "religious," are just as authentic as those generally considered as such. Whether festive or filled with grief, these moments are occasions of celebration; the festival is the natural time for a meeting with the numinous.

We cannot shut God up in a temple, even though we need not, for that reason, become the kind of iconoclasts who render judgment regarding the precise place in which the divine ought or ought not to fix its residence. We ourselves are temples of the Holy Spirit.

What we call the "sanctification of feasts"—all religions celebrate holy days— cannot be reduced to the atavism that prohibits "servile work," a practice that was established in earlier times to protect the poor. Such sanctification reminds us that God is the God of festival, and that celebration is a privileged place for meeting God.

We have spoken of joy. The festival underlines the communitarian character of joy, participation, and the interchange between three worlds: the material, the human, and the divine.

These moments—that I have called "crucial" because they reveal to us a crossing of the ways among the many ways—constitute, so to speak, moments of discontinuity and therefore place us, in an existential manner, before what certain Scholastics have called "continuous creation," and Buddhists the constant re-creation of everything, because, in a certain sense, no permanent substance exists. The Gospels themselves speak not only of a new heaven but also of a new earth—in a passage that need not be interpreted in an exclusively eschatological manner. One of the phenomenological traits of God is novelty and perpetual surprise. If I were not afraid of being too paradoxical, I would say that the readiness to be surprised and to admire is, almost, a requirement for experiencing God—who does not permit Himself to be imprisoned in either physical or metaphysical forms. The God of the past is nothing but a simple "construction" of the mind: it is *not* the "living God."

Among these moments, the dominant one is death, in all its aspects. Death is undeniably the point at which we encounter the mystery. Although, day by day, we are incapable of a personal experience of death, we are capable of experiencing the death of others, in particular of those we love. This love liberates us from an individualistic prison: the death of a loved being suggests that our self ends neither with our body nor our individuality. We cannot directly experience the death of the other, but we can experience something that, at that time, also dies in us, something that belongs to us, something of which we can have full and lucid consciousness, inasmuch as the subject of our experience continues to live. We are not saying that the mysterious, the ineffable, the incomprehensible, is in itself identical to the experience of God, but that it is a privileged occasion for that experience.

But there is more, because death is not a simple physiological experience. The death of the ego, which is spoken of in virtually all the world's spiritualities, is something very real. The *jīvanmukta*, the risen one, the grace-anointed, the fulfilled one, who is dead to the old Man or has ontologically overcome his own egoism, is ready for the experience of God. In order to experience the Creator of nothingness in ourselves, it is necessary to become "nothing."

In dealing with crucial moments, we are not thinking only of what Stefan Zweig called the stellar moments of humanity, that is, the events that took place at Sinai, at the Jordan, at Bodh Gayā, at Vṛndāvana, or of other acts of historic transcendence, whether social or personal. I refer to small, humble moments that seem to flow between two acts of life that apparently are much less important: we have missed a train, the mail does not come, a visit is late, a coffee taken in haste is too hot, and we arrive late for a rendezvous. We are ready to "waste time," and it is as if the divine dimension of reality were hidden in these small, unimportant facts. It is written that God is a hidden being—whose tabernacle is found in the shadows and whose recreation consists in amusing Himself among people, cooking and sex included. Neither a fall from a horse nor an encounter with an angel is required: sometimes, all that is needed is a misstep on the street in order to find "the God of little things." Sometimes God takes us without warning, and at other times He supplies us with energy and inspiration. The kingdom of God does not arrive with great fanfare; neither the bridegroom nor the thief arrive at the anticipated hour.... Additional explanations are perhaps unneeded. Some schools of spirituality have called this kind of experience "the practice of the presence of God."

Nature

The absence of an *advaitic* experience—even though it is the key to a philosophic vision of the Trinity—has led Christianity to fall prey to a panicked fear of a so-called pantheism. In order to avoid monism, Christians fall into dualism. God and the world are radically separated, which means that the transcendent God becomes progressively more superfluous, relegated to a *heaven* that is not the *sky* of the astronomers. Not only did the Creator rest on the seventh day, but it seems that He also withdrew into a celestial vault, and thus ceased to create, leaving just an evolutionary "super-automatism" on.

Man is Man in community; human community, however, is not limited to its fellow creatures. The human community is also cosmic, since Man is an integral and, even, constitutive part of the cosmos.

Nature is one of the places in which the average person is capable of the most profound encounter with the divine mystery. Our contact with nature is not primarily conceptual but existential; I would say cutaneous—that does not eliminate the participation of our intellect in the experience of nature.

In saying "nature" we are thinking of everything that is natural, not restricting ourselves to a refined and perhaps artificial view.

This leads us to an idea that underlies this whole chapter. For Man, the experi- ence of God, not paradoxically but spontaneously, is the most obvious and natural experience. St. Thomas in his *Summa theologica* (I, q.60, a.1, ad 3) even goes so far as to say that natural inclinations (*cognitio*, *dilectio*, *inclinatio naturalis*) are always true and right; otherwise we would withdraw all trust (*derogari*) in the Maker of nature.

Although nature as the temple of God is a well-known image, it is generally interpreted in such a way as to keep His transcendence intact, at the price of forget- ting His immanence. Every positive teaching of pantheism is perfectly acceptable; its error consists in omission, rather than in excess. All is divine, although the divine is not exhausted in that Whole we call reality. A less imperfect metaphor would perhaps be one that certain religious traditions have developed: the world is the body of God, not understood as a Cartesian separation but in a positive symbiosis, one that does not eliminate differences but overcomes separation.

The experience of the divine in nature is not reducible to a tellurico-numinous feeling regarding a *mysterium tremendum et fascinans*. The relation is much more intimate. It is not a matter of performing a pirouette by our causal thought, in order to leap to a first efficient cause, separate and separable from what is caused. "Creation" is inseparable from the "Creator."

If the "Creator" stopped creating even for a second, creation would return to the nothingness from which it proceeded. By means of causality, the intellect is capable of soaring all the way up to God, but Man is not simply intellect; his relation to God is immediate and therefore does not require the mediation of reason.

Nature is not only a privileged but also a natural place for meeting God. It is an experience capable of assuming several forms, and it has been the object of innumerable interpretations.

The experience of God in nature is not primarily the experience of the one who makes it, whether creator or artist; nor is it the experience of another force that sustains or gives existence to what we call the natural order—be it the one discovered by our aesthetic sense, or by calculation, or thanks to the microscope, the telescope, or our rational thought. It is not a question of raising ourselves to His level or penetrating the mysterious depths of the cosmos. It is primarily a simpler and more profound experience. Not an experience of either immanence or transcendence, nor an experi- ence of an Other, but the experience of a Presence, of the most real presence of the actual thing in itself, from which we are not absent ourselves. Some interpretations can be suggested (put forward) in consequence (as a consequence?). As we will have the opportunity to repeat, the experience of God is the total experience of Man, in which nature is not absent.

Silence

As we already mentioned at the beginning, silence is an indispensable condition for preventing our discourse about God from degenerating into a "logomachy." It seems opportune for us to insist once again that silence is not only the condition but also the atmosphere in which the experience of God is capable of breathing without getting drowned in dialectics.

Apophatic theology, frightening as it may have so often seemed, directs our atten- tion to contemplation. To know how to listen is the gate to contemplation, and, by listening, to realize that the highest knowledge is not to know, and that every time we name God—that is, as a concept—we almost commit a profanation, a blasphemy.

Some verses of Angelus Silesius exhort us not to leave the sphere of silence in order to arrive at the experience of God, inasmuch as God is silence itself. The following lines are part of his work *Der cherubinische Wandersmann* (The Cherubic Pilgrim), and we will translate them a bit freely, since the reader will anyway be able to compare them with the original text:

Gott ist so über alls, dass man nicht sprechen kann,
Drum betest du ihn auch mit Schweigen besser an. (I.240)
God is so far beyond everything that we cannot talk to Him,
Therefore worship Him silently.

Schweig, Allerliebster, schweig: kannst du nur gänzlich schweigen,
So wird dir Gott mehr Guts, als du begehrst, erzeigen. (II.8)
Remain silent, beloved, silent: if you can rest completely in silence,
Then God will give you more blessings than you asked for.

Mensch, so du willst das Sein der Ewigkeit aussprechen,
So musst du dich zuvor des Redens ganz entbrechen. (II.68)
Man, if you wish to utter the being of eternity,
you must first cut off all discourse.

Niemand redt weniger als Gott ohn Zeit und Ort:
Er spricht von Ewigkeit nur bloss ein einzigs Wort. (IV.129)
No one speaks less than God, "without time or place."
From all eternity He says only a single word.

Wenn du an Gott gedenkst, so hörst du ihn in dir,
Schweigst du und wärest still, er redte für und für. (V.330)
When you think of God, you hear Him in yourself.
You remain silent and peaceful, then He will not stop speaking to you.

The only way of speaking of God is in the vocative; the nominative does not exist, and all other cases are but anthropomorphisms or idolatry. The vocative is the exclamation that bursts from the depth of our soul, from such inner depths that it is not even heard by ourselves—only when the left hand does not know what the right hand is doing is the action of the right hand authentic (Mt 6:3); only when my prayer bursts from the depth of my soul and remains in the secret chamber of my being is that prayer genuine (Mt 6:5ff.). Everything else, Christ says, was already performed by the heathens too (Mt 5:47; 6:32): they pray, sing hymns, praise, and chant, but none of all that reaches God. These are only preliminaries, gestures that are likely to be successful if performed with goodwill, but run the risk of making us believe that we have the power of manipulating God.

God is an untranslatable symbol, and probably an irreplaceable one for many people. But we ought to be aware that we are dealing with a symbol that expresses itself in a word—a word trying to say that which, by its very nature, is inexpressible. We employ it in order to point at something "beyond," a "space" that is the space of freedom, a realm that is the realm of the infinite.

From a Christian standpoint, it is impossible to know God in the sense that we currently give the word "to know." The only possibility of knowing God is to become Him. Access, if we can call it that, cannot be simply gnoseological. No concept, no idea, can replace that "substantial touch" that we can neither know nor reduce to any language. Again the German mystic tells us, repeating a unanimous tradition:

Je mehr du Gott erkennst, je mehr wirst du bekennen,
Dass du weniger ihn, was er ist, kannst benennen. (V.41)
The more you know God, the more you realize
That less and less you know of what He is.

"Let the wise man practice wisdom and not fall into long speeches, that are empty words," an *Upaniṣad* says (*BU* IV.4.21).

As a synthesis of what, in different forms, the religious tradition of humanity teaches us, we can say that the experience of God is possible only when we have arrived at the triple silence—immediately adding that silence does not mean keeping quiet. Silence does not mean artificially quieting human desires, nor any form of repres- sion. The *nirodha* of yoga does not signify an active rejection, just as the taoist *wu wei* does not recommend laziness, nor Molinos's "quietism" the modern *pasotism*; neither does Ignatian "indifference" entail an insensibility to what is human. In the same way, neither should the *ataraxia* of the Epicureans or the *apatheia* of the Stoics be interpreted as an inhuman impassibility—despite the abuses all these words have undergone. Courtesy does not eliminate courage.

The three silences we mentioned are:

The silence of the mind, that is, the tranquilization of our mind in such a way that ideas no longer dominate our lives, as if human existence were the conclusion of syllogisms based on first principles. The mind keeps silence when it remains respectfully quiet as it confronts the ultimate questions of nothingness, which had probably been posed by the mind itself. To take this into account, to be aware that we cannot understand everything, liberates the mind from a weight that is often oppressive. The Latin liturgy does not speak of *vivere secundum rationem*, "living according to reason," but *secundum te*, "in accordance with yourself "—through Christ and in the Spirit. This in no way implies that the mind possesses neither rights nor a domain of its own, but that it is not our ultimate guide; it does, however, have the right to veto every irrational action. "It is neither through great instruction nor by means of mental effort nor by the study of Scriptures that we obtain ātman," repeats the *Kaṭha-upaniṣad* (I.2.23).

The silence of the will, more difficult to achieve, is not obtained when we wish not to wish, nor even when we simply do not want anything, but when the will no longer makes any noise—that is, when it moves harmoniously in the Whole—we could also say, in the Tao—and wants what it wants as to be wanted, to express it in a paradoxical way. Free will is not individualistic libertinage but the intrinsic dynamism of Being, which is not determined, not constrained by any external factor. It is what many schools of spirituality call purity of heart; others prefer to interpret it in terms of an empty heart.

The silence of action refers to the nonviolent action that directs life like an expert helmsman (one of the first meanings of *sophos*, the wise one) who does not exactly follow the direction of the wind, but simply utilizes it. Strong and fruitful action is not measured by either the effort or the revolutions it engenders, but by the force with which it rules the events of life, on the personal, historic, and even cosmic levels. The "profound meaning," so often badly understood, of so-called duties or commandments consists precisely in their reference to the *karma-yoga*, to adopt an expression from the *Gītā*. "Your commandments are joyous and liberate the heart," proclaim the psalms of David.

Saying it in another way: Man experiences infinity both through the intellect, since knowledge never reaches its end, and through the heart, since love never totally attains the object it loves, and also through the action, that never arrives at its fulfillment. That is why silence is required.

The experience of God is, paradoxically, this very experience of contingency, which, just by discovering itself as contingency, reveals the tangential point between the finite and the infinite. It discovers that both our thought and our will and action never exhaust either their origin or their purpose. The self-awareness that we are without beginning or end is, precisely, the experience of divinity. There are as many psychological paths that lead to this experience as there are people; as many traditional paths as there are religions; as many personal paths as there are religiosities. God belongs neither to the one nor the other, neither to the good nor the wicked: He transcends all our words and faculties. In this experience of empty transcendence, we experience the void, the emptiness, and ultimately silence.

Silence is the only place of freedom. Thought, in fact, is not totally free inasmuch as it is constrained by the principle of noncontradiction. Nor is the will totally unconditioned, inasmuch as it finds itself constrained by the good, even though this good is partial, or the will can make mistakes. Action is not mere movement: it moves toward an end, which directs it in its turn. Silence alone offers a space for freedom: God is freedom, and silence is the "space" needed for experiencing God.

Epilogue

Those who have lived the experience of God, in one way or another, have lost their common-reference identities. All that is left to them is their deepest identity.

The experience of God is then understood as subjective genitive: the experience *of* God himself, not *my* own. God is not an object—either of faith or experience. It is the experience of God that passes through (*experiri*) me, in which I participate more or less consciously. In this sense, however, the phrase is inexact, since to say that God is part of my experience requires Trinitarian precision: it is the Son in the Spirit that constitutes this divine experience.

Our experience of God is the divine self-consciousness in which we participate as we become, in Christian language, part of the "whole Christ," the *Christus totus*. That is divinization.

On this basis, we can say that "the man of God," to use a traditional expression, does not have an identity that differentiates him from the others. His identity identifies him more and more with the whole of humanity and the entire universe—he feels himself, as St. Paul says, more Jewish with the Jews, more Greek with the Greeks, more all with all.

One example: "The man of God" does not consider himself identified, limited, by any given label: Spanish, Indian, academic, philosopher, believer, Catholic, priest, or male. He does not even think the label of human being or living being is appropriate.

This is the experience of total stripping that the mystics speak about. Those who consider that the label "Christian," for example, separates them from "nonbelievers" confuse the experience of God with their own interpretation of the experience of God. The one who speaks as "American," as "scientist," as "male," except on specifically scientific subjects, leaves aside or confuses the experience of God with his experience of God. Such an experience is not the oceanic, prelogical or primitive feeling that has frequently been criticized; rather, it is the ultimate and universal experience embodied in the concrete and the particular. The experience of God cannot be separated from a stroll with a friend, a shared meal, the love that we feel, the idea that we defend, the conversation that unfolds, the pain that we endure—discovering in all this a third dimension of depth, of love, of the infinite, and hence of the inef- fable. It is a discovery that discloses the value that lies hidden in the deepest and most real of our human acts.

The experience of God is simply the experience of the third dimension of reality, which can show its effect in the profound manner of conducting a human activity, among things or among people, or in concentrating itself in the world of ideas.

In this experience, we—like the classic mystics of many traditions—see the dimension of *emptiness* in all things, which is not their nullity. Utterly real as things are, they nevertheless do reveal something like a void, an *absence*, a something *more*, if you will, which is not "something in addition," as rather "something less" than the absolutizing of the thing or the event that we are living through—something less than the substantiation of the thing or the event. Because of this *Gelassenheit* or sense of renunciation, this attitude of a "holy indifference," *asakti* (the act of detaching oneself from things, independence with regard to them), and *wu wei* (nonaction) are perceived as the fundamental attitude of the mystic, if we may use that name for those who hold their third eye open.

If deprived of the two other dimensions, of course, this vision of the third eye is a simple hallucination. The interpretation of this experience, nevertheless, depends on the cultural milieu of the one who interprets it. One of those interpretations gives it the name of "God"—which, in turn, is open to a great variety of meanings.

One clarification is necessary. It is not a question of pantheism or even panen- theism—except when we complete our thought by calling it a "panen-psychism" and a "panen-cosmism." Everything is in God just as, analogously, everything is in Consciousness and in the Universe. Each of these dimensions is interwoven in the other: that is what we have called the cosmotheandric experience, the *perichōrēsis* or mutual interconnection of the real, the life of the radical Trinity.

The practice of silence lets us "hear" the music of this third dimension. Nor should we overlook the fact that the very opportunity of enjoying silence is already a grace.

In this sense, the experience of God coincides with the fact of seeing God "in" all things—and all things "in" God, if such is the name we wish to give Him.

We understand then that the mystic is the one whose activity is completely free, because in all things and events he sees the empty "space" that prevents him from being fatalistic, making it possible for him to act trustfully, being sure that what he does is not in vain—even though he should never judge his action by its immediate effects (see the notion of *ni@ kāma karma*, or *nai@karman*, in the *Gītā*).

The experience of God, therefore, distracts us from everyday activities, whatever they may be. Once again, we are not talking about the experience of an object called God, since God is not a thing. We are talking, rather, of an experience of reality in its three constitutive dimensions.

By employing a different language, we could say that it is at once the experience of the thing, of ourselves within the thing, and of God who embraces both. It is the experience of the cosmotheandric icon of reality at a given moment of space and time, from our personal perspective and in the light of our limited and concrete vision.

We have said that the experience of God ought to be understood in the sense of a subjective genitive, that is, as the experience that God has, not of a solipsistic self, but of a Trinitarian and hence relational and participative Being in which we enter, and all creation with us.

Seen from this side, experienced as starting from us, this experience consists in recuperating our original—that is, our natural—state, which in traditional language is the paradisal state before original sin. That is why we say that the way is redemption, liberation, and fulfillment. Although it originates in us, this original state needs to be recuperated, restored, as the Victorines of the twelfth century said. In this state, we experience what the Greek wisdom cited by St. Paul says, when he recalls that "in Him we live, move, and exist" (Ac 17:28).

This is not the supposed "presence of God," like the *prae-essentia* of a Being in face of us, but the more interior, more personal experience; not as if we were moved by another, but conscious that the source of our actions and the ultimate subject of our being belongs to that infinite sea that we call God.

We repeat that the experience of a transcendent God is literally impossible: we would turn His spotless transcendence into something solid. Experience requires immediacy. Such a God does not exist: He is a projection of our mind, the fruit of a monarchical civilization.

The Trinitarian God is different; we are inserted into the divine *perichōrēsis*. I experience myself then as "son"—to repeat a traditional designation which, as St. Thomas remarks, is only a metaphor. For this reason John the Evangelist speaks of the Word, not of the Son (*Compendium theol.* I.40; *Sum. theol.* q.27, a.2).

This experience of God is the experience of my deep Self, the paradoxical experi- ence that we are most intimately our own and at the same time superior to ourselves. The necessary condition is to have a pure heart.

The experience of God consists in touching the totality of Being with the totality of our own being : to feel in our body, our intellect, and our spirit the whole of reality both *within* us and *outside* us. And paradoxically, it is the experience of contingency: we touch the infinite at one point (*cum tangere*).

The experience of God is the experience of the Mystery that leads our lives from both within and without.

Part Two

THE CHRISTIAN SPIRITUAL JOURNEY*

So that you too may share our life.
Our life is shared with the Father
and with his son Jesus Christ.
We are writing this to you
so that our joy may be complete

1 John 1:3ff.

* The three short pieces that make up this second part appeared in a single volume published in 2007 by Jaca Book (La gioia pasquale, La presenza di Dio, and Maria), but the author wrote them long before (published separately by La Locusta, Vicenza, in 1968, 1970, and 1972, respectively). Not only are they characterized by the same direct and accessible language, as they are transcripts of what was said during spiritual retreats, but together they express an introduction to the Christian experience that, in addition to having aged well, enables us to avoid reducing Christianity to a moral, a doctrine, or a philosophy. We are thus involved in a mystery that accompanies us, that envelops us as it enveloped Mary in her yes to the call of God from the annunciation until the foot of the cross.
It deals with a journey of the "fullness of Man," a fullness that resides not in a simple religion but in Christ, to whose resurrection all people have been called from the beginning. "Paschal joy" is for all people. Christ's message has too often been reduced to a doctrine or interpreted with a biased spirit both by Christians and by non-Christians!

Introduction

Republishing a book, or rather three small books, nearly half a century after their first edition can mean that the author stopped there and has therefore stopped living, since life is constant change. However it can also mean that he believes he has attained an immutable truth, an eternal core that is immune to the passing of time. In this case it would only be repeating the lesson.

The author does not believe in either of these two possibilities. His thought and his life have not "stopped at Eboli," as in the famous book by Carlo Levi. Now he would write differently—and in fact he does. The author does not even believe in the immobility of truth. It is true that one can sing a "Lied" by Schubert, but we know that each song is new and old at the same time. The score is the same, but the song is new and different each time it is sung : it is not the same song. Life is not repetition.

What I have said would already be a justification to dust off an old manuscript, and indeed the author trusts that each reader can re-create the score—in fact it is precisely what he/she is invited to do.

This re-publication also has another ambition: that of inspiring the reader to create a new song just as great musicians created new music from old cantatas. Being traditional does not mean repeating oneself, but introducing change and continuity, as in any growth. These three short books would like to be—that is to say, words bearing joy, words that are always new because they are always renewed. The original words were spoken—and they wish to remain thus even if they are written.

For this reason the author has not wished to change almost anything of the language of the time. That language, which at the time seemed new because it was traditional, can be an inspiration for the new music of our life.

I will then be asked if I still personally believe in what the texts say. I must confess that, after a first quick glance, I was tempted not to publish them because, in order to avoid misunderstandings, I thought they would need a more complete revision and important explanations such as: "God is not reducible to substance," "Christ is not an individual," "the Church is not just the institution of the Church nor is it only Christians...."

My response is in any event affirmative, with a simple request addressed to today's reader to consider the thoughts expressed here —and that in any event they can never reach their fullness. The language is varied and different because faith is in the Mystery and not in its conceptual translations. This discernment is on the contrary very healthy as it frees us of fanaticism. As old Aristotle once said, "The Being (and therefore also the Truth) can be told in many ways."

I could have inserted many notes in the text, referring to other traditions also, and added comments of a more "up to date" and universal spirituality, but in that case it would have become another book. I prefer instead that it can be seen that there has been a journey in spirituality.

*

The first text comprises a triduum of preparation for Easter held for the students of the university campus chapel of La Sapienza University in Rome in 1963. The oral style of the retreat forms part of the meditative style of the triduum. Years later, in 1968, the text, taken from assistants' notes and revised by me, was published by La Locusta, a publishing house in Vicenza.

Allow me a further personal reflection. After those now far-off years, I left the shores of the Mediterranean and never returned to Rome, except for some occasional, sporadic appearances. On that occasion, the university chapel was packed. My heart was there. With a few exceptions, I have never again seen my friends of that time. My words have been scattered by the wind. Many may have forgotten not so much my words as those of the Gospel that they echo, but the seed, I hope, has remained, or even better, has died in becoming fruit. I would like to dedicate this new edition to all those friends—also those who will read me. Life passes, but friendship endures.

*

The second text dates from another retreat held in about the same year in the hermitage (Casa San Sergio) of a dear friend, Divo Barsotti, whose memory remains alive in my heart. The title of this text is the original one, although, for reasons I will explain later, I would have preferred it to be *The Presence of Christ*.

In the course of nearly two thousand years, except for the first centuries, Chris- tians have lived honoring the Trinity only in words, while remaining monotheistic. It was therefore possible to speak of the "presence of God" without integrating it with the presence of Christ. Either Christ was God, therefore the presence of the One God was sufficient, or God was a man, so His humanity was a means to reach the God of monotheistic mysticism. The humanity of Christ, indeed, was somewhat of an obstacle to reach the heights of "spiritual" life—that is to say, of a disincarnate spirituality, since God was considered a "pure spirit"—and therefore all of us, usually, "impure spirits." Hence also the idea that mysticism was a privilege for exceptional souls, totally purified of corporeal ties.

In prayers we said, *per Christum Dominum nostrum*, as in the liturgical texts. The Son takes us to the Father; He can be a means to reach the One God, but it was thought that once He had been reached there was no further need for the *per Dominum*. He is the way, but the ultimate end is the One God, pure spirit. We forgot that the same liturgical prayer does not stop there, but continues, *per Dominum nostrum*; the *nostrum* is not superfluous nor is the continuation incidental: *in unitate Spiritus Sancti*, and this unity is inseparable. Indeed, the complete prayer adds, *qui tecum* (with the father) *vivit et regnat in unitate Spiritus Sancti, Deus: per omnia saecula saeculorum* (For Jesus Christ our Lord, Your Son, who [being] God, lives and reigns with you in the unity of the Holy Spirit, for ever and ever). In brief, there is no Father without the Son in the unity of the Spirit—but also vice versa. The Trinitarian *perich¯or¯esis* is not unidirectional. The Trinity is a perfect communion in which nobody predominates: the three persons are equal, according to the conse- crated formula. Therefore, the so-called presence of God in the Christian regime is the presence of the Trinity.

In brief, the Christian "presence of God" is not the awareness of a disembodied God, nor of a "pure Spirit" or a Plotinian God, an Âaṅkarian or a Spinozan—even without entering into historical-religious considerations to demonstrate that also there the Trinity shines through.

We should immediately clarify that, if speaking of the "presence of God" without Christ is misleading, speaking of the "presence of Christ" leaving out God is even more erroneous. If there is no God without Christ, neither is there Christ without God—without us and without the world.

This implies a different conception of divinity. However, here we want to concentrate on the presence of the Christ of the Trinity.

Let us start from the Christian affirmation that Christ is "perfect God and complete man" and that the theme of this meditation is therefore "the presence of God." This is the Christic experience.

Since the Sibyl's oracle at Delphi in the West and the *Upaniṣad* in the Orient, "knowing oneself" has been the highest aspiration of human perfection. Knowing what I am is the starting point to reach full awareness. This is, according to India, "fulfill- ment." The Christian response is clear, but its comprehension less so: "Anyone who sees the Son sees the Father and anyone who sees the Father sees Him in the Spirit."

Our "presence of God" is thus the experience of a Christ who gives Life to things. In Him was the Life—and the Life is our light, says St. John. So God is seen in everything and everything is seen in God.

Experiencing the presence of God as a Christic presence is to live the experience of the continuous incarnation in all creation, to see creatures as limbs of the Mystical Body of Christ, to discover the divinity even of our own body. To live then in the presence of God is to experience the radical Trinity, that is the Trinitarian structure of all reality—which elsewhere I have called cosmotheandric.

Seeing Christ everywhere does not mean being conscious that Jesus is present. Even those to whom He spoke did not know that Christ was present in the poor; they saw and they loved (or ignored) those who were hungry, thirsty, or in need of anything. This presence of Christ is as subtle and discreet as the presence of God. It is not the awareness of Jesus of Nazareth, even if Christians reach this consciousness through him. We can describe it, inversely, as the awareness in us of the divinity of all structures of creation, but a divinity that is not a substance. The Trinity is not three Gods. So it is not a projection of our mind to see God in everything, even in matter itself. This vision is not a pantheistic vision, nor is it the vision of a monotheistic religion.

The third text, Mary, also has a story of its own, which (providentially) changed the author's life. It was because of it that I went to India. A foreword should, however, concentrate on the content of the text and not on the life of its writer.

This text is the simple confession of my love for Mary, mother of God, symbol of humanity in which the divine is fully manifested—not in an abstract humanity, but in each person who knows how to utter Mary's unreserved yes, so in me, in you, dear reader. That is why I spontaneously address you informally as a friend. Is it not only to a friend that one can confess the profound feeling of love?

I must say that I myself had almost forgotten the pages that we are now reprinting, having integrated them in other works. It was the initiative of Jaca Book to encourage me to republish them without substantial changes, and I am glad because, as they represented an important phase of my life, I think they could also have a meaning for the contemporary reader. My thanks to the publisher and to Milena Carrara, who has supported me in the painstaking rereading of the texts.

Tavertet, Epiphany 2007

4
Paschal Joy

Faith as the Condition of Joy

We are gathered here to prepare for Easter, so that this year's Easter can be, once again, a new and renewed Easter, more conscious, more real, and above all fuller.

For this reason, conscious and aware preparation is needed (and the whole of Lent, all in all, is only a preparation) so that, one Easter after another, each one of us can achieve his or her fullness, his or her total joy, the goal of human life.

As the retreat is addressed to people who for the entire academic year have demonstrated their intention to live their faith integrated and incarnate in the world, it was obvious that the theme of Easter was this: the Church as a source of joy, culminating in Easter.

We will seek to meditate following a threefold procedure, and we will make some considerations about Christian joy, because it is evident that, if our faith, our hope, and our charity do not lead us to a deeper serenity, do not give us back a positive sense of life and a true delight, there will always be tension, unease, and dualism in our life.

The danger for a Christian life is to content oneself with a faith that is not on the same level as the rest of our life.

Dualism derives from a faith that has not penetrated our being in every cell, until it makes it divine even at a physical level.

The great danger is that of a half-religious life. The great danger is to stop before reaching Easter.

Stopping halfway, not climbing the hill of the Easter events, not reaching Jeru- salem to die and rise again there, this is our great danger.

Contenting ourselves with a moral, with negative commandments, with not committing serious sins, contenting ourselves with following from a certain distance what only some have the courage to do, imitating them with a second-rate imitation, this is our danger: believing, in a word, that the Holy Spirit does not exist, that Easter is pure romanticism, that Christian perfection and Christian life are the destiny of a privileged few who succeed in attaining it, unlike the others.

But Christ did not come to preach the gospel to the elites, to special or highly gifted people: he came speak to the poor, to men of flesh and blood, fully immersed in the normal life of any historical age.

So often we lack the humility and the courage to once again live Christianity with all the freshness and immediacy of a faith lived to the full.

To achieve this, for us who call ourselves intellectuals, beings who want to be aware of their situation, it may be appropriate and opportune to proceed in three successive steps. Today, we will deal with faith as a condition of human joy: a talk, therefore, about philosophical anthropology. Tomorrow, religion as a source of joy: the opposite, therefore, of how those of a certain mentality see it. According to them, when one speaks of religion, one becomes a little too transcendental, losing freshness, spontaneity, and joy; and following this principle, we have so often let our Christian existence degenerate. The third day, we will see Christianity as the message and realization of perfect joy—since, indeed, he who is not happy is responsible for his unhappiness. God is not a tyrant who wants us to suffer. I am speaking of happiness, not of absence of suffering. So today we want to see how faith is the condition of human joy. As I have said, it is a talk about philosophical anthropology, of philosophy, to rediscover the value of a word that has so often been vilified, not in the modern sense, but as an integral effort to reach the threshold of Christian truth.

Today we will dwell on three precise and very elementary points. My task is to try to demonstrate how faith is a condition of human joy—that is, how, without faith, one cannot know that joy to which every man aspires.

The first point is to realize that happiness, even in the most normal sense of the word, is the ultimate goal of all human activity.

In the world in which we live, everyone is seeking a foundation that can be universal. The great crisis of contemporary spirituality, religions, and many other things is precisely a crisis of universality: when it is discovered that a dogma is no longer accepted by everyone, it seems it no longer has any value; when a moral is found not to be accepted by everyone, it starts to be considered a specialty of a few; when, in any problem, we cannot reach unanimity, this means that there is already a sort of limitation, a biased mentality, something that hinders the establishment of a universal order that may be accepted by all.

And when we seek a common foundation in the modern world, in this world which is tormented by so many different "engines" each pulling in their own direction, we find that there are very few universally accepted values.

Perhaps there is unanimity in only one thing : in the acknowledgment that man wants to be happy.

Man, all in all, always seeks fullness, happiness, of some kind: depending on his conceptions, on his way of life and his ideology, he will give one interpretation rather than another, follow one route rather than another; but at the basis of everything there is Jesus who says—and it is in today's Gospel: "Whoever is thirsty come to me." And man is thirsty, thirsty for happiness, thirsty for fullness, thirsty to achieve something, to become something; it is a thirst we all feel, this dissatisfaction or anxiety, or stimulus to succeed—since we have not succeeded yet—in filling ourselves with what is not yet inside us.

The most universally accepted value among believers and nonbelievers, spiritualists and materialists, the good and the bad, the underdeveloped and the overdeveloped is precisely this thirst for fullness, for fulfillment, or in other words, this thirst for happiness and peace, a value that can be called so many names but that at bottom is always one thing : one's own fulfillment and joy, the peace men have always sought in all their labors and quests.

When a sinner sins, when a saint practices the greatest virtues, when Man follows a passion or an ideal, when all is said and done, behind each thing, he is seeking its essence: that fullness that should not always be interpreted in the egoistic sense, but in the sense of a total fullness, a *beatitudo*, a filling of the voids that the human being has, a strengthening of what is within us, the development of what has not yet flowered fully, has not emerged, and has not completely developed.

We want to attain being because, as yet, we are not. And it is precisely this that characterizes the itinerant state, the pilgrim state of man, or of anything on earth: because any dynamism in the end is always a dynamism toward something, and this something is precisely, even by dialectical definition, the fullness of the being that moves toward this goal.

Happiness is truly the ultimate goal of human activity. Man wants to be happy, he wants to be at peace with himself and with others. Man has this longing for happiness, fullness, coming to be and, over and above any interpretation that can be given to these phrases, this means that there is a constituent dissatisfaction with the natural order; but it could be said, likewise, that there is a lack of total development, a potential, and a provisional character of any temporal order.

The very fact of living in time means that we have not yet fulfilled ourselves. The fact that my life is stretching out as time marches on means that I have not yet managed to realize what I must and can be tomorrow. It means that my life always tends toward a kind of infinite that I cannot reach, because I cannot live all my time at once; I must live today, and tomorrow, and the day after, and then gather the fragments of my past and, loaded with these, walk toward a future. But it also means that I cannot live the day after tomorrow without having passed through tomorrow, that I always have a tomorrow and a day after tomorrow, I always thirst for infinity, I always have an infinite goal that I will never realize.

Man seeks the infinite in the finite, and here lies all the greatness and the mean- ness of the human being. It is a search, a thirst for the infinite that nothing can satisfy because everything is limited, because there is always a tomorrow and there is always a more, in everything. When something stops having a tomorrow, and no longer has a more, it is no longer a value. We are saturated, and this causes boredom. When a thing here on earth no longer has the possibility to have a tomorrow, or to have a more, when a thing stops and the dynamism ceases to exist, what was or seemed to be the greatest value becomes a source of boredom, tiredness, and disappointment.

Man seeks the infinite, but he seeks it in the finite because he has no other place to look for it.

The infinite is not at arm's reach; if it were, it would no longer be infinite.

And here lies all the greatness and the meanness of the human being; all the greatness, because nothing can satisfy him, because there is a truly infinite dimension to his being, because he truly wants to rise ever higher, and he never arrives; and, on the other hand, this "more" that is sought cannot be tomorrow or ever: the only way to seek it is to seek it in things that permit another "more," another tomorrow, a constant overcoming.

Thus Man is infinite on the one hand, but on the other he is closed, rooted, a prisoner—some would say—of the finite itself.

And in this search for the infinite in the finite we find all the tension, all the danger, all the beauty of human life.

Virtue is none other than this, and sin is none other than this.

Now, obtaining human joy, this minimum or maximum, I do not mean of tranquility, but of fullness, feeling that we are on the right road and that we can really rest in Being, all this is possible only when one has faith, a transcendent faith, which is possible, even anthropologically.

This is not a mathematical demonstration, because here we are not dealing with mathematics; we are dealing with human life, still warm with personal experience.

Without faith one cannot be happy. One cannot be tranquil or calm without a certain faith, without, that is, a bridge that already has a column, a pillar near the other bank, and serves as an orientation through all the variations, the highs and lows of life, and permits a rest every now and then, and reassures both psychologically and ontologically that it is worth walking because we are walking toward something that really exists.

Once again you see—a long speech would be needed, but this is so clear for anybody who has had experience of the human soul—that happiness is always a gift.

We cannot make ourselves happy.

When you have a difficulty, try to go beyond your own shadow; if you feel unhappy or anxious, try to overcome the obstacle only with the good that you have within yourselves; just try to go forward in a car without petrol; try alone, without going out of immanence, to overcome this *pondus vitae*, this *taedium existentiae*.

When something is not going right, it is absolutely impossible to overcome the impasse, whatever your psychological attitude. If one does not have a point on which to anchor oneself, something external toward which one can orient oneself, it is impossible to straighten oneself out and get out of the situation in which one finds oneself.

Happiness, peace, and joy are always a gift, something that is given to us, and only those who have this sense of gratitude are sensitive to this happiness and this peace.

I am never self-sufficient, especially in this, which is the most important thing in human life: having peace, having cheerfulness, having joy.

We are always bound to an "other," or another thing, or the circumstances, what surrounds us: nothing, never, depends solely on me.

I only have within me the condition, the female principle that must be fertilized; I cannot make myself happy. I can perhaps make others happy, I can perhaps give peace, happiness, advice, joy, love, everything to others; with myself I am impotent, I can do nothing unless I receive from outside and I open myself up.

But it is pointless to use theoretical arguments here. Try to have an experience, of any kind, such as, for example, on a purely biological level, a toothache: if nothing external intervenes (which can even be the mind, which is able to transform physical pain) I can do nothing. Man, at this level, is not self-sufficient.

We can therefore conclude that there must be something transcendent, something which is for me an ideal point, a love, a person, an object, a truth, a mission, that is outside me, in which I believe, and which can truly orient me, lift me up again, make me overcome crises and walk in a certain direction, giving a sense to my existence, to my suffering, and to my fall.

Without a firm point a little above or beside me, but anyway outside me, it is impossible to get out of the vicious circle of human life, out of our limited nature as creatures.

Without transcendent faith, Man does not have a point toward which he can direct himself and walk, which allows him to go out, create himself, arrive, and not continue to go round in circles, wasting time and energy, without the possibility of realizing (his) being.

But there is even more: if I must believe in something to be able to give a sense to my life, not just any support is sufficiently strong to carry the weight of my weakness as a creature; not just any ring is strong enough to hold me for long.

If to go out occasionally it is necessary always to have an ideal, a firm point, something transcendent; if I have to give my faith an object, this object is not indifferent.

In particular moments any passion, any love, any hatred, can save me by making me overcome the obstacle, tearing me from myself and changing my course. But life is not over in a few moments, and not every support is strong enough to guide me according to a constant line: I cannot lean on it for long if it does not possess certain features.

If this thing in which I believe is not superior to me, stronger than me, then it cannot support my faith and it cannot save me from daily failure.

A love, I said, can make me take a leap forward. But if I, then, can do what I want with this love, if it turns out that the object of my love is weaker than me; if my boyfriend or girlfriend, or science, or discipline, or sport, or any value in which I believed turns out to be weaker than me because I can, overturning the order, use it for me, for my pleasure or service or use, then what should have been a support can, yes, be of use to me temporarily to climb up and save myself from the danger of falling. But, once it has been used, it becomes a toy in my hands, an object of my egoism, a doll of my passion, an instrument for my vanity and my pride; then it is no longer useful to me.

Any object that is not stronger than Man, and superior to him, cannot help him. Its reality limits itself to the contingent moment of a determined place.

If Man does not find something external and superior and stronger to which he can cling when he vacillates, he loses himself among the many attractions that confuse him.

To have faith, cheerfulness, peace, serenity, to give a sense to life, faith in an object is necessary: not in any object, though, because life is more than a second, it is longer than a day, it is more difficult than a week.

Without something that is above and that is stronger, then, one cannot be in peace and overcome anxiety, this illness of modern Man.

Nowadays Man has become aware that the base under his feet is crumbling, that nothing preconstituted is acceptable; he no longer lives in the innocence of believing that there is a preestablished order and that there is nothing to be modified.

Nowadays this innocence is no longer possible.

If once Man could somehow believe that an order existed, and move forward with this faith, now he can no longer believe in an inferior order and therefore he must believe in a superior order that is stronger than him.

The basis of joy is inherent in the anthropological constitution of the man who believes in a value, in something above him and stronger than him.

And I cannot believe for long in a thing *as* stronger than me, unless it really is stronger than me.

I cannot believe in the love of a person or in an ideal, if this ideal and this person are not stronger or, to express it better, superior to me: only thus do I not run the risk of converting a superior value into an instrument of my egoism.

Have we not often seen people who transform God into their whimsical toy? Have we not observed that there exists a form of prayer in which I transform God into the dispenser of what I ask Him, and I make use of Him exclusively insofar as I can make demands, and I offload onto Him my impotence, my laziness, or my ambitions?

This God does not support prayer, nor the object of true faith: an object that has to be real and stronger than me, so that I cannot convert it into an instrument, as we are instinctively tempted to do, even with God, rendering Him a whimsical toy, a powerful being there to satisfy our requests when we have been good.

Today our talk is rather philosophical, as I have already said, but everything becomes simple if we translate it into Christian language.

God loves me, He cares for me, He knows what I am like, not what I think I am like or how I would like to be.

Accepting myself as dependent on Him and believing in Him who thinks of me and loves me: this is how perfection is no longer seen as autarchy, or self-sufficiency, nor is it a theoretical perfection yearned for according to an ideal concept of Man, which does not exist.

If I am convinced that my life has a sense because He exists, because He is there, He loves me and thinks of me, and the hairs on my head are counted, and the reason of my existence is in Him, then I can do this experiment, this act of faith which is so simple, so childlike: believe that God is my Father; that God loves me; that God, more than any father, is proud of me (to speak anthropomorphically) and that even my faults make Him smile (to continue the anthropomorphic metaphor); that I have nothing to fear, because, if He exists, He is much more responsible than I myself am, and if He called me into existence, it is He who carries the weight of this call, the weight of this existence.

It is absolutely false that Man is free with an absolute freedom, in imitation of divine freedom.

Faith is this simpler faith, in which all the extremes touch. It is believing that everything is harmoniously ordered, that I am truly loved by the Lord, and that there is no need to play a part, and say that He does not love me as I am. He is more responsible (if we can say this) for my weaknesses than I myself am. They are more His than mine, because I am also more His than mine.

Wanting to be a little God and support oneself is not possible. Man is nothing without God or independently of God.

Man tends to make himself into an autarchic, responsible center, as if moral responsibility were ontological independence. In fact, the reverse is true, and whoever does not understand this has no peace.

Instead, whoever has this simple, almost infantile faith, but which is the deepest, because it rests on the very foundation of his being, possesses this serenity, this acceptance of reality as it is, not as he would like it to be.

Let me say, by a pun, that self-love, in the sense of egoistic love, is a sin, because the only really authentic love that I can have is love that does not belong to myself: God's love for me, in which I participate and through which I see myself as I am, with all my faults, a creature of God and therefore having value of reality. But my ideal concept has no value; the infinite, wise, perfect idea that the ego has of itself does not exist. It is an imagined idea of philosophers, who have projected in God the idea of a perfect world.

I am much more perfect with my faults than this idea of my "I" in the divine mind that has already reached a Platonic perfection that exists nowhere: not in God, because in God there is nothing that is this "I"; not in me, because I am a reality of flesh and blood very different from the ideal that I have formed.

This is the outline of our first meditation of today: faith is necessary for human joy and joy is either possessed completely or not at all.

Therefore, to conclude, faith is a condition of human joy, and human joy in turn disposes us to make faith arise and appear—the very opposite, therefore, of an artificial and at times morbid tragic view.

Faith is the normal expansion of this joy, which can naturally laugh, which does not have this anxious preoccupation of those who want to save themselves on their own and do everything by themselves. Faith means to be able to receive all things, even one's own being, as a gift.

And this is really the secret of happiness, this minimum of faith that always knows that there exists an external point on which it can lean.

And as we are talking in Christian terms. It is in our Christian faith that we should seek the source of true peace, tranquility, and human joy.

This first step is important for a deepening of our faith.

A faith that does not lead to this peace, serenity, and tranquility is not a true faith, and a tranquility and a peace that are not founded on faith, as experience has proved, cannot overcome human tension, doubt, and anxiety, and cannot therefore last for long.

Religion as the Source of Joy

Yesterday we saw how faith is the condition of human joy, and happiness the ultimate aim of Man's activity; how necessary a transcendent faith is for this joy, and how the object of this faith must be superior to and stronger than us. We saw that Man aspires to happiness and that faith is the condition to achieve it.

Today we will talk a little about this happiness. And we will say that religion is the ultimate and true source of joy.

Yesterday our talk was fundamentally philosophical, albeit not in an overly abstract form; today our meditation will be fundamentally religious, in the sense of religion in general, and not specifically Christian religion. Unfortunately, Christianity has indeed often been separated from religion, and as a consequence Christian discussion has often been separated from religious discussion, forgetting that true religion is that feeling of religiosity that Man has possessed from the moment he appeared on earth.

So, today we will say that religion is the source of joy.

Yesterday we saw how Man aspires to happiness; today in conclusion we will say that happiness is salvation, and nothing else.

Salvation, such a simple thing which is sometimes forgotten. Salvation, what each religion professes to give, and what each religion at bottom gives. In terms which are more familiar, more heartfelt, simpler if you like, this means happiness and nothing else: *brahman*, God, heaven, *nirvāṇa*—these are other words to say, in a full and not just in a psychological way: joy, peace, mercy, happiness.

Religion claims to be the way of salvation, and this is synonymous, or rather it is identical, to being the way of happiness.

And if religion is not the way of salvation, it cannot keep the promise; a kind of dichotomy is created between an earthly life of unhappiness and suffering and a future life as a reward: but this is Manichaeism, which is considered heresy in all religions, because if there is anything that religion or religions wish to teach it is that there is no such separation or total transcendence between this world and this life, and the next world and the next life.

Religion is the bridge that aims at uniting the one thing with the other, and it puts them in direct relation to each other.

It would be the object of a really terrible and cruel psychoanalysis to think that between this world, whose existence depends in some way on a God, and the other world, there was such an inadequacy that we may accept the rule of living a miserable life here, in order to have a reward there.

That is false.

If religion wants to be the way of salvation, it also wants to be the way of happiness, joy, peace, and mercy, where evidently these terms are not to be understood exclusively in a psychological, individualistic, egoistic, mean, narrow sense.

There has been—and we still suffer from it—a deformation of the idea of religion, by identif ying it with a certain moral (I say "a certain" because what has almost exclusively been emphasized is its negative side), so that we have been limited to following the regulations dictated to Men by a more or less powerful and capricious God, and we have often lived our religion in conflict with life and even with love.

Instead we need to say, and see clearly, that joy is the religious category par excellence, just as a festivity is the manifestation of this religious category.

In fact, all religions are joyful, full of festivities, and cheerful: even those of the so-called primitive peoples, those that ethnologists of varying degrees of superficiality, seeing things from outside, will call religions of fear. Fear is an inherent element of religion precisely because religion wishes to free man from fear of things, nature, earth, himself, and others.

All religions are joyous, and the festivity is the primary manifestation of each religion. There is no religion without festivity, and all in all there is no festivity that does not have a transcendent and religious content.

The fact of having lost joy and happiness is a sociological phenomenon belonging to a certain Western culture of today; so that even Christians, when they enjoy themselves, do so with a certain guilt complex, or perhaps even guiltily, because they have let joy and festivity lose their holiness.

Sociologically speaking, all religions are uneconomic, as they are rich in community festivities.

No religion has a criterion of inexpensiveness, or economy; all religions are in favor of festivities, always for a sense of community, when our epoch is rather—or has the tendency to be—economic, and to exploit time, to earn everything possible, to be efficient and hardworking.

All religions have one, two, three, and sometimes more festivities per week, and all religions conceive the meaning of life as what has value of existence and permits us to reach fullness—not life in order to work.

We have perhaps reached a point of exaggeration in this, and therefore our epoch has wished in a certain sense to reaffirm and recover the sense of work, but let us not now go to the opposite extreme, and let us not think that Man is exclusively a being that must work like a slave, and that the most important things are efficiency, results, and "business."

The three great antireligious values, according to a phenomenology of religion, could be economy, efficiency, and individualism, because religion is uneconomic, joyous, and community-minded: every religion, without exception.

I was saying that the festivity is the principal manifestation of joy and the primordial religious category.

At bottom, festivities are always religious, because they are always festivities of joy and gratitude, even those for the dead, or for catastrophes, or for the sad moments in life. They contain a sense of community and they are an outlet, and weeping and other demonstrations of grief always end in a regained peace, a reacquired serenity, a joy that returns.

There are also festivities that at the beginning seem to be just full of weeping, precisely because weeping can remain no longer in the soul and the body of the sufferer. After a funeral, after a commemoration of a catastrophe or a defeat, the initial motive no longer exists. There has been an outlet; the festivity has acted as a kind of valve.

All festivities, including these festivities, are always of joy, gratitude, and grace. And we must rediscover in ourselves this sense of festivity, this category which (literally) re-en-acts the union of Man with all of reality, this gathering, *ecclesia*, this "return to unity" of people who have common ties: all sinners, and yet they all possess something that unites them, and this "something," when they gather to celebrate a festivity, assumes a religious value through purification.

When Christ said, "When two or three meet in my name, I am with them," he was expressing—I paraphrase it in more academic words—the fundamental law of the festivity and human gathering, *ecclesia*, and human congregation.

Festivity is what unites us to our fellow men, and to mankind, both past and future. A festivity does not create itself; it re-creates itself, repeats itself. It is linked to a certain tradition that renews itself, but always connects us to Men, to our past and to the ancestral past of mankind.

A festivity is a thing that makes Man more of a Man, because it drives away the great danger of his detachment from his brothers of the past and the future; thanks to it, a chain is created between one thing and another.

In the festivity, and I am speaking fundamentally of the religious one, Man is not only united with past and future mankind, but also with the cosmos. There is no religious festivity that is not connected to the moon, or the sun, or the harvest, or the rain, the rocks, a cave, a place of pilgrimage, or to something material, earthly, or cosmic, because Man cannot alienate himself from all other things.

By dint of believing so seriously that Man is a different being from things, a kind of alienation has been created. There exists a kind of human racial madness, and maybe trees and birds laugh a little seeing that Men consider themselves so extraordinarily separate from and superior to things that they no longer have the possibility to establish a dialogue or a relationship with things, animals, and everything else.

A festivity is always something that makes us more real, because it makes us more creatures.

A festivity is always linked to the equinox or to the four seasons, or the earth, or fertility, or a river, or the sea, the sun, stars, the sky, heat, the rainy season, or any other thing. There is no religious festivity that does not have this essential link with the cosmos, with things. It makes us feel the true "humility" of Man—that is, to perceive oneself as a creature, *humus*, earth, a thing, and this not in a pejorative sense but in a realistic sense. Humility does not mean feeling humiliated, but being aware of one's real situation in the cosmos.

The festivity therefore creates the union of Man with mankind of the past and the future, of Man with the cosmos, with everything. It unites Man to time and eternity.

A festivity is always something that, although happening in time, through the commemoration of a primordial time, of an *in illo tempore* that becomes present in the present, connects itself with eternity.

What else is all worship if not an anticipation of heaven, of eternal joy on earth, in time?

What else are all liturgies if not a mirror and an anticipation of the celestial liturgy? It is a heaven on earth; thus, in the liturgy in its most profound sense, song, dance, praise, incense, love, and peace have their place and a role to perform.

Now that we are preparing for Easter, we see that in the liturgy of Easter Saturday, from the *Exultet* to the *Gloria*, it is all none other than already living in heaven on earth, because it is precisely through worship and liturgy that Man can touch the Incarnation, the temporalization, if you will allow me this word, of the eternal in temporality—which I have elsewhere called *tempiternity*.

And each festivity, all worship is a commemoration that unites not only the present with the past through tradition but also time with eternity through the liturgy and faith.

This at least for those who live their religion as it should be lived. I repeat: religion is intended here in the general sense, with whatever name it calls itself, and perhaps even atheism is a name for a form of religion still in progress.

We are also children of our age, which is experiencing a certain profanation of joy. The concept of joy easily slides toward that of a type of pleasure, but he who says "joy" does not say "pleasure." Joy is not a pleasure. It is not even absence of work; it is not wealth and success and lack of problems. It is something much more profound: one can be in joy and have a stomachache and an economic problem to solve.

"O Brother Leo," said Francis of Assisi, coming from Perugia, "perfect joy is not there. Even if the Friar Minor were to give sight to the blind, chase away devils, resuscitate the dead after four days, bring to life any dead, write that this would not be perfect joy. And if he converted all infidels to the faith of Christ—write, O Brother Leo—the Friar Minor does not find perfect joy in this."

He had understood that perfect joy is a much more profound thing.

And he, Francis of Assisi, knew how to speak about it much better than us.

We are so academic that, to understand the same subject, perhaps we must say that happiness and joy is the Being itself, God, joy, salvation, and happiness. God is effectively joy, God is beatitude; God, the Being, is joy, and joy means precisely the communion with Being, the awareness of *being*: not of being good or nice or intelligent or great or healthy; all these are more or less important accidents that do not invalidate the essence, the true substance of my being.

Since all of us are so attached to our being that we would like the intelligence of one and the beauty of another and the savoir faire of a third, but all transferred to me, everything in my deepest "I"... it is the discovery of this "I" (different from the ego) which causes me joy, because it is the discovery of the direct participation of God.

Joy means precisely this awareness of the being itself, this ontic growth of my own person, which I do not want to exchange with that of another.

I want to have all that my ambition may want to have, but I cannot want the being of another; it would have no sense.

Beati pauperes, blessed are those who know how to rid themselves of the super- fluous and then discover the true reality, because the stars can only be seen at night.

In our world we have let joy be profaned, deconsecrated, slide toward pleasure and wealth, success, and so many other surrogates.

We have reduced our Christianity to a negative moral, a religion of death, a religion that shuns life, a negative consolation.

A wind of Puritanism is blowing on these Atlantic and Mediterranean coasts, and it tells us so many beautiful things that are not false, but that can be deformed if interpreted unilaterally, be they about sin, grief, or punishment.

For us who are preparing ourselves for Easter, to be able to receive the total joyful message of the risen Christ, cosmos, and mankind, what we need is the religious reconsecration of happiness and joy that has been profaned and deconsecrated by a base mentality and culture. We need to understand again that religion is really the source of joy, understand again what is said to Christians in the *Epistle of Barnabas* (AD 150). They are called "children of joy," *tekna euphrosynês*, of *euphrosynê*, children of serenity, children of joy, of pleasure: this is what Christians were called in the *Epistle of Barnabas*.

We know, without having to look too far, that Pope in 1745, in his constitution *De servorum Dei beatificatione et beatorum canonizatione*, added a fourth condition to the three classic conditions for the canonization of a saint: "... and a constant joy, even if it is of a melancholy temperament," which is not incom- patible. Constant joy is truly a sign of holiness and religiosity.

It is therefore necessary to have a religious reconsecration of joy, a rediscovery of something we have lost.

Today I am simply remembering events; the memory is enough to bring them alive, if their seed is not dead in us.

We need to rediscover the meaning of the word "grace," and let me play with this word here.

It is said that the Christian religion is based on the concept of grace.

Grace is fundamental for Christianity; through grace we are children of God, through grace we participate in the divine nature, through grace we are saved. It is grace that enables us to reach God.

Well, have you ever thought how many things the word "grace" means?

In more than one European language, "grace" means something we are grateful for, something at which, like a banknote, everyone smiles. Grace is not a sad, dark thing, a thing before which we behave as if it were ugly. And the religion of grace is a grateful, gratifying, amiable religion.

Grace can also mean gracious, in its ancient English sense—that is, beautiful; grace means beauty, it means *doxa.* But we have forgotten all this. We have founded a theology on truth and we have forgotten to found it also on beauty; we have decided to erect a moral on good, and we have forgotten to found it also on light. It is written: "God is light," *doxa*, "glory," *shekhinah*.

But we have belittled religious life, forgetting that grace also means this: beauty, *doxa*.

So often religion presents itself as not very acceptable because it is founded on an intellectualistic conception of truth that no longer has light, no longer has color, no longer has a body, is no longer incarnate, no longer has that glory of the Lord that always accompanied the chosen people, wherever they went.

Religion is a bearer of grace, and grace means precisely a grateful thing, and also a gratuitous thing, which was unexpected, a surprise, a present that arrived unexpectedly, which we could not have aspired to because it is much bigger than anything we could have dreamed of.

Grace has these dimensions of surprise, gratuity, a gift that one could not have expected.

Religion is what makes it possible to regain the paradise lost, to reach the super-human, and the fulfillment of all the dreams that Man has in the depths of his being.

It is religion that says: your trouble is that you do not love enough, your trouble is that your ambition is still too weak, you are still too small, you are not yet sufficiently bold or brave, Man enough, you do not yet go deep enough or leap high enough: your trouble is the exact opposite of what you think.

Religion did not come to eliminate the anxieties and ambitions of Man, but to sublimate them with what has been given to us gratuitously because Man alone would not be capable of doing it.

Grace consists in considering existence as a gift, something grateful, "gracious," and *gratis* and also something that one is grateful *for.*

Grace also means giving thanks (*gratiam agere*), receiving existence and salvation and happiness that can be had only if they are received as a gift, with hands opened toward heaven to give thanks with gratitude and thanksgiving.

Yes, grace is a fundamental religious category.

Only if one places himself in this vision does he manage to discover reality, as is said precisely in a Hindū holy text, an *Upaniṣad*: "He understood that *brahman* is joy, because in truth all beings were born from joy, and once they are born they live in joy, and they are supported by joy, and when they pass on, they return and re-enter joy."

This is the religious vision: that things come from joy because God is pure joy, they return to joy and they are sustained by joy and in joy when they appear in this world.

Without religion it is impossible to remain at this height, to admit this vision, not to be driven away by small things, by banal existence.

So religion is not only a source of joy; but, what is more, without religion, without this *religatio* to something that is above us, without this discovery of one's self, which is already direct participation, a gift of the Absolute and of perfect joy, without this hope, one cannot have joy, one cannot endure daily troubles and overcome them. In the long run, intelligence is not needed, nor can instincts and feelings be dominated for long, if one does not possess an interior strength.

We need a religious reconsecration of joy, and this is our mission; I would say it is fundamentally a mission for intellectuals and the young.

Joy cannot be disincarnated, because joy cannot be a thing that is exclusively (I repeat, exclusively) internal, hidden by fifty layers of superstructures of another kind.

So often we have considered a central part of faith or religion some problems that do exist, but that are not fundamental. And yet from a simple analysis it transpires evidently that the fundamental category of religion and the most universal nature of each religion is precisely joy.

Many religions do not have priests, temples, and other things that may seem essential to us, but there is no religion that does not have festivities.

So we must recover the sense of festivity and joy in ourselves and others, at all levels of our existence.

Only living in this dimension are we a little nearer and more prepared to receive the legacy of joy—the good, joyful news of the New Testament, of Easter, in time, in history, and in eternity.

Happiness is salvation, and salvation is precisely this perennial and total joy, this communion and communication with God, which is not so much a source of joy as perfect joy.

Tomorrow we will see how all this reaches its fullness (not exclusivity) in faith, which is the historical and cosmic personal message of perfect joy.

Christianity as the Source of Joy

On the first day we tried to explain how faith is the condition of human joy. On the second day we described, very briefly, how religion is a source of joy. Today we will have a simple, and I would like it also to be classic, Christian meditation.

Let us leave aside so much erudition and general religious talk, and attempt a collective study in depth, here, in the chapel, that is, in a holy place: a meditation of ours on Christianity as a message of perfect joy, an attempt to understand what the evangelical message is.

The word itself says it: *euangelion*, the gospel, the good and joyful news. This is indeed a task for us, for each one of us.

If faith, if Christianity does not present itself to us as good news, it is no longer the gospel, it is no longer what it should be; it will be a thing received by routine, by habit, something that others preached to us but that is not a living thing; and you cannot pass on a dead body. It is useless that all books are full of good scholarship and that the church contains something like a dead deposit, if this thing is not vivified and resuscitated within each of us.

The first condition to understand what the mystery of Easter is—what all the gospel is also—is to receive it as what the gospel professes to be, that is as an "evan-gelical" message, an *euangelion*, a happy, good, beautiful, joyful news.

And there is an intrinsic, not only extrinsic relation in this neologism that expresses the evangelical message: only if it is new, if it is news, only if it is something that shakes you, that one believes and lives almost as he did the first time, with admiration, even with a reaction of slight amazement (because we have never thought of it, and what in fact is natural does not seem so to us), in a word like a personal discovery, a thing that is new and renewed, each day can be gospel—that is to say, it can be beautiful, happy, joyful news.

The *euangelion* is truly good news, news of salvation and joyous news, only if it is truly news, something new, something that has never been said before now, that has never yet been heard, that is discovered for the first time and admired.

At bottom, when I do this act, which is more than a simple rational comprehension of something I know by heart, but which is an act of faith, it is always fresh, always new, always something that has never happened before.

It is like skiing on a slope of virgin snow where nobody else has yet skied; you ski down it the first time, know that you are opening a track in snow that is virgin because nobody has yet touched it.

I repeat: the new news, the gospel, is good, happy, and therefore bearer of salva- tion only when it is new and fresh, when it is discovered each day. We need this virginity of mind and spirit and body to hear it and receive it.

After this initial introduction, what is the content of the gospel, its message? As I told you, it is a message of perfect joy.

The Precursor John the Baptist already knew this: "It is the bridegroom who has the bride; and yet the bridegroom's friend who stands there and listens to him, is filled with joy at the bridegroom's voice. This is the joy I feel, and it is complete" (3:29).

At times the message of the gospel has been explained to us in a quite overcomplicated way, so that it seems to want to communicate so many things to us.

What Christ came to tell us and to bring us is the message of full, total, and perfect joy; nothing more, but also nothing less.

It is the entire message of the Precursor to prepare the way for the Lord. John himself (they are almost his last words in the Gospel) says that he was filled with joy because he heard the bridegroom's voice; he listened to it, and he is filled with joy at his voice. And the same John continues with the phrase with which he finishes and closes his mission as Precursor: "He must grow greater and I must grow less."

All the Old Testament is full of this hope, this song of praise, this sense, which is the only thing that the "revelation" can truly reveal.

For us, with our very limited cognitive capacity, God can reveal himself much more in our most infinite aspects: Man is more infinite in his desire, and more unlimited in his love than in his cognitive capacity.

If we are told that God is great, we understand it exclusively as a thing that transcends all that we can imagine.

Instead Man's desire is infinite.

His knowledge is limited, but his love and his desire have that capacity of infini- tude that his mind does not have.

When the young Thérèse of Lisieux wrote in her diary that she had infinite desires of love, her good spiritual father thought that the word was not very theological, and he crossed it out and substituted it with "incommensurable." At bottom it means the same thing, but perhaps he was afraid of this desire for the infinite that the little Carmelite felt within her.

And Man really has an infinite capacity for desire; therefore, the greatest revela-tion, most appropriate for our capacity for infinite desire, is God, joy.

"A woman in childbirth suffers, because her time has come; but when she has given birth to the child she forgets the suffering, in her joy that a human being has been born into the world. So it is with you: you are sad now, but I shall see you again, and your hearts will be full of joy, and that joy no one shall take from you."

This comes from John 16:21–22, in the Lord's final testament.

It is such a human comparison, so material, so concrete: the woman has pain, the woman screams, but when a man is born, she no longer remembers her suffering. "I shall see you again, and your hearts will be full of joy, and that joy no one shall take from you," which is what He has left us: "I leave you my peace."

His commandments are beautiful and joyful.

Yesterday we were speaking of grace, and we said that grace means being grateful, gratuitous, "gracious," and it implies a sense of thanksgiving (*gratiam agere*).

Let us go back to the original word, *charis charà*. It means much more: basically, it means joy.

If you open any dictionary or if you read any secular or religious work, under the word *charis* you will not only find joy, but also—it is one of those words that include many things—beauty, amiability, honor, preference, gratitude, and also prize or wages.

It is in this polyvalent and full sense that Christ speaks to us.

And also in his testament, in his priestly prayer, he says to us, "I have told you this so that my own joy may be in you and your joy be complete."

Have we ever meditated a little more deeply on these words?

"I have told you this, I have spoken to you"—His words are the cause of our joy, his *logos*, his revelation, his prayer, his liturgy, his obedience; "I have told you this, I have shown you this so that..."—and then there is such a marvelous exchange—"so that my joy (*gaudium meum*, *chara emê*), my grace, my joy, what is mine, what is my deepest characteristic, be in you and live in you."

My joy, his own, the joy of the Lord, the joy of the intra-Trinitarian beatitude: so this is my characteristic, this *charis* that is joy, beauty, amiability, that is all the benignity of God appeared to mankind, which is honor, gratitude, gratuitous, grateful beautiful grace, that this *charis/chara* "be in you"; "and your joy be complete" (*plêrôthê*), may achieve *plêrôma*, fullness; that infinite desire may be filled with this thing which I have come to share with you.

His joy, that intra-Trinitarian joy of being the Son of God, he communicates to us so that our joy may achieve its fullness, its fulfillment, its *plêrôma*, its summit, its end: the joy of being children of God. And in John 17:13: "But now I am coming to you and I say these things while I am still in the world." Earlier it seemed he was only addressing his own (in John 15:11): "I have told you this so that my own joy may be in you and your joy be complete," so that your joy will reach this fulfillment, this *plêrôma*. But then he does not want only to limit himself to his own, and he repeats the same idea with a different nuance: "I say these things to the world, but now I am coming to you (Father) and I say these things in the world to share my joy with them to the full." That they may be filled, that they may have fullness. The verbal form *peplêrômenên*: that they may truly arrive at this *plêrôma*, that they fill themselves fully until the end and they have it *en autois*, *in semetipsis*, in themselves, not only as a legal adoption, as a thing that I have infected you with today and I have told you of, but that belongs to them, that is something that truly resides in them.

These things, all I have done, I have said, what I have revealed in my life, I have said it so that they may have the fullness of joy and my joy may remain and be in them, *en autois*.

Something much greater than a simple adoption: it is a gift, but a gift of which one becomes the owner and that turns into something that belongs deeply to oneself.

If we do not meditate on these things that are so fundamental to our Christian life, how can we really understand what it means to be Christian, and thus draw near to the message of joy and Easter, understanding that the Lord has spoken to us exclusively so that we may have joy and the fullness of joy?

The Christian is the lord, the Christian is not the man who lives on earth with an inferiority complex, but the opposite: the Christian is the one who has received the message, the testament, the legacy of full and total joy. There is no chance or obstacle that can overwhelm it.

This is our faith that overcomes the world. This is our joy, which is the joy of being children of God, which is the perfect joy, reserved to all those who exercise justice (*dikaiosynê*).

Do you remember the echo of today's gospel? It is Christ who speaks in a some-what argumentative way with the Pharisees: "Is it not written in your law [rather a polemic 'your']: I tell you, You are Gods" (Ps 82)? Now if those to whom the word of God was addressed were called Gods—and Scripture cannot be cancelled—how much more?" This is perfect joy. *Theoi este*, "You are Gods."

It is interesting to notice how often (and for me it was an unexpected discovery), in environments not too distant from that in which we now live, the idea that the essence of Christianity and what Christ came to bring to Men on earth is perfect joy—because we are children of God and because we are one thing with God and we divinize ourselves totally in order to form a single unity with God—is found to be a little strange, something that was not known, that seems a novelty, while it is all that the Lord wanted to leave us and the reason why he came down to earth: divinization, the perfect joy of being God.

Not only to be like God, imitations of God, surrogates of the Highest; not only what Adam and Eve perhaps wanted to be-come, to come to be, a little too quickly; thus the serpent touched the depths of their mental fibers when he told them that they could be like God, while their destiny and their vocation were much higher than that of becoming like God, similar to God: it was to become God himself.

Ego dixi: dii estis, et non potest solvi Scriptura.

Theoi este, you are Gods, and Scripture cannot be cancelled.

We are called to become God, and this is the message of Christian joy.

If John the Baptist, before the message, had understood, John the Evangelist, after the message, wrote it explicitly. In his letter he says, "and we are writing this to you so that your joy may be complete."

Always the same idea; he had also understood and was imitating his Master, "so that your joy may be perfect, complete."

And to reach this, evidently, the condition is to listen to the word, receive it, and put it into practice.

Easter is the Christian and non-Christian feast par excellence, that feast that is the unity of all festivities precisely because it comes not only to proclaim, but to realize this new life, this divinization, this *koinônia*, this communion, communication, participation, and unity with the Trinitarian God.

But the condition is what is realized in our life and what was realized in the life of Christ: the cross.

The only condition to rise again is to die.

The only condition to live a truly Christian life is to rise again.

But only the one who dies will rise again. Whoever does not die, who is afraid, who does not die to his/her own ego, cannot rise again.

So many Christians are neither fish, nor flesh, nor fowl, neither one thing nor the other: they feel uneasy in the world because they are not of this world, they have not risen again and so they walk depressed, like people whose place is neither here nor there.

So we can neither be light of the earth nor salt of the world, because we have not had the courage to die fully to ourselves, to our egoism. And as long as this latter is not truly transformed, it is impossible to be Christian; one is perhaps a catechumen, but nothing more.

The only obstacle to being a Christian is not that of being a sinner (this is not an obstacle); it is not being mediocre or normal: on the contrary, being a poor man is the condition for which the gospel was preached.

The only condition is really that of dying, total abandonment, letting the Lord do and undo. Dying in and with Christ, letting the former Man go and disappear.

The Easter message, which is repeated constantly because everything grows in an upward spiral, is precisely this: if wheat does not die, it does not rise again. To use stronger words: whoever does not hate his own life will never live the true Life.

This is the only condition.

When one accepts to say, "Lord, You have won the contest," then new life begins, the life of the person who has risen again.

This does not mean that you are not a sinner as before, but everything is already on the other bank, in another dimension. Christ has taken possession of you and you can begin to feel, to enjoy this perfect joy.

"I have told you this so that my own joy may be in you and your joy be complete." So it is a true rebirth; but if I am not born again, I cannot have this joy. However, when a Man is born in the world, when he already has something divine and definitive, he even forgets the labor and pains of this birth and rebirth.

This is perfect joy: being aware of reaching this divinization, our total transfor- mation in/into Christ.

Today we have been inspired by John.

In the sixth chapter he says the phrase heard so often, and so often meditated on, but that we are afraid to live wholly, which is why our reason tries to give interpreta- tions that are in the end only impoverishments: "Whoever eats my flesh and drinks my blood remains in me and I remain in that person."

"Remains": residing, being already inside, to live "in me" and "I in him."

And so that there may be no doubt of any kind, he continues: just "as the living Father sent me and I draw life from the Father [through the Father I live none other than the life of the Father, *dia ton patera*, with the full sense of an active accusative], so [not in another, more imperfect form] whoever eats me will also draw life from me" (*dia eme*, same preposition, same accusative, same identification).

This is Easter, this is the Christian vocation: truly to be God, to reach the ultimate bosom of the divinity, to be one with Christ and thus fully to become a part of the divine, of the full and total joy, to continue the creation, the redemption, the constantly and totally renewed development of a life that is then true life.

And when one lives this, then one truly understands how perfect the joy is and how the message of Christ can be reduced simply to this: I have spoken to you so that your joy may be perfect and nobody (as he will say in chapter 16) may take it away from you. Nobody can take this joy of yours, because it is yours, because I am yours and you are mine. "Whoever eats me, lives in me and I live in that person," and the union is total and perfect.

The Christian himself, this Christian who has risen again, who lives another life that is the full and total life, and who thus goes beyond things and at the same time is fully incarnate in them; things that, on the one hand, do not touch him, as water does not wet the leaves of the lotus plant, but on the other hand and at the same time he is incarnate in them: it is he who directs, who leads, who makes history move forward because his point and his fulcrum are outside any movement and any change of history itself.

It is, once again, about the divine paradox: the poor will inherit the earth and those who weep will be happy, he who seems persecuted and poor will be the one who really rules supreme.

This, then, is the Easter spirituality that brings us this message of perfect joy, this spirituality that overcomes any negative asceticism, any negative morality, any situation and attitude of opposition.

Let us prepare ourselves for this Easter with a little more trust and faith.

The only obstacle is this small ego, which must disappear; this egoism, which I must overcome. Then joy will spring forth.

Let us prepare ourselves for this *hallelujah*, which can already be sung from now here on earth, which is compatible with so many other things because nothing and nobody takes from us the perfect joy, this jubilation that He gave us and that He came to reveal to us.

We must only listen to His words and put them into practice.

This, then, is the outline of our Easter preparation.

We said in the first place, in Advent, that the Church is the hope of mankind, peoples, and individuals. But let us not forget that the Church is not a simple insti- tution, but the people of God.

During Lent, we saw how this Church purifies us and forgives us: this is the sense of penitence, because alone we are not able to receive, listen to, and put into practice the Christian message.

And at Eastertide, which is the acme and the climax of the Christian message, we have tried to show how joy is what the Lord left us. Joy is not solely preached, because it must not be preached, it must be contagious: it is the present, the gift that God gives us.

Let us prepare ourselves in this Holy Week truly to receive this joy.

So many times, when we speak of preparation, it seems to be an active thing, that there is something that must be attained.

Now I would ask you to prepare yourselves for Easter in the most actively passive way, the most masculinely feminine, the most authentically Christian; in an attitude of receiving, as one receives a gift, as one who knows how to hope, as one who loves trustingly, as one who believes firmly.

Therefore faith, hope, and charity are the doors that open us to this message from the Lord.

Let us prepare ourselves then to receive this gift, this perfect joy, knowing that the only obstacle can be our egoism, which refuses to die.

This is a great, unique personal experience, and it is worth each of you saying, "I want to try to take this step." Try to take this step, to let yourselves go, to let yourselves be led by heaven.

Then you are born, you are reborn, and the peace of god, His *charis*, which is joy, which is beauty, which is amiability, which is this total bliss, comes to us, remains with us, and nobody can take it from us.

5
The Presence of God

Living the Presence of God

We have come here, to this sacred place, for a day's retreat.[1]

But what is the use of having a retreat, distancing ourselves from the things we usually do, if we then bring with us all that we have distanced ourselves from? Do we use this day to better project ourselves into the future, or to return again to what we came from before the retreat?

Today, this retreat could, perhaps, try to break this vicious circle, this almost constituent lie of our life that makes us live projected into the future, that is always problematic, laden with the past, full of expectations, and that never lets us live the present.

If we have climbed up to San Sergio, it is not only in order to have a retreat but also to stop for a moment.

Now we are celebrating the mystery of God, the mystery of Christ, the mystery of the Church, the mystery of the world, the mystery of each one of us. And this is in itself an end; so let us stop there. If we could stop, even for a minute, everything would already be realized: discovering and becoming aware that we are in God.

"Lord, may I see" is the most important prayer of the message of the Church on this *Quinquagesima* Sunday. I would like this to be our prayer today. "Lord, let us see, so that we become conscious of reality—that we do not live always either without understanding or without seeing, or seeing and understanding only what in the end is unimportant."

Living the presence of God: this will be the theme of our private and collective prayer and our meditation today. Living the presence of God means, in the first place, living, and living fundamentally in the present. "And at once," says the Gospel, "his sight returned." At the very moment

1 Held at Divo Barsotti's hermitage in Settignano (Italy), 1966.

that Jesus says to the blind man, "Your faith has saved you," he is cured and he can see.

Salvation is discovering, seeing. "At once." It is this instant that we should live, without being weighed down by the past, which is an obstacle to us, which makes us old and with no vision of the future, which makes us adolescents, dreamers, utopians. The experience of the presence of God begins with that of the presence of the moment, of the present.

Living the Mass, the sacrifice per se, is something truly greater than a past or a future. It is a present.

And then a dimension of verticality begins to open itself, which, together with our temporality, forms the cross, the symbol of every authentic existence.

Living the present means living without a past, without a future, having overcome time and having also transcended space. Space, this other structure that weighs on us, because we would like to be here or there, to be in one place or another, to be in the East or the West, and in the meantime we are nowhere, we are always absent.

I do not wish to preach a sermon today. I would like us to stop here, at this altar, and discover that this altar is the center of the world, and that this moment is a moment that overcomes the present, past, and future.

It is an experience that must be made here and now.

Here, on this stone where we are celebrating, is the center of the world. Here is realized that only thing that we then see as a prism of a thousand colors, but which is in the end one thing only: it is the creation, redemption, and glorification of all reality.

And in me is the whole cosmos, all of it!

It is faith that we must ask of the Lord to be safe, to see. "Your faith has saved you." And this faith then discovers that the important thing is not "prophesy, philan- thropy, science [I am commenting on the epistle you know well], nor moving mountains, nor the government of the world, nor money, nor wisdom, but what counts is one thing alone: charity."

And if we analyze this hymn to love (1 Co 13), we see that St. Paul first speaks of love as "patient."

Why is it patient? Because it awaits nothing. It has come to a halt. It does not expect anything else.

An impatient person is someone who wants to go elsewhere, who wants to do something else; and he looks at his watch and perhaps he can wait, but his patience is an artificial one, it is not that patience of which the Lord spoke to us last Sunday, when he said that "in patience you will possess your lives." It is not that patience which is the fruit of charity.

And charity hopes everything, believes everything, does not become irritated, does not pursue its own interests.

Oh, how artificial all our spiritual approach can be! How it can be a spontaneous revelation of all that we really are, and we are much more than beings in time and space!

Everything can be overcome, both the temporal and the spatial, if we live with truth.

And we cannot have a life of contemplation, nor can we have a life of true action (two aspects of what is fundamentally the same reality in this double dimension), if we do not overcome, if we do not transcend time and space, if we do not live this presence of God, of reality, of the present.

It would be sad if we were to make so many efforts to be good, but we remained in the superstructure, without ever living this simple thing, this love, this faith that saves us.

Living in the presence of God.

Being once again like children, being free, which is the necessary condition for joy. Whoever has a lot of responsibility, a lot of public appointments, may perhaps

take his work too seriously, while it should be considered as a game that is played with one's full attention, but with detachment, never taken as an end in itself, which would be ridiculous.

We are sad, at times, because we give too much importance to the past in our life, which does not allow us to be as we would like to be, or because we are projected toward the future with our desires, and thus we are not able to discover reality in the present.

A day of retreat, therefore, is much more than "retreating." It is this stopping, here, now, in this Mass, to offer ourselves, to offer the world, to receive the whole creation, to receive Christ, to offer and receive everything in a total transformation of what I see; to embrace all the past and, by squeezing it in our hands, make it disappear; to take on the future and, by assimilating it, see that it was—I don't say *māyā*, but not the whole of reality.

And now I start living, and if I die in five minutes I have lost nothing, and if I live fifty years more I have lost nothing : I am not saying that I have gained nothing, but I have lost nothing.

And so we enjoy this freedom, this joy, and we begin to live.

"Walk in my presence and be perfect," said YHWH to Abraham; and since the word of YHWH is always causative, Abraham *was* perfect, as all tradition will say.

So, what should I do? Strange things? No!

God said, "Walk before me and be perfect": like Abraham, you will be perfect by walking in His presence.

In this Mass, today, now, here, we are asking the Lord to make us realize his presence. "Lord, may I see": this vision, this awareness, this faith. "Lord, may I see." Vision does not have an object; it is not what you see. If I want even to see a

small thing, it is limited: I see that, but I see nothing else.

"Lord, may I see." "Your faith has saved you." And at once he saw.

And then another thing, for us who are still pilgrims: "... and he followed him, praising God." Let us also do the same, now.

Being Able to Live in the Presence of God

Being able to live in the presence of God is fundamental for a Christian life.

We could indeed say that those who can live in the presence of God have already attained what they wished for.

The beatific vision is none other than the presence of God, so the presence of

God, here, on earth, is already the end.

I said "presence of God," not presence of oneself, not self-awareness, not sense of stoical perfection or, according to the humanistic conception of Man, always being irreproachable, impeccable, one's own master, in control of oneself, and... thus never angry!

What about Jesus? How often he got angry! "After so much time I have spent with you, you still have not understood anything !..." *Irascimini, et nolite peccare*, says a psalm.

The Christian is not some kind of perfect being, with a television smile playing on his lips!

Presence of God does not mean presence of one's self; it does not even mean human perfection. Nor is presence of God a feat of memory: saying thirty or forty prayers, performing acts of love, doing an act of humility on each step you descend, uttering an invocation at each step you climb, thinking of death—or of life—at every crossroads, greeting first the guardian angel of everyone you meet: all these can be wonderful things, but don't let us confuse the means with the end!

What can be a means can also become an obstacle.

No, the presence of God is not simply a feat of memory... even those who have no memory can live in His presence.

And it is not even a simple act of willpower, nor a technique, which can be learned as one learns to drive a car.

Hence the disappointment that one can feel when one goes on a spiritual retreat and would like to learn something, a recipe in the ascetic, mystical, or practical field, that could be useful to us.

And it is not even a feeling, a sensation that makes us feel at ease or uneasy. How can I perceive the presence of God if I have to focus on driving my car, or doing an algebra calculation, or if I must cook, sew, and so on?

The presence of God does not distract me, nor does it divert me from what I am doing or from my daily tasks.

In brief, it is not a dual experience; it cannot be presence of myself, it cannot be a feat of memory, it cannot be an act of will, it cannot be a feeling.

This morning we have tried to underline an aspect of the presence of God as "ever-present," as the overcoming of time and space, and therefore of the past and the future and any spatial dispersion.

Living in the presence of God means to live in the present, *hic et nunc*, "here and now," it means to make one's own life one, reunited (the exact opposite of today's dispersion), and here I would like to use a classic word of all Christian and non- Christian schools of spirituality: "concentrating oneself."

What does "concentrating oneself " mean? Centering everything as in a circle whose radii reach all the circumference and branch out from a single center. And one is equidistant from everything : from me, from my life....

Con-centrate. In the "con" there are two elements.

The first is this convergence toward the center in a harmonic way, where nothing is dispersed, and we do not forget either our own body, nor our appointment for the following day, nor what we have to do. It is not a question of abstracting oneself. There is a radical difference between concentration and abstraction, precisely in that they are two opposite poles.

Abstraction leads to losing oneself in the clouds. It is evasion, it is wanting to have a more or less spiritualistic idea of oneself; then one cannot recognize what one is. It is a temptation toward angelism, which often takes hold of those who are projected toward a certain ideal (I am not saying "toward God").

Concentration, on the other hand, is as much the opposite of dispersion as of abstraction. It is—as the Italian word *raccoglimento* suggests—an inward gathering, which, however, does not mean abstracting oneself from things because I do not care about them and I just want to be left in peace.... Second, "concentration" also means to center oneself "with" ("con"). We are not alone; God is with us and helps us to achieve this total reunification.

It is a question of the presence *of God*, which is not a dual presence. God is not another, who is outside, like an eye that watches me and checks on me so I can never let myself go.

A Chinese proverb says, "You cannot stay for a long time on tiptoe." Any artificial position cannot be maintained for a long time; sooner or later we return to our normal position.

The presence of God must not be identified only with that pressure that in particular moments God exerts on our soul to spur it toward a certain function, not leaving it in peace until it says "yes." How many examples there are in the Old Testament! God begins to persecute somebody and does not leave him alone until he accepts to be a prophet, or to go to Nineveh, or to do whatever else.

This is God's free initiative, but the presence of God of which we are speaking is more "natural" and less obvious.

The presence of God is not a kind of surveillance, so that we cannot be ourselves because we are always in a state of artificial tension, nor is it a projection of our idea of God.

If in the presence of God we cannot be as genuinely as possible "ourselves," *that* is not the presence of God. It could even be a kind of spiritual schizophrenia, so that we project another "I" that stays there and watches us, and that, in accord with our idea that it should have of our perfection, makes us always vigilant and careful to do ever more, ever better.

I am not saying that all this is bad, but it is not the presence of God, which is more natural, because God is not extraneous to us.

The presence of God is not firstly "a presence," and then... "of God." It is the full Presence of Reality.

The presence of God displays three aspects: two can be explained easily, while the third, the true presence of God, is almost impossible to explain.

The first aspect belongs to intelligence, the gifts of the Holy Spirit of knowledge and science.

It is a kind of capacity to see things as they are, but also to discover their true dimension, a third dimension, which may not be seen at first sight.

The presence of God is that light that enables us to discover this dimension of depth in every thing, every action, every behavior, every word, every creature, every instant.

The presence of God enables us to discover that things are much more profound than they seem, much more beautiful than they appear, much more real than we believe.

It makes us perceive how everything is unique and linked (*religata*) to God, how everything is a manifestation of the unique Presence, a revelation of the Only One who unveils Himself; which is, yes, appearance, but of the only thing of which it can be an appearance.

It is vision that enables us to discover God in things, which enables us to discover that everything is God, in the form of a child, a bird, a headache, a bus we have missed, a law of physics, a letter we must write, spaghetti that has gone cold, sleepless nights.

Everything must be discovered in this new dimension, in this concreteness, which is none other than a form of the cosmic symphony that is creation.

The presence of God is this awareness of the Sacred in every moment, in every thing. "Everything is sacred," God will say while revealing himself to Peter in the vision of Joppa. Everything is sacred, because everything is God, from God, in God, with God.

Whoever perceives the presence of God will respect everything and everybody; he will have, on the one hand, an extraordinary boldness and, on the other hand, an extreme diffidence.

Everything for him is sacred and marvelous; so he has no restlessness, anxiety, or uneasiness.

It is that state that all ascetic authors call "holy indifference" (but note the *holy*): health or infirmity, living in the West or the East, staying in one's own country or going to India, what difference does it make?

This is not indifferentism: on the contrary, it is profound passion in everything we do, in every reality we come into contact with. It is the sense of the Sacred, it is the sense of God not as *another* being, but as the Only One, as the Spirit, the Creator, giving the word "creation" its truest meaning, as expansion and multiplication of God.

The second aspect of the presence of God consists in discovering God as present in everything in His dynamic form—that is, as love.

If the first aspect emphasizes what philosophers call the immanence of God, the second aspect emphasizes His transcendence. It makes us discover that in this cosmic dynamism all things move toward God, that God is the object of every desire.

If Man begins to live in the presence of God, he not only discovers a new dimen- sion in things, but he also discovers that everything belongs to the economy of the Holy Spirit, who is spirit of love, who gives life and loves, who makes the Son—and with the Son all of creation—return to the Father.

These are the first two aspects; about the third, of which one cannot speak, I will just make some allusions, but I do not have the words, because if I say "love," it is too little; if I say "consciousness," it is unilateral; if I say "experi- ence," I do not render the idea; if I say "recognition," it is too intellectual. I do not have a word to explain this experience. Perhaps one could say : being alive in God and with God.

That means: when I live myself as a "pre-essence" of God, as a "pre-God," as a God who is about to become God and as a being called to be God, but who is already God inasmuch as this call is the only thing he has, and which—although he is not yet God, he has not become it yet—will lead him to be God.

However, "not yet being God," or "still being not-God" because about to become

God, should not be interpreted in a total and absolute sense.

This vision of me as God, and at the same time as not-God, because I am not yet God and not because I am not God, but because I am "still not-God"... this, let us call it for the sake of brevity, experience of me (and in this "me" all that is in contact with me is involved), all this is none other than a "presence of God," a divine "pre-essence."

However, all words are inadequate, so I can only be silent.

The Presence of God Is a Mystical Vision

The presence of God: it is a mystical vision, a vision that goes beyond concepts. It is already an anticipation of the beatific vision.

We must, however, be realistic and know that things have a rhythm, and that we have not yet arrived. We are all pilgrims, walking with the hope of arriving, but we cannot forge ahead; indeed we must not forge ahead.

In any event, even when we have to forge ahead, we do not even realize it; it is God who works in us.

Even this awareness of our limits is important.

The presence of God must be cultivated, evidently, and we must not forget what is commonly called the practice of the divine presence, nor all those little means that lead us to live in this state of conscious ecstasy, which is not ecstasy but a much more profound vision than it appears.

The Church, in many an *Oremus*, tells us that we must love God *in omnibus e super omnia*. Love God in all things.

But our love must not be a prisoner of things, it must not exhaust itself in the more profound vision that we have of them. It is not enough to see God in things; we need to see things in God. Any love that makes us prisoners, without freedom, is nothing but idolatry.

If one loves God in all things and above all things, then one can live in this presence of God, in this awareness and consciousness that we are "presence of God." This presence of God also makes us build the much-needed bridge between biological life and the life of grace. This construction is certainly more difficult than it may seem.

The osmosis between our life of work and effort, and our life of prayer and offering, is often quite poor, and it is not easy to attain what should be the ideal of life, one single life, where work and prayer are no longer separate, although the time to be devoted to one and to other remains distinct.

As the Lord penetrates us, He also transforms our body and divinizes it (we have a confirmation of this in the most recent dogma proclaimed by the Church, concerning the Assumption of the Virgin Mary), until there is a union of life, which is the fruit of a life of the active and real presence of God.

Only an action made in the presence of God dominates all the possible consequences that this action can have.

So, what is to be done?

There is no exhaustive answer; there cannot be one.

Only someone who does things with another sense, with this sense of freedom, with this sense of a presence that trusts him and that pushes him to do this or that, no longer worries.

Someone who lives the present can truly achieve anything, and is already beginning to unify his or her life.

We must be a truly single thing; body, soul, and spirit must be unified. The human and the divine must again form a total unity within us, and in this our process of transformation and divinization, in this lapse of time and space, we will bring the entire cosmos to become a part of the new earth and the new heavens.

The presence of God, therefore, is not only necessary for a life of contemplation, for strictly sacred actions, but it is also necessary for every action, every decision, every act of everyday life.

The unification of our actions, the unity of our life, will make us discover what God means, in a truly personal form.

Lectures, practices, readings, everything helps, but at bottom they are only opportunities so that afterward a personal experience occurs, so that a flash of inte- rior light makes us realize what our intelligence has perceived; otherwise everything would remain just theoretical.

The presence of God will lead us to live our lives in depth, to change each of our meetings into an event of communion; every occasion that may seem banal into a revelation; every activity, effort, or sorrow into a manifestation, that is, a theophany.

He who lives in the presence of God lives constantly discovering God in His most varied forms.

God is not only in what is beautiful, He is also in what appears less beautiful to us; He is not only in what we have done according to our moral principles, He is also in what may look not so good to us.

The Man who lives in the presence of God lives all theology and all things in one, in a simple intuition, which perhaps he cannot even explain, because he does not have the words or the concepts. Despite not knowing how to explain it, when he listens, or these things are taught to him, for him it is like remembering what he already knows.

I believe we really should live with a new style of life, with greater trust.

All my talk, which could be extended and developed, can basically be summarized in a very simple piece of advice: we must have unlimited trust in the Lord. Let us listen to what the Lord said to St. Catherine of Siena: "Catherine, think of me, and I will think of you." So let it be Him who thinks of us!

This trust teaches us that we should not worry, in a rational sense, but trust, and trusting is not only entrusting, but having a real trust even in the things, the circum- stances through which God leads us, and not only in our conceptions of what is good or bad, of what is worthwhile or not worthwhile, continually judging everything.

The criterion to detect the presence of God is not the fact of always being in the clouds, nor of being absorbed in great contemplation, outside what people normally call reality. The contrary is true: I discover all of reality in its most concrete dimensions; it is in the divine presence that I discover both God and the world. So, *in omnibus* I find peace, because the *Super Omnia* gives it to me. This is what the Man who lives in the presence of God and walks *in conspectus Domini* is called to.

Let us close this last meditation of our retreat trying to do what is traditionally called an act of the presence of God:

Lord, You are there and also here, You see us and I see within you. I would like to penetrate until I see nothing but what You see, and as You see it. We are a vision of Yours, so that all our relationship should be converted and inverted, and I would like to experience myself as a divine *you*. Lord, I call You "you," but You are the "I"; I am Yours, Your "you." You see me, and so I can close my eyes, not to walk with closed eyes, but to see—increasingly—the totality of everything.

6
Mary

The Mystery of Mary

Ecce mater tua!

—John 19:27

To a friendly reader:

Please excuse me if I address you informally: not so much to be fashionable, but as a sign of familiarity, as I believe these things can only be discussed in an atmosphere of closeness.

Everything is important: theology, science, culture, progress, everything is very important, but, without Mary, our Christian life is incomplete and any conception that one tries to give to Christianity fails.

From original sin onward, Man has acquired the tragic prerogative (by the science of good and evil) of being able to possess the truth in some way, without being possessed by it; of being able to get close to reality and even of being able to recognize good, without this making him true, genuine, and good.

The only exception is Mary. When we, human beings, put ourselves in contact with

Mary, the Immaculate, it seems that her original privilege is transmitted to us, too.

One can have faith in Christ and not love him, one can be a theologian and not be in grace, one can possess the truth and be in the wrong, one can, finally, be orthodox and go off track. With Mary something special happens, which cannot be wholly explained; it is certain that one cannot have faith in her without loving her, that one cannot think of her without her exerting an irresistible force over us.

Quando gyro vallabat abyssos, aderam! (I was there when He marked out the horizon on the face of the deep!).

Thus all the tradition of the Church considers the devotion to Mary as the best guarantee of perseverance.

You will understand, then, my friend, that I cannot coldly offer you a meditation on the Virgin, without pouring all of myself into it. But, in order not to go beyond the limits of a simple meditation, I will try to tell you briefly what, for a long time, I have been craving for. I would like you to understand me well, and to read between the lines: *Legas et intus legas.*

First of all, I would like to address you as a person who is immersed in the hubbub of modern life, with economic worries, professional problems, family affairs and situations, political responsibilities—in a word, with little time to "waste" on simple lucubrations that are not immediately lucrative or directly useful. Your intel- lect, however, can still be attracted by a topic as exclusively devotional as that of the Virgin, and the proof is that you are reading this!

You are immersed in life—that is to say, you are an active person—and yet there is a contemplative tendency in you which makes you "waste time" (which is a form of giving and gaining one's own life) on a topic that has nothing to do with your everyday interests. However, you may realize that in the Virgin you can solve many problems whose fittest horizon would be difficult to find in other ways.

Years ago, I recommended that a friend of mine, an active man who was involved in important and urgent business, as a remedy to dispersion, which he considered inevitable, not only have a filial devotion to Mary, but also study her figure intellectually and theologically. When, after a certain hesitation and resistance, he decided to do so, he understood the sense of my advice and he experienced the fruits of it: Marian theology offered him a climate of serenity and contemplation, but above all it gave him a detachment when facing his immediate concerns, so much so that he was able to overcome them. The vital union with Our Lady also made him discover the transcendental deception of our intelligence and immunized him against the constituent temptation our intellect is subject to: on the one hand, participation and the image of God with unlimited projection, and, on the other, limited participation, tributary of matter and time, which instinctively absolutizes everything it touches, forgetting that in this sublunary world only one thing is necessary. Without any contact with the Virgin, our intelligence easily loses the sense of proportion, the sense of relativity, and intellectual serenity—things, in fact, normally lacking in most people. God save us from the *furor theologicus* outside its field, from the dogmatic extrapolation with which people sometimes try to justify earthly actions.

This is not the moment to explain how an authentic Marian theology may have this cathartic function for our mind, this soothing action on our spirit, this feminine influence on our intellect. Finally, we must turn to the complete, perfect, ancient synthesis that Mary, the *gratia plena*, *pulchra ut luna*, *electa ut sol* ("full of grace, beautiful as the moon, exalted as the sun") realizes in the creation. Only in her as the *sedes sapientiae* do we find the criterion for a correct, complete, intellectual, affectionate, axiological development of the created being.

Mary, perfect creature in her human and divine nature, is the hidden guide who naturally attracts those who seek even the slightest perfection that is integrally human. *Ab aeterno ordinata sum* (I have been ordained from eternity).

You are a member of the faithful and you have the right and the duty to make your voice heard in the Church, not so much to teach, but to contribute to its orientation. The helmsman guides the ship, but it is the lighthouses on land that light up the coast and the rocks.

Laypeople also are Church, and every Christian has a personal and not-transferable mission to accomplish in the Mystical Body of Christ. I would like to remind you here that it is not necessary to belong to the official authority of the Church to be a real theologian. We must once and for all overcome that false pharisaic respect that our era, in this respect still post-Cartesian, reserves for theologians, as authoritative bearers of the doctrine of a religious confession. Theology is not a matter of confes- sion or of school, but of faith: every Christian must be sufficiently sincere not to leave one's own faith at the margin of one's thought or to use it only as an extrinsic corrective, almost as if his or her very reason were not enlightened by this superior form of knowledge that gives us true wisdom.

Theology as *theologia viae*, itinerant theology (and theologians know it well, but at times it is appropriate to recall it), is not a ready-made medicine that was given to us to automatically cure our ills. True theology accompanies Man in his pilgrimage on earth, and it is none other than the worship which Man, his mind, his *logos*, so to speak, renders to God, listening to His message and His Word and seeking to clarify it. This is not a privilege of priests, but a need of the Christian mind and, as such, heritage of all Christians, as well as the universal aim of the Church. Theology is not only a *logos* addressed to God, as the explicitation and human revelation of the *logos* of God. *Ipsum audite!* (Listen to Him himself !). Do not forget that theology, according to St. Thomas himself, is none other than a normal expansion of a life of faith. *Fides quaerens intellectum* (Faith in search of knowledge). We need to revive this Christian practice, which was never wholly lost, to make our intelligence work integrally—that is to say, theologically.

I would now like for a moment to proceed more directly into the mystery of Mary. In Marian literature we find that, on the one hand, the so-called narrative books are almost apocryphal gospels on the Virgin, very pious and poetic, which make Mary say what she did not say and make her feel what the author personally feels; or they are interesting archaeological and historical narrations, more or less adequate, which revolve like a spiral around the Virgin, but do not know how to give us what we seek in these books. The systematic books, on the other hand, leave the historical shell aside, as they suppose that the historical part is a simple covering, and profess to reach the core of Mary, losing themselves either in pleasant personal reflections or in abstract Mariological speculation.

All this is nothing but an excuse, because I too would like to speak to you about Mary, about Myriam, that dark-haired Jewish woman, humble and feminine, who did not know she was full of grace until the angel revealed it to her, disturbing her with his greeting.

This little essay contains many years of hope and life. What remains now is a dense liqueur decanted from experience and filtered by prudence. I will therefore be brief and schematic. Only passions that have passed through the fiery phase, and concentrated themselves, are those that really deserve to be called passions. The others are ephemeral fireworks. The same breath that blows out a match can light embers.

It is written that, if we do not become children, we will not enter the kingdom of heaven. But can a man, once he is old, enter his mother's womb again to be born again and thus be a newborn baby? This is the question that Nicodemus, the lawyer, asked Jesus.

I will not spend time theorizing on evangelic spiritual infancy, neither quoting St. Paul, who anxiously formulates the doctrine, nor St. Augustine, who comments on it, nor even St. Thérèse of the Child Jesus, who lives it, but I will simply say that we are (and will be) children to the extent that we have a mother.

For our blood mothers—and I do not say "earthly," because the Virgin is also earthly and corporeal—we will always be children. We could be the most famous people in the world, but they will always consider us as children and they will never take us too seriously, and rightly so. As long as one loves one's mother, as long as one responds to maternal love, one preserves one's heart of a child.

Love toward Mary is therefore necessary to enter the kingdom of heaven, because the door is open only to children. This does not mean that love for Mary is a strict obligation. Strict, that is, as the explicit subject of a formal rule. This type of love cannot be commanded. This, however, does not mean that such love is not already implicit in our infantile state. In all moments of human life, from the most important to the most ordinary: when she loved the Lord, when she worked doing her duty, when she practiced charity and acts of mercy, when she was under the fig tree, when finally she lived in divine friendship, she was with you, from the begin- ning, although you did not know it, like a discreet woman, tidying everything up, sensing everything, smoothing much roughness, sweetening so many things.... Isn't it true? Think of your mother when you were very small and you knew nothing ! There is another life in you, which is not born of flesh, nor of blood, nor through man's work, but through the will of Woman... *Fiat!*

The love of the child leads me to speak of human love. Christianity is a divine religion, and consequently it seems unfathomable, cosmic, and mysterious to us human beings. But it is also a human religion, and as such it possesses, among other things, a dimension of love that cannot be better transmitted than by a woman, the blessed one among all women.

The human heart has its rights, and the Christian believer is not unaware of this. Christ came down to earth to make us more than men, but this elevation does not mean that we must cease being human; on the contrary, the Christian needs more than others to refer to Mary that human dimension, which is even more than human, which integrates our life on earth. This is why Christ gave us His mother.

Furthermore, Christian life is not without this dimension of the heart, which is just as important as the cerebral dimension. Faith itself is something more than the affirmation of a statement that is considered certain. It is also essentially a free act, that is to say, an act of love. Christian fullness does not violate the rights of human desire: the most important and *only* rule of the "New Law" (so to speak) must be fulfilled by the entire extent and intensity of our being. I must love God with all my mind, with all my soul, with all my energy, even physical, with all my being. This means that outside this love for God there can be no capacity for love. But I do not possess a special organ to love God, other than those that nature has given me, to be raised to the same order as the divinity. I must love God with what I am and how I am. In other words, we must love Him as we love our fellow Men, creatures of God, with our heart of flesh and blood; this heart remains even if it is filled with grace or, to express it better, Christ.

More still, it is with our love, true and real, concrete and human, that we love our God, who has become man, and we also love His mother, who was left to us as a legacy.

Because of a certain irreligiousness that has little by little entered our Western culture, we have lost our innocence of spirit and, as a consequence, the spiritual strength of language. And thus we are nowadays ashamed to speak naturally, and we seek palliatives that sterilize our life. The basic feature of the marvelous Marian devotion in the medieval Church consists in the fact that its love toward the *Madonna*, the Virgin Mother, is not a spiritualized love, a disincarnate affection, but a preeminently human love. It is the same as the love of men when they truly love. Christian sublimation is not a Jansenist sterilization, nor a Manichean calcification. And the Christian faithful have been preoccupied, since ancient times, with defending like a treasure even the physical purity of the Immaculate Virgin, who conceived by the Holy Spirit and gave birth without a violation of her virginity. The Church continues to celebrate Mary's integrity solemnly and devoutly.

Christian tradition has always distinguished the cult of *hyperdulia* dedicated to the Virgin as something essentially different from the cult of saints, without this making it a cult of *latria* and adoration. God is worshipped; the saints are venerated; the Virgin... the Virgin is loved.

Let us be clear. Our language is poor; we lack words. Worship and veneration imply a certain love, a fondness, a voluntary donation or the recognition of supe- riority. Without this sureness of love we cannot worship God, nor venerate the saints. The cult toward Mary, on the other hand, requires a different love, a new relationship, which is more similar to human love on earth. It is what we on earth call "being in love."

This dimension of our religiousness, which I would venture to call feminine, certainly does not exclude the other aspects of Christian life. The mystery of Mary's Assumption into heaven, in body and soul, allows us a fully human relationship with her. Indeed, in heaven, that is to say in God, *in sinu Patris*, there exists at least one Man's body and one Woman's body; and on earth the Christian loves Christ, but also his/His Mother (the mother of both), Mary. Just, I will not speak to you of Jesus on this occasion: only of the Blessed Woman among all generations. This blessing is not a formula. The Church reveals to us a realist and human love, which expresses itself in the sincere and simple expressions of the liturgy, teaching us to love with supernatural naturalness, to call things by their name, and not to scorn matter and the body. There is only one love.

Sometimes we need to open our heart, we need a place where we can cry and laugh; we need to give vent to our feelings and really be ourselves, ceasing finally to hide behind a mask or a role; we need, in a word, the opportunity to be children. And if our Christian life is true and authentic, and does not degenerate in the cold official recognition of a series of more or less connected affirmations, as a substitute of true faith, then we need Mary, who is a woman and a mother.

It was necessary (although our reason does not see it) for Mary to have a body, for her to have it still, if she is to attain the fullness of her mission in the Church of God. The Madonna is in heaven in body and soul in order to be able to continue being a person, a mother, so that we can find in her the warmth of the body and the physical embrace (the love of the soul is not enough), to be able to establish with us a communication of fully human sentiments, sentiments that require the collaboration of the last emanation of God that is physical reality—these are words of St. Thomas.

In fact, sentiments, this specific feature of the human being, which neither angels nor animals possess, spring from the meeting or the clash between body and soul. What we call feeling, and which is not pure sensation nor simple awareness but a complex knowing and desiring with all our being, body and soul, these profound sentiments and presentiments of the human being, who foresees and senses, trembles and vibrates, enjoys and desires, trusts and fears—the Virgin could not have unless she had in herself the integrity of all her being, her body itself. If Our Lady must continue to be a mother, then she must perceive our sentiments, she must feel them with us, she must enter into a relationship with our being.

Mary is "the mother of fair love, and of awe, and of knowledge, and of holy hope." But, at the same time, with God, she is *terribilis sicut castrorum acies ordinata* (terrible as an army arrayed in its encampment), she is the warrior who crushes the dragon's head, who dominates and rules the destinies of creation from the beginning. This is why our contact with the "Full of grace" must have a sweet personal intimacy and an unfathomable cosmic depth. All the texts of the Church which speak of the sweet and terrible "Our Hope" possess a double polarity, familiar and unusual, maternal and objective, terrestrial and heavenly, unintelligible for the nonbeliever and shocking for those who do not love her.

It is not only the liturgy, in an excess of lyricism, that attributes the most dreadful and bold phrases to the Virgin: all the unanimous tradition of the Church attributes to Mary a series of functions, in the administration of grace and even of nature itself, which makes the Madonna truly the queen of the entire creation. The Virgin generates us in a real manner, she is our mother and also the mother of the Church, she is the *Dei genitrix*, she who begot God, pattern and epitome of the Church, intermediary of grace, co-redeemer, and so much else.

Nowadays there are some valid texts on what the Church and tradition say about the mother of our Lord and her relationship with God, with Christ, with the cosmos, and with us. We try to read them with a true and solid Christian mentality. The soul (Latin: *anima*, a feminine word), which is converted to Christ and baptized, affirms a common patristic thought, is called "Mary," as *she* also generates Christ. Hence the beautiful old Christian tradition, at baptism, of adding the name of Mary to that of the patron saint.

The Virgin is co-redeemer. If divine maternity was a grace, her maternity in our regard was a consequence of her co-redemption. Mary offers what she has: her heart. Let us take seriously what the Church says in the feast of Our Lady of Sorrows. True co-redemption, even for us on earth and from all standpoints, is redemption through the heart. For precisely this reason she was given to us as a mother under the cross, she generates us to the life of her Son, and she cooperates as a wife, in this sense, with the work of the Holy Spirit. However we will not understand any of all this until we have also baptized our mind and overcome rational paganism, until we have learned to think as Christians and let ourselves be penetrated, that is to say enlivened, by faith. The first words of the Precursor and those of Christ himself, at the beginning of their public mission, were to proclaim the need of a true *metanoia*, that is to say, a radical change of heart and mind.

Permit me at this point a brief theological excursus. I do not wish to break with Christian tradition, but, on the contrary, unite more authentically and profoundly with it, and in the last instance with Christ, with Him who with His person is also the Truth as well as the Way and the Life. *Until* we go beyond the rationalist models of our thinking, divergent from the "rational obligation" to bend "all intellect to obedience of Christ": *until* we vanquish the idealism implicitly disguised by certain universal concepts, colorless, disincarnate, and inexistent in themselves; *as long as* we attribute more reality to some ideas, which to be accepted need to be hypostatized in God but which in themselves do not exist (that is, the ideas of God on things are God in Him—*Creatura in Deo est creatrix essentia*, says St. Thomas—and outside Him they are the things themselves; when God, in the intra-Trinitarian process, thinks the *Logos*, He thinks the entire creation in him and with him); *as long as* we attribute more reality to some of our ideas than to concrete existence; *until* we redeem the formal categories of a thinking of pure essence to make them able to open to the absolute singularity and vibrant reality of Christ himself; *until*, in a word, we impregnate our intelligence with our faith, our intellect will never grasp the Christian message (which is not so much a doctrine as a life, a person), nor its profound meaning.

Thus, for example, Christ is not my model because he realizes an idea that must be exemplary for me. Christ does not "realize" anything; rather, the various things are realized in him and reside in him. Everything has been made by him and for him; he existed before anything was made, alpha and omega of all creation and recapitulator of all the universe.

Furthermore, Christ is not simply an example for me, not even the greatest of all, as a saint can be; he does not have a mere function of exemplarity so that I realize fully in my own way the idea of Man, but he is my model because he forges me in his image and likeness. He does not push me to be a "a Man," but to arrive at being "Christ." The ontological *mimêsis*, which constitutes the fundamental duty of my Christian existence, is a true *homoiôsis*, and consists in the fact that, without losing my I (and "my I" is none other than the "you" created by God), I identify with Christ, that is he who lives in me and renders me "a single thing" with him, and through him the whole Trinity resides in me. A Christian is not an *alter Christus*, but the *ipse Christus*, Christ himself, who—"in the unity of faith and the knowledge of the Son of God"—is reaching the perfect Man, so that, the Christian being wholly subject to Christ, Christ can in turn subordinate him wholly to the Father, so that, in the end, "God may be all in all."

Christ, who is truly man, is not on the one hand God and on the other *a* man, one more specimen of the species; he is not the most perfect example of human nature. Christ is not a special case, a concrete realization of a universal unalterable idea, and therefore dependent on it. Priority belongs to Christ and not to "nature." Here, too, we must speak of the supremacy of the person. Christ, *perfectus homo*, is not *a* man, he is *the* Man—*Ecce homo!*—and so are all of us, in as much as we come from him and we seek him....

But all this would take us very far; it would lead us to recognize the urgent need to think seriously with Christian categories.... Let us content ourselves, for the moment, with thinking of the attitude of Mary and her personal, living, direct relationship with us. Myriam is not an idea; it is she, the mother of God and my mother, who in her definitive body remains beside her Son on the right hand of God the Father, according to the traditional metaphor.

I would also like to highlight the double function of the mother of God in us. Mary is a model of interior life, it is often said, and in fact it is true, but the word "model" simply suggests, again, the idea of an example that I must imitate. The Virgin is a master of interior life, Christian terminology says more exactly. She teaches with her example and her action. Mary does not have a doctrine. She lives and acts. She pushes and supports. She attracts and convinces. We can see it with two examples.

I would venture to call the first example the passive principle of interior life. There exists, widespread in bigoted circles, a pernicious spiritual selfishness and a pseudo-Christian self-worshipping meanness that sterilizes more than one interior life. It seems that Christ preached a mere supernatural eudemonism, and that he was content to give us a simple recipe to succeed in being eternally happy in the other world. This is the unconscious egocentricity of those souls who receive the Eucharist in order to attain purity, of those people who pray to have good luck, of Christians who are good so that things go well for them. This is none other than pure self-worship. *Deus non debet aliquid alicui nisi sibi* (God owes nothing to anyone other than Himself), says St. Thomas (*Sum. theol.* I, q.25, a.5, ad 2).

The Holy Communion is certainly nourishment, but with a function that is the precise opposite of that of the material metaphor: it is not the nourishment that turns into my substance, but mine that becomes its. *Nec tu me mutabis in te, sicut cibum carnis tuae, sed tu mutaberis in me* (And you will not transform me into you, as food of your flesh, but you will transform into me), says St. Augustine (*Conf.* VII.10). "Seek the kingdom of God and its justice" is what we have been told: that we do not pray like Gentiles and that we do not have worries about ourselves, because our heavenly Father, who looks after the birds in the sky and the flowers in the field, already knows what we need. Often we let ourselves be overwhelmed by a lot of personal and even objective pseudo-problems, so that we do not see things theocentrically or, more still, Christocentrically. This, in the final analysis, is the mission of faith: a supernatural, ontological, and not just morally Christocentric vision of the reality of things.

The purpose of our life is not ourselves, and therefore it is neither our betterment nor our sanctification. All this comes and is given to us in addition. The ultimate object of our life is not even to give glory to God. A creature does not possess a category that can give God true glory. He/she can give Him, in case, a kind of accidental glory, of what kind it is not easy to understand, in a God who does not have accidents. The purpose of our life is simply God, union with Him, communion with the divinity. God created all creatures not for His happiness nor for theirs, but *ad manifestandam perfectionem suam* (to manifest His perfection), says the First Vatican Council. I wish to say that the purpose of my life is not to give glory to God, but simply God. His glory, not the glory I can give Him, which does not exist, but His own. The purpose of my life is, therefore, His glory, if you like, or, better still, His communication with me, His union with me. *Omnia propter semetipsum operatus est Dominus!* (God has worked all things for Himself !).

This is what has been believed, felt, and foreseen by all the souls who have followed and follow the path of inner life, the ways of love, the straight roads that lead all to the very end of their existence. Therefore, in this adventure of life, Man realizes that his task is predominantly passive, with a passivity that is not always easy to accept, but which can even be joyous. The human being who journeys toward his God is conscious of being somewhat pushed, attracted, led. One certainly must not fall into a proud quietism, but neither into an ingenuous activism. Expressed differently, God is more interested than me that I reach my ultimate goal, if I can put it this way. Even more, He is the principal and prime cause, the decisive factor in my journey of sanctification toward Him. My perfection is more His task than mine. My work is limited to not hindering Him, not disturbing Him, letting Him act, sayingyes—like Mary.

It is in this that the Virgin has a particular role. From the beginning, in all mystical theology, although one speaks of love, of wedding, of spiritual marriage or simply of union, fusion, communication, the creature has always been the passive part, the negative principle. In other words, only the Virgin, fertilized by the Holy Spirit, can teach me how I should behave. In God's union with me, in the purpose of my life, He is the active principle and I am the passive one. I have only to say, *Fiat!* or better, *Ecce ancilla!*

"The Creator is enraptured by the beauty of his creature," says St. Catherine of Siena; the divinity has found some *ad extra* reflections of itself, and wants as soon as possible to reabsorb them all.

"Listen, daughter, bend your head and listen. The King has been taken with your beauty." He follows me and watches over me, He does not tire, and He urges me, He adulates me, He appears to me and hides from me.... Whoever does not believe me should read the Song of Songs, and not be shocked....

And who will teach me, "a child who cannot speak," nor write, nor love? This is the mother's mission.

My friend, do not forget this feminine principle of inner life....

Mary is a master of "inner life" in a second sense, too, although this phrase, which has become sanctioned by custom, is slightly ambiguous. There is only one life, which is neither exclusively inner, nor exclusively exterior. An exterior life is not in the strict sense life, nor is the authentic Christian life, like that of Mary, uniquely inner. The mother of Jesus, like all the women of her class and her time, worked and performed the roles befitting her state of mother, wife, and neighbor in a Jewish town. This complete life, authentic and full of supernatural naturalness, has sometimes been given the ugly name of "mixed life."

Christian life is first and foremost one: if we break the unity, it is not authentic life of Christ in our being.

The vital teaching of Mary, virgin and mother, bride and consecrated to God, active and contemplative, in the world and above it, is unique and singular. She, in achieving the perfect synthesis of human life, teaches us that action is none other than the material fruit of contemplation and its expression. It is not a vicious circle, but rather a vital one. Contemplation stimulates activity in the world, and this activity feeds our mind and our heart to know and love God in creatures, until we reach the face-to-face vision.

Life has not been given to us either to give or to receive, that is neither to act, to do (what?), nor to see, to contemplate, to judge (how ?); it has freely been given to us so that we can live it, burn it in a sacrifice of praise, *sacrificium laudis*, to the Creator. I do not justify myself for what I do, but for what I am. Life, Christ tells us, does not consist in possessions (Lk 12:15). Priority belongs to the Life, the greatest approximation possible to the Life, to the Light of Men, to Him in whom the Life was.

Authentic Christian life is the synthesis between Martha and Mary. Certainly, Mary, the sister of Lazarus, chose the better part; supremacy belongs to contempla- tion; but not for this does it cease to be part of a whole, and the whole is the Life. True contemplation sees God in things, but to reach this point we need to see things, become acquainted with them, know what they are like, experience them—that is to say, that we need to act, fail, win, suffer, in a word: live.

At times, there exists a not very clear idea of Christian life in the world, and Christian laypeople have lived for a long time with a certain inferiority complex.

The Virgin remains the shining example of the person who fully realizes this perfect—natural and supernatural—life. For the expression of this spirit I would like to go back to a mystic, a friar, not modern but ancient. Although the quota- tion is long and archaic German is difficult to translate, I believe it is worth trying.

Let us listen then to Meister Eckhart in *Reden der Unterweisung*.

> Once I was asked: many people rigorously keep themselves apart from men and are happy alone and go to church and thereby find

their happiness. Is this best? I say: No. And this is why. He who is at peace with himself is of course at ease anywhere and with anybody. But he who cannot feel well with himself, does not feel well anywhere or with anybody.

He who feels well with himself truly has God with him. But he who truly has God has Him everywhere, in the street and with everybody as well as in church, in a hermitage or in a cell. Nothing can deceive or mislead the man who has God and truly cleaves only to Him. Why? Because he has only God. But he whose intention is pure, only in God, carries God with him in all his works and everywhere. And all the activity of such a man is performed directly by God. Indeed, any work belongs more to the One who is the cause than to the one who performs it.

If then our intention in truth is pure and only in God, He himself must perform our activity, but nothing can impede all His works, neither place nor feeling. Thus nothing can induce such a man into error, as he wants and seeks only God, and he will not be satisfied by anything other than God, who unites with such a man by his intention. And thus, as God is not dispersed in any multiplicity, likewise nothing can dissipate nor multiply this man, as he is united with that One in which all plurality is unity and nonmultiplicity.

Man must live God in all things and must accustom his spirit to keep God always present in his feeling, his intention, and his intimate love.

It is the same if you busy yourself for your God when you are in church or in a cell. Try to keep this same spirit among people, in the tumult, and in the external world. But as I have often said, when we speak of being the same in everything, it does not mean that any activity should be considered on the same level, or that all places and all men should be considered the same. This would be very unfair: in fact it is better to pray than to spin, and the church is a more noble place than the street. Nevertheless, in your work you must have the same spirit, the same loyalty, and the same seriousness as you have before your God.

Believe me, if you keep this equality, nothing will prevent you from havingyour God present. However, he who does not have his God truly thus, within him, but distant, will always have to go and look for Him outside, here or there. Whoever seeks Him by using other means, in one activity or another, in various men or places, does not have God. In that case, it can easily happen that anything will be an obstacle for that man, because he does not have God intimately, nor does he seek only Him, nor does he always maintain his intention exclusively in Him. For this reason, not only does bad company disturb him, but even a good company damns him; not only is the street, or a bad word or deed an obstacle to him, but certainly also a good word or deed will impede him. Therefore, the obstacle is in him, since all things have not become God in him. If for him everything were God, everything would be right and good, everywhere and with everybody, because he would have God within him and nobody would be able to take Him away from him, nor would anybody be able to hinder him in any way in his actions.

But where then does this true possession of God lie, so that it can be really attained? This true possession of God is in the spirit and in an intimate and conscious turning to and hurrying toward God; not, however, in a uniform and constant thinking of God, given that by nature it would be impossible to aspire to this, and furthermore it would be very difficult and not even the best thing. Man must not exclusively content himself with having a God in his thoughts. When the thought went away, this God would also disappear. On the contrary, we need to have an essential God, who is far beyond the thoughts of men and all creatures. This God does not go away, nor does He dissolve, unless it is the man who voluntarily distances himself from Him. He who possesses God so intimately in his essence understands Him in a divine form, and for him God shines in all things, given that all things appear divine to him, and furthermore everything forms in him the image of God. In him God always has His eyes wide open, in him there is a restful separation from external things and a penetration of the God who is always present in his intention.

For this precise reason we need to have passion, a profound care of our inner selves, a wakeful conscience, clear and sure about how our spirit should find its way before things and men. But Man cannot learn this by avoiding things and retreating into solitude, far from the outside world; he must learn to be alone, private, everywhere and with anybody.

Man must learn to go into things, to grasp his God there, and he must succeed in forming Him efficiently within himself like one who wants to learn to write. In order to possess this art we need to try often and hard, however bitter and difficult it may be, even if it may seem impossible. If one practices with application and

> frequency, then he will learn and master this art. Certainly one must think first of each letter separately and conceive it clearly; but soon, when he has assimilated the art, then he is no longer in thrall to the picturing of letters and thinking of them. Then he writes freely and easily whether his works be small or bold. It is enough for him to know that at a given moment he must exercise his art; and then, although he does not think about it constantly but thinks about what he wants, he nevertheless creates his work with his writing. In the same way man must irradiate the presence of God without special effort. More than this, one must see things in their true form and remain totally free from them. For this it is necessary, above all, to think of them as the pupil thinks of his art of writing. Thus, if Man must be permeated by the presence of God, he must be impregnated and molded in the form of his beloved God; he must be essentiated in Him in such a way that His presence shines effortlessly.

Who achieves this full life? Have you not seen—are you still unaware of Mary, who achieved it and who wants to complete it in you, too? Are you not aware of her very essence, present and discreet in all the virgin, fecund lines of the Dominican mystic? Mary is a master of Christian life. A normal woman without complications, she teaches us to simplify. There is not action on the one hand and contemplation on the other; plans here, and rules and caution there. Everything is simpler and easier. There is simply life, that is to say *fiat*, the shining *fiat*, a double echo of the creator one and the virginal one, which we repeat with our lives: a "yes" according to her *logos*: *Ecce ancilla Domini!*

Marian Dimensions of Life

I would now like to speak about what could be called the Marian dimensions of our human existence, of our life. I would like briefly to outline three dimensions, so that they become a personal meditation, having, I believe, a value of their own, and able to give a certain sense to Marian devotion.

Superficial devotion is of little use, as it disappears upon impact with the problems of existence. The only soul that can profit from it is one that, with a more profound and so more contemplative vision of things, can see reality and can understand the message without words, the message of a simple existence, which is much more than a sermon or being always busy. In fact, Mary said almost nothing and did very little. And despite all this, her "being," her existence, has rightly led her to be called "blessed among women."

The Human Dimension

The first dimension that such contemplation of Mary reveals to us is what could be called the human dimension of religion, of our faith, and therefore of our life.

Mary is not the Absolute; the inaccessible, invisible God whom nobody has seen; the ineffable Creator, who is infinitely distant from us and whom Man will never be able to reach in the mystery of His abyss. Mary is not even Christ, who is Mediator, man and God, Redeemer, and with whom we can certainly have a profound but not merely human contact: our relationship with Christ is a sui generis relation- ship, theandric, which cannot be defined with our commonly used terms for merely human contact. Mary is something different.

The first dimension of life and the first Marian dimension of life is the human one. Mary is a simple creature, associated with everything : with redemption as well as with love. She was the first believer. It is precisely this human dimension of religion that is symbolized—embodied, I would say—in Mary. A religiousness that is not human, that is not concrete, that is not earthly, that loses itself in a vague mysticism, that dissolves into a more or less disembodied yearning, that has perhaps understood the profoundly unfathomable and mysterious sense of all religion, but that loses its sense of naturalness, humanity, and concreteness, is no longer and cannot be a religiousness that is concrete, human, earthly and therefore full.

It is here that the dangers become very visible: the danger, in fact, of an overly sentimental or weak religion exists. If we compare Christian religiousness inspired by this Marian dimension with the religiousness of some religions that sometimes lack somewhat this human element, then we will see the enormous difference between a Christianity that is incarnate and human (and that is often too incarnate and too human) and a pure religiousness or transcendence, of mystery that may well be fascinating but "on the other side," and makes people live with the constant fear or obsession of a destiny that is hanging over them. Religion thus appears to be something that cannot be an everyday reality because it is too sublime, because it is absolutely inaccessible: it has lost its very, primordial dimension of humanity and naturalness.

All the greatest theology—that which concerns the great themes of redemption, creation, love, distribution of graces, divinization of Man—has been associated with a poor peasant woman in virtue of the *fiat*, of an annunciation.

The mystery of the annunciation lies precisely in this dimension that is human, terribly human, so that the religiousness of Christianity at times risks seeming too banal.

But one extreme does not justify the other, and one abuse is not eliminated with an opposite abuse. Whoever has a remotely personal relationship with Mary automatically and spontaneously acquires a sense of naturalness, a dimension of humanity for all his religion.

It is unlikely that someone who has established personal contact with Mary can have a negative religion or religiosity, made of inhuman asceticism or wielding a willpower that seems to separate him/her from the other people.

The Feminine Dimension

A second dimension of the Our Lady and Christian life is centered on the mystery of the Immaculate, on the *Ecce ancilla*.

It is the feminine dimension of spiritual life, inner life.

Mary is a woman on the one hand and a mother on the other.

She is a woman—that is to say, she embodies that eternal feminine of which poets speak. She embodies human love; she embodies all the polarity that lies in sex, all the need that Man has to find a complement and a pole that is equal but wholly different, at times almost contradictory.

Whoever does not discover this side, and does not integrate it into his or her personal life, risks making a serious mistake: it is false to think that the body is only male or female.

Man, in his complexity, has this polarity, this tension that begins within oneself and then extends to the relationships with others.

The Christian who does not have a vital relationship with Mary easily tends to reduce his religion to one of those factors that constitute one of the most serious dangers of our times: detachment from life.

Then religion is of use to very good people or to great sinners, but it is of no use to our human life, and so it cannot be a complete religion that grips a man's whole life.

Mary is a woman: every epoch can symbolize her in the form that is most suit- able, but at bottom she will always be the same thing, and she will represent the need for the eternal feminine, the need for a complementary life, the need that on earth and in heaven there be only one, unique love.

Whoever thinks he can love God differently from how he loves his girlfriend, mother, or a male or female friend is already starting to detach himself from life and beginning to make his religion into something so pure, so sterilized and aseptic that then it will not help him to be a man and live with others.

Perhaps he can live the first part of the greatest commandment; but to say that I must love my neighbor as myself, and think that this love does not have the same meaning as human love on earth, this is not love.

Man has only one heart, which is made in one way. He who loves God, and who loves his fellow men for God, does not love in a different way from how he can love with the most passionate and sexual love that can exist on earth.

There is only one love, and this is fulfilled almost automatically and harmoniously when one has a relationship of faith and love with the Madonna.

This female dimension of life and existence, this need for the feminine exists within us because at bottom every human being is androgynous, and it also exists beside us.

Mary is the mother of Christ and our mother, and in fact, according to the astonishing and dogmatic form of Ephesus, she is the mother of God.

Perhaps the human dimension is lacking in some religions, or at least in some manifestations of religions, but the dimension of the mother-goddess, of divine maternity, is lacking in almost no religion. Quite interesting, isn't it? Not that we should think that Mary is the mother-goddess or the substitute of the mother-goddess of other religions, but the formula *Mater Dei*, in all its strength, remains and will always remain a dogmatic formula, which does not content itself with saying that Mary is the mother of Christ, but says and repeats that Mary is the mother of God.

According to an interpretation of mine, Mary is the "temporal mother of God and mother of the temporal God." The Latin definition *Mater Dei temporalis* can in fact mean both "Mother of the God-made-time, of the temporalized God" and "temporal Mother of the eternal God."

Not the mother goddess, but the mother of God, which gives a dimension of concreteness to our religion. There exists, I repeat, the great danger of detaching religion from life, of making religion a beautiful, sublime, superior thing, which is kept apart so that it does not dirty itself in daily life, with the danger of an atrophy of Being.

Only when we discover that our heart is made to love are we not ashamed of our feelings and our human dimension.

A certain relationship and a minimum of devotion to Mary help to humanize our being and our religion.

I should perhaps make an exegesis of the Song of Songs to explain everything well, but I will limit myself to advising a careful reading of it.

The Corporeal Dimension

There is, however, a third dimension that the Marian devotion shows and reveals to us. If the first mystery is that of the Incarnation and the second that of the Immaculate, the third is that of the Assumption.

The devotion to Mary helps us to discover that religion concerns our life in its complexity, in its human, and therefore also corporeal, dimension. Religion is not for spirits, neither for pure nor impure spirits. It concerns Man in his indestructible and consubstantial unity of body and soul.

A religion that is not corporeal is not a human religion, so it is of no use to Man. A religion that wants to present itself only as spiritual purity will be stoic, gnostic, platonic, but it will not be fully Christian.

In this connection, I maintain that the belief in the immortality of soul is a platonic and not a Christian dogma. There is no passage in the Bible or dogma where the immortality of soul is mentioned.

It is Man that is immortal. It is Man that is unity. It is Man that has a religion. And Man also means this flesh, this body, these bones.

The resurrection of the flesh is not a kind of appendix added at the last moment: it is a reality that is at the beginning of all life, all Christian life.

Religion must therefore be corporeal.

The dogma of the Assumption clearly states: Mary in heaven is a creature, she is a human being, she is body and soul. Bodies alone do not exist—a corpse is not a body—and souls alone do not exist. If they did, people would be only abstractions.

Just as there is not only one will, or only one intelligence: I can speak of intel- ligence, body, soul, and so on, but it is only a manner of speaking. I can say: finger, nail, and so on, but I cannot hypostatize and make the nail walk alone, or the body alone, or the soul alone, like those beautiful paintings in old churches where one sees only the upper half of the souls in purgatory, which lead children to ask their mother if souls in purgatory have pointed ends....

The value of a body is *as* a body, not in as much as it serves something else. The body is not an instrument, but a constituent of Man.

The value of a body includes the value of human feelings, of human purity, of all the senses, of civilization, of the sum of corporeal values, of the concrete world, and of time.

All this must be deified, all this must be transformed, all this asks for an "assumption."

This third corporeal dimension must be a dimension of Christian life, of mystical life, overcoming—if necessary—the gnostic, stoic, Neoplatonic, and spiritualist influences.

St. Paul, culturally speaking, certainly could not have the degree of reflective knowledge we have, and yet, when he experienced the highest ecstasy, he did not venture to say he had abandoned his body. "With my body or without my body, God knows." Enraptured to the third heaven, he repeats, "Whether with my body or without my body, God knows." Obviously, with his body.

In Christ dwells all the fullness of the Godhead bodily.

Why do we say that God is spirit, and not that God is body? When we say that God is spirit, we do not mean that He is spirit on the model of our spirit: that is clear! But why should only half of my being have value—perhaps after having been purified, sublimed? What about the other half ? Or perhaps I will say that the body is worse than the soul, like Plotinus, the Gnostics, the Stoics, and so many others?

What about the corporeal dimension of inner life, of Christian life! The divine and supernatural value of the body!

God is not a corporeal being. So be it. But nor is God a spiritual being ! And if it is said that God is a spiritual being, purifying the concept of spirit, then I say that God is corporeal, purifying also the concept of body!

If it is purified and applied in an analogical sense, the problem is solved!

In Mary, with the dogma of the Assumption, we have a creature associated with the redemption of humanity and united in body and soul to God, according to traditional terminology.

Body and soul: I am not a spirit, nor am I spirit on one side and body on the other. So my religion and my faith, if they are authentic, will be equally corporeal and full of the values of the body and gravitation, just as they are full of the values of the spirit.

Hence, once again, a religiousness that integrates and fully penetrates human life and the life of the body. Hence the importance of respecting the other's body as well as one's own—and not for questionably valid moralistic reasons, which then some try to almost hygienically justify.

Hence the function of fasting and eating, of the act of procreation and dance, of any needed corrective to the body, and of hygiene and physical beauty: all these values cannot be external and independent, nor can they exist only in a negative relationship to religion.

It is not a matter of saving the soul: it is a matter of saving Man! Not only the soul is the temple of the Holy Spirit, the body is, too!

During the Eucharist, Man is slowly transforming all his body into a glorious body by virtue of this supernatural metabolism.

"All his body." Which does not mean it will be less of a body because it is more spiritualized.

It will be more united, so the will will be ever more intelligent, and intelligence will have an ever stronger power of freedom and decision.

So the spirit will be more incarnate, more flesh-made, and the protein will be more spiritualized, more spirit-made.

So there will be more unity of life, more union between body and soul, between will and intelligence, between feelings and desires: Man will achieve an increasingly deep, ever simpler, unity.

All these considerations are variations on the one theme of the Assumption: "Therefore all the generations will call me blessed."

O, the breadth of the value of the human body! The importance of our feelings!

We are used to considering that the essence of sin and human action is the will, sovereign and decisive, which does and undoes things. Poor will, which dances to the tune it hears! Feelings are at least as fundamental as the will! The combination of causes and aggravations and contributory factors that influence the fulfillment of an act are at least as fundamental as the decision that we believe to be free, and which under a certain aspect is.

This is the corporeal dimension, therefore, of inner life.

A religion detached from the body is not a human religion.

To a religion that considers this body merely as an instrument at the service of the soul we could reply that the soul helps and is at the service of the body. Exactly the same!

Neither one is working for the other: they are both a single thing in a double manifestation.

It is certain that anyone who enters into a personal relationship with Mary immediately and instinctively finds this recovery of the value of holiness for all the body and what is corporeal, and gives a value of transcendence, that is of religion, to all human life.

I was saying that an excessively voluntaristic education had made us think that we are only responsible for what our will decides.

But we are much more: We are responsible for what our heart feels.

When Peter reprimands Ananias with harsh words for his sin, his lie, when the apostles reprimand Simon Magus in the same way, they do not speak of will, they do not say he has decided, agreed or disagreed, but that his heart has been stained for the very fact that a thought or desire or idea found a place in his heart.

Woe betide us if we believe that our inner cleanliness consists only in washing our hands, later thinking about this or that, and concluding with a "as I do not agree to anything..." or with a "I do nothing...."

It is here that a much more profound education is necessary, which makes us feel responsible and which permits those who have a bit of faith and charity the catharsis and the purification of their own feelings and body, their tendencies and desires, all that combination of deepest values of our human existence. It is here that faith also transforms, purifies, and changes.

Epilogue

We have described three dimensions of interior life from the Marian standpoint. Mary is the living symbol of a human religion, and of a religion that has a female aspect: we are the female principle that God fertilizes, and the whole of Man's relationship with God is none other than a relationship of created femininity toward the Creator.

The "wedding" theme is one of the leitmotifs of all the Old Testament.

Mary is also the symbol of the third dimension, the corporeal one of life, of spiritual life and the life of faith and Christian life.

Here are the three Marian dogmas: the dogma of the annunciation, which reveals this human sense; the dogma of the Immaculate Conception with its feminine dimension of *ancilla Domini*; the dogma of the Assumption, finally, which renders her aware that all generations will call her blessed because God has done great things in her, that is in all the being of Mary, which will then be raised in body and soul, into heaven.

And now, as a farewell, friendly reader, I would like to repeat Mary's only phrase to Men, which the Gospels have given us as a testament: "Do what he tells you."

Even if she were to tell us to fill the jars intended for good wine with water, let us not hesitate: let us fill them completely, *usque ad summum*!

SECTION II

The Path of the Monk

Part One

Blessed Simplicity

The Challenge of Being a Monk

Introduction

This book deals with simplicity in a very complex way. Perhaps the solution of the dilemma between holy simplicity and harmonious complexity does not depend on a dialectic-but-static attitude forcing us to choose the former or the latter as the ultimate structure of reality. It is most probably about a dynamic process, personal and cosmic at the same time—a process I would define as rhythmic. We start with an undifferentiated simplicity: this is the original innocence. After its awakening, our conscience starts to consciously become enthusiastic over simplicity, and it starts to lose itself. Reflection is not simple: it is the splitting of the conscience into two. So we try to regain the original simplicity, but a lot of conditions are needed for this. This is the beginning of the discovery that the complexity of life and reality must be harmonious, they must be placed together (as the Indo-European root *ar* suggests). Truth, reality, cannot be all that complicated. But this very conception is already very complex. Complexity is harmonious only on condition that it does not stop, it does not fall into self-congratulation, and it searches for simplicity without further complications. The harmony of complexity is precisely the attempt to step beyond it, the intention aiming at simplicity. But, after it has been reached, this very discovery puts us in the position of losing it. It is what I have called elsewhere the passage from *mythos* to *logos*, and from *logos* to *mythos*—from spontaneity to reflection, and vice versa. Innocence is not a thing we possess; it is something we have to regain endlessly. To sing the heights of innocence is already a complex task. The attempt to harmonize complexity leads toward simplicity. These are the two poles of reality. The third is invisible; it is the power pushing them both, the energy moving them, the love attracting them, the Spirit inspiring them. The whole of it makes up what I have defined the "cosmotheandric structure of reality."

The aim of the title of the first Italian edition, *La sfida di scoprirsi monaco*, that is, *The Challenge of Surprisingly Being a Monk*, was to show that it was not a book only for monks, but for everybody, both believers and nonbelievers (a widely used phrase, though a wrong one: a Buddhist monk is not a "believer" in the Western and monotheistic sense of the word, but he is a great "believer" nonetheless). This book tries to help us regain the deepest dimension of the human being, which is so often neglected in our current, shallow culture; and to do so without confessional distinctions. I used the term *monachos*, surely not a Christian one, because every novelty (and we are dealing with novelty) must be rooted in tradition, if it is to be anything more than a passing fashion.

The ideal of the *monachos* was to become the integral, complete man, who aspired to have in his being the *microkosmos* that mirrors the *macrokosmos*, the entire universe—although, all too often, our idea of the *kosmos* is quite poor, and the person is reduced to the "individual."

I take the monastic ideal as the human archetype who has always wanted to overcome banality, insisting particularly on the vertical dimension of life (*zōē*, rather than *bios*), as an antidote to a superficial existence—with no defense or criticism of the current or ancient monastic institutions. Anyway, today's monk cannot simply "copy" his ancient brothers.

The issue that is dealt with in this book is the rebuilding of the whole man, based on nine aphorisms where ancient forms of wisdom have been crystallized: they are commented on here, then supplemented according to contemporary needs.

A basic assumption, in this work, is that we are living at a crucial moment in the history of mankind, which requires *a radical change* in the dominant culture, and which is not content with more or less moralizing reforms. That's why we must start from the beginning : man. Scientists *experiment* with things; philosophers with ideas; artists with shapes; a monk tries to *experience* himself. According to many traditions, those who know themselves, know God, while other traditions add that they also know everything else. Thus experience is "co-birth" (although the exact etymology of this term is uncertain)—that is, being born jointly with the thing we know. I will present three ideas which seem pertinent to today's world and for which the monastic archetype could be a symbol—a symbol, I say, not a model.

1. The first thing we need for a more human life (in order to attain Life, *zōē*) is to rediscover the value, or better, the centrality of *silence*. "*In* the beginning was the Word," many African, Asian, and European cultures teach. But none of them, as far as I know, claims that the Word *is* the Beginning. The Beginning is Silence, the Void, Non-Being, the Abyss, Darkness, or other symbols in many other traditions.

Obviously I am referring to that Silence from which, in the Beginning, comes the Word. The word is not silence, nor is it an interpretation of silence. The word enjoys its *ontonomy*; but the true word emerges from the silence, "shattering" it, going beyond it, overcoming it. In traditional language there is the expression: "The Word is the Sacrifice of Silence." Silence doesn't speak, it says nothing, but it makes the saying possible; Silence inspires it, since it dwells there. However, Silence does not interpret anything, but as we become conscious of it, we are invited to interpret it. This is a basic, difficult point. Better said, it is impossible to explain, because Silence is simple (*simplex*), it cannot be ex-plained (*ex-plicare*): its "folds" already have sound, and besides they can be manifold. Silence is Freedom because it is not; it is not yet something, therefore it can be anything.

A bit more in detail. He who does not live Silence—does not experience it—that is he who hasn't existentially passed through it cannot be a tolerant person: he is necessarily rigid, he cannot feel happy when things do not go as he "would like," or as he "thinks" they should go. This means that both freedom and pluralism, as well as tolerance and happiness, are based on the experience of Silence. By living this Silence, you understand that things can be said, done, conceived, in many different ways. Silence does no violence to things; it puts them in their own place, their own site (*situs*), a concept that is etymologically related to silence (*sighv*).

Nearly all religious traditions stress the importance of Silence, not because they are giving us some good moral advice: Don't be noisy, be humble, don't bother the people around you.... Much more than that. They stimulate us to discover ourselves by discovering the original Silence we come from. The last line in Plato's *Letter* 13, to Dionysius the tyrant of Siracusa, reads, και αυτος ισθι (and always be yourself)!

"Noble silence"—Buddha says—is the basic virtue of a monk. "A monk either speaks to God, or talks about God," according to a Christian aphorism—a God, however, who is everywhere, "even among pots and pans" (St. Therese). The wise man is silent, according to Taoism. "The words of wise men must be listened to quietly," as Qohelet writes. When Darwin had to express his opinion on a young candidate, after the usual academic interview, he exclaimed, "How can I give you my opinion? He didn't stop talking from the moment he arrived!"

Silence is not the result of suppressing words; it is not about silencing the ques- tions that concern us. Silence is a preceding, original, originating dimension; it isn't the result of anything else. It is the origin of everything that will spontaneously rise from us, if our heart is pure and our mind is free and unbiased. "When they hand you over, do not worry about how you are to speak or what you are to say," says the Bible (Mt 10:19 NRSV); otherwise, you will curb the Spirit. Monks cultivate, or try to cultivate, all this. This is the archetype but it cannot be the goal, as the *Dhammapada* teaches: "Not just by embracing silence do you become a wise man." This book is not a *vademecum* on contemporary spirituality. Spirituality—provided that the word fits, but I doubt it—is something we have to build, together, by actually living it.

It is not at all easy to live silence in a noisy and agitated society; this art probably begins with simplifying our lives. Maybe we need to experience it, rather than talking about it too much—where "any Becoming is silent," "stands still" (*jedes Werden stand still*, as Rilke wrote in one of the first verses of his *Buch vom mönchischen Leben*)— vaguely echoing an *Upaniṣhad* (*TU* II.4): "There, where every word retreats" (*yato vāco nirvartante*).

2. The forced specialization of modern life, connected to the use of machines, has led us to what has been termed "the barbarism of specialization." But the worst aspect of this fragmentation of knowledge is that it includes the danger of a *fragmentation of the knower, Man*. Here, again, *simplicity* plays a central role.

Modern culture is schizophrenic. Man has torn himself away from the Divine (as if God were something else), from earth (as if we weren't bare material beings), from other living beings (as if we weren't animals), from other people (as if we weren't essentially a community), from the other half of humankind (as if men and women didn't belong to the same species), not to mention further divisions, castes, apartheids in the economic, social, and cultural fields: probably more superficial ones, though not less destructive. Differences, our intelligence shows us, are not the same as divisions, which are unjustified extrapolations.

This book would like to appeal to modern humankind from this further point of view. Our current life banalizes us, automatizes our bodies, mechanizes our hearts. It is true that philosophers and monks, in order to make the necessary leap beyond superficiality, secluded themselves from the world, and specialized. I don't mean to deny the wisdom of this decision, nor that it might be fundamental to many people. A full human life can be reached only by going beyond the banal routine of existence and overcoming what, "falling into the same syndrome," the Germans call *Alltagsmensch*, the English "man of the street," and the Castilians *los de a pie*. But everyday life, streets, and feet aren't despicable at all; on the contrary, that's precisely where we must find the "third dimension" which, having superficially put itself above the other two, must not therefore deny nor despise them. Any elitist attitude is suspect.

And this is the challenge to traditional monasticism, which begins with the dualism between spirit and matter, as the very word "spirituality" shows, although probably we currently lack a better one, and we can employ it as the realm of the Spirit, which exists where liberty reigns. As a consequence, the description of the monastic archetype is not simply the defense of small monasteries, which are more or less discreet enemies of the world (a very healthy thing, on the other hand); instead it aims to describe human life as *cosmotheandric* fullness.

The monastic archetype is not a specialization; therefore, we are not being requested to seclude ourselves from the world. The three eyes with which we see the world according to several traditions—that is, the eye of the senses, the eye of the mind, and the eye of faith—give us an accurate vision of reality only if we keep all three wide open at the same time. Understandably, not an easy task. The existence of "high places of the spirit," say, the Himalayas or Montserrat, can help human pilgrims to open the third eye, but we couldn't do it if there were no refuges (monasteries, brotherhoods, small groups) on the way, to remind us that the other two eyes are also indispensable. "Leaving everything" is necessary, and it is the first step, but "embracing everything" is the second step. And this is love, which is not possession but a gift. This is the challenge that elsewhere I have called *holy secularity.* Precisely because being a monk is not a specialization, monkhood represents a human archetype, including family life and political or professional activity. This is indeed something new, because if once monks had political and economic power they did so despite being monks. Nowadays, on the other hand, a monk does it as a person who has renounced not the world, but his ego(ism). Monkhood, at its core, is not an institution, but a vocation; a human vocation.

3. A third aspect of the monastic archetype seems very important and "burning" to me. In other texts I have called it "ecumenical ecumenism."

To put it more simply, to speak of a "Buddhist Salesian" or a "Muslim *dashanam*" would be stretching words beyond their limit. On the other hand, a Christian monk or a Buddhist monk is not forced language, just as a scientist monk or an artist monk is not. To put it another way, monasticism is a primordial religious and human phenomenon, and therefore predates the divisions between religious confessions and specific social classes. As monks, a Jainist and a Christian can understand each other, although each speaks his own language. But, in order to do so, they must know each other, and no deep knowledge can exist without a personal relationship. This recalls a typical feature of Western monasticism: hospitality. In this period of great migratory movements, we have a great opportunity to practice this virtue, which has been forgotten as a consequence of rampant individualism.

Without embarking on other types of debate, Man has a core that I would term "religious," using this word as a synonym of ultimateness, which is deeply human as it touches a person's very essence in which the members of different religions and cultures can meet and be in communion. This should be a side effect of our current situation, and a duty for today's monks: a "hearty ecumenism" that, while not denying differences, does not insist blindly on them, because, after all, we are primarily people who are aware of our own contingency. Nowadays there is no doubt that not unity but *harmony* between religions and cultures is a *human imperative*—for peace, the survival of our planet, and a fullness of life that is not egoistically encysted in its own individuality. And, once again, without *simplicity*, which is not artificial simplifica- tion, what we have been saying cannot be fulfilled.

⁂

Why did I choose the monk as an archetype? Why not, instead, the nobleman, the gentleman, the knight, the honest man, the wise man, or the saint?

First of all, because all these models have so often been used and misused that they have lost much of their paradoxical strength.

Second, because I thought that it might be worth recovering an age-old tradition which played such an important role (though not always necessarily a positive one) in the history of mankind. There exist unnecessary iconoclasms, and most are counterproductive. It seems to me more pertinent to be connected to tradition, maybe to criticize it, and above all to continue it.

Third—why not—in order to urge and stimulate those groups that still call themselves "monks," who won't be damaged at all if they breathe a bit of fresh air.

Fourth, as a kind of respect toward the word itself. "Monk" is in fact the translation of *monachos*, a term with a refined ambivalence: on the one hand, it means alone, silent (*muni*), solitary, lonely, that is the most usual rendering of it. On the other hand, it means "unique," therefore impossible to be classified, to be reduced to quantity as one specimen of a series. According to the latter interpretation, the monk becomes the unified person, the full one, the one who aspires to fullness of being, and therefore not numerically identifiable, since he embodies the Whole, not as a sum of the parts, but as a *solidus*, something consolidated, and therefore able to be solitary. It is significant that a great monk of our times, Thomas Merton, wrote a book called *No Man Is an Island*, suggesting that nobody is "isolated" according to the first meaning of *solus*, but that a man is *holus*, full, a whole.

Nor should we ignore the fact that Merton quotes a verse by a famous poet. A direct translationof Psalm 24 (25), v. 16, from the Latin Vulgate reads, "Have mercy on me, Lord, because I am poor and *unique*."[1]

To recapitulate:

- Monastic institutions cannot monopolize the monastic ideal as I have described it, nor can "religious" people, nor Christians. There is a perverse principle of ownership when trying for exclusive possession of the sun and the rain that God sends to everybody. A little more trust in the spirit may seem frightening (to cowards) although it is beautiful and dangerous—like life.
- The crisis of "religious life" is basically a crisis of Life. And life needs air in order to breathe. St. Therese mocked "rigid souls."
- I think that it may be healthy to begin speaking about "the monk" without traumas or resentment.
- Above all, we must help people to live life in all its vitality with depth and joy (ānanda), two dimensions that are essential to it.

⁂

The occasion for this book was a conference in 1980 in the United States, which I had the honor of chairing.[2] Some eighty people took part, most of whom were nuns and monks belonging to different religious traditions. A fourth part, in the original edition, included contributions by Abbots Cornelius Tholens and Armand Veilleux, Professors Ewert Cousins and Michael von Bruck, also Father M. Basil Pennington and the architect Paolo Soleri, and other participants who helped to make it an unforgettable event. Over the years since the first edition, the text has been translated into many languages. This book contains my essay, enriched by the subsequent debate.

My thesis is simple. Contemporary spirituality—or, better, a full

---

1 Current translations read: einsam und gebeugt (M. Buber and Neue Jerusalemer Bibel), soletto e misero (Istituto Biblico di Roma), sol i desvalgut (Bíblia Catalana Inter- confessional), lonely and oppressed (New English Bible), desolate and afflicted (Authorized Version and Revised Version), solo y afligido (Nàcar Colunga), solitaire et malhereux (Bible de Jérusalem), etc. The Latin version had pauper et unicus. Although the direct translations from the Hebrew text are more faithful, it is interesting that modern times do not love this "unique" (monogenē, as the LXX version says). That's how, anyway, I translate a mysterious text by St. Paul: "By the grace of God, I am what I am" (1 Co 15:10; see Ex 3:18); our uniqueness as a corollary to our divinity, which is a work by God's grace.

2 The conference had been arranged by the North American Board for East-West Dialogue, a committee belonging to the Aide Inter-Monastères.

human life for modern man, cannot be satisfied with the imitation of ancient patterns, that of the monk, for instance. We need a much more radical novelty.

So we must go back to the roots (*radici* in Italian). Monkhood has always wished to be a journey toward the radicality of the Absolute—even though it doesn't exist, as such. But modern monkhood is experiencing a crisis in the East and the West. Our task here is not to deal with the problems of monks. Our interest is in a full human life for our time which, as it is original, must go back to its origins. One of those original elements is the root, which, as has been mentioned, monks tried to cultivate. The new monk is not an imitation of the institutionalized monks of different traditions: he must learn from the monastic tradition, in order to launch himself into the new spaces of contemporary life.

This book does not seek to present contemporary "spirituality," but only to take a deeper look at its foundations, so that we can face our responsibilities in modern life. Sometimes, we are so concerned with our efforts to "save the world," heal the earth, or contribute to its survival that we forget the profoundness of this very life in which we are part of the illness—and of the cure.

This text has seen various editions, and the author has suffered for each one the "trauma" of trying to "improve" the text without spoiling its inner unity. This time, too, he would have liked to write another book. But he has learned from Master Kung (Confucius):

> Meng Sun already knows *tao*.
> He went beyond wisdom.
> He made his life simple.
>
> —*Chuang Tzu* VI.5

It is this simplicity that this book wishes to have.

Tavertet, August 15, 2006 (Femininity Day)

Prologue

The Monastic Vocation: Is the Monk a Universal Archetype?

ός πορεύεται απλώς,
πορεύεται πεποιδώς

—Pr 10:9

Qui ambulat simpliciter
ambulat confidenter.

—Vg.

He who walks simply,
walks confidently.*

The topic is ambiguous, but its ambiguity is revealing. If I hesitate it is because I feel I am breaking rather than constructing something. It is painful to break into pieces what one sees whole; and yet to speak, to explain, to unfold, to spread out in time and space is to break things apart. Like the body of Prajāpati dismembered in the act of creation, it seems that this simple and ineffable vision which is for me the symbol of the monk can only be communicated in fragments. I must begin by taking a hammer and destroying "the universal archetype of the monk," not unlike a child pulling apart its beloved little toy to see what is within. And within, we may discover emptiness...

My presentation will have one Prologue and four unequal Parts. The

* Cf. Pr 3:23; 28:18; Ps 23:15–16. The text is commented on by Meister Eckhart, Sermon XV.2 (no. 162). It is significant to read the modern translation of this aplos, which was so central to the Patristic and monastic spirituality and echoed so strongly in the New Testament. (Cf. Mt 6:22–23; Lk 11:34–35; etc. The Hebrew word has other connotations. Cf. also the leitmotif of homo viator, of Man the itinerant being). Here are some of the modern examples: "A blameless life makes for security" (NEB). "He walks secure whose ways are honorable" (KJ). "He walks secure, who walks pure" (Knox). "Chi va con rettitudine, va sicuro" (Istituto Biblico). "Chi si conduce con integrità, cammina sicuro" (Nardoni). "Qui va franchement va sûrement" (BJ). "El que anda en rectitud va seguro" (NacarColunga).

Prologue is a confession on method. The first Part will deal with the central understanding of monkhood as a human archetype. The second Part will try to spell out the contemporary monastic vocation in some chapters that develop a general principle. The third Part comments on the vision of the Hindū monk with some texts and examples. The fourth Part will be what we called the Synthesis at the symposium, which takes the form of general reflections on this unending topic.

Since my early youth I have seen myself as a monk, but one without a monastery, or at least without walls other than those of the entire planet. And even these, it seemed to me, had to be transcended—probably by immanence—without a habit, or at least without vestments other than those worn by the human family. Yet even these vestments had to be discarded, because all cultural clothes are only partial revelations of what they conceal: the pure nakedness of total transparency only visible to the simple eye of the pure in heart.

I feel perplexed about the way to proceed. Probably the best method would have been to take some seminal figures like the Buddha, Anthony, Milarepa, Âaṅkara; possibly also more modern ones like Bruno, Ramana, Dōgen, Maharishi, and others, and derive from these the monastic archetype. This course would have been relatively easier, and certainly more interesting, especially for those who may already be somewhat familiar with these giants of monastic spirituality. We would then have witnessed a quality of life and a human maturity that could serve us as beacons for our shaken human pilgrimage. From their examples we could have arrived at the monastic archetype.

Two reasons have induced me to undertake a quite different method. First, the monks already know many of these materials, and second, it would not contribute enough to the emerging mutation just to present traditional monasticism at its best. Such a presentation would have made all of us proud of such ancestors, but perhaps have veiled from our eyes what I consider the challenge of our times. It would have put us in line with the "try harder" mentality that would imitate their exploits, but it would distract us from considering whether our present-day predicament does not require of us a new *metanoia*, a new *conversio*, another radical change of mind or conversion, instead of just a renewed *imitatio*, a modernized imitation. To a nonmonastic audience, I would say that this presentation speaks to the monk in every one of us and does not wish to supplant or correct the rich literature on monasticism. I would indeed like to inspire the reader to delve into the sources of this rich human tradition.

The two reasons are connected. I am not so much directed to recount the history of the past or even to venture into the historical future, as I am concerned to probe the transhistorical present—for us here and now.

In other words, because I am existentially concerned with our daily lives and present situation, making use of the ambiguity of the phrase "monastic archetype" I shall address myself not to describing the monk as archetype—that is, the monk as a paradigm of human life—but to exploring the archetype of the monk—that is, monkhood as a possible human archetype. In point of fact, the phrase "monastic archetype" may mean that there is a monastic archetype of which the monk *is* the example, or of which the monk is the manifestation.

The distinction is *important* and subtle. *The monk as* archetype may be taken to mean that there is such a thing as an *ideal* monk, and that monks have incarnated this ideal in different degrees. This might be the best way for a *renovatio*, a renewal of the pristine purity of the monk. It is a legitimate and urgent concern, but in a certain sense, it freezes human creativity inasmuch as it ties us to an almost Platonic and immutable essence of the ideal monk. Archetype here means a model, a prototypical form (*morphé*). It allows only for explications and clarifications. All that is left to us is to be good or even better monks. To speak of *the archetype of the monk*, on the other hand, assumes that there is a *human* archetype that the monk works out with greater or lesser success. Traditional monks may have reenacted in their own way "something" that we too may be called upon to realize, but in a different manner, which expresses the growth and newness of the *humanum*. Archetype here means a product of the different forces and factors, conscious and unconscious, individual and collective, which go into shaping a particular human configuration. In a certain sense it gives us a free hand to launch an exploration into the very dynamism of the many factors that shape human life. In a certain sense, this leaves us free to explore the dynamics of the many factors that shape human life. Since archetype here does not mean a model, but rather the product of human life itself, this very archetype is thus mutable and dynamic.

But the distinction is also subtle, because it does not allow for any separation. We may have no other entrance into the archetype than to study or come to know the monk as archetype. We cannot create out of nothing, nor can we concoct an archetype according to our fancies. It is the crystallized experience of the elders in the tradition, and the reinterpretation of that very tradition, that will give us real wings to fly on a human journey and not to disintegrate in midair because our feathers were artificial. A noteworthy corollary of this distinction without separation is this: to consider the monk as archetype—namely, as a model—helps us to delve into the sources and to investigate the beginnings of monasticism.

We have to connect with tradition. To study the archetype of the monk, on the other hand, as well as the accumulation of human experiences still ongoing, brings us to observe the signs of our times and directs us to the future. We have to decipher the riddle of modernity. I say "riddle" because we shall have to discriminate between fleeting and superficial fashion and the real contribution that enriches and continues the value of tradition. This means that in spite of our stressing the differences between tradition and modernity, as we shall do for heuristic reasons, we should not overlook their continuity. In point of fact, the new monks are precisely those who contribute to the crystallization of the archetype that I shall endeavor to describe.

The topic is so enormous and the literature so vast that I can do it but minimal justice even if I limit myself to the quintessence of monkhood. And I shall attempt to do this from an anthropological perspective only. That implies not only a limitation—otherwise, almost anything can be said about monks and archetypes—but also a particular direction: a method that not only takes into account common sociological features, doctrinal resemblances, or religious common denominators, but also those aspects of the human being that are most deeply rooted in its nature. We shall do this, I repeat, neither by disregarding the traditional monastic ideal, nor by just explicating things from the past.

To be, then, quite specific: Is the monk a universal archetype—that is, a universal model for human life? No. The monk is only one way of realizing a universal archetype. Yet it is in and through this (monastic) way that we may gain access to the universal archetype—of which the monk is a manifestation. This allows us to speak of the universal archetype of the monk, provided we do not freeze the inner dynamism of monkhood, and also allows us to speak of the "new monk."

The method for this enterprise is rather special. It requires the phenomenological, sociomorphological, and historical methods simply to account for the manifestations of monasticism, but it has to proceed a step further. And for this we need recourse to a kind of philosophical approach and personal introspection. I assume the first step is sufficiently familiar, and shall concentrate on the second.

We shall have to take into account not only the past, as we know it, but also the present, as we understand it, and ourselves as we experience our lives.

One simple reflection may provide us the required mood. Whatever monkhood may be—and there are scores of definitions and descriptions—it seems to have exhibited a symptomatic polarity. On the one hand it is something special, difficult, even sometimes queer, with tinges of social and cultural nonconformity; on the other hand, it is something so very much human that it is ultimately claimed to be the vocation of every human being, what everybody should be or is called upon to be—in some way or other, sooner or later. An enlightened awareness of this polarity will, I hope, put us on the right track in our quest.

7
The Archetype of the Monk

By monk, *monachos*, I mean a person who aspires to reach the ultimate goal of life with all his being by renouncing all that is not necessary to it—that is, by concen- trating on this one single and unique goal. Precisely this univocity (*ekāgratā*), or rather the exclusivity of the goal that shuns all subordinate though legitimate goals, distinguishes the monastic way from other spiritual endeavors toward perfection or salvation. The monk is at least in the state of *mumukṣutva*, or desire to be liberated, and is so concentrated on just this that he renounces the fruits of his actions (*ihāmutrārthaphala bhoga-virāga*), having distinguished the real from the unreal (*nityāmitya-vastuviveka* or *ātmānātma a-vastuviveka*), and for this is ready to undertake the necessary praxis (*sādhana*).* If, in a certain sense, everybody is supposed

* I am very much worried about having to say monk/nun, he/she, and his/her all the time. I could replace "monk/nun" every time by "monkhood," but this abstraction goes against the genius of the English language. Besides, I would prefer to reserve the word "monkhood" for the archetype. I could say "she" instead of "he," but what we really need is a third article, not the masculine or the feminine or the neuter (which is Solomon's judgment, "neither the one nor the other"—for then you kill the child). Not the neuter but the "euter," the utrumque, the "either" gender that would include both male and female. For the moment, I shall use Man as Mensch, puru@a, anthropos, and not give males the monopoly on Man or split human beings into men and wif-men, males and fe-males (other etymologies notwithstanding). This split does not cover the entire human being either. Where are the children? Where are those who are not comfortable being either a he or a she? Curiously enough, gender only appears when we speak in the third person and objectify others. When I say "you" or "I," this invokes the fullness of the androgynous human being. In dialogue, we address each other as persons, whole and complete, with no need to make distinctions like adult or child, or black or white, or male or female. Only when we start talking about "third persons" do we have to say "he," "she," and the like: because they are not encountered directly and in person. When God is a You—or as I would rather suggest, the ultimate "I" to whom the You is "me"—the gender does not enter either. It is interesting to note that in some African languages the only difference between "he" and "you" is a distinction in tone. Every word should be a prayer and should be directed to a person. Hence also my uneasiness in talking into microphones.

to strive for the ultimate goal of life, the monk is radical and exclusive in this quest. All that is not ladder is ignored; all that is not the way falls apart.

The thesis I am defending is that the monk is the expression of an archetype that is a *constitutive dimension of human life.* This archetype is a unique quality of each person, which at once needs and shuns institutionalization. Such a conception has always been an underlying belief of tradition. The great monks have always been worried when the monk becomes a well-accepted figure in the world and receives the blessing of society. Being a monk is a highly personal adventure. It is with this belief in mind that tradition has considered the hermit—the idiorhythmic—to be the perfect monk: the *saµnyāsin*, *monachos*, *muni*, *bhikṣu*, *rāhib* (in spite of the doubts of the Qur'an), and so on.

We shall have to ask ourselves a difficult and only partially answerable question: not what monks think of themselves or what society thinks about them, but what ultimately has compelled them to embrace monkhood; not what sociopsychological motives they had, but—insofar as this is possible—what deep anthropological urge there was behind the languages of the different religious traditions that impelled them to walk such a path.

The monk ultimately becomes a monk not by a process of thinking (about death, the caducity of all things, *nitya*), or merely of desiring (God, human perfection, heaven, *nirvāṇa*), but as the result of an urge, the fruit of an experience that eventually leads him to change and, in the final analysis, break something in his life (*conversio*, *metanoia*, *ihāmutrārthaphala-bhoga-virāga*...) for the sake of that "thing" that encompasses or transcends everything (the pearl, *brahman*, peace, *shama*, *moksa*, liberation, God, *satori*, enlightenment...). One does not become a monk in order to *do* something or even to *acquire* anything, but in order to *be* (everything, yourself, the supreme being, nothing...). The monk does not become a monk just because of a desire. He will be told time and again to eliminate all desires. I speak of an inspiration and a need. It is not because one wills it that one becomes a monk. The monk is compelled, as it were, by an experience that can only articulate itself in the praxis of one's life. It is an experience of the presence of the goal of life, on the one hand, and of its absence (of not having reached it), on the other. Monastic spirituality has developed this topic of the initiation into monastic life in preference to almost any other theme. In a certain sense the monk is both the aspirant and the perfected one. There is a tension between the experience of the fullness of the goal, on the one hand, and of being still on the way, on the other. The monk has heard and believed the *tat tvam asi*: this is you (a You), but his being is not yet the You of the I.

It is the existence of such an ontological aspiration in the human being that leads me to speak of monkhood as a constitutive dimension of human life.

Now, this understanding of monkhood as a human dimension has been obscured by the juxtaposition of other elements, which have led to the common belief that the monk represents the highest type in the human scale; and from here it is but a small step to consider the monk to be the perfect Man, from the ultimate or religious point of view. Most traditions, in point of fact, will tell us that only the *muni* attains *mokṣa*, only the *bhikṣu* reaches *nirvāṇa*; and thus everyone is called to be a *saṃnyāsin*, in this or another life, as only the *sadhu* burns away all of his *karman* and is not born again; the Christian *monachos* is the only worthy successor of the *martyr* and thus the perfect Christian—and, of course, the perfect Man.

What is this human perfection? Let me explain by means of an example. According to Greek and Latin Scholastic theology, each angel is a species. The angel, by the very fact of being an angel, has reached the full "angelicity" of its particular order. Each angel is as fully angel as it can be; every angel exhausts its own nature and completely realizes its own specific potentialities. Once created, an angel completely fulfills its nature. It has reached its natural perfection.

Not so with human beings. A human being, unlike an angel, is not its whole humanity—nor can it become the whole. If one human being could exhaust the perfection of humanity, it would leave no place for anyone else. A human being is not the Adam, not the *puruṣa*, nor human nature. The perfection of the human individual is not the fullness of human nature; it is not nature, but personhood; it is not the essence of humanity, but the incommunicable and unique existence of the person. An indefinite number of people can realize, each uniquely, their own perfection. Humanity is manifold. In this sense *the* perfect human nature does not exist, nor does it exist in a particular being. It would have to embrace the whole of humanity, actual and possible, and this is not feasible for any individual person. Yet there are people who actualize their dormant potentialities and others who don't, people who reach a high degree of humanness, as it were, and others who don't.

We should emphasize this point because a certain monolithic conception of the hierarchy of values—again under Platonic influence—has given the impression that there can be *the* perfect human nature: say, first of all Christian, then male, and then adult, white, English-speaking, and so on. In point of fact, a perfect human nature is a contradiction in terms. It would have contradictory attributes: quick and slow in reactions; white and black, or brown, in skin color; masculine and feminine in gender; Spanish and Chinese (etc.) in language; introvert and extrovert in character; young and old in age; and so on and so forth.

From this it follows that the search for human perfection cannot have a single model. The word "perfection" has to stand for a meaningful, joyful, or simply full human life, whatever and wherever we may believe this "fullness," "meaning," and "joy" to be. Each person will have his own way of realizing the perfection of "humanity." I shall call the *humanum* this core of humanity or humanness that can be realized in as many fashions as there are human beings. Humanity is one; the *humanum* exists in the particular form of each and every individual person who realizes that fullness of being. Even if this fullness is considered to be a merging with Brahman or a total annihilation, this could be called the *humanum* of that specific person.

Each human being has to conquer the *humanum* in a personal and unique manner. The endeavor of every religion is to give a concrete scope and possibility through which the human being (individually or collectively) may achieve the *humanum*. In this endeavor to acquire full humanness or the *humanum*, many ways are open. A traditional name for the gamut of these ways is "religion." Religion is a path to the *humanum*, be it called salvation, liberation, or whatever generic name.

Now, not only can this *humanum* have many interpretations, it also has many aspects that show the whole richness and complexity of human nature. The poet, the intellectual, the craftsman, the man of action, and so on, all express different facets of it. Each of these facets represents the cultivation of one aspect of the *humanum*. By and large, the human person tries to find a harmonious conjugation between several of these human qualities, just as persons of good taste combine the several colors of the different pieces of clothing they wear.

One ideal has very often crept into this human striving for perfection. We could call it the Supernatural, or the higher level. Realizing that many human virtues can turn into obstacles to higher goals, and having experienced the mutual incompatibility of many otherwise desirable human qualities, most religious traditions have opted to save the *humanum* by raising it up to the "superhuman" destiny of the Supernatural or *paramārthika*. You attain perfection by jumping over the "natural" or *laukika* perfections and, by short circuit as it were, you reach in another sphere the fullness of your life. This "supernatural" saint can seem rather a quaint figure here on earth, but we are told that later, in heaven, he will be radiant with light and suffused with all perfection. And in fact there does seem to be something in the *humanum*, as we have defined it, that transcends mere humanity and points to another degree of reality not to be found on the merely "natural" level—assuming simply that *nature* is whatever is *born* (*naturam* coming from *natum*) on earth, be it spiritual, intellectual, or material.

Most religious traditions have this somewhat transcendent conception of the *humanum.* The search for it is what characterizes the *Homo religiosus*, but we have not yet arrived at the monk. The monk is neither the *homo* on his way to the *humanum*, nor the *Homo religiosus* in his search for the *superhumanum* or supernatural.

My hypothesis is that the archetype of which the monk is an expression corresponds to one dimension of this *humanum*, so that every human being has potentially the possibility of realizing this dimension. Monkhood is a dimension that has to be integrated with other dimensions of human life in order to fulfill the *humanum.* Not by bread alone does Man live.

And it is such an archetype that we find under different names in most human traditions. It is quite understandable that precisely those religions that have most diligently cultivated this dimension have tried to institutionalize it. And here is the paradox: once monkhood becomes institutionalized, it begins to become a specialization and it runs the risk of becoming exclusive. Not everybody can or should enter a monastery, but everybody has a monastic dimension that ought to be cultivated. Monkhood is a constituent, a part, a dimension of the human being, an archetype; but the monastery is a *totum*, a total organization of human life. The monk within the institutionalized framework often suffers from the fact that his vital impulses toward full humanness are curtailed merely because they are absorbed in the total institution—and sometimes sacrificed for the benefit of that institution. Experience shows that all too often the monk finds himself/herself looking outside the monastery for that human perfection to which he aspires. (I shall later defend the monastery as a living organism and not, primarily, an organization.)

Institutions are necessary, and the more human a need the more necessary the institution. Marriage could be an example, and monasticism another case in point. But the moment that the institution monopolizes the very values it represents, the danger of "institutionalization" appears. The institution is the ritualization of the means, but when the means become ends, the institution becomes totalitarian. I will not deal now with love outside marriage, because we are concerned about the quest for the Absolute outside monastic institutions, of all sorts.

I surmise that one of the crises of present-day monasticism is precisely this kind of quid pro quo, that something that belongs to human nature as one of its constitutive dimensions loses a good part of its force and its universality once it becomes a particular form of organized life. Thus monkhood—which, properly understood, is intertwined with other dimensions of being human and could be an essential element in reaching human fullness—becomes a totalitarian ideal and loses sight of its own potential. And yet, conversely, there is no organism without organization. I am simply echoing tradition, which sees the monk as a solitary (not an isolated) being, living perhaps in a (spiritual) family, but not as a member of a world closed in on itself. The monastic vocation is essentially personal.

Something similar happens when other dimensions of human life, like sexuality, sociability, playfulness, or even art, and so on, become institutionalized in an institution that purports to encompass the entirety of human life. The *humanum* is multidimensional, and no single dimension can encompass the complexity of human life. We shall return to this theme.

But I have not yet said precisely in what this dimension of the *humanum* consists. It is this: In the search for "perfection," Man has very often looked for oneness, the *hen*, the *monos*, the *ekam*, the *unum necessarium* (of the Vulgate). I may use a metaphor here, a most traditional one in both the East and the West, in spite of the differing emphases: *the center*. If we look for oneness on the periphery we cannot reach that equanimity, that *shama*, that peace peculiar to the monk; we cannot have that holy indifference toward everything because we are not equidistant from everything. Monkhood is the search for this very center.

Inasmuch as we try to unify our lives around the center, all of us have something of the monk in us. This center, by virtue of being a center, is immanent to the human being; but at the same time, by virtue of being as yet unattained, it is transcendent. We should bear in mind that we are not speaking of any specific monastic institution in any specific religion, but rather of an anthropological dimension. Monasticism is not a specifically Christian, Jaina, Buddhist, or sectarian phenomenon; rather, it is a basically human and primordially religious one.

To speak of a Buddhist monk or a Hindū monk or a Jaina monk or a Christian monk does no violence to the words. The Christian, the Buddhist, the Jaina... are only qualifications of the search for that center, for that core that any monk seeks. The monastic vocation as such precedes the fact of being Christian, or Buddhist, or secular (we shall speak about that, too), or Hindū, or even atheist.

In short, we must recover the monastic dimension of Man as a constitutive human dimension. If this is indeed the case, then monkhood is not the monopoly of the few but a human wellspring that is either being channeled in different degrees of purity and awareness by different people or thwarted altogether. Every human being has a monastic dimension, which everyone must realize in different ways. Monasticism in its historical forms would then be not only an attempt to cultivate this *primordium* in a particular fashion but also to commit oneself publicly to developing, in an exemplary way and according to the cultural environment, the deepest core of our humanness.

I am saying that there is a primordial monastic dimension prior to the quality or qualification of being Christian, Buddhist, and the like. Moreover, this distinction is *transcendental*. This means that, while for everyone there is only one particular way of being a monk, the distinction is nonetheless real and not just a distinction in our mind. My way of living the monastic tradition may be the Jaina, the Christian, the atheistic, or the secular way. But the monastic dimension is prior to and different from the way in which I may live it out. The way I am to live my being a Hindū monk is simply by living my monastic vocation in the Hindū manner. We do not speak *the* language; when we speak, we use only *a* language.

If we go so far as to identify the Christian monastic way with the monastic vocation or with monasticism per se, then we commit a serious mistake that will have more than merely theoretical consequences. Fanaticism, misguided missionary zeal, Inquisitions, and "holy" wars have something to do with it, to say nothing of the self-destructive practices too often found in monastic institutions. Christian monasticism, for instance, should not be the unique point of reference for an article on monasticism—as it still is in the *Dictionnaire de Spiritualité*.

Let us reflect for a moment on the metaphor of the center and on the different ways in which this center is experienced by describing in a very approximate manner two classical ways, commonly called the Eastern and the Western ones.

In fact, the major differences today exist not so much between "East" and "West" in traditional parlance as on the interface between tradition and modernity; after all, ours is the epoch of multimedia and a multitude of spiritual seekers experiencing "other" traditions. I should emphasize that these two centers, the "Eastern" and the "Western," are not geographical locations but anthropological categories. Each one of us has an "East" and a "West," an Orient and an Occident. "East" and "West" are symbols that denote two main emphases that have been stressed in some traditions more than in others, but that can in no way be considered the exclusive possession of one or another religious family.

First, the center is in the center of our being. It is in the middle, equidistant from every single factor of our existence. It is not only a geometrical center, as it were, but also a gravitational one. All stimuli, good and bad, joyful and sad, converge on that center; all arrows tend toward it. But all impulses and all movements also originate there, insofar as we are centered beings. To the extent that we are con- centrated beings, while the blows and scrapes of life may still pain and wound us, when we are thrown into the air we shall land again on our feet, like the cat, who is a well-centered being. And again, all of our actions, words, and thoughts will have the power not only of the particular muscle we employ in each case, but they will have the weight of all our being, like the blow of a Zen master trained in the art of hitting with the hand.

The center, furthermore, has no dimensions. Ultimately, it does not exist; it is void, and inasmuch as this is so it will remain immobile while the surface is all awhirl. Another word for it would be to say that it is absolute—that is, unbound, untied, free, and for this reason, compatible with everything inasmuch as it remains independent.

As a consequence, the center has no value in itself. It is a function of all the things for which it is a center. Eliminate all the other things around it and the center disappears, or, rather, reveals itself as what it "is": no-thing. An entire monastic spirituality could be derived from the study of this metaphor. Indeed, Zen monasticism could tell us something about it.

As for a typology of the center from an Eastern and Western standpoint, I will say only the following. Even if every center has to be inside, the Eastern center is preeminently immanent. Every center is immanent, but the Eastern center is immanence itself. Immanence does not mean a kind of interior transcendence, as it is so often interpreted. It means that the immanent "thing" is really in the very core of that entity and somewhat identified with it, though without confusion. Many images suggest this concept: cave (*guhā*), point, emptiness (śūnyatā), no-thought (*mu*), womb, clear mirror, Non-Being, and so on. The way is introspection, the inward journey.

Within the pattern of immanence the classical acosmism of the Eastern monk is readily understandable. The *saµnyāsin* can be acosmic because in the center he has, or rather "is," everything. He can totally ignore the world because the real is within and not outside. Thus he can be absolutely carefree regarding an illusory world.

The center for the Western monk, on the other hand, is certainly equally inside and interior, but it is transcendence. Again, here, we have to warn against the common misunderstanding that interprets transcendence as exteriority, when what it means is ultimate difference (just as immanence denotes qualified identity). This transcendent center is *semper maior*, ever-elusive, other, nonassimilable. It evokes the images of the mountain, the infinite, the sphere, fullness, *plērōma*, and even progress, or using the neologism of Gregory of Nyssa, *epektasis*, that is, constantly going forward, reaching further, toward the beyond (the Father, the New Jerusalem).

Within the pattern of transcendence, the classical involvement of the Western monk in the religious issues of the contemporary world is easily comprehensible. The monk can preach crusades and open "schools of prayer" or simply schools; he can write books and judge the world as a "guilty bystander."

Let me be more specific, at the risk of overemphasizing my point, by taking the examples of Christian and Hindū monasticism: Christian monasticism is a *way* of life. It is the commitment to the uncompromising search for the Absolute and the readiness to break through all the obstacles on the way. It is the path toward the center, and the vows are the *viatica*, the means for this pilgrimage toward God.

Hindū monasticism, at least in the traditional understanding of the *saṃnyāsa*, is a way of *life*. It is the very Life of the end of life, the goal of the Journey, the *āśrama* beyond all *āśramas*, only improperly called the fourth one. If Christian monasticism is a *vocation* (you have to follow), Hindū monasticism is an *answer* (you give). The *saṃnyāsin* does not renounce the world, or whatever, in order to achieve something. Because he has seen, experienced, *lived* the real, he discards all the rest. He is not the novice, the *brahmacārī*, but the *comprehensor*, the *jīvanmukta*. There is nothing he has to do, because all has already been done. He is at the center, peaceful, quiet, and serene. No sacrifice, no vow, no anything is required or remains to be done. The texts are quite explicit.

We have here two different patterns of understanding, two different ways of living and experiencing one and the same archetype. From the beatific vision to the symbol of the mountain, to the sphere of Parmenides, to the fullness of Christ taught by Paul of Tarsus, you have the same paradigm, which should be compared and contrasted with the paradigm of total emptiness, thought-less-ness, one-pointedness (until this point itself disappears), the cave of the heart... to which you *in*-gress, not *pro*-gress. There are in this latter model no schools of *pro*gression in spiritual life, but only of *in*gression to the depths of darkness; because in the center, the *guhā*, the cave, there is no light.

Discussion

Why do you have such a negative view of institutional monasticism?

I am not against institutions. Society cannot exist without institutions. But I would make a distinction between institutions and institutionalism, which is when institutionalization takes over the life of an institution. I think an institution should be not only an organization, but also an organism. The distinction between organism and organization is a very delicate one. An organization works when there is money; an organism runs when there is life. And I think this is more than a metaphor. No amount of money (read "arms") will protect the institutions of the first world (or of the second, for that matter) if its organism is sick. The organization needs a frame; the organism requires a body. The organization needs a boss, a leader, an impulse from the outside to let it function. The organism lives by virtue of its soul, health, the harmonious interaction of all the parts of the whole. An organization is entropic; an organism is diectropic. An organization equals the sum of its parts, and each part is replaceable by an identical replica. An organism is more than the sum of its components, and no component can be replaced by an exact duplicate, because each is unique. If at all, the organism has to regenerate itself from within when it has been wounded. An organism dies when the soul departs, when the heart ceases to beat or the brain to vibrate. An organization has much more resistance because its structure is stronger and can function by inertia, provided some kind of elementary fuel is pumped in; it has a higher power of inertia.

I would not like my explanations to be interpreted as if I were making every effort to liquidate monastic organizations as superfluous and senseless. My point is that, if I am correct in saying that monkhood is a constitutive human dimension, then this dimension can never find its full expression in a closed institution that is bound to be the privilege of only a few. If the monastic dimension exists at least potentially in everybody, the institution of monasticism should be equally open to everybody. We should then distinguish between monkhood and monasticism.

Of course, people who share a common ideal can and should come together to discover meaningful ways to realize that ideal. This is more than legitimate. But this tends more to justify other collective forms of religious life than monasticism. A religious congregation in the canonical sense of the Roman Catholic Church, for instance, certainly aims at the sanctification of her members, but her raison d'être is the specific purpose in view of which it was established: looking after the poor, teaching the people, defending the holy places, catering to the spiritual needs of priests, healing or helping the sick or the pilgrims, or extending the kingdom of Christ, and so on. Monasticism as such has no purpose or ideal of this type—that is, it does not aim to fulfill something *ad extra*, despite the considerable evolution of the idea of monkhood in Western Christendom during recent centuries. The monastery, then, would not be the "establishment" of the monks, but the *schola Domini*, the school where that human dimension is cultivated and transmitted.

I would like to add a philosophical remark. As long as the *logos* holds sway over the *mythos*, the impasse is almost impossible to overcome. We need, then, constitutions, laws, contracts, and constrictions. We have, instead, to regain a new innocence that will allow the myth, and the spirit of the whole enterprise, to take over our lives. The *logos* is strong; it relies on evidence. The myth is fragile; it relies on faith. As soon as faith weakens, it is like when the salt loses its "saltiness"; it cannot be restored. Then we need a new myth that, in its turn, produces a new *logos*.

And here we hit upon the vast problem of overorganization, of preplanning and preprogramming everything and anything, and often forgetting the essential. It seems that the function of education in this country is to impart purposefulness to life, a certain notion of success, which I take not only as an assault on the very etymology of the word education (*e-ducere*—to bring out, to draw forth), but also as counterproductive of the very purpose of education, which ought to be to free the subject from very many sorts of conditionings. That is why education has been made compulsory by the state. Indoctrination and socialization take place in the early years of mandatory education. One of the aims of monastic or religious education is, or should be, to undo or correct that kind of compulsory education that tend toward competitivity and consumerism. And yet, despite the difficulties, one probably cannot do without a certain institutionalization. Once again, it is a question of proportion and balance.

If monkhood is just one of the many human dimensions, is a monk closed in his monastery an incomplete being?

Incompleteness remains in all of our experiences as long as one has not reached the true goal, the *moksha*, the liberation from all finitude. The ways by which monasticism has traditionally tried to overcome the incompleteness of the radical simplicity of monkhood have been either by immanence or by transcendence. The first way is by interiorization: you, as it were, eat up the outside world, you internalize everything, and you feel that in this internalization you have overcome that incompleteness. It is an overcoming by immanence, as it were. It is the way of mysticism. In the second case, you go to the Father of all lights, the Source of all being, and there, at the top, beyond any limit, you attain everything. It is an overcoming by eminence, as it were. It is the way of eschatology.

So you may fill up that incompleteness by reaching the center, in the interior of your being, where all the radii converge and everything coalesces—

and then the world is there already. There is no dichotomy between me and the world. This is the first way. Or, second way, you go up, or out, or beyond—even if you have to wait until the end of time—where again you also attain everything. It is the *panta en pasin* (God "all in all") of St. Paul.

But contemporary mankind does not seem to agree wholly with either of these two paradigms, which are typical of an Eastern and Western mentality, respectively. I believe, however, that the elimination of the tension between East and West, of itself, is not enough. If we are to speak of monasticism today, we must take into account the impact, the challenge, the revelation, or the temptation of secularity, which is not secularism. I see this as the great task of our time: The two paradigms, the one of immanence and the one of transcendence, do not seem to suffice anymore. We will have to work at this, and try to see if there may be any alternative.

May Christianity be understood as a combination of these two ways, the Eastern and the Western one?

This is an interesting opinion from the point of view of a tradition, and it is indicative of how this tradition conceives itself nowadays. A present-day Hindū and Buddhist would express themselves in more or less the same way, and all of them would be right, to some extent. This is what I consider the deep impact of secularity, which makes us feel unsatisfied with either pattern. Certainly, the trap of modernity would be to say, "Let us create a new religion." But this is naïve and insufficient. We are too burdened both by the weight and the richness of tradition just to sweep it out altogether, throwing it onto the garbage heap of history. But the impact of secularity might very well lead us to say, "Let us have a better understanding of tradition." Then I, as a Buddhist, would call for a renewed comprehension of the *pratītyasamutpāda* (the radical relativity of everything that exists), which would bring me to a new understanding of the Buddhist message. Or, as a Hindū, I would begin to look for a new understanding of *karma*, or of *dharma*, which would in turn lead me to a totally revised understanding of the modern *saṃyāsin*. Or, as a Christian, I might try to overcome the immanence/transcendence pattern when speaking of incarnation.

In this I glimpse the proper role of modern secularity. If we find something vital in what I call secularity, we should graft it onto our own tradition. Yet, to be vital, the graft must draw its nourishment from the roots. On the other hand, within the traditions themselves there have been evident examples of both attitudes and remarkable efforts to overcome unilaterality.

What do you mean by the "trap of modernity"?

The trap of modernity means uprootedness, *déracinement.* That is, thinking that the world began yesterday, or the day before yesterday; that what we learn at school or can know from everyday life is everything that there is in the world; that the technocratic megamachine in which we live constitutes all reality. This cuts us off from the roots of the real, roots that grip deeply down into Reality as a whole. This is the trap of modernity. But I would also warn against the stagnation of tradition, which occurs when a tradition is so old that it does not allow any new growth, nor change of any kind.

I should maybe add what I mean by the word "modernity" without the trap. In this case, I prefer to use the word "secularity," that is, the conviction that the *saeculum*, the temporal structure of the world, is something definitive, something irreplaceable that we cannot ignore, and that therefore we have to take into account even at the ultimate level of reality.

When the contemplative finds the center, be it in the guhā, the cave, or on the mountain, in the Beyond, doesn't he reach a point where all categories, all ideas about immanence and transcendence fall away, and only God is left, as All in all?

Yes, certainly. But everyone describes their own experience trying to render in words what they see within. Here lies the challenge, the danger as well as the appeal, the temptation and the weakness, of cross-cultural studies. From within, once we have found the pearl, we have found everything. Then there is no longer "in" or "out," as with the kingdom of God in the *Gospel of Thomas*. We can still wonder whether we are "in" or "out," but the question has meanwhile become pointless.

However, since Time is not finished yet, and we are in this cross-cultural situ- ation, we have the legacy of many rich traditions, we have been "thrown together" (*sym-bolon*), and we are not the only people who have had this experience; for these (and probably many other) reasons, we have not yet attained that state of absolute freedom, total unconcern, and simplicity. Otherwise, I should simply go my own way, with no need for us to meet and talk about it all. But as soon as I hear of other people's experiences, I break that unity, that blessed simplicity, and then I find this typology of immanence and transcendence to be valid. By looking at it from the very center of experience, however, even this becomes superfluous.

This raises another problem: the risk of being carried away by statements like, "Oh, you are wrong, you are so primitive-minded! You did not get it, because you only went into the *guhā*, you remained inside the cavern." Or, "Yahweh is respon- sible for all the crimes committed in His name." This attitude is wrong because we commit the sin of *katachronism.*

Anachronism is what our grandmothers do: they judge the modern world on the basis of their old ideas. We are all inclined to accuse our old people of anachronism. *Kata*-chronism is the exact opposite kind of perspective mistake: it is when we use present-day categories to judge the past. This is not typical of grandmothers, but of teenagers; it is what we—as teenagers in this world, which develops too swiftly—too often happen to do. It is naïve, besides being false, to judge the past by our contemporary categories of understanding. We need categories that have been tested in the crucible of past times, and can survive in the present time. It is important to bear in mind that our typology does not authorize us to judge, let alone to condemn, other such efforts that mark the history of mankind.

Could you explain, in simple words, what contents you put into the word "archetype"?

Hiraṇyagarbha, the gold cosmic egg. I cannot say it in a few words. I would say that an archetype is a paradigm that naturally becomes the center of the myth we live in. Myth is what we believe in, without even knowing it. This is why we can only deal critically with other people's myths.

The word "archetype" has a long history, and was reintroduced by C. G. Jung. I use it in a sense that only partially corresponds to Jung's. I don't like the term "model" because it sounds too objective, too exterior, and too strictly linked to consciousness. Nor would I say conviction, belief, faith, or doctrine, all of which appear to be too "essentialistic," too conscious or too conceptually connoted.

An "archetype," in my opinion, is—literally—a fundamental type (*arche-typos*), that is, a basic constituent or relatively permanent feature, in this case, of human life. It is used as the contrary of a fleeting appearance (*phainomenon*). It represents a basis upon which at least a part of our life is built. I take from Jung not so much the notion that it is submerged in the collective human unconscious as that it is a *dynamis* that on the one hand directs, and on the other hand attracts, human ideals and praxis. I have also used the expression "constitutive dimension" as the anthropological counterpart for what in the history of human consciousness crystallizes or appears as an archetype.

The word is polysemous, as most living words are. It may mean a sort of Platonic essence, a prototype that is immutable and gives identity to its participations. It may also mean something that is hidden in human nature, because it is cause and effect of our basic behavior and convictions.

8
The Canon of the Disciple

The reflections that follow are not intended to be a new "Rule of the Master." Rather they hope to express "The Canon of the Disciple," that is, to formulate the aspiration of contemporary Man in search of unification as he is confronted by the manifold character of his being and the surrounding reality.

Following a time-honored custom, as much Oriental as Western, I will formulate a single principle that will then be developed in one corollary and nine canons, each of which will be followed by a gloss and a commentary. The gloss will present the canon in its traditionally valid form, while the commentary will interpret it according to contemporary lights and distinguish it from the traditional understanding. The gloss emphasizes continuity; the commentary, change. The two together will describe the contours of growth.

For the sake of presenting more strikingly the facets of the new monk, I shall sometimes overstress certain aspects of the traditional interpretation, overlooking the fact that any living tradition is much richer than it may appear and that generally it already contains a potential for the more contemporary aspect that I underline. I present this contrast more as a heuristic device than as a historical description.

I know and foresee the reaction among the best representatives of the traditional monastic spirit: "But this is exactly what we want and what we stand for! Why then all these caricatures?" I am in full sympathy with this reaction, which only stresses the continuity of the monastic vocation. But we cannot be blind to appearances either, and to the manner in which things are often seen. It may be that some do not sense the conflict between the old and the new. But one side alone is hardly in a position to pass the verdict that there is no conflict if the other side does indeed see a conflict. And in fact the uneasiness of the younger generation, and the prolifera- tion of religions and schools of spirituality, demonstrate that there is an apparent conflict between tradition and modernity.

The problem arises as to whether this contemporary spirituality I shall describe can still be called monastic. The answer may be semantic, but it should not be nominalistic. Names are more than just arbitrary labels. Should we still speak of monastic values even though they have changed? Should we still speak of a modern "monk" when he has abandoned so many of the trappings of the past? Is it altogether the same archetype? Before deciding on the alternative, I would voice a double convic- tion: the first general, the second specific.

First, in the crisis brought on by the encounter of religions and cultures, the words that express fundamental human experiences cannot be identified with a single conceptual interpretation within one culture. They must rather be amplified until they embrace the homeomorphic or functional equivalent in other traditions. The word "grace," for example, cannot be reduced to what the Tridentine Christian tradition thinks of it, but must embrace what the follower of *shaivasiddhānta* thinks of it as well. Thus, in order to determine the meaning of a word, a functional approach is imperative. The modern monk might have changed in his understanding of many values, but if the thrust—that is, the existential intentionality—remains, he can still be called a monk.

Second, this approach is strengthened in the particular case that concerns us now. In order to know what a monk, a *rāhib*, a *saµyāsin*, a *muni*, a *bhik@u*, and so on, is, we must know not only what each tradition says about him but also what prompted the monk to take the stance he took.

It could be that in the last analysis we would prefer to do away with the word "monk" altogether and find another, less overburdened one, but this would not prove that what the contemporary monk intends does not correspond to what the ancients were trying to do. It is still an open question, which probably has no theoretical answer. If the modern monks—I mean the new monks, not those of our contemporaries who legitimately follow the traditions of the past—call themselves monks, there seems no reason to oppose them in this. Here "apostolic" continuity is probably more important than doctrinal uniformity. But we shall still have to see whether the archetype of monkhood has been split into two, whether we have here a mutation or simply another species of religious life altogether. It will all depend on whether we can find a single principle for both traditional monasticism and the new variety. The enterprise is not an easy one.

We may recall that the great scholar and Benedictine Jean Leclercq has written that "monasticism is not a matter of speculation, nor is it a problem; it is a mystery," and that the great Trappist monk Thomas Merton speaks of monasticism as "a problem and a scandal."

The issue is important not only for the status and future of monasticism, but for religious existence in its entirety. In our present times, when religious values are suffering a profound transformation, perhaps monkhood will become the central religious archetype, so as to offer a continuity that may save modern Man from falling into a more than cultural schizophrenia—a split within himself due to a break with his own past.

Our hypothesis about monkhood as a human dimension will have to stand the analysis of the archetype of monkhood in all of its manifestations. History shows without exception that the monk in all traditions has been a sign of contradiction. Monkhood has been hailed as the divine life on earth, and the monk as the *jīvanmukta* and enlightened being; but he has equally been scorned as the *vulgus pecus* (herd of cattle), the *novum inauditumque monstrum* (new, unheard-of monstrosity), the hypocrite, and alienated fellow par excellence.

Here appears the consequence of our distinction between the *monk* as arche- type—that is, the monk as a paradigm of religious life—against the archetype of the monk—that is, the human archetype lived out by the monks, but which may also be experienced and lived today in different ways.

We all know not only the *Rule of the Master*, but also the different masters of the venerable monastic traditions, East and West; but who are the disciples? Who is the disciple who writes these Canons? Who is the modern monk about whom we are going to speak? The author of the *Canon of the Disciple* is as anonymous as the writer of the *Rule of the Master*. The new monk is represented by the young generation of men and women entering into traditional monastic institutions but carrying with them, sometimes in spite of themselves, the spirit of secularity. The new monk is further represented by all those who do not even dream of entering traditional institutions, but who nevertheless are attracted by a life that could well be called monastic. They have, in fact, started new movements, new religions, and new forms, and sometimes revived old patterns. In sum, and especially, the new monk is an anonymous being who voices the aspirations of many, and of older colleagues as well: the new monk is an ideal, an aspiration that lives in the minds and hearts of our contemporary generation. I have found this new monk among the poor and among the rich, in the East and in the West, among so-called believers and nonbelievers alike. I have found an equal number of men and of women, and I have found them active in secular institutions as well as in religious organizations. The new monk has not yet acquired self-consciousness, and the Disciple is not always aware that he or she is following the Master. You will find this new monasticism in the slums, in the marketplaces, in the streets, but also in the mountains and the valleys, and even in the corridors, classrooms, and lobbies of modern society.

Similarly, you will often find the new monk living in the old monasteries. His name is legion and his surname is "dissatisfaction with the status quo," but his pedigree is as mysterious as the sources of the waters: they emerge from every slope because it has rained, and rained heavily over all the earth, and the clouds are still hovering overhead....

Now we shall try to analyze the main traits of monkhood, and to formulate that unifying principle to which we referred.

The Monastic Tradition: The Fundamental Principle: Simplicity

Gloss

At first sight, human life is complex: Our body has many organs and divergent uses; our spirit has a plurality of faculties and manifold functions. We are attracted to many things, and our very being is the result of diverse factors constituting a complex being. We become aware of reality when we begin to distinguish, and we begin to know when we discriminate. The human person is not a single entity but a network of relationships. All that is in us and around us seems to be manifold. We live under the sign of multiplicity, and human civilization tends to further multiply knowledge, distinctions, methods. And life itself: there seems to be a natural dynamism toward complexity. Furthermore, the very many parts of the universe and of our own being seem to be in strife with one another: the mind against the heart, the parts of the body in conflict with each other and with the spirit, dissension among families and nations, the law of the jungle among animals, cataclysms in nature....

Nor is this all. Everything seems to be ephemeral, inconsistent, fleeting. Tempo- rality is unsatisfactory; we feel the uneasiness of proliferation. *Sarvam duḥkham*: suffering everywhere. *Ta panta mataiotēs*: all is vanity. Plurality is a fact. The world is complicated, and so we are often worried and perplexed because we appear to be incapable of handling the many things that interest and yet trouble us.

Monkhood is a radical reaction against such a state of affairs. If Man has been defined as the only animal that knows how to say No, monkhood could similarly be described as the radical articulation of this No to the excruciating multiplicity of all that appears to be. The monk is the nonconformist. The monk down the ages has been seen as the only one who sails against the wind propelling all things, in search of the simplicity of the source. The monk is the one who tries to swim upstream, against the current, searching for the—supposed—simplicity of the origin. God is simple. Brahman is utter simplicity. The monk believes the Absolute is simple and that the goal of his life is to attain that very simplicity. The way may be hard, and at the end there may even be no way, but it is all simple. No thing, nothing can quench his thirst, *tṛṣṇā* (Skt. Pali: *taṇhā*). The monk will not be satisfied until that very thirst has disappeared, not so much because he has found an object capable of appeasing his desires (he would soon look for another object), but because the very cause of that urge has disappeared.

This simplicity as a feature of monkhood is not indiscriminate simplicity. It requires an essential qualification. It has to be a *blessed* simplicity, that is, a blessed simplicity conquered with blood ("blood" and "blessed" are etymologically linked) and then made holy, sanctified (*sanctus* also means "set apart"), isolated within that uniqueness of experience that has reduced everything to its quintessence and reached the ultimate transparency of truth. In other words, the monk does not seek simplicity by doing violence to the real, by chopping off real values, by abusing some of its realms and exploiting others. Rather he aspires to simplicity by respecting the rhythms and the nature of things, ultimately because he is convinced that the truth of the truth, so to speak, the core of being, the *satyasya satyam*, is simple.

As an example of this traditional mentality, I may adduce without commentary three fundamental texts chosen at random. These texts do not, of course, speak of the novice, but of the fully realized monk. Aspiration here has already given way to fullness. I translate the first and the last, and reproduce Abhishiktananda's version of the second.

The first is a famous hymn to the monk in the tenth mandala of the *Ṛg-veda.*

At Home in Both Seas, East and West
Within him is fire, within him is drink,
within him both Earth and Heaven.
He is the Sun which views the whole world,
he is indeed Light itself
the long-haired ascetic.
Girded with the wind, they have donned ochre mud
for a garment. So soon as the Gods
have entered within them, they follow the wings
of the wind, these silent ascetics.
Intoxicated, they say, by our austerities,
we have taken the winds for our steeds.
You ordinary mortals here below
see nothing except our bodies.
He flies through midair, the silent ascetic,

beholding the forms of all things.
To every God he has made himself
a friend and collaborator.
Ridden by the wind, companion of its blowing,
pushed along by the Gods,
he is at home in both seas, the east
and the west—this silent ascetic.
He follows the track of all spirits,
of nymphs and the deer of the forest.
Understanding their thoughts, bubbling with ecstasies,
their appealing friend is he the
long-haired ascetic.
The wind has prepared and mixed him a drink;
it is pressed by Kunamnamā.
Together with Rudra he has drunk from the cup
of poison—the long-haired ascetic.

The second text is a free rendering from the *Bṛhadāraṇyaka* and other *Upaniṣads.*

In this world,
out of this world,
seer of what is beyond sight,
he goes secretly and hidden, unknown;
mad with the madness of those who know,
free with the freedom of the spirit,
filled with essential bliss,
established in the mystery
of the nondual.
Free from all sense of otherness,
his heart filled with the unique experience of the Self:
fully, and forever, awake.

The following verses of St. John of the Cross declare the way to ascend the Mount of Perfection, and warn against following twisted paths.

The Way to Come to the All
To come to what you do not know
you must go through where you do not know.
To come to what you do not enjoy
you must go through where you do not enjoy.
To come to what you do not possess
you must go through where you do not possess.
To come to what you are not
you must go through where you are not.

The Way to Hold the All
If you wish to know all
wish to know nothing of anything.
If you wish to enjoy all
wish to possess nothing of anything.
If you wish to be all
wish to be nothing in anything.

The Way Not to Hinder the All
When you stop at anything
you lose your thrust toward the all.
For to come altogether to the all
you must altogether leave all.
And when you come to hold it all
you must hold it desiring nothing.
For if you desire to have something at all
you have not your pure treasure in God.

The Sign That One Has the All
In that nakedness the mind finds quietude and rest
because, as it covets nothing, nothing
pushes it upward, nothing forces it downward,
for it rests in the center of its humility.
For when it covets anything, in that it is fatigued.
Nothing, nothing, nothing, nothing, nothing.
And on the Mount, nothing.
Here there are no paths—for there is no law for the just.

In sum, this blessed simplicity appears to be the monastic principle as such, as so many witnesses from different traditions confirm. It could be easily be called a Quest for the Absolute, too. In fact, this Ab-solute is "un-bound" precisely because it is both free from multiplicity and frees us from every constriction. The Absolute means not only the liberation from multiple concerns but also from multiple beings: in a word, from multiplicity.

I call it "principle" because it is at the very root of the monastic aspiration, and it characterizes monkhood generally, serving as a criterion to distinguish the monastic dimension from any other. This is all the more important as we are going to underscore some facets of the "new monk," which are conspicuously different from the traditional ones, and this principle will serve as the criterion of continuity with tradition.

Commentary

While traditional monasticism tends toward simplicity (*haplotēs*) through *simplification*, with the accompanying danger of reductionism, contemporary "monasticism" seeks simplicity through *integration*, with the consequent danger of an eclectic juxtaposition. If the temptation of the first is pessimism, that of the second is optimism. Nothing is said about whether or not this new attempt will succeed.

Fuga mundi, contemptus saeculi, kāyotsarga, tyāga, nityānityavāstuviveka, or, in other words, scorn for material values, contempt for the temporal, abandonment of the body, indifference to the political, sense of superiority before cultural values, neglect if not condemnation of the profane, renunciation of the world and of the immense majority of values cherished by mankind, and so on, constituted basic points of the traditional monastic spirituality, whether Jaina, Hindū, Buddhist, Christian, or whatever. The monk's only concern, at least in theory, was the supernatural, the *pāramārthika*, how to acquire *nirvā...a*, the one and only thing : to eliminate *duḥkha*. In order not to do unwarranted violence to the real, this simplification must justify itself by a doctrine that relativizes all those other values and has them appear as secondary in comparison with the quest for the Absolute. If you truly simplify, you should not eliminate any real thing. That would indeed be reductionism. You must simply get rid of appearances, "privations," burdens, and complications. Ultimately, you are bound to say that nothing is lost when you suppress the superfluous, because in truth you are "already there." "There is nothing to lose. It's just that you do not know it yet." Or, as the *Tirukkural* says, "Whatever thing a Man has renounced, by that thing he cannot suffer pain."

Here we have the existential role of doctrines like original sin, *karma*, the intrinsic evil of matter, the provisionality of time, the caducity of the world, and so on. What is certain is that in the search for the one needful thing, the *unum necessarium*, traditional spirituality forgot that this *unum*, to a certain extent, has parts, and that although Mary's portion may be the better one, Martha's is equally a part of the *hen* (the one) toward which the *monachos* or *monotropos*, as the monk was called in the Greco-Christian literature, strove. It tended to forget that if you are overconcerned with looking for the real always beyond everything, you may very well leave reality behind. Or, as Abhinavagupta says, "The essence of reality is to appear."

In sum, what is abandoned is deemed superfluous, if not bad or negative. The monk renounces the flesh and the world either because they are bad, or ultimately unreal, or at least not definitive. The authentic monks, states Dom

G. M. Colombàs, never cared to bear witness. They would have considered it presumptuous, proud, and even hypocritical. They were humbly satisfied with not giving scandal.

The present-day way of thinking is definitely different: the mysticism of transcendence or immanence has been supplanted by the mysticism of integration among all possible values, in the belief that such a synthesis is possible. It is not necessary to be a eunuch, or lame, or maimed to enter the kingdom—perhaps because this kingdom is no longer seen to be situated in a transcendent heaven. One is reminded of that cry of Augustine: "Those who have maimed themselves for the sake of the kingdom of heaven are no longer males. Oh, peculiar foolishness!" How is it possible to consecrate to God a human life if we renounce living it? This was a catchphrase in some Christian monasteries some years ago.

Theologians and exegetes will thus undertake to adapt the texts to their new understanding, but this is not our concern now. We hear it said that Buddha was the first Marxist, and that the Hindū *saṃskāras* were the first rules of hygiene, that fasting purifies the body as much as the soul, that unquestioning obedience strengthens the will, and so on.

The modern monk does not want to *renounce*, except what is plainly sinful or negative; rather he wishes to *transform* all things. Will he succeed? He does not want to destroy but to build; he is not interested in stripping himself of everything but in assimilating it all. The Christian cross itself is seen not so much as a sign of suffering and death as of the intersection of the four directions of the real in one harmonious point equidistant from the four extremes. He strives to be at the center, converting it not into a point without dimensions, but into a perfect sphere that embraces everything.

New winds are moving through millennial monastic institutions, be they Christian, Jaina, Buddhist, or Hindū, and new forms of monastic life are springing up in many places. We have to ask ourselves whether this is a betrayal of the monastic calling, or a new mutation in the same direction or, finally, another form of spirituality that may be experiencing the pangs of its birth within the womb of the old institutions, but which must eventually go its own way once it has reached a certain maturity. We must ask ourselves if what we have here is rupture or continuity.

We could have located the essence of monkhood, as so many texts would confirm, in the effort to unify one's life and reach a unification with the rest of reality. We could have given a true but too general (and flattering) definition of the monk as the *monachos*, that is, a person who aspires before all else to be wholly *one*—not, however, a solitary, "isolated" person, but "all-one," unified. The monk would then be the person seeking, first, a unity within himself, and then a unity with the entire universe. This would apply to any serious person in search of his or her own humanness, and so I would extend the meaning of the word to other human efforts at integration that have never been related to monkhood.

The whole challenge of *modern* monkhood, it seems to me, consists in the impos- sible attempt—at first sight—to acquire by its simplicity the *fullness* of human life. This is what I have called "simplicity through integration," which is properly the archetype of complexity. In order to come to grips with the importance and the challenge of such an attempt, we may now consider the other possible method for reaching the *humanum.*

The Alternative: Secularity or Harmonious Complexity

We have declared blessed simplicity to be the principle that most fundamentally distinguishes monkhood and renders it intelligible. This principle organizes and arranges human life according to that paradigm; but we know that there are many other human efforts at living a full human life that do not draw their inspiration from this archetype. When Abhinavagupta, for instance, says that in order to reach liberation one has to integrate and transform all the elements of the world, he also seems to be expressing a principle alien to the monastic spirituality. When Nicholas of Cusa, for instance, presents God as the "*complexio omnium*," as the encompassing integration of all things, he is no longer in the traditional monastic mood but displays a trait of the European Renaissance. When Teilhard de Chardin sees the evolution of the universe as an increasing complexity, he equally departs from the monastic ideal. On the other hand, when St. John of the Cross tells us that the way to the All is to renounce everything, or when many a tradition tells us that the ultimate reality is void, nothingness, śūnyatā, these voices all express the monastic ideal. Not without a deeper reason than that uncovered by philosophical inquiry did the founder of the most powerful monastic institution in the world, the Buddha, defend the *anātmavāda*, the doctrine of the non-self, as the very center of Buddhist life: there is no substance, no permanence, no ātma*n* underlying the flux of events.

In point of fact, there seems to be a double attitude possible regarding the authentic approach to reality. It could be expressed in two words: simplicity and complexity.

As we have already indicated, these two fundamental human options—that of monkhood and that of secularity—are not taken up merely because of the private opinions of their followers. They are undertaken because they represent two basi- cally different conceptions of reality. You follow the way of simplicity because you believe that the world is reducible to a single point, because you believe that the nature of reality is simple, so that you *really* do not lose anything in the process of simplification and, on the contrary, you win not only a subjective well-being but also an objective truth. You follow the way of complexity because you believe that the structure of the world is pluriform, because you believe that the nature of reality is complex, so that your task is to collect all the seemingly severed bits and pieces of yourself—and, in the final analysis, of the universe—into one multicolored pattern.

Simplicity, as the etymology of the word suggests, indicates a single *plicus* (fold), singleness, a one-without-a-second, without duplicity of any kind. Sim-plicity on the ultimate level is only possible if the multi-plicity is but the fruit of a single reality unfolding. Ultimately, the manifold character of reality is viewed as only secondary, contingent. Simplicity as an ideal implies the belief that either the multiplicity is reducible to unity or that there is no way of salvaging all those "inferior" elements, since they belong to a merely apparent world. There is no point in wasting precious life and human effort in utopian fantasies of a paradise on earth, of a just human order where everybody will be happy, and the like.

This attitude of simplicity entails a kind of universal and ultimate pessimism regarding the secondary structures of reality. These structures cannot be redeemed. And yet we have also to offer a full human life to those who live in an unjust society. This they may achieve by simply stepping out of it—and into another world. We have already mentioned the underlying monistic underpinnings of the way of simplicity: the ultimate reality—what really matters—is monistic, namely, it is unequivocally one. This is an implicit assumption not always patent, because most of the time we do not draw out the ultimate consequences of our attitudes, and also because many other cultural and religious factors with their clear-cut dualistic doctrines often counterbalance these latent monistic tendencies. Life, after all, does not need to be consistent; or rather, it is in fact not always logically consistent.

Reduced to its bare bones, this first basic attitude reposes on a monotheistic belief in a perfect, and thus simple, God at the very source of reality. To return to that source is the meaning of life.

On the other hand, *complexity*, as the very word suggests, implies the result of "joining" all the elements so that they may fit together in a whole, in a concordant and superior unity. Complexity is only possible if the internal tendencies of the different constituents can be compounded with one another and if, in the final instance, all of them form "parts" of a whole from which they have originated, or evolved, or become somewhat detached. Complexity as an ideal implies the belief that there is a supereminent unity holding everything together. It entails a kind of universal and ultimate optimism regarding the possibility of establishing a cosmic or personal order in this universe of ours. It does not believe in tragedy. It assumes the compatibility of all that there is, and the possible reconciliation of the disparate elements of reality. It minimizes evil.

Those who take the attitude of complexity believe that the structure of reality is pluralistic, so that you commit a sin of reductionism against reality if you attempt to reduce everything to a single principle. Reality is complex, and realization implies reaching the highest possible complexity.

Reduced to its bare bones, this second basic attitude reposes on a pluralistic belief ultimately incompatible with the symbol of a monotheistic God as a perfectly simple reality.

It is also clear here that the belief in a plurality of irreducible elements is a basic assumption of this attitude. It is worth the effort to bring together the diverse constitutive factors of reality because they are all real, and the jigsaw puzzle can indeed be assembled into an orderly picture. It may very well be that the real solution exists only on a transcendent plane, in a later world or an eschatology still to come. Both simplicity and complexity are, in fact, dynamic attitudes that do not need to be immediately realizable on the given plane of ordinary existence. This reference to a superhuman point is expressed in the two adjectives we are using to qualify these two basic human options.

Blessed simplicity underscores the fact that it is not an automatic process, but one that has to be wrought with total dedication, by an "extra-ordinary" grace and through a transformation of the very structures of reality. The monastic spirituality is not so naïve as to launch us on a trip in which everything fades away at the end. On the contrary, it will assure us that in the end nothing is lost, all is regained, but in a higher, incomprehensible sphere in which "things" appear as what, in reality, they are. It is not, as the novice may tend to believe, that the rivers and mountains are *again* rivers and mountains, but that for the first time the rivers and mountains are *real* rivers and mountains, because the reality of rivers and mountains is more than their geological appearance.

Harmonious complexity means above all that everything has to be transformed in order that it all may be joined and fit together. But here transformation does not mean an ontological change, as it were, so that beings (*entes*) are converted into the Being (*Esse*), for instance, but instead a thoroughgoing enhancement of their actual being; although the language, in English, is bound to sound the same, the meaning is quite different.

Both attitudes then imply a process, a becoming, a change. Yet again the difference becomes clear when we consider that the former attitude stresses a change in consciousness, and the latter a change in external structures. Monastic spirituality is directly concerned with changing our awareness, with transforming our very selves. Secular spirituality, on the other hand, is mainly concerned with altering the circumstances, the surrounding world.

We could go on describing these two apparently irreducible views or rather experiences of reality, but we might best now turn our hand to sketching their possible relationship, and leave for the final chapter of the book our attempt at reconciliation.

The first thing to note is their respective insufficiencies. The whole of reality cannot be reduced to one single principle. In spite of all the subtle ontological distinctions on the ultimate level, a single principle would necessarily annihilate all the rest. There has also to be dynamism and a certain type of pluralism within the highest unity. On the other hand, reality cannot be sheer unrelated plurality either. In spite of all the differences and irreducibilities, the very awareness of plurality entails a higher unity. There has also to be a certain relationship between the ultimate ingredients of reality. This is, I submit, what the doctrine of the Trinity as well as that of *advaita* stand for. Here is where I speak of the *cosmotheandric* character of reality. Or we could equally put it in the remarkable words of Parmenides, at the inception of the Western tradition: Reality is given at every moment as totality (*pân*), oneness (*hen*), and complexity (*synechēs*). This is probably the language of most mystics, and to it we shall return after having presented the announced nine *sūtras* with their corre- sponding *bhāṣyas* and *tīkās* (glosses and commentaries).

Nine Sūtras

In order to provide an overview of the nine canons, we give them here before the corresponding glosses and commentaries.

1. *The Breakthrough of the Primordial Aspiration*
2. *The Primacy of Being over Doing and Having*
3. *Silence over the Word*
4. *Mother Earth prior to the Fellowship of Men*
5. *Overcoming Spatiotemporal Parameters*
6. *Transhistorical Consciousness above Historical Concern*
7. *The Fullness of the Person, Rather Than of the Individual*
8. *The Primacy of the Holy*
9. *The Memory of the Ultimate and of His Constant Presence*

Sūtra 1. The Breakthrough of the Primordial Aspiration

Gloss

Simplicity is not just given. It has to be conquered by overcoming the world of multiplicity. Dazzled by the many facets of the world and the many desires of our hearts, we have to retrieve the essential unity of things and of ourselves if we are to be what we really are. In our first incursions into life we might have been deceived, if not wounded.

The monastic archetype lies hidden beneath the ordinary appearances of things and of human life. It is not a superficial whim. One cannot begin the quest for blessed simplicity just by abandoning things or wandering around to escape the burden of one's own duties and responsibilities. World literature is hard on monks. The harshest words against fake specimens of monks are spoken by the monks themselves. It suffices to read the *Rule of the Master.* Of the four kinds of monks only two are worthy of the name, and the other two are condemned in the most execrable words. The monk is not just someone who wishes to be a monk. It requires a breakthrough, an initiation, a *dīkṣā*, a new birth. You have to be a twiceborn, a *dvija*, in order even to begin. All monastic traditions stress the *compunctio cordis*, the *conversio morum*, the true *metanoia*, the firm resolve to leave behind the "things of this world," the *laukika* and the stern urge for liberation, plus the practice of all the virtues. Âaṅkara's *Vivekacūḍāmaṇi* could serve as a classical example here. The desire for liberation (*mokṣa*), *mumukṣūtva* has to be a burning fire. You have to knock again and again at the door to the monastery, or touch repeatedly the feet of the guru to be taken seriously. Not all who say, "Lord, Lord!" are fit for the kingdom.

There has to be a rupture of planes, as any initiation requires, but the proper plane here is especially the tissue of one's own heart.

The heart here stands, of course, for the core of the person. This heart has to be broken, or, rather, once the heart is broken open one can begin anew by setting out to make it whole again in a wider and deeper way than before. The heart breaks because *hamartia*, sin; *duḥkha*, suffering; *avidyā*, ignorance, injustice... per vade the world. "Save me from death, afflicted as I am by the unquenchable fire," is the typical plea of the Hindū candidate to the monastic way, as Âaṅkara writes. Monkhood is not merely a continuation of "ordinary" or empirical life. Initiation is needed. But the initiation is not automatic. It presupposes an aspiration: the primordial aspiration of Man, that of becoming what he truly is—or is supposed to be—has to break through. A discovery or revelation, dim as it may be, has first to be there. The Christian tradition can speak of the baptism of desire only because the desire for purification is essential to the Christian initiation. The primitive monks, for instance, never claimed to do anything but take seriously the baptismal initiation, the plunge into the waters of death and resurrection which begins one's growth into that Christic sphere where the entire renewed Body of creation commences its expansion. Christian monks did not want to be special Christians, but just Christians. It was only when people felt that the praxis of evangelical demands had begun to relax that the monks were singled out as an example for all Christians, not because they did something peculiar, but merely because they tried to practice Christian virtues—which Paul twice summed up as *haplotēs kardìas*, *simplicitas cordis*, simplicity of the heart. Even at that time, this simplicity already meant also the purity of the total person at the core, at the source.

This break has to be both personal and public or sociological. It is not enough to have felt in one's heart the all-pervading reality of *duḥkha*, the prison of *saṃsāra*, the *hamartia tou kosmou*, the sin of the world; it is also necessary to fall at the feet of the guru, to leave your house and/or your family, to "go to the mountains," to renounce the world, to publicly become a renouncer, to enter the *saṃgha*, to practice *xeniteia*, expatriation, or some similar act. You need to break with society, even if this means that you no longer perform the sacred rites. The entire monastic literature bristles with sarcasm against those who deem it possible to be monks while living with their families or in the bazaar or town. The *fuga mundi* is more, although certainly not less, than a merely "spiritual" attitude. The habit does not make the monk, but certainly it is the monk who makes the habit. You may ignore the pearl for a time, but at a certain moment you have to sell all that you have and buy it. The monk goes *extra mundum.* Monastic asceticism is both inner and outer.

It is necessary to underscore this first canon, not only because it is essential to monkhood, but also because it is perhaps its most visible and probably most specific trait. This *sūtra* has a sociological aspect that is specifically monastic.

It is also necessary to stress its importance because there are misunderstandings, on the one hand, and difficulties in putting it into practice, on the other.

There can be no monasticism without this experience of conversion, of turning around and turning inward, of stripping off the very many hindering things, of abandoning the "usual," the "normal," and even the secure and often reasonable way. As one *Upaniṣad* says, "On the very day one is 'brokenhearted,' on that same day one becomes a renouncer"; one brokenhearted, that is, one indifferent to the world, a disillusioned person.

This experience can take, obviously, the most variegated forms. It does not need to be a psychological shock, but at any rate it has to be a break from which there is no return, as texts from East and West confirm. *Vairāgya* means disgust for the world and, literally, hostility (*vaīra*) to it. To be a man (a hero, a *vīraḥ*) is to fight the world, as this etymology suggests.

The "broken heart" is only a one-sided metaphor, for in truth it is only a nega- tive expression when seen from this shore of *saṃsāra*, of mere creatureliness. It is the "old" heart that is broken open, often with violence, so that it may give way to a "new" heart and a healed person with the incipient throbbings of the new life of compassion, love, and true understanding. The metaphor is one-sided because, seen from the far shore, from the new life, it is not a broken but a renewed heart.

Monastic life is also a life of peace, joy, and serenity. The heart that has been— that could be—broken was a wounded heart, a sinful heart, a heart of stone. It had to be broken because the human condition is unjust, ignorant, sinful. The monk has to break through the thick walls of this heart, the walls of callousness and selfishness in himself and around him; he has to break through mere temporality and inauthenticity in order to be on his way. *Ahamkāra* and *abhimana*, selfishness and conceit, have to be, so to speak, "exposed," broken wide open, so that the true ātman, the real "I" may emerge.

Opening oneself to primordial aspiration is the very beginning of spiritual life. Now this aspiration alone, necessary as it is, cannot produce the effects to which it aspires. Here the will is impotent. The aspiration is only the condition for what follows. It does not produce the goodness it aspires to.... For this, something else is required. Now, who is going to open this heart? You cannot do this by yourself, try as you might. No degree of personal suffering or of social disorder is sufficient to cause this *metanoia*. Many see this, and escape or fall into despair. Their hearts remain closed. Here we touch the mystery of this first *sūtra*. Somebody, something, God, the *ātman*, the *guru*, grace, love... has to touch or strike my heart and open it up. I am somewhat passive throughout. It happens to me. And for this, I can give no ultimate reason—because it is a gift, although it may often appear as a burden and even as a curse.

Moreover—except in a very few cases, and even these exceptional people have to work to maintain that heart open, pure, and simple, time and again—for most people this is a continuous process, an increasing openness, a constant purification of the ego that persists in returning to the level from which it has been dethroned. Here is the place of sacrifice as a constitutive element in the actual nature of the real. Sacrifice performs this exchange of hearts, this opening up of our lives, this rupture of planes, this throwing off of the banality of merely instinctive life.

Some of the classical Indian *sūtras*, precisely because their study is for the sake of *mokṣa* or salvation, begin with the adverb *atha*: here, now; and tradition has interpreted this to mean exactly this new beginning on the path to liberation, which implies a rupture with the past or with what has been learned so far. Thus begins the path of the *yoga-sūtra*, *brahma-sūtra*, etc.

For reasons we cannot develop here, I have called *aspiration* this primal dynamism of the human being—fruit of the spirit, rooted in the very spiritual nature of Man—and not desire, mainly in order to dispel any possible misunderstanding from some monastic spiritualities, especially the Buddhist, which condemn straightaway any sort of desire, be it for a bad or even for a good object. Desire is the activity of the empirical ego. Aspiration is the breath—and even the blowing—of the spirit within.

Commentary

The modern monk cannot bypass the need for conversion; he cannot do without initiation. And every initiation not only means the beginning of a new life, it also implies a break with the previous stage of existence. But there are at least two impor- tant variations in the way this *vairāgya*, this *compunctio cordis*, *penthos*, repentance, may be experienced.

First, many practices of the ancient style seem not only obsolete, but harmful and negative. The corporal mortifications, for instance, and the detachment from the affairs of the world often appear incompatible with the contemporary monastic spirit. The "world" has shifted from meaning "bishops and women," to quote a face- tious remark of the first Christian monks—that is, from the dangers of the social life of the community, civil and religious—to the political and socioeconomic structures, along with the ideologies of all sorts that represent a danger to combat and an enemy to conquer. To fight the world and its demons today may mean to combat the system and its technocrats.

This shift of the parameters of the world is all the more important to emphasize since many of the traditional forms of monasticism still operate in the institutional way with the old pattern while, anthropologically, the new pattern has already emerged—thus creating sometimes unnecessary tensions. It is not that the world and its ways are not to be renounced; it is that the world is no longer seen in the theatres, in the schools, in "profane letters," in sex, or in political activity. The world is seen, instead, as we shall still have occasion to show, in the "worldly spirit" that today takes most prevalently the forms of social injustice of every sort, political manipulation of all kinds, and, in general, the prevailing system of a competitive society in which people just do not have the same tools, talents, opportunities, and desire to compete. Perhaps here money (*mamonas*) is the invariant.

Much has been said and written about world-affirming and world-denying spiritualities. All too often one has not sufficiently considered the different conceptions of that world which some spiritualities are supposed to affirm and others to deny. If a certain Vedantic monasticism, for instance, rightly or wrongly according to our opinion, but nonetheless in fact, believes the world to be sheer illusion, then the corresponding world-denying attitude amounts to a true life-affirming and reality- affirming attitude. The modern monks are interested in many of the things of "this world" because they believe that the shaping of this world is a religious and even a contemplative concern not alien to or at odds with the monastic vocation. The dichotomies between the temporal and the eternal, the sacred and the secular, the humanist and the Hindū or the Christian or the religious in general, the natural, and the supernatural, and so on, are no longer considered valid. I shall call this the impact of secularity, and undertake to explain it later.

In other words, while traditional monasticism often insisted on the sinfulness of the world and the need to break one's heart, the contemporary monk would like to discover the positive side of Man's primordial aspiration to the infinite, to full- ness, to perfect joy—and almost takes it for granted that hindrances will have to be overcome and obstacles conquered.

The modern monk stresses the distinction between that primordial *aspiration* of Man, which triggers the dynamism toward liberation, justice, and peace, and the *desires* of the human being, which entangle our lives in trifles, banalities, selfishness, and sin. The new monk, having heard so much about the suppression of all desires, sometimes fears that the basic aspiration of his being may also be somewhat dulled or blunted. It has happened more than once that young aspirants are "turned off " and go away because of the long faces and lack of joy that they seem to have discerned among the elders who were supposed to be their models. I am not blindly approving the fact that most modern gurus appear as smiling figures. I am just saying that joy, *ānanda*, is also a monastic virtue and an essential ingredient of the primordial aspiration of Man. Tradition and modernity would agree on this. It is only that this bliss seems, sometimes, to the modern monk, either too high, because postponed to another life, or too deep, because hidden beneath too many cautions, warnings, or just unfriendly appearances.

The *second* variation that the present-day mentality introduces to this first canon is the secular link between the individual monk and the rest of the world, including all the social values and secondary causes that seem to maneuver the destiny of humankind. In other words, the disciple goes to the master because his heart is broken, or because he aspires to the infinite, and he asks for instruction and guidance; but too often he is uneasy and may even revolt if he feels that what the master wants is to further break his will by obliging him, for instance, to do irrational things. The famous watering of a stick could serve as an extreme example. The new monk, first of all, has lost the innocence or naïveté needed not to see clearly through the psychological motivations of his superior. Second, he feels humiliated—not in his pride, but in his dignity—to be treated in such an artificial manner. Third, he is also concerned with the stick and with the real plant and takes it to be an affront to the earth, the possible plant, and the stick to indulge in such a mockery. Or maybe he should interpret the injunction as an attempt to check on his sense of humor? The Zen Master or the Desert Father may still command irrational things, but the disciple must nevertheless understand that the rationale behind the injunction is to help him transcend the mental level.

The breaking of the heart surely does not mean that others have to break my heart artificially, but only that I have truly arrived at such a conviction with the painful aid of authentic experiences—and not by means of artificial experiments. Without a doubt, the monk wants his will to be set in tune with the will of God or the master or simply with the nature of things or of reality, but not just to be broken for the sake of breaking it so as to be prey to whatever injunction may come at him. To be sure, I have forced the colors of a certain traditional spirituality in order to put the variation more forcefully, but we may perhaps have succeeded in doing that.

Sūtra 2. The Primacy of Being over Doing and Having

Gloss

Being is one, or it can be unified. Doing and having, on the other hand, entail multiplicity. Monastic spirituality in its search for simplicity defends the primacy of being although it may consider it empty, *śūnya*, and in fact nonbeing, *asat*, *mu*; or full, complete, *plērōma*, and in fact supreme or absolute Being. In every case it is to being before doing and having that is given primacy. Different schools consider the Being as more or less static, or instead affirm that the Being is pure act. But what is essential is just *to be* (grounded in reality).

One of the words consecrated by tradition to express this second canon is "contemplation." And contemplation, in spite of the origin of the word, stands for *theoreia*, *jñāana*, a knowledge that amounts to being. In point of fact, contemplation is the activity that situates us in an open space from which we can observe and contribute to the course of the universe; or as the *Gītā* will say, that activity that delights in the well-being of all beings, or that maintains the world in cohesion (*lokasaṃgraha*). Contemplation begins by purporting to be the ultimate means to attain the final end of human life, namely, to sustain the cosmos or, in terms of Christian mysticism, to create, redeem, and glorify (divinize) the universe along with God. But soon it is recognized that the human condition cannot transcend itself. The ultimate means thus became in itself the very end of life, the fullness of existence. Put another way, the means have evaporated; there only remain what appeared as means, converted into ends. Therefore, for the contemplative, it does not make sense to speak of a model to imitate or even of a path to follow. The contemplative life is simply life, life in its fullest sense: for some it is the discovery of the person or of the humanbeing; for others, the discovery of the being of all beings. At any rate, the value of each being lies in its being what it *is*, not in what it does or has. The intuition of the Being, thus stripped of all spurs or inducements: this is what the monk glimpses. We do not have to justify our existence by what we do or how useful it is to others. That would only instrumentalize our lives and convert them into mere means for some other thing, for a better future in a vertical or a horizontal line. Life is an end in itself. In this manner contemplation became more and more opposed to action. And in this way the monk became the contemplative par excellence, as against the active religious people. The *saμnyāsin* does not perform any rites, the hermit lives long periods without the sacraments. The monk is normally not engaged in action.

We would need many other reflections in order to deal more thoroughly with this issue. The monk, for instance, is a monk because he is in search of enlighten- ment. His whole life is geared toward this. And yet he knows that the very desire for enlightenment is somehow an obstacle to it. Paradoxically, we could say that enlightenment is thus the goal of monasticism, but not the aim of the monk. You are after *satori* and to get it you become a monk, but you do not look for it, as it were. You are open and perhaps full of hope, but you have no expectations.

In any event, monkhood is not primarily concerned with doing anything or having something. The central point is the development of the core of the human person to its fullest, in whatever sense this core or this fullness may be interpreted.

Commentary

But what is this life? Traditionally, the primacy of being came to be regarded as a primacy over doing : as *theoreia* before *praxis*; as the *jñānavadins* before the *karmakāṇḍins*; as contemplation being more important than action; or, as the Scholastics formulated it, *operari sequitur esse* (action follows being). Further, this being aspires to become the absolute Being in which there is no distinction between having and doing, being and becoming—or even between "being" and "Non-Being." The contemporary monastic spirit equally defends this primacy, but being is not considered to be merely a theoretic vision, pure *gnōsis* or mere *darśana*; it is not just an intellectual operation that relegates praxis to an inferior plane or a secondary role. To refer to the Scholastic dictum cited earlier, its reverse is equally stressed here: *esse sequitur operari.* Praxis and theory are not put in dialectical opposition. It is not a case where the former rules the latter or vice versa, because ultimately the one does not exist without the other. All praxis has a nucleus of theory, and all theory is the fruit of some praxis. True action is contemplative, and authentic contemplation acts. Such a dichotomy does not exist in reality.

The new monk stresses the unity of being and doing, but at the same time under- scores the distinction between being and having. Having is not simply riches, it is also the power of the means. And having can exert a deadening weight on being. A task of monastic spirituality is, also, to lighten being in order that it may truly be. Having is everything that being has not yet been able to assimilate. I have stocks of food, but the daily bread is not having; it is being. Having is all the artificial trappings that we accumulate; it is the knowledge stored in our computer hard disk or in books and not really transformed into our very being. Having is about all the accessories that serve some purpose at first, but further down the line leave us entangled in the means without allowing us to reach our true goals. Having is all that bows us down under the weight of our sacks of provisions. Having is what prevents us from acting in a contemplative way. Having is the equivalent of the many fabricated interests that impede the truly purifying action that many would call revolutionary. The Eucharist is to be eaten, not displayed on a golden throne; the Buddha is to be discovered in oneself rather than worshipped in emerald or in a *stūpa.* The contemporary monk does not so much want to wash his hands of all doing as to free it from all having, *parigraha*, precisely in order to let it achieve its proper ends. He wants no chains on his feet. He wants to be able to go where the Spirit leads with all his being, which no longer "has" any having, because it is pure act.

The modern monk resents the fact that the traditional monk has often been "condemned" to social inaction under the pretext of just being, as if the two were at loggerheads. He would like to be active in the world as an outcome of his own being; he stresses poverty of having in order to attain a higher freedom in doing. Will they succeed?

Sūtra 3. Silence Over the Word

Gloss

Silence is one. Words are many. Strictly speaking, this gloss should be left blank, but priority does not mean exclusivity. In Trinitarian categories we could stress the attention the monk gives to the Spirit over the Word, without this implying absolute priority. It does imply, however, being ever attentive to the spirit in the word. Expressed in philosophical categories, we are dealing with the priority of myth over the *logos.* And, speaking with moral overtones, we could explain this canon by saying that it deals with a new innocence that no longer has anything to say, because it feels that everything has already been said, and that speech is nothing but the cloak of reality and all too often its tomb. Those who listen to the silence out of which the word emerges often have no need of words, and from those who have not discovered this silence the very word will conceal it. The *kevala-jñānī*, or the *kevalin*, the perfect Jaina monk who has already obtained omniscience, neither thinks, nor speaks, nor preaches. The three *yogas*, mind, speech, and body, progressively disappear. He has even dispensed with teaching the saving doctrine, except for the *tīrthānkara* whose mission is preaching. The monks speak and write little and often do not sign their writings, although through their disciples we know their names. The Buddha commends the noble silence, and "the silent one" is a synonym for the monk. Each word comes out of silence and when possible accompanies it.

The experience of silence is itself silent and therefore does not compete with the word. The very formulation that speaks of priority is misleading. From the side of silence there is no priority. Silence does not say anything. Nor is there any priority from the side of the word. It would represent a contradiction for the *logos* to affirm by means of that very *logos* that there is something preceding it. Nonetheless, human experience through the ages tells us repeatedly that the *tao* that can be expressed is not the *tao*; that those who know do not speak and those who speak do not know; that it is understood by those who do not understand and is not understood by those who understand; that only those whose spirit is poor shall truly see God, and so on. There is a spiritual experience that is not conscious of itself. There is a meditation without thoughts: it does not think, nor does it even think that it does not think; and yet it is not simply a dream or total unconsciousness. There is something awakened in us that later on can possibly be incarnated in word, but which allows us to see that the word is word precisely because it is itself incarnated by the work and grace of the spirit.

True "orthodoxy" is not the correct formulation of doctrine but the authentic experience of the "glory of the truth." It is nothing but the other side of orthopraxis. The monk does not understand doctrinal disputes when they are extrapolated outside of their context. What in modern times has come to be called the "sociology of knowledge" is what monks of all time have experienced; that is, that every formulation is dependent on a set of factors that relativizes it.

To cite more than one tradition: "In the beginning was the word," but the word was not the beginning, since it emerged out of it. It is not that there exists a thing that cannot be said, or that there exists an ineffable something behind the *logos.* Silence does not speak, nor has it anything to say. Silence has no message. Authentic silence is not the repression of the word, but rather the nonreflexive consciousness of the very womb of the *logos*; yet this is true in such a manner that if the umbilical cord uniting the two is severed, both miscarry—the silence is dispelled and the word dies. For this reason, the cultivation of silence cannot be commanded, nor can it consist in repressing the word. Recalling the classical distinction between nature and culture, the word belongs to the latter, and silence to the former. There is no culture of silence; silence is natural, or it is not silence. We naturally keep quiet when we have nothing to say.

Paradoxically, albeit understandably, the traditional monk takes relief from his silence in prayer, be it individual and silent or communal and vocal. It seems, more often than not, as if the silence is not broken by "talking" to God or by reciting interminable mantras. In a cenobitic setting, the most marked characteristic of the traditional monk is a life of prayer. Silence blossoms in prayer. The monk only speaks to others on rare occasions, but on the other hand he chants, recites, studies, and meditates constantly—his *politeuma*, his *conversatio*, his homeland, "his citizenship is in heaven." It is the others from below who climb up to the high places where monks live, to ask their advice. The monk does not speak but is questioned. Curiosity is a sin. It does not even interest him to preach by example. He has submitted everything to God, to the *Dharma*, to what is, and he is not concerned with interfering directly in the course of events. His silence is acosmic. Not everything needs to be expressed in words. Life, gesture, attitude: all may be equally expressive. But there is no need, either, to express everything. Things can find their proper place in the abyss of silence.

Silence does not mean to be numb or dumb. Monastic silence is what it is because it has overcome the mental and passed beyond words, because it has transcended thoughts. This is why monks are not at ease among intellectuals. And, of course, monastic discipline will recommend silence as a regimen against dissipation.

Commentary

The modern disciple has learned well the lesson of his predecessors and will not fall into the temptation of trying to use the mass media to make himself known or to influence others. However, he is equally aware of an unbreakable bond between silence and the word, and fears that the former will degenerate if it is not incarnated in the *logos*, if it does not descend into the marketplace of Men and, at the very least, listen to them. He fears that his life will be short-circuited if he isolates himself from the clamor of his fellow Men who ask for bread, demand justice, and sing and dance to the sun, the moon, the seasons, or to the religious and civil events and festivities of their time. The disciple wants to listen to the world, although this may later trouble his silence. But it may also make his silence more vital and perhaps more fruitful. The demons and *asuras* of the cold and lonely regions have been converted into the shouts and cries of the human crowds. So there they go, these modern monks.... The daily papers with their news have been converted into spiritual reading because they are the subject matter of meditation.

The silence of the modern monk is not only at the beginning, holding fast to the very source of the word. The modern monk does not like high walls, enclosures, and lonely places where all the noise and stirring of the world cannot reach him. He tries to find the silence at the end of every word as well; he would like to let the exuberance of the world land again in the silence, so that the *perichōrēsis*, *circumincessio*, or circular dynamism of the word might complete its return into silence. There has been a continuous descending of monks from the high mountains of the gods to the lowly plains of their fellow humans.

This canon shows clearly one of the places where the mutation, the split, or simply the possibility of the other option in favor of complexity, may become more visible. There is the danger that the modern monk may pay lip service to the primacy of silence without ultimately believing in it—and here the metaphor of "lip service" is ironically appropriate: to speak about silence is already to betray it. Silence does not speak, does not bear witness, does not even hint at anything, because ultimately silence *is not*. In the beginning *is* the Word. Silence is fully acosmic. Silence *is* the absence of *logos*. Silence is not intelligible. Silence does not hide itself, because there is nothing to hide. Silence is not in favor of silence, because it is not in favor of anything. Nor does silence defend and justify itself either, because silence has nothing to defend: silence is not a subject matter about which you talk. Silence is not against the *logos*; it is simply prior to it. The *logos* is the sacrifice of silence, its immolation in the word. Silence is the Father, source, and origin of the whole divinity, according to a Christian interpretation of the Trinity.

In point of fact, only very few monastic movements have been radical enough to consider the *muni*, the silent one, as the perfect monk. The Jaina monks and the Zen monks are probably the most representative, together with some Hindū *saṃnyāsin* and a few Christian solitaries. But most surely the true silent ones are invisible to our eyes and totally hidden from our consciousness. Even they don't know about their silence. Nevertheless, even without taking extreme positions, the traditional monk reveres silence and values it more highly than the word.

The modern monk is often torn apart on this issue. He loves silence, indeed, and would like to keep a balance between the apophatic and the kataphatic, but it is hard for him to believe that he has not to speak when it would amount to repression not to allow his thoughts and words to penetrate and influence his surroundings. He is conscious of having a mission, and this fact alone makes pure silence impossible. He might have lost that innocence that he still may admire in the "fools for Christ" and the *mauna*, hermits or wanderers. But the lost innocence cannot be recovered. And a *second* innocence is a contradiction in terms! Perhaps he may strive toward a *new* innocence, but this new innocence has already crossed the threshold of the *logos* and proceeds apace into unknown realms. To put it more simply: the modern monk knows how to read and write; he cannot pretend to be illiterate.

We know very well—see Dom Leclercq and his fascinating book on the subject— that this tension is not just a relic of yesteryear, as the Buddhist tradition also demonstrates. Yet what was once the personal vocation of the few today becomes the general situation of the majority. The fact that so many Christian monks were also ordained as priests, one of whose functions is the *diakonia tou logou*, the "ministry of the word," shows that this dilemma is all too real.

Sūtra 4. Mother Earth Prior to the Fellowship of Men

Gloss

The earth is one; people are many. The earth is simpler than Man, who is more complex. If it is certain that the monk has his gaze fixed on the invisible, often called "the beyond," the "center," transcendence, God, *ātman*, *nirvāṇa*, and so on, it is no less certain that he has his feet firmly planted on the ground. The monk stands, in a certain sense, between heaven and earth, with the consequent danger of forgetting the intermediate world of his fellow Men. Of the three worlds, the *triloka* of which almost all traditions speak, the monk seems to live more in the netherworld of spirits, demons, *asuras*; more in the telluric than in the human social world in which so-called civilized humanity moves and bustles. The monk has a certain chthonic-telluric consciousness that characterizes him; he does not belong like the ants or bees or other humans to a productive society, but to a living cosmos like the wild things and the seasons, even if it is called the kingdom within. The monk cultivates this earth and all the spirits that vivify her. The monk lives in communion with the cosmos; he is in touch with the sap that runs through the earth—and with good and evil spirits alike. At the same time he looks toward the heavens, the beyond, the first world, and it is as if he almost bypasses the second world, the human sphere that is often seen as transitory, provisional, and rather irrelevant, if not straightaway illusory and unreal. But our point here is the monk's rootedness in the last of the three worlds.

Certainly it is not solely the privilege of monks to live with the seasons and celebrate the arrival of spring, advent, new year, and the festivals tied to earthly, astrological, and atmospheric cycles; but it is the monk who primordially celebrates such festivities with the greatest independence from their sociological or agricultural effects. The monk leads a cosmic existence that then allows him to forget, or at least neglect, the historical aspect of human life. Social issues, for example, have never been his strong point, nor have historical problems much concerned him. Between heaven and earth the monk seems to live in a vertical posture, inclining toward Mother Earth only the better to lift himself up to look toward God, or the Gods, or the nameless Mystery above his head. He wants to live alone because he feels in his being the vital current that descends from above to the depths of the earth. He has little time or interest for the horizontal currents that circulate between human beings. Only when heaven and earth seem to meet (as in the Crusades of the European twelfth and thirteenth centuries) will the monk take an interest in "politics." And often he betrays a singular lack of historical understanding (as the same example of the Crusades shows). The monk is a cosmic being who tries to disentangle himself from this cosmos; he is not a social worker. The monk struggles and deals with the elements more than with his fellow beings.

Alchemy, even more than astrology, was a monastic occupation. Alchemy is not a means to riches or power, but to a total transmutation that only begins with matter. Alchemy is "the art of bringing to completion something which has not been completed," as Paracelsus put it, paraphrasing the common belief of his time that all things had been created incomplete. The monk undertakes this task by beginning with Mother Earth and her elements, which are not only the physical but also the psychic ones, to utilize the modern parlance. Indeed, all the elements are also spiritual forces.

Commentary

The Canon of the Disciple faithfully follows the Rule of the Master here: *ora et labora*, and this labor consists in the cultivation of himself and Mother Earth. But the population of the earth's primitive inhabitants—*bhūtas*, angels, *asuras*, elves, *yakṣas*, and marauding demons—has dwindled nowadays.

What is important for the modern monk is earth herself. She, too, is a victim of the voraciousness of human beings, who have abused her more than all the other living beings put together did. Humans have not simply taken their sustenance from the earth. They have further exploited and violated her, trying to climb to heaven— although this Tower of Babel is beginning to crumble, if indeed it was ever built. It is not so much the living spirits who still populate the earth that worry the modern monk as he tries to reestablish a relationship of harmony and collaboration with her, but the living earth herself. To work the earth does not mean to exploit her for one's own gain. It means to cultivate her as one would a friendship or a garden, not as one would plunder a mine. Traditional monasticism offers us plenty of examples of such cultivation: cheese, wines, honey, and crafts. Mother Earth is returning to life and recovering the soul that from ancient times she has always been believed to possess: *anima mundi.*

The attitude of the monk before the earth should not be confused with a fundamentally aesthetic posture. It is not so much the beauty of a garden that engages him as it is the pulsing life of a forest; it is not the immensity of a landscape as much as the freedom of the waters and the spontaneity of the natural cycles. The monk is not a "primitive," but he can claim to be a *primordial*, not limiting his life to the merely rational or aesthetic or social. It is not only that he attempts to recover his own body, but equally that he tries to save Mother Earth.

We are not referring here simply to a Franciscan or Zen attitude with regard to nature; we are trying to point out the more generalized sharing of a community of destiny and a vital metabolism with all that is earthly. A major part of cult, or sacrifice, consists in linking Mother Earth with all her elements for the revitalization of life; from the Vedic *yajña* to the Christian Eucharist, examples can easily be multiplied. The Vedic *keśin* and the Jaina *digambara* do not go naked; they walk clothed, but clothed only with the wind and covered by the air. As in the hymn we cited earlier from the Íg-*veda*, "Mother Earth protects them."

The unification of life cannot be carried out without the collaboration of the earth and without integrating her in the process. Not only is the body exalted; so, too, is the whole earth. The monk seeks solitary places, but he does not exile himself. He does not flee from the earth; he roots himself in her. Most monks caress her with their bare feet; and the *sādhus* when they die are not cremated like everyone else but buried in the bosom of Mother Earth, or more often thrown into the abyss of the Waters.

But the modern monk is not satisfied with this alone. Can he live in communion with the earth and in community with his fellow beings as well? He conserves a certain wish to retire to the deserts, but he has seen these invaded and occupied by instruments of atomic destruction. There seems to be a shift from the cosmic to the human, and also an inclination to find the divine more in Man than in the cosmos. He likes the earth, feels close to her, but he cannot dispense with the fellowship of Man. Modern science has demythicized the earth. The modern monk may not go along with this all the way, but he has suffered its impact. He reacts by adopting a less cosmocentric and more anthropocentric attitude.

It is here that the canon of the disciple situates and frames monastic prayer. The monk is traditionally the Man of prayer. But his rite is as much cosmic as human.

His prayer is not so much petition as praise, and in many traditions is more a partici- pation in the rhythms of the universe than a hymn of glory or a cry for help. The monastic prayer of the disciple is all of this, but it is primordially a contribution to the interactions that govern the universe, an active introit to the coredemption of the cosmos, a revitalization of the spiritual content of the world, and a contribution to the total atmosphere of reality breathed by all beings. Cult is the celebration of the order of reality.

Sūtra 5. Overcoming Spatiotemporal Parameters

Gloss

Monastic existence does not move solely or principally in time and space. Interiority, on the one hand, and transcendence, on the other, are classical monastic categories. The spatiotemporal involvement is foreign to the monk. Reality goes beyond time and space. Human destiny is not exhausted by us achieving our goals in time and space. Again here we see the principle of simplicity at work.

True life, traditional monasticism would say, has little to do with this mundane life that unfolds in time and space. The monk bears witness to the beyond, to the overcoming of worldly, temporal, transitory cares and tasks.

"The life above is the true life." At best, this one here below serves to make us aware and worthy of the other.

Naturally, the overcoming of spatiotemporal parameters cannot be achieved overnight. Monastic formation takes this into account and leads the candidate through a lengthy process of purification and enlightenment. There is room for growth and becoming in traditional monasticism, but the goal is clear: total disentanglement from the structures of this cosmos, *saṃsāra*, world.

Commentary

Here also there exists a tension between the classical monastic spirituality and its contemporary interpretation. While the former understands this "going beyond" to necessitate an abandonment of material parameters as a prerequisite for achieving the definitive end, the latter reinterprets this same "going beyond" as the discovery of a new dimension that does not render superfluous the material elements of reality but rather complements and transforms them. While the first emphasizes transcendence, the second underscores the immanent. We have already remarked that immanence should not be considered merely as a negative transcendence, that is, as a transcendence interior to each thing. Immanence is not something that is so interior to a thing that it has somehow already transcended the thing itself, but rather something that dwells in the very marrow of the being in question and constitutes it, without thereby being totally identified with it.

The contemporary monastic mentality seeks a spirituality that is not exclusively "spiritual." It wants to integrate, not exclude, all the spatiotemporal parameters of human existence. Its fundamental category is transformation, metamorphosis, transfiguration. Not by bread alone do we live, but certainly by bread as well, and without bread we cannot subsist. But the bread must be assimilated, that is, *transformed* and *converted* into the very material of our being. We have already said how the modern monk wants to recover the ancient alchemy. Here the monk rejoins existing but somehow neglected threads of tradition. Many a mystic, Eastern and Western, displays an extraordinary contemporaneity.

The reality that the monk tries to discover, and to which he attempts to adjust his life, is not supra- or infra-temporal. Perhaps it could be called trans-temporal in the sense that it is inherent in temporality itself, although it transcends it imma- nently. The lived experience of *tempiternal* awareness, for example, is not that of an existence faced with an atemporal and, in the last analysis, posttemporal eternity, but rather the experience of those tempiternal moments of this very existence in time and space. The monk is a child of our contemporary time and shares many insights of what might best be called a *sacred secularity*. He does not await an "other" life, but cherishes the hope of discovering in "this" life his own soul, that is, the very Life of life, including his own. Today's monastic formation is or ought to be aiming toward the aperture of the "third eye," toward opening our senses to a reality hidden in the most ordinary things and events, a vision that reveals itself spontaneously as long as our own vision is pure and our hearts untainted. The monk does not cultivate the expectation of the future but the hope of the present; he does not want to live looking toward the past, but tries to drink in the whole transtemporal content of the present. The redemption of time and space implies an integral transformation, an "opus" of spiritual alchemy that comprises all his asceticism, *sādhana*, *tapas*, training, and ardor. Many trends, ancient and modern, meet here.

And here the unification of being, toward which the monk strives, becomes more arduous. Not only will he not scorn any human value, but he actually attempts to cultivate them all. Nonetheless, he is more than ready to offer any value in a sacrifice intended not to annihilate, but to transform it. True wisdom here consists in the transfiguration of all values. Because of this, the monk loves everything that exists and is even passionate about everything human, without excluding the material and the temporal. In a certain way, the more ephemeral the value, the more likely it is to awaken his interest and attention: it becomes all the more urgent to rescue and redeem it before it disappears. The modern monk is ecstatic about the flower that blossoms today, and tomorrow fades away.

The contemporary endeavor is audacious and difficult, because all that glitters is not gold. *Viveka*, the discernment of spirits, is needed here. There are pseudovalues and there are allurements that distract us from the ultimate meaning of life. It has been written that no one can serve two masters, that *nitya* (the permanent) is not *anitya* (the impermanent), that *paramārthika* (unchanging order above) has nothing to do with *vyavahārika* (the natural order below) nor the world with God, nor flesh with the spirit: "Render to God what is God's and to Caesar what is Caesar's," and cease to lead a divided existence. "Take quick action, because it is better to enter the kingdom crippled than to remain forever excluded from it." "I have come only to teach the way that will free you from suffering; all the rest is superfluous and therefore an obstacle to obtaining *nirv*āna." The majority of monastic spiritualities teach this, albeit with some major refinements due to the exigencies of human nature.

Present-day religious consciousness tries to realize an integration without falling into a compromise, to achieve unification without degenerating into mere juxtaposi- tion. Is this possible? The theoretical answer that has long been proffered still holds: the devil, too, is a servant of God; the temporal is the very manifestation of the eternal and its shadow; the world is the creation or the body of God himself and as such is good; the real human spirit is an incarnated spirit; Caesar himself belongs to God; true simplicity is that which has integrated all the elements of reality; amputation is not necessary when the organism is alive and retains its regenerative powers; freedom from suffering is only the other side of that first step necessary for the achievement of happiness; the very obstacles in our path are what allow us to overcome them and ourselves in the process; and so froth. Reality is neither monistic nor dualistic, but *advaitic*, Trinitarian, and vital—that is, pluralistic (although) without separation.

But theory is not practice. Current monastic asceticism intends to make possible what until now would have seemed inconceivable. It is asked, "How is this possible since I do not know Man?" Is the faith of today's monk powerful enough to realize such a harmony and effect such an integration? The answer that encourages him is to hear that "There is no word impossible for God." And this is precisely the task: to achieve what at first glance seems quite impossible—to unite heaven and earth, flesh and spirit, the world and God, masculine and feminine, secular and sacred. "The Buddha's Way is unattainable. I vow to follow it!" runs the last of the four vows of the Rinzai tradition.

This dilemma of modern spirituality is formulated without palliatives and carried to its ultimate consequences by the contemporary monk. Either the perfection to which we have aspired down the ages is a pernicious and alienating dream, since it cannot be realized, or else we must be able to achieve it by overcoming but not abandoning the spatiotemporal nature that constitutes us. A perfection that is not also in some way corporeal ceases to be human; a happiness that must be left for later ceases to merit the name. Is there a middle way between an obviously insufficient and ultimately nonexistent Humanism and an equally unreal Angelism? The monk poses the problem in all its acuity to cure us of half-measures and beguiling short-term solutions. This is the challenge of monastic spirituality in our day. Many pray "on earth as it is in heaven," but sometimes they understand "since not on earth, then at least in heaven." The modern monk retorts, "If not on earth, then not in heaven," because "to him who has, more will be given" since all that we have is what we are. The monk also "has heard it said" (*itivuttaka*), the kingdom is neither within nor without, but *between* us, in the interregnum of the cosmotheandric interaction. And to this end he strives "to be a light unto himself."

Discussion

It seems that, when the spiritualities of the East or the West encounter the spirit of modernity, a fearful impact occurs. Could you more thoroughly explain the relationship between the modern world and the modern monk?

This is an issue I had intended to deal with later, but I will take the opportunity to describe briefly what I consider to be the very essence of modernity.

Undoubtedly, any tradition has its past, its present, and its future. Furthermore, it is conscious of what is modern. Every tradition knows the meaning of living in the present day, renewing itself, modernizing itself, or doing whatever is needed to keep the path toward the future open. A tradition is alive only when something is passed on to another, transmitted; when a new sense is stripped away from the old age, and therefore something else is left behind—which is what the very word "tradition" means. There would be nothing extraordinary, in a context of this kind, in speaking of modernity. When I used the words "modern monk, or nun" and "modernity" in my presentation, I did not use them with reference to what is totally past. I would like to stick my neck out and present the thesis that an all-pervading *secularity* is the fundamental feature of today's modernity.

By secularity, I do not mean the well-known process of secularization that has occurred in the history of the European churches. Nor do I mean the realm of the profane. I would make a fundamental distinction between "secular" and "profane." The profane is, by definition and etymology, that which is not the sacred, that which lies before the *fanum*, namely the *pro-fanum*, in front of the temple; that which is not included within the holy space (*sanctum*). So, the dialectic between the sacred and the profane should be carefully distinguished from the dialectic between the secular and whatever else. The sacred/profane distinction refers to the priesthood. The realm of the priest qua priest is the *fanum*, the temple, the numinous, the sacred. The realm of the layperson, of the nonpriest, is the profane. The monk has little to do with this dialectic—although, in the *Rule of the Master*, the tonsure prohibits calling the monk a layman. Yet monks are generally not *purohitas*, priests. The tendency of monks to be also ordained as priests is a peculiar trait belonging to Christian history, due to a never completely overcome tension between Christianity and monasticism, because of the Christian tenet of Incarnation. The Incarnation, in fact, seems to relativize the Absolute. A process of secularization was perhaps needed in order to bring about the fuller meaning of secularity as I conceive it.

Until now, because of many factors on which I shall not elaborate, the secular has been more or less identified with the profane. I think it is time to disentangle the profane from the secular, and to discover that the secular does not necessarily mean the same as the profane, but something else as well.

Here again I align myself with that accumulated and crystallized wisdom that we have in the words themselves: *saeculum* comes from the Etruscan, most probably, and is connected to the Greek *aīon*, aeon, as well as the sanskrit āyus, which means life span. *Saeculum* means time, or rather time span, the *life span of the world. Per omnia saecula saeculorum*: What does it mean? Not "forever and ever," either in an atemporal eternity or in an indefinite linear temporality, but "for the entire time span of all the moments of life of the world": a kind of time to the second power that I have called *tempiternity*. Secularity, which I now relate to modernity, means the *saeculum*—that is, the temporal span, the temporality, *time*, the flow of time, the temporal character of things. This temporality is now being taken not only as something that matters, but as something definitive. The most significant mutation factor in our time—for good and probably also equally for ill—is that the temporal structure of reality is no longer considered somethingyou can dispense with, or even utilize (that is, manipulate), in order to reach something more important. Its fleeting, passing, ephemeral character notwithstanding, the temporal structure of the world now represents a coefficient of reality that cannot be eliminated. Therefore, temporal structures can no longer be dealt with as mere instruments or means.

So, secularity is the basic trait of today's modernity, and an *advaitic* approach would be the best method to prevent us from falling into pure secularism, or some other kind of atheistic or, anyway, one-sided view of reality. Reality is so rich that it has life in itself, and having life, it has a fullness that I, from my limited point of view, cannot help seeing as complexity, though in truth it may not be so.

If the monastic dimension is constituted of the humanum, as has been said, three questions arise: Is it possible for everyone to give expression to this dimension? And to what extent is it necessary? And who gives the right expression to it? Who can help us identify it?

I would not like to quibble by giving a subtle answer. I feel it is necessary for everybody to try to live that dimension. To use the metaphor of the *vertical* dimension, I think that this dimension is constitutive of every human being, so that to achieve the fullness of the *humanum* you have to try to unify your being. Something of a monk must be present in all of us; something religious is hiding within every man.

Now, if by "expression" of this dimension we simply mean expression, I would say it is absolutely necessary. If you stifle it, you will not only suffer from stomach troubles and psychiatric disorders, but will have other problems. I add that any culture that represses/stifles the expression of this innermost core of the human being risks a possible explosion from within.

Yet this expression does not need a conscious formulation. Man is more than reason alone; the human being is more than *logos* alone; and cultures cannot be built on the *logos* alone but need also the *pneuma* and the *myth*. So the expression with which I subscribe to the tenets of a church or join some religious organization or even consider myself "religious" in the current sense of the word is not necessarily a conscious one. The exterior manifestation of the monastic dimension of man can appear in a thousand other, different ways. As when the Gospel says, "The prostitutes will precede you into the kingdom," their existence is difficult to approve as a recognizable expression of religious life, but it seems that they enjoy a certain right to precedence—at least in the Christian kingdom of heaven. This is in answer to your second question.

The third question asked whether there are *specialists*, *keśin*, enthusiastic people like the ones we found in the hymn from the *Ṛg-veda*, God-intoxicated people. I would say yes, without a doubt. There are people whose lives are geared that way, centered in this dimension (and the using of the pejorative word *specialist* under- scores the difficulties you may have in accepting what I am trying to say). There are people whose main concern, whose fundamental vocation, whose essential calling lies in bringing together the other two factors that the question hierarchized; so that the unconscious, unformulated, unarticulated expression (the first level, which is necessary for everyone), and the second (the conscious expression), become really incarnated in *you* as an institution. And the "you" can be in the singular or the plural; and that is what would be called monasticism *strictu sensu*. This does imply a certain type of institution, that is, the institution as a living organism, not necessarily an organization.

"Specialist," as I said, is the wrong word, because we cannot speculate about personal vocations. We cannot institutionalize them. Forcing them to become "normal," "ordinary," "common," would be the same as destroying them. But they exist. You cannot but admire some *sādhus*, but you are not supposed to imitate them. Woe to them, if they ever become conscious of being admired as models. Nevertheless, the ideal of the perfect monk, as tradition presents it, is often more like an icon to wonder at than a model to imitate.

Sūtra 6. Transhistorical Consciousness Above Historical Concern

Gloss

Although the *avatāras* of monasticism on this earth have contributed substan- tially to the histories of their people, the monk as such lives primarily within an ahistorical compass. The concepts that we forge of the Absolute or of reality certainly fall under the historicity of the human being, but the monastic invariant does not lie in such notions. Rather, we find it in the yearning for total unification, which can never be content with the distensions inherent in historical events. Time is always fragmentary, and the monk would like to embrace all the three times together. Yet history does not allow it. There is no event complete in itself; it must always have an antecedent and a sequel. The Absolute does not exist in history because history must always advance, and the Absolute is immutable with reference to time. Witness to that is the existence in us of a consciousness that is not exhausted by historicity. We may call it mystical, supernatural, intuitive, or wisdom, *anubhava, prajñā, jñāna, dhyāna, samādhi*, love, or whatever we wish, but there is something besides history to which the monk perennially bears witness. What use is it to conquer the whole world, if you lose your own life?

Once again, we find the principle of simplicity at work here. Not only is time threefold, but history is also manifold and polyvalent. The monastic urge is to transcend such multiplicity. The problem is how.

Commentary

While the Rules of the Masters have insisted on the eternal, perennial, *nirvanic*—in a word on the *suprahistorical*—the Canon of the Disciple emphasizes a *transhistorical* awareness of reality. The former attitude permitted the monk to place himself above the disputes of Men. He was a valid eschatological symbol for all those who believed, in one form or another, in eschatology. But this attitude loses its force the moment its power is not recognized. A symbol is always a symbol for someone, but the symbol is at one and the same time trans-subjective and transobjective; its (subjective) interpretation is as necessary as its (objective) position. A symbol ceases to be a symbol when it is not recognized as such.

Transhistorical consciousness, which can already be found in a certain kind of mysticism through the ages and across the continents, recognizes no kingdom "above" or "beyond" this world; rather it discovers a hidden dimension of reality, one that in a certain manner transcends history and yet still remains immanent to it. This is the experience of *tempiternity* I dealt with briefly in the previous pages, which is neither a more or less perfected temporality nor an eternity impervious to the temporal, but the perfect and thus hierarchic integration of what apparently seem to be two factors (time and eternity) in the one integral tempiternity. Salvation, *mokṣa*, *nirvana*, and other expressions of the ultimate end of human life are not projected into a future that has been somewhat perfected and idealized, but are discovered in the very fullness that we are capable of experiencing in time, not "later." This awareness discovers, *in* and *through* the temporal, the tempiternal nucleus of the plenitude of our being—or however else we would choose to describe this reality.

The consequences for a contemporary spirituality are incalculable. It is not a question of projecting into a linear future what once was formulated in a vertical future, as it has often been attempted by a certain kind of dialectical materialism. Nor is it a matter of merely interpreting the vertical existence of the other life by means of new cosmological and/or metaphysical parameters. The crux of this experience lies rather in experiencing this other dimension in the midst of the very everyday reality that normally presents itself to us as spatiotemporal. Human salvation will then be the realization of the greatest fullness and happiness of which we are capable "while" we are living, although it also means transcending the merely temporal duration. Once again, we may call this the experience of Life in life, if we may thus be permitted to paraphrase the prophet of Israel. The monk will try to live this reality, and his life will remind others that the meaning of life resides not so much in anxiously striving to obtain what we do not have as in being so intensely concentrated that we break through and discover, or even conquer, that which we *are*. It is not the historical victory, whether of the individual or the collectivity that matters, but personal (and thus also communal) happiness, the *re*-velation that strips from us the veil of inauthenticity so that we can become what we truly are.

Here the Christian symbol par excellence is the Transfiguration. The apostles see, feel, and speak with a Christ who is a reality in time and space, but nonetheless transcends that sphere. Not only is the past (with Moses and Elijah) made present, but the future as well, since the one they have with them is not the historic Jesus but the resurrected Christ, and in fact they speak of the forthcoming events. The Taboric experience is for me a paramount example of what I call *sacred secularity.* The transfiguration of Jesus on the mountain—not in the temple—breaks down the separation between the *profanum* and the *fanum*, the profane and the sacred. The everyday secularity can be transfigured if one but has the "single eye" to see it. This seeing is the kingdom of God, here, now. The Buddhist symbol manifesting the same intuition is the Buddhic nature of all things, which only needs to be discovered as such. The Mahayana tradition will express it by saying that *saṃsāra* is *nirvāṇa* and *nirvāṇa*, *saṃsāra*. Vedantic Hinduism will emphasize that we are already *brahman*, even though we fail to notice it. And Jainism together with Gnosticism will tell us that the ātma*n* and the real are simply buried or enclosed in *karman* and matter, and that one need only be freed of such shells.

Cosmologies, anthropologies, and theologies vary and are often incompatible; but the deepest intuition always cuts in the same direction. In modern parlance, history is not the sole dimension of the human, or even the central dimension of reality. Nonetheless, it is not a matter of denying the reality of history or of temporal events, as some of the traditions mentioned have done. Nor is it a question—and here is the relative novelty of our times—of superimposing upon temporal reality a second atemporal, superspatial, eternal story and relegating to this Above or Beyond the ultimate meaning of life. Rather it requires that we open ourselves and our lives to the—Taboric, if you wish—revelation that reality is adualistic, Trinitarian, and simple, but with a simplicity that is at the same time multifaceted, and whose interpretation—*perichōrēsis*—is not always within reach of our experience.

Perhaps the lesson of the last six thousand years of human historical consciousness will be to convince us that history leads inevitably to war. Perhaps the monk is the harbinger, on a totally sociological plane, of the awareness that we cannot be reduced to merely historical beings without thereby more or less schizophrenically dividing our existences between a world here below and a kingdom above and beyond.

Transhistorical consciousness confers on the monk an irreplaceable calling in the realm of the secular, as we will later describe. It is not only a matter of emphasizing intimate, personal, or transcendental values, the "peace of soul" and of "mind" of the traditional language. Transhistorical consciousness summons the monk to cultivate that hidden core of the human being which assures that this being is not less but more than a merely historical being. Perhaps humankind is beginning to become aware that it is on the threshold of a new and radical mutation: that of ceasing to be an animal species with a historical consciousness. I understand historicity as something more than just the remembrance of the past; it is an intellectual memory that enables Man to accumulate his past, to relive it, to assimilate it in spirit in order to enrich his present. Perhaps History, and not only a historical period, is coming to an end: the nuclear catastrophe is in the long run inevitable, the ecological deterioration inescapable, and the violent explosion of the present paneconomic and technological system all too probable.

After the catastrophe, the human being will no longer live looking forward to the future, and will not experience time as the Western world now mainly experiences it, that is, as a succession of more or less homogeneous and therefore quantifiable temporal fragments, but as a new and instantaneous creation with no other guar- antee than the immediate experience of the transtemporal moment. The dimension of interiorization, which is characteristic of monastic spirituality, is translated here into a conscious breaking open of the temporal shell of existence in order to savor its tempiternal kernel, not only at the individual level but at the level of the entire humankind. It is not necessary to subscribe to millennarian, eschatological, Joachimist, Teilhardian, Aurobindian, messianic, or evolutionist theories of any kind to accept what I want to point out here, although all of these can be seen as concrete insights into the fact that the present-day human species is not the end of the whole creation or the full and complete actuality of what a human being carries within. Monasteries would then be the "high places" of this transformational alchemy of Man on his ascending way toward a cosmotheandric reality that surrounds him, and which he himself is, although it surpasses him.

Transhistorical consciousness lets us perceive that the meaning of life consists of reaching the greatest happiness that each of us can, at any and every given moment; freeing us in this way from the desire to chase after happiness where it cannot be found. Salvation, as most religious traditions teach, consists of joy, *chara*, *ānanda*, *sukha*, *nirvāṇa*, heaven. The fact that this happiness was not seen to be fulfilled in the lives of the majority of mortals during this life, as well as the fact of being steered by a certain cosmological interpretation of time and space, has deferred and transplanted happiness to another otherworldly sphere. It is for this reason, too, that the majority of traditions believe that it is only the very few who are saved: very few reach complete happiness and peace in this life. The rest are either miscarriages that do not carry through to the true life (and this failure is hell), or else they must return to recommence the cycle of inauthentic existence with the hope of someday freeing themselves from it—or even without such a hope, as in the Jaina *abhavyatva* or the Calvinist predestination. Even in the adualistic conception, few are those who reach this fullness, compared to those who might otherwise have reached it, had circumstances been more favorable. Hence the religious importance (although never ultimate or definitive) of sociological structures. The monk is precisely the one who bears witness that we can still reach the peace and joy of our plenitude even in a filthy slum. Even in a concentration camp, salvation is not beyond our reach. Not without reason do many thinkers consider *hope* the central problem for those who physically live in this industrialized world.

There seem to be two answers of the human heart to the almost universal experience of the ultimate frustration of most mortals. It does not need to be a consciously psychological frustration leading to envy, hatred, or depression, but there is no denying the deep feeling that our lives have not been lived to the full, that we have not had the proper opportunities to awaken all our dormant talents. The one answer is eschatology: later on, in another life (or lives) we shall be given our retribution or our chance. This is the way of a transcendent transcendence. The other answer is the way of interiority, be it of the individual person, or of the corporate person of the community (*Dharmakāya*, Body of Christ, Communion of Believers, Humanity, etc.). In the first case, we feel that at certain moments of our existence, or at least at the moment of our death, we will reach that human depth, that center that will compensate us for an entire life only half-lived. In the second case, it is the corporate Self, the vicarious nature of personhood, the totality of the cosmos... that compensates for the individual shortcomings. This is the way of immanent transcendence. In the first case, an individual reaches "salvation" within himself. In the second case, it is attained within the "real" or larger Self.

In spite of cultural trends and systems of belief often defending the eschatological view of reality, it should be clear that monkhood has always been more inclined to the path of interiority.

Sūtra 7. The Fullness of the Person Rather Than of the Individual

Gloss

By individual I understand that which results from the expedient of cutting off a sizable and useful part of the human being, generally coextensive with the material body. An individual is the result of a pragmatic slice through a certain number of the diverse constitutive relationships of the human being, in order to create a practical subject of operations. The individual is an abstraction, in the precise sense of the word: all that would make Man too involved and unmanageable is *abstracted* (drawn away) from the human being. An individual is a manageable entity with clear-cut boundaries. It is an identifiable piece standing on its own, isolated. It responds to an "identification card" (wrongly called "identity") and has a social security number.

The person, on the other hand, encompasses the whole complex web of the constitutive relationships of Man with no limits other than those that spontaneously appear in each case. An *I* is a person only to the extent that he does not isolate himself: a *you* is needed, precisely in order to be an *I*. And vice versa. Further, both need a field of action conditioned by the so-called third person, even if this be a thing. And all this takes place not only in the singular but in the plural as well. The *we*, *you*, and *they* belong equally to the person, which is in its entirety neither singular nor plural, nor feminine, masculine, or neuter. The gender of the person is the *utrumque* (both). It embraces all that we truly are because we participate in it without the obsession of private property or exclusive possession. The person can reach to the very limits of reality; it reaches up to where, in fact, we stand when the stance is authentic, that is to say, when it is the true dwelling place (*estancia*) of our being. *La persona es, en donde está.* The person is there, where-it-is, in his *Dasein.* Personality is measured precisely by the differing limits in the stance of each individual. "Be attentive to the place where you stand" is a well-known Zen saying. The isolated Man has no personality—he is drowned in himself—whereas the *bodhisattva* or saint has a personality that reaches to every place where his action makes itself felt, because he has put his heart into it, even unto the limits of the universe. The monastic ideal does not seek an egoistic perfection (viz., of the individual), but locates the meaning of life in the total perfection of the person, which reverberates in its benefits unto the entire reality. Monastic spirituality does not try to reform the world by direct action but tends rather to reform Man with the conviction that such reform affects not just his egotistical individuality but his whole person, which on the one hand reflects and on the other hand influences all of reality. Here there is a striking difference from other forms of spirituality. The emphasis here is on the human person and not on the reform of structures, be they social, material, or even intellectual.

Traditional monkhood was able to achieve this without great difficulty because the sense of individuality was not as developed or pronounced as it has become in recent times. The fullness of the person was felt to be in the *saµgha*, in the community, in the Body of Christ, in the totality.

This is a salient feature: the person is the community, even if it is only a solitary monk. The monastery is more than a family in the modern sociological meaning of the word. The monastery is the full person. The *saṃgha* is one of the three jewels of life; it is necessary for liberation. The links between the members of the *saṃgha* are stronger and more intimate than blood relationships. The *guru-cela*, master-disciple bond is the strongest bond on earth. The abbot is *abba*—that is, father; the *saṃgha* is a *saṃskāra*; the monastic community is a sacrament. Just as in the traditional societies the spouses do not choose each other, but are chosen, so the members of the *maṭha* or monastery are equally bound to each other by a sort of ontological link. Monastic life is more than just communitarian life, it is more than just an association for the sake of reaching or realizing some common goals. Only when the limits of my person extend to the limits of my entire world can I truly stand alone, all-one, as a solitary hermit, as a *muni*, in silence and solitude.

There is a fundamental difference between the *koinōnia* of the monastery, the brotherhood of the *saṃgha*—or even, in more general terms, belonging to the *dharmakāya*, the *buddhakāya*, or the Body of Christ—and membership of any other kind of association. The external difference is clear enough: whereas the latter binds us together with a view to the realization of a partial goal of human life (wealth, education, health, political concerns, etc.), the former claims to have a "holistic" character embracing the totality of the human being in its ultimate perfection, goal, liberation, salvation. But the internal difference is more subtle and depends precisely on the degree of adherence and trust (faith) of the person concerned. Membership of the *ecclesia*, the *umma*, the *maṭha* is not with a view to doing anything special, but of being—and being (perfectly) what (I believe) I am. It is a natural relation- ship, while the other is a technical one. As members of an ordinary association we are individual parts and can go in and out without any fundamental damage to our being or to the association concerned. We are one part of the machinery, and this part can be replaced by another individual. We are simply members of an organization. Not so with the membership of a religious community of the monastic type. I am not only a *pars in toto*, but also a *pars pro toto*. I am unique and indispensable. The monks with whom I lived recently in a Tibetan monastery would not understand that you "enter" a monastery. You do not enter into a family, you are born into it. The whole is prior to its parts. If I leave, I kill my very being and also do irreparable damage to the *ecclesia*, the *saṃgha*. This is hell to me, and an incurable wound to the organism. The hand cannot live cut off from the body, nor can it be replaced by the eye—although in due time there may be regeneration (*kalpas* and the law of *karma*) and reconciliation (forgiveness and redemption). The famous dictum *extra ecclesiam nulla salus* (outside the *saµgha*, Nature, the *buddhakāya*, the *dharmakāya*, the Church... there is no salvation) is an essential feature of that "communion of the saints." That a specific group can claim ownership of that *ecclesia* or of the knowledge of its boundaries, this is another matter altogether. The community outside of which there is no salvation cannot, obviously, be an organization. It has to be a sacrament, a *saṃskāra*, a *mysterion*. By burningyour passport you may renounce the State (and its protection or oppression), but by this act you do not cancel your language or your nation.

Now, the monk discovers his roots within the entire reality. His fidelity is to the whole, to the earth, as we have said in order to stress that he is not ontologically linked to humankind alone. To be a person, here, means to be a living center of the whole of reality.

The principle of simplicity is at work here in a peculiar way. It entails getting rid of the complexity of the individual in favor of the simplicity of the person. An individual is a closed system. Its boundaries are clear-cut. The "mine" and the "yours" cannot be mixed. A person is an open system. Its limits depend wholly on the power of the center. Each person is an expanding universe. You need not keep anything for yourself, because the real Self is not a private property of your own.

Commentary

In our times we are witnessing an anthropological change regarding the awareness of the boundaries of personal being. The new limits refer both to those of a certain conception of the Absolute and to those of the world around the person. Monastic consciousness has become universalized, so to speak, by grounding itself in what is specifically monastic and thus placing monkhood before the historical ties of belonging to a nation, race, or even religion. Buddhist and Christian monks, for example, seeking a shared monastic experience, will not be deterred by the fact that they happen to belong to different religions.

But the fundamental distinction between the traditional and the contemporary understanding of monkhood consists in the surreptitious dualism of the traditional monastic anthropology contrasted with the underlying monism of the contemporary conception, although in both cases they try to avoiding falling into their respective temptations. The traditional monk is a *monachos* because he is not a *dipsychos*, a being with a twofold soul, with a double end and a double life. Between the *pāramārthika* and the *vyāvahārika*, *sat* and *māyā*, God and the world, the temporal and the eternal, *nirvāṇa*, and *saṃsāra*, and so on, the monk has chosen the first and renounced the second. Or rather, in moral terms, he has refused greed, envy, worry, sin: all this belongs to the world. The monk wants to jump to the other shore where he will be free from all this. We need only read the Buddhist and Jaina scriptures along with the Christian books to be convinced of this. There are two cities: the city of God and that of the Devil. To be sure, the monk is not yet an *arhat*, a *bodhisattva*, a saint, but he is on the way. Now monastic spirituality, in order to circumvent the dualism of the two Men, two shores, two realms, will have to say that perfection consists in realizing that *saṃsāra* is *nirvāṇa*; that one has already arrived, at least potentially, at being a *comprehensor* and no longer a *viator*; that we *are* all *jīvanmuktas* and not *mumukṣutvas* saints, and not only aspirants who still live in confusion and distortion; that the union with God, who is all in all, is the destiny of everybody. But this perfection is only at the end of the path, in the completion of the *sādhana*. Monastic perfection is reached by living with one's face turned toward the Absolute and one's back to the relative, by "seeking God only," concentrating on the One, the *ekam*, with that single intention in one's heart and mind, *ekāgratā*, without any kind of compro- mise. Liberation, *mokṣa*, is all that matters. Everything that divides—*amerimnia*: women (for the male, and men for the female), passions, pleasures, and especially one's fellow Men—is scrupulously avoided. One must live free from all cares and worries, stripped of and unattached to all that is earthly, contingent, and perishable. Personhood is forged only in contact with the Absolute. God alone suffices, "*Sólo Dios basta*," *kaivalya*.

The fundamental category in classical monastic spirituality was obedience, *vinaya*, discipline. Through docility the monk attains his perfection, by it the *bhikṣu* conquers *nirvāṇa* and the *muni* reaches his goal. Fidelity to the path, to the *dharma*, the rule, the ideal came to be symbolized in and through obedience, the *ob-audire*: knowing how to listen to the mysterious and ultimate voice embodied in the *tao*, the *dharma*, the *śāstras* or the will of the guru, the abbot, the father. The objectivity of what is commanded matters only in part. What is important is the subjectivity, and from this point of view it amounts to the same whether you are watering a dry stick or caring for a sick person. What matters is the intention. What is important is the subjectivity that is expressed in fidelity to the master, which is the only thing that will help us free ourselves from ourselves and reach the other side of the river, since our own will is the final refuge of *ahaṁkāra*, egoism, and *abhimāna*, the vanity of the individual's sense of self-worth. We have already pointed out, in commenting on the first canon, that all this is not sheer irrationality: the monk should see that he must obey, that is, he ought to be able to discover the power within the command that evokes obedience (its "obedientiality"), but he does not need to see the intel- ligibility of what is commanded. The limits to obedience are set not by my seeing the rationality of the command, but by my agreeing to the obedientiality of the injunction—that is, I have to see the reasons for obeying, even if I do not see the reason for the command. Obedience does not seek to be blind, but intelligent. All the vows, *vratas*, can be reduced to this "fidelity above all," where objective judgment is transferred to the superior and we are left with the inalienable subjective insight of our willingness to obey because we are convinced of the obedience due to the rule, the "will of God," the *dharma*, the Absolute, the very voice within us that can only be discerned when we hear it echo from the lips of the Master, *ācārya*, or whatever we may call him or it. Obedience must be interiorized; there is no true docility unless it stems from the mind and the heart without any constriction: these are obvious stages that must be reached in the ascent of the mountain of perfection "until the morning light dawns in our hearts."

The winds of contemporary spirituality may come from the same source: God, *vāyu*, *pneuma*, but they seem to be blowing in opposite directions. They are aiming at the same perfection and plenitude of the person, but this is not seen so much in getting rid of all the unnecessary ingredients of the person so as to be self-sufficient, as in the realization of the person through cultivation of the bonds that unite him or her to the unfathomable riches of creation. The monk does not want to be a man set apart, but one integrated into the whole. Perfection is not seen in the immolation of the person on the altar of obedience in order to arrive at *apatheia*, "holy indifference," but in the possibility of actualizing all the dormant potentialities of our being through obedience to the Spirit, at once immanent and transcendent.

These new winds are being felt in three almost antagonistic areas, although at heart they are perhaps complementary: corporality, intimate personal relations, and political awareness. The famous Plotinian saying about living alone with the Alone does not strike a chord in the modern monk, who envisions the *monachos* as a unified being. But then this unification is certainly not an individualistic one. It can be realized only if we assume the entirety of our being, unify our divided existence, and integrate our own life with the destiny of the community. In other words, the body, sexuality, and politics belong to the perfection of the human person. Let us try to describe these new winds without too hastily attempting to direct or judge them. I am not venturing any answers here.

We shall only present the problems.

Corollaries

Corporality

Without necessarily reaching gnostic, angelic, or *arhat*-like extremes of scorn or radical forgetfulness of the body, there does seem to be common to the traditional monastic mentality a certain neglect of the body and of corporeal values. The body is considered at best a collaborator and more generally a mere servant whom it is necessary to treat well in order that it might serve us well; but at bottom it is dead weight. And if some traditions, like the Christian, speak of the resurrection of the body, they also do not forget that it is not yet resurrected and that in the meantime the flesh is treacherous, or at least ambiguous. It is interesting to observe that, while the Hindū monk goes as scantily clad as possible, and the Jaina *digambara* completely naked, the Christian is weighed down with robes. By exactly opposite signs, all of them want to show that they have overcome the body, that they really have no bodies because they do not want to be their bodies.

The contemporary monk wants to be able to say that he *is* also his body, that the body is not an enemy, not even a friend or a servant, but rather is he himself; that health is an element as much physical as psychic; and that the soul depends as much on the body as the body on the soul, if one were to use such dualistic language. A man is not literally a body, but he is his body and without the body there is no man. The *monachos* is not "one" through his soul or spirit only, but because he aspires to succeed in realizing the union that exists between the diverse elements of his very being. The present-day monk understands what etymology merely suggests, that meditation has to do with medicine (*medéri*), salvation with health (*salus*) and freedom (*sōtēria*), and the two together with *sarvam*, the totality, being whole. And if it is true that the monastic ideal attempts to go beyond humanism, this is not so in order to take refuge in some nonhuman angelism or in some disembodied and thus inhuman spirituality, but rather to achieve a human fullness from which no truly human value is missing. Asceticism is no longer the mortification of the flesh so much as the vivification of the body, so that it too might participate in the destiny of the person. There is no doubt that the monastic *viveka*, *madhyama*, *sobrietas*, and *discretio* prevented many abuses, but the overzealous ascetic exploits of monks, East and West, are also well documented.

Here mention ought properly to be made of tantric monasticism, be it Hindū or Buddhist (especially Tibetan) and better known under the name of *yoga*. *Yoga* is a polysemous word. It does not need to mean only the ascetic "yoke" that keeps the body docile to the rule of the spirit. It can also mean the integration of body and mind in a harmonious union. *Tantra* is equally a multivalent word. It does not need to connote only bodily experiences, or otherwise forbidden practices. It also means the sacramental view of reality, the conception that everything is both material and spiritual, and that salvation consists in the transformation of both. The *cakras* of the yogic spirituality and the practices of the *tantrikas* try to incorporate the body into the spiritual *sādhana*. The body is the seat of power. The coarse dichotomy between body and soul is overcome by discovering a continuum formed by many kinds of bodies and different sorts of souls.

The practical question today is how to integrate or reintegrate corporality into those monastic traditions that have thus far neglected the body. This would mean much more than simple body-awareness or care for material needs, which already had a place in the monasteries of old.

The Canon of the Disciple cannot provide a set of rules here, but only express a need that is felt and direct our attention to it. If it is true that we *are* also our bodies and not only *have* them, the consequences are revolutionary.

Sexuality

With no need to emphasize the noxious and all too prevalent extremes that have cropped up everywhere throughout human history, the traditional monastic mentality has always defended the proposition that "*entre santa y santo, pared de cal y canto*" (between a holy male and a holy female, a strong firm wall), which is to say that human perfection should sublimate in one individual the androgynous nature of the human being. In most cases, monastic spirituality is simpler and not overly concerned with the androgynous character of the person. It tells us that this life is provisional and fleeting, and thus that any consummation experienced on this plane is not the consummation to which we are finally called. So it does not much matter if the human being does not reach fulfillment in this field. In the other world, the true one, there is neither male nor female, nor any giving or taking in marriage. Celibacy, *brahmacarya*, and the renunciation of family were all seen as essential to traditional monasticism, in spite of a few notable exceptions. Eschatological perfection has no sex; monastic formation treats Man as an asexual being. If sexuality doesn't make itself felt, you can simply overcome it by ignoring it. If, however, it exacts a price, we are told that it is a fruitful sacrifice, one that places us on a higher plane than the merely biological. Being "capable" of living a celibate life has often become the standard by which it was possible to measure the authenticity of a monastic vocation.

Contemporary monastic spirituality tries—with various degrees of success—to recover the sacred sense of sex and the positive function of human sexuality. This function reveals itself when we find ourselves confronted with our own limitations and realize that we need an exogenous complement and not simply an endogenous supplement. We seem to need some*body* else and not just some*thing* else. We feel the need for intimacy, interchange, friendship, and love, not as distractions from the one needful thing, but first as a spur and inducement, and finally as a culmination. The word that in this context has transcended the boundaries of a single religion and culture to enrich others is *tantra*, that form of spirituality that I have translated as sacramentarian, which suggests that the path to perfection passes not only through the correct use of all created things, but also through the mutual co-penetration of human beings. People are not just instruments for the perfection of others; more than interaction and collaboration is needed. Community, friendship, and intimacy are required. The issues here are burning, and once raised cannot be ignored. To be sure, sex here should not be reduced to the merely genital, nor to the exclusively physical. Sex is the very sign of differentiation of the human being (*liṅga*), just as in biology it is the cause of differentiation among individuals and species.

The human person is, to varying degrees, the harmonious conjugation of all the personal pronouns. The strong monastic emphasis on the *we* made the relation with a *you* less urgent, and the filial/paternal relation with the guru or abbot diminished the importance of any other intimacy between two people. Moreover, being heed- less of the body could permit a certain personal intimacy between two brothers or sisters without sexuality apparently becoming an issue... the well-known warnings against "particular friendships" and the naïveté shown in averting pairs in the *maṭhas*, *vihāras*, and monasteries notwithstanding. But the problem becomes acute when the divine *You*, the bridegroom Jesus, the Kṛṣṇa of the *gopīs*, the devotion to the Blessed Virgin, etc., is demythicized and deanthropomorphized. What Ferdinand Ebner has called the *Dulosigkeit*, the deprivation of the "you" for the realization of the "I," is being experienced more and more dramatically as a distortion. So, modern forms of spirituality that do not want to break with tradition emphasize the *plural* "you"; the apostolate, the mission to accomplish, service to others, external activity, and so forth. This work, called mission, apostolate, *seva*, and the like, then becomes the surrogate for a living "you" (singular). We often hear the exclamation, "I am not married because I have no time (for it)." But experience shows that the "work" in the complexity of the modern world becomes very rapidly bureaucratized, ceases to be a "you," and turns into an *it*. Then you get married to an "it": this is your spouse....

All of the pronouns must be properly declined for personal fulfillment, but the contemporary monk suffers from this debilitating lack of the (singular) *you*. The "you" is the friend, the beloved. The "you" is that person who best enhances the dimension of intimacy, caring, delicacy, attention, and, finally, love in any human life. The *nyingma-pa* school of Tibetan Buddhism—the most ancient, as its very name indicates—countenances married monks without even requiring that the spouse also belong to the monastery. But the Lama with his red cap was perhaps more married to the plot of ground he worked and the community with whom he lived than to his wife. Technically speaking, Lamas are not *bhikkus*. Perhaps marriage is not the real issue, but rather friendship. Nor is this really a problem of concupiscence. The issue at stake is whether the *monachos* can be "all-one" even though he is "alone," whether monotheism (and dualism) or *advaita* (and trinity) is the authentic para- digm of perfection. Tantric spirituality emphasizes time and again that the śakti must be internalized. But the śakt*i* is not the Ego; it is the "you." And yet it has also to be the "Self." The celibate, as the very word suggests, is the *kevalin*, the single one, the alone. Sometimes I suspect that the spirituality of "foolishness" may be the instinctive reaction against the diabolic temptation of the monk: *autarkeia*, to be self-sufficient. These "holy fools" become totally vulnerable and, thus, insufficient.

In any event, the problem is paramount. The perfection of the human being is at stake. The Canon of the Disciple cannot go further, but it can still add a methodological proviso and insert an excursus.

The methodological quandary is the following : We need a new anthropology to deal with this question. Now, on the one hand, we cannot stick to the old customs just because they were good and yielded good results (if this is indeed the case); we have to find convincing reasons that fit our understanding of the human being. On the other hand, we cannot defend a new anthropology based, say, on recent discoveries in biology and psychology, and throw overboard centuries and millennia of human praxis. Deeply human problems are not just mathematical puzzles that can be solved theoretically. They need the marriage between theory and praxis, and this may very well be one of the tasks incumbent on present-day monks.

The excursus will let us have a look at the problem of celibacy, which is not the same as what we have been speaking about, although this is very often the way in which the issue is put. The problem of celibacy should be distinguished from the sexual question.

To justify celibacy a priori implies that we have before us a convincing anthropology that tells us that virginity is a higher human status, or family life a burden in the quest for human fulfillment, or a spouse a sort of bondage, or individual androgyny a valid human option, and so on. Then we could also adduce historical reasons like the shortness of time before the Last Days, or sociological reasons like the tempo of modern technological society, or cosmological arguments like celibacy marking the end of a karmatic line so that there should be no progeny to perpetuate that person's karma, or spiritual ones like divine marriage, and so on. I might even venture an astrological reason, which would claim that for the hero of the newly inaugurated Aquarian Age the biological family has no place. A cogent and powerful incentive, mainly Christian and Hindū, is the conjugal argument. Christ, Kṛṣṇa, or God is the divine spouse, jealous and unique. *Quia iucundum Deo in tua virginitate habitaculum preparasti*, "because you have prepared a joyful dwelling place for God in your virginity," says the Catholic breviary in singing the praises of St. Lucia. We could easily multiply this list, but it can all be reduced to accepting one particular view as powerful enough to justify the theory of celibate life.

The Disciple's stand here, in our times of crisis, may be closer to having convincing power, mainly because it is at least humbler. It is not a justification, but an explanation a posteriori.

It is a fact that celibacy is a widespread human institution, mostly linked to monkhood. It is equally true that there are today many celibates who voluntarily chose celibacy, even if many of the reasons for which they did may now even to them appear questionable. The argument a posteriori could start from the fact that you are a celibate, and then say, "What about now ? You did it in good faith and it is not a bad thing in itself, even if it may not appear as the ideal. It may be worse to break it now, and you may not know how to do it without causing real harm to yourself and those around you." In short, celibacy does not need the claim to be a superior form of spiritual life, or to have any theoretical justification. We may even find many advantages to celibacy, if positively accepted; much as a not very pretty young girl may try to counter with sympathy and intelligence the effect of her long nose. And thanks to that nose, she may very well have developed many another more important virtue.

This should not be taken as an invitation to sheer passivity, or a neglect of the mystical reasons for celibacy. It is a call to real prudence and respect for the praxis. To want to justify celibacy may indeed become the beginning of its condemnation. It may expose the loss of innocence; it may jeopardize the spontaneity and freedom with which the option was originally taken; it may betray a secret disenchantment, triggering the need to justify it by something else. When you pray, you are not asking for proofs of God's existence.... Why are there so many books today trying to justify religious celibacy? I would be the last to deny that there can be an advaitic androgyny within a single person. I am only indicating the present-day state of affairs.

Political Awareness

If in traditional monastic spirituality the human person is realized through contact with the Absolute and separation from the world of Man, this segregation, signified by the enclosure, seems to have acquired a negative character in contemporary consciousness. If we are political animals, then the contemporary monk seems unable to believe that he can attain his human fullness without cultivating the political dimension. Obviously, we are not referring to mere "political parties" with their partisan squabbles or to arguments over the technical methods for achieving some preconceived ends, but rather to the well-being of the *polis* as the symbol of human community, and to a participation in the problems of our fellow beings that would allow us to realize the importance of the basic structures of human conviviality.

Undoubtedly, monastic praxis has not always been consistent with its theory. History shows us monks, Eastern and Western, ancient and modern, involved in the affairs of their local communities and often unmasking with perspicacity the machinations of political power. But this was either simply accepted and tolerated—although hardly in accordance with the acknowledged monastic spirit—or it was justified as belonging to a suprapolitical realm, be it the "kingdom of God" or the "salvation of the people."

At any rate, the modern monk still wants to be solitary, but he will not tolerate being isolated. And as he has perceived all too clearly the functioning of secondary causes, he cannot be content with a union with the First Cause that would prevent him from contributing directly to the life of the community of which he feels himself to be an integral part. "God has left the world to the quarrels of Men," yet the monk today realizes that true prayer is not an excuse for inaction in the world but is actually an intervention in the dispute itself.

When cultures and religions live without major conflict within a single myth, there are values that are respected without argument and attitudes that are accepted without debate. Where monasticism enjoys such recognition, the monk can remain outside and above political and temporal options because he is granted a superior sphere by the whole community. The recognition and acceptance of his stance of renunciation by the community at large confers on him the power and influence that he himself has renounced. The monk is not a marginal being, although he might have flown to the fringes of society. But in the contemporary world, if the monk renounces the world, the world also renounces him and can get along quite well without him. And it seems certain that this attitude begins to prevail even in parts of Africa and Asia as well, where the renouncing ascetic is beginning to feel alienated due to the passive ostracism of society. He can no longer threaten to hold back the rain if the people do not believe in him... or if they have a reservoir close at hand.

In the modern political situation there is no neutral ground. Taking refuge in the so-called supernatural sphere already represents a decision of a political nature, generally in favor of the status quo. The Buddhist monks in Vietnam and the Christian monks in Latin America could be adduced here as examples of this awareness, which throws the monk into the strife of everyday life—perhaps to bear witness to nonviolent means, perhaps to the relativity of our ends and goals themselves, or perhaps simply to elevate the level of the dispute, but without claiming a sphere of privilege or a recognized superiority that would permit him to act as the final recourse. And if he were consciously to reserve this function for himself he would commit a great hypocrisy. The monk does not offer his services if others do not ask for them. The monk does not enter into the games of a competitive society. Moreover, the human situation is today so complex that we cannot hope to find any unanimity on political questions even among men and women consecrated to a monastic life. The person is forged in the crucible of these very contentions between human beings.

The world is left in the hands of the strongest and of destiny, as are human conflicts. Or, as the Arabic refrain goes, "The world is God's, but the Merciful One has rented it to the most courageous." We cannot aspire to the kingdom of God without seeking first its justice, but this is no longer a merely supernatural righteous- ness, it is also a political problem that cannot be sidestepped. Put in another way, the great religious problems of humanity today all wear a political face: hunger, peace, freedom, justice, happiness, human dignity.

The quandaries accumulate. Political involvement cannot be left to the initiative of the lone monk: today's problems are too complicated. To enter meaningfully into the political world, personal preparation and social backing are both needed. Otherwise the monk will be used against his own intentions, as the experience of the worker-priests in France clearly demonstrated. But can a monastery take a political stance? Sadly, as noted, not to take one is already a decision in favor of the status quo. When the reigning order is generally accepted, when we all live within the same myth, there is no problem. And when the persecution is obvious, it may be a matter of courage or of prudence to stand against the tyrant. Christian and Buddhist monasteries in communist countries, however, are a telling example of how difficult it can be to agree on the path to follow. When the reigning order is seen by some as evil and by others as only questionable, the dilemma becomes even more excruciating. Whatever position we may eventually take, to ignore these issues is no longer possible or acceptable.

Summation

The ultimate reason for the triple change discussed above is simple. We will see it more clearly in the next Canon, but we can, perhaps, anticipate ourselves a little here. The classical monastic attitude teaches that true human perfection is transcendent and situated in the beyond; so, the fact that all desire to obtain it here below is a childish illusion, unable to distinguish between the temporal and the eternal. We should not dream of realizing happiness and perfection in this "vale of tears," in this realm of *duḥkha*, of suffering and pain. Monks should not worry about being Apollonian models of beauty, Socratic examples of wisdom, Renaissance paradigms of global knowledge, or Olympic athletes of physical prowess. They have renounced all that. Their perfection is in heaven, in *nirvāṇa*, or in a transcendent *mokṣa*. The monk is supposed to be available for any service because he does not look for his perfection on this earth. "What does it matter if you ruin your health, or fail to study sociology, or live a few years less, if by so doingyou gain the kingdom of heaven, attain enlightenment?"

The contemporary mentality rebels against this attitude. The contemporary monk does not want to palliate his thirst for the infinite, but he also resists believing that the path to human and even divine perfection must pass through the immolation and deprecation of human values, or even simply that it lies above them. He does not renounce the transcendent but he does not want to be separated from the immanent.

This attitude does not discard all the virtues implied in Canon 1: *penthos*, *tyāga*, *compunctio*, penitence, and, especially, the purification of the heart. But the new monk would like to go beyond what he is likely to consider only the first step toward sanctity: the stripping off, the negation, the renunciation. He would like to go beyond the mentality of the novice and the fervor of the junior in order to reach a more balanced and mature second level, all the dangers of lukewarm spirituality notwithstanding.

The problems here remain distressingly unresolved since there does not yet exist an adequate formulation, let alone an experience, that would warrant and ground a greater optimism. The nondualistic solution that timidly emerges from these pages is still far from possessing the patina of a multisecular experience or the seal of a sufficiently generalized acceptance. The Canon of the Disciple is not a substitute for the Rule of the Master; it is only a voice calling for a fruitful dialogue.

Sūtra 8. The Primacy of the Holy

Gloss

Reality is complex, and so is human existence. The unification toward which the monk strives is effected under the aegis of the Holy. The monk is not like the priest, the dispenser of the sacred mysteries; nor like the sage, the receptacle of liberating knowledge. Neither is he like the scientist, the expert who understands how things function; nor like the artist who shapes the invisible realities into sensible forms; nor like the worker who carries out the labor necessary for the accomplishment of all these things. The monk endeavors to attain an unqualified holiness. He strives for holiness only. He seeks the Absolute; if God is the Holy, he strives for God. But the monk does not necessarily need God; it is holiness that he needs. The Buddhist and Jaina monks do not have God as a Supreme Being and Creator, yet their search for absolute truth is no less intense than in the theistic cases.

Many people besides the monk will try to become holy, but they will do it in and through something else: marriage, art, work, good actions.

Monkhood stands for the quest of ab-solute holiness, unrelated to anything else, insofar as this is possible. The holy is neither the sacred nor the profane. The profane is everything that is celebrated outside the temple. The sacred is the realm within the temple; it is the domain of the priest, not of the monk. The *saṃnyāsin* performs no rite at all. Many Christian monks retire to solitude without priest or sacraments. The hermit does not leave his cave to attend festivals in the temple. "*Quid facis in turba qui solus es?*" asks Jerome: What are you doing among the crowd, you who are a solitary?

The sacred stands in a relation to the profane, but the holy is the center of everything and of every activity. The center remains immobile while everything else turns about it; the center remains equidistant from everything circling around it, which is precisely what constitutes it as center. This equidistance of the center from all that is peripheral thus translates into the equanimity, sobriety, and indifference of the monk. But the center is also separated, segregated, apart from everything else. This is one of the meanings of the word "sanctity," and historians of religion will link it with the meaning and function of tabu. The monk is set apart; he severs his links with society. Monkhood is a dimension of human life but does not exhaust its possibilities. The monk wants to realize the integration of his person by choosing the better part, but in no way does he claim to have a monopoly on human perfection. Reality is not the center alone. The sphere could not exist without its center, but the two should not be identified or confused. Monkhood is only a part, and only the whole of humanity can reach that plenitude to which all human beings aspire. The plenitude is communal, and ultimately theanthropocosmic.

Commentary

For classical monasticism the center of holiness is found in the transcendent, the eternal, the other world. The religious spirituality of our day seems to have effected a mutation of considerable import: *the holiness of the secular.* The secular, too, belongs to the very center of reality, although it is not its only constitutive factor. Expressed inversely, the holy is also the center of the secular and acts at times as a catalyst, which activates a process without in the final analysis intermingling with it.

From the preceding canons we can clearly infer that contemporary monkhood tends toward the secular, without thereby diminishing its pursuit of holiness. It cannot renounce the secular world because it does not believe it to be secondary; it cannot renounce activity in the world because it believes this to be indispensable. The monk does not give up his struggle for a total personal perfection. He would be unsatisfied with saving only a human misfit. He does not believe in an ill-structured world that has to be cancelled in order to reach the goal of Man. He will abandon neither time nor space because these are his dwelling place, and his dwelling, like his body, forms part of his life. He cannot believe that perfection entails alienation from the structures of the real or exile from this earth. Nonetheless, he claims still to move within the compass of the holy. Is this feasible? Is it not a compromise? Is this not a naïve optimism, explicable perhaps only as a reaction to an earlier pessimism?

The mutation alluded to above suddenly places the monk in the center of our troubled times. Awareness of the secular has been growing in tension—and all too often in conflict—with the holy.

Traditional religions found themselves, and still greatly find themselves, in opposition to the secular. Today, however, we begin to glimpse that the movement of secularity is not necessarily directed against the grain of the holy. Secularization, certainly, has been a fight waged against a special regimen of the sacred that had accrued to itself privileges little less than unbearable to those outside of it. But secularization was only a process. The crucial feature of secularity lies elsewhere. It lies in surmounting this dichotomy between the temporal and eternal worlds and in recognizing the ultimate and indispensable character of temporality. Thus the *saeculum* is not in jest, nor passing, provisional, unreal, a shadow, or whatever we would like to call it in order to attenuate the impact of an unjust and violent status quo. Secularity represents the affirmation that the body, history, the material world, and all temporal values in general are definitive and insuperable, although not exclusive or complete. They are to be found alongside of other values that also make up the warp and woof of the real and the human.

The monk's entrance into the secular realm cannot but represent a mutation of considerable religious import. That the world is not evil, that it is legitimate to become involved in temporal affairs, that time has a positive value, and that the religious person must occupy himself with reforming the very socio-politic-historical structures of reality—such ideas do not today encounter much resistance. Indeed, most of the religious movements and orders, Eastern and Western, since the sixteenth century are already operating along these lines—to the extent that they sometimes incur the opposite extreme of mere social activism out of touch with the center. Yet it does seem as if traditional religions had reserved for themselves the definitive reality of another superior sphere called the other life. And if the priest straddled these two worlds, the monk, surely, represented the one whose acosmic vocation placed him already on the other shore and made of him the eschatological witness to the definitive human state.

Either the monk remains outside the secular sphere, or if he enters it without ceasing to be a monk, then this must signify that the secular is also somewhat definitive, ultimate, and, in its way, equally as important as the so-called other life. This means that the two lives cannot be separated, that the one does not exist without the other, that the true life does not belong to another world. It means the incorporation of the divine in the human and its impregnation of all the structures of the material world; the descent of the real into appearances; the eruption of the noumenon into the phenomenon; the transformation of the divine *avatāra* into the human. Either the monk ceases to be a monk, or the secular ceases to be profane and is integrated into the holy.

This change is of no little import because it announces to us in no uncertain terms that the separation between the holy and the secular is no longer sustainable or, at the very least, that temporality with all its consequences is as holy as that which traditionally was maintained apart from the noise of the world and the servile chores of temporal affairs. But if this represents a mutation in the conception of the holy, it equally signifies a parallel revolution in the experience of the secular.

The secular is no longer that which is fleeting, provisional, perishable, contingent, and so forth, but is rather the very clothing of the permanent, the eternal, and the immutable—to continue using for a moment categories that must soon be superseded. The secular should not be abandoned in order to achieve the real in the way a snake sheds its skin to continue living and growing. Or, to put it in Christian terms, the resurrection of the body is not unto an everlasting life with another body and another kind of flesh than that which we now have, feel, and are, but rather in this very flesh that now constitutes us, as more than one Conciliar text will tell us. First, "resurrection" "*in hac carne, qua nunc vivimus*" (in this flesh in which we live), and second, in "eternal life."

In various periods of human history, mainly in times of emergency, monks moved by compassion and a sense of duty descended from their "high places" into the political arena. But once order was restored or duty fulfilled, the monk withdrew again to his seclusion. It may well be that the situation of the world is now so desperate that it has awakened the monastic conscience to this new step, but the fact remains that when the Buddhist, Christian, Hindū, or Jaina monks today enter the struggle for a more just world, they do not do so as if this were something alien to them or to their calling. It entirely behooves them to enter the territory of the secular world. They will no longer accept being shut off from true participation in the full human reality. There is no "other" life, even though the existence led by the majority of humans does not often reach even the minimum standard of what could be called truly living the one and only life that exists. And this is precisely hell. It is with the redemption of this life and not any other that we are dealing, as the doctrine of the resurrection of the flesh will remind Christians, or as the Vedantic intuition will show Hindūs, and the teachings of Gautama, Buddhists. But this life must be won and, as the majority of religions emphasize, this true life is hidden in our present everyday existence. It is necessary to "believe" in it, or to "be able" or to "know how" to penetrate it, discover it, realize it. Salvation is within reach of our hands—it is nearby and even within us—but we are in need of a revelation, a word, a redeemer, a gift of grace, a personal effort, a spontaneous decision, a teaching, a guru, or an awakening of the very best that is in us in order to attain it.

The monk bears witness to the primacy of the holy, and today discovers its hidden nucleus in the very material structures of reality and in the yearnings and strivings of humankind. The classical Buddhist conception of the momentariness of creation or the equally traditional Christian one of the continuing creation, on a par with the Hindū concept of the simultaneous creation, preservation, and destruction of the universe, could all serve to express the human experience of the unity of each and every moment of existence, the incommensurable importance of all that is, the irreducibility of every being. Things and events are not mere means for some other thing. It is precisely this which constitutes alienation of human beings: the race toward an end that does not exist, the anxiety about a future that will never arrive. And if the danger in former times consisted in being projected into a vertical future, the modern temptation lies in wanting to throw oneself headlong into a horizontal future. Neither future is any longer operative, namely, sufficient to give us fullness and peace. The enterprise of building a better world is not a mere technique of manipulating or programming the future, but the very art of the present. Authentic human work is not a means to an end, but a basic form of human creativity, that cannot be reduced, under penalty of slavery. And when the machine imposes its conditions on human productivity, it dehumanizes and condemns that activity. Modern technological society cries out to be redeemed from the enslavement into which it has fallen. The contemporary monk withdraws from that society, not to abandon it to its slavery, but to incarnate the authentically human—which turns out to be the most divine.

The secular function of the monk in the modern world could perhaps be described in the following manner. There are four sociological groups of capital importance in society:

1. Church or religious groups
2. Academia, or teaching and research institutions
3. Government and military
4. Industry and commerce

These are as valid in an agricultural civilization as in the emerging *technículture* (a word that would like to signify the positive and civilizing aspects of a technified world). Strictly speaking, the monk belongs to none of these four groups. He is neither priest, nor intellectual, nor public officer, nor producer. A great number of traditional societies admit a fifth state: that of the person who has abandoned the world, the monk, the *saṃnyāsin*, the renouncer, the one who has forsaken all the rules of the game of human intercourse, who has leaped over the wall and yet remains as a symbol to the majority of mortals of the provisionality of all human enterprises. In his own eyes the monk is one segregated, set apart, but in people's consciousness he is holy and thus by no means a marginal or peripheral being. The monk resides in the very center of society, and when the people are faced by what appear to be technically insoluble problems, they approach their saints, their monks, hermits, and ascetics.

Since time immemorial there seems to have existed—more or less underground—a sixth group as well: the guerrillas, the so-called counterculture, the dissidents or revolutionaries, those who are not content with merely reforming the immediate shortcomings of society, or simply rotating the seats around the tables of power, but who strive to radically change the whole system. Now these voluntary marginal "citizens" are, however, to a large extent dependent on the countersystem, which is, in the final analysis, dependent on the very system they claim to combat. In dialectically opposing the system, one has no choice but to accept the rules of the game that the system defines, albeit with the aim of over- throwing it. The contemporary monk may well belong to this sixth group, but with one fundamental difference: he has, as far as possible, eliminated the negative factor of simply opposing the system. On the contrary, he takes a positive stance. He tries to acquire the greatest possible independence with regard to the system, and then attempts to actualize in his life and experience a radical alternative to that system. Many esoteric movements also tend to belong to this group. It must be said that many of the already existing groups of men and women who strive today to realize this new style of life, or who dedicate themselves to studying and formulating its bases, are authentic successors to traditional monasticism—imperfect and provisional as these first essays may be.

There is also a seventh group: the true marginals, those without a voice, without means of subsistence, those exploited, neglected, or ignored by all the others. The monk also establishes a singular relationship with these rejects of the earth, but in this case as well there is a marked difference: while the genuinely destitute have a vague consciousness of their own marginal status, the monk preserves the traditional conviction that he is centered in the very heart of reality.

It is just this that permits the monk not to be violent. Authentic nonviolence must be more than a mere means for obtaining whatever is sought. If the case is put on this level, the active monk is going to appear hopelessly naïve to, say, his Marxist partner in revolution. Nonviolence is an end in itself, because it embodies a form of life that believes ultimately in the harmonious structure of reality. Without this faith in the radical goodness and integrity of existence, nonviolence is not only impossible but ceases to be nonviolent and contradicts itself. If evil is located on the same ontological level as good, it is not enough to oppose it nonviolently; it is not sufficient merely not to collaborate with it in the confidence that it will thus—some day—burn itself out and the basic harmony of the universe be reestablished. No, if evil is granted this status, then it must be eradicated, pulled out by the roots without any sentimental consideration for the good grain that might be growing together with it in the same soil. This is why nonviolence can only have meaning in an adualistic conception of reality. It makes sense only if the world is not a battlefield between Ohrmazd and Ahriman. The monk's entrance into the secular world may make all the difference here, if his witness concerning both the means and ends of our human struggle continues to be an expression of his vocation to an unqualified holiness. (And, yes, you may well read this to imply unilateral disarmament.)

Sūtra 9. The Memory of the Ultimate and of Its Constant Presence

Gloss

The combination of a psychological presence and an ontological memory belongs most especially to the archetype of the monk. It is not an ontological presence: it is simply a "given fact." To ponder the Ultimate may be the mark of the philosopher, but the monk as such is not a philosopher and is even rather suspicious of a certain predominance of mind and thought in Man's life. This *sūtra* speaks of an ontological fact brought constantly to one's memory—that is, a psychological calling to mind of the ontological fact of the reality of the Ultimate.

Nor is this a psychological remembrance of the entrance into the Ultimate reality. Such remembrance is the lot of almost any human being, at one time or another. It is rather the ontologization of this psychological fact—that is, the remembrance is to some extent considered an ontological fact. In other words, ontology is psychologized and psychology ontologized. Ontology is brought to mind, and psychology is given an ontological weight. The ontological fact of (the existence of) the Ultimate is converted into the psychological center of the monk's life, and the psychological fact of the convenience and usefulness of such a remembrance becomes the ontological pivot of the monastic way of life. Let me explain this a little more clearly.

The Ultimate has many names: the Absolute, God, Brahman, *nirvāṇa*, Nothingness, Absolute Future, Justice, and so on. Its entrance has also had many connotations, the most important of them all being Death, but it may equally be called Justification, Innocence, Initiation, Love, and so on.

The monk is fascinated by the Ultimate Reality. His life is geared toward it as the only thing that really counts. But this Ultimate Reality has a gate, and this entrance is what concentrates all of our efforts and energies. To have the Four Noble Truths ever before our eyes; to constantly recall the caducity of all things; to meditate on death day in, day out; to see every event in our lives under the perspective of death, not to be affected by anything that passes away or has no immediate bearing on the ultimate goal of life or nothing to do with the gate conducive to that goal; to conserve equanimity and serenity in the face of world calamities and social upheavals because they do not belong to that ultimate level; to be free and prepared to face ultimate reality—these and many similar injunctions are well-known by monks.

As a matter of fact, the psychological motivation for most monastic vocations comes from the seriousness of this fact, be it called death, the transient nature of visible things, or by whatever name. As David Steindl-Rast tells us, "It is in confrontation with death that the monk situates his encounter with the Ultimate Reality." This is "the basic experience that makes a man become a monk." At any rate, the monk is carefree, serene, nonattached, uninvolved vis-à-vis all the ripples agitating the common human affairs of the majority of mortals because he has already squarely faced death. He has died the Great Death, as Zen puts it. The monk is something of an aristocrat. He belongs to a minority fully dedicated to that final goal, and he may also be living such a life vicariously for everyone. He is not selfish, but somehow an exception. Yet he very much relies on the existence of the others. The whole world would collapse tomorrow if everybody were to become a monk, and the monk himself would not be able to survive were it not for the fact that there are nonmonks around (and devotees).

Death and Ultimate Reality are facts of human consciousness, but the monk has a psychological relationship with the Ultimate and ontologizes its gate. The Ultimate is there not only as the goal of existence but also in the mind and heart of the monk all the time. Death is not only recognized and accepted, it is given a status of its own and allowed to dominate and condition all other human activities. It is precisely because of this that monkhood has a tendency to be institutionalized. The presence of the Ultimate and the reality of death are far too serious matters to leave to the caprice of freewheeling human nature or to the will or whims of the individual. Monasticism, as it were, institutionalizes the presence and the reality of the Absolute. The monastery is an institution where death is present and the Ultimate constantly remembered. It becomes a witness to and a sign of the reality of the Absolute.

It is this constant reenactment of the Ultimate and the permanent presence of the way to it that has led most monastic institutions to cultivate the liturgy in a special manner and to live human life in its entirety as a ritual that expresses and unfolds the very destiny of the individual and that of the whole universe. The real clock of the *vihara*, the monastery, is not the movement of the sun, or the events of history, but the clock of the anthropocosmos on its way to liberation.

Nowhere, perhaps, is the principle of blessed simplicity more evident than in this last *sūtra*. It is the experience of the Ultimate, the reality of God, the Other Shore, that magnetizes the monk and allows him to simplify his life. This would not be possible if the gate to this Ultimate were not a new life, which can be put forward and symbolized in many ways (initiation, profession, etc.), but which culminates in the mystery of death. Death is the gate. But death kills everything. So the monk is not much concerned with anything mortal. Death simplifies everything.

Commentary

The modern monk is equally "God-intoxicated," as some people still say today, but he would not like that this intoxication be a merely cutaneous eruption. He fears sometimes that the constant thought of death may paralyze the human efforts for mortal values that are nevertheless worth our energy and attention. The modern monk is fascinated by the intuition that *nirvāṇa* is *saṃsāra* and *saṃsāra* is *nirvāṇa*, that one's talents have to yield their fruits here on earth as well and that the hundred- fold is also for this life. Yet he can equally be torn apart because his elders tell him, and his own experience confirms, that this ideal synthesis may be unattainable and any mere compromise lethal.

In the face of the easygoing contemporary efforts at harmonizing these two extremes, the monk feels inclined to underscore the traditional that abandoning the world contributes to its salvation, and so on, but the monk's concern is that he has only one life, and often he wonders how all this can be possible.

The old masters knew well that one has to integrate death into life, that you should look at the lilies of the field even if their existence is fleeting, and they knew also that the monk is not life-denying—but what is this life? The life that does not die or the mortal life? The sociological pattern of monasticism was turned toward everlasting life. The winds of secularity seem to be blowing in favor of mortal life. Can a monk, therefore, be secular and still be a monk?

It is this last *sūtra*, especially, that will prompt us to examine this underlying tension in a more philosophical light in the final part of this presentation.

Epilogue

The Canon of the Disciple does not intend to replace the Rule of the Master. The *kanon* is only a "cane," a walking stick, a measure, something used for comparison so as to have some kind of standard. The canon does not offer a model or even provide answers. These have to be elaborated through line, harking back to the "one thing only" that the Buddha taught to h disciples and which the Christian gospel equally emphasizes. He shuns instant spiritualities and superficial gratifications. But he senses as well that a certain preoccupation with death and the centrality of the eschatological may not only dehumanize him and alienate him from his fellow beings but also make it all too easy. In a word, he fears spiritual selfishness. He is uneasy chanting psalms while his brethren suffer or struggle for economic or political liberation; he feels uncomfortable looking after his own perfection while many of the urgent tasks to be done for the world would require a certain renunciation of his own good manners and "virtues." He knows very well the ambivalence of all these thoughts, and also the excruciating pain of disentangling himself from the common affairs of the world out of love and interest and hope for them.

Certainly, naked we came into this world and naked we shall return to Mother Earth, in spite of all Egyptian and cryogenic mummifications. Certainly the monk submits to being stripped of all inauthentic adherences and is ready to concentrate on the essential, but is not the Ultimate linked with the penultimate and from there on down to the least grain of sand? Is the Ultimate so foreign and transcendent, so wholly other that it has no relation to the strivings of Man? Undoubtedly, death sets all our perspectives aright, ... double reaction to death: it may be seen as the end form of growth coming from both an internal dynamism and an external grafting. And in the *fuga mundi*, we may have an example of precisely this.

And this is the second part of my answer. In point of fact, in the traditional *fuga mundi* I see a very positive aspect, though I shall not dwell now on what *mundus* meant to those generations. In my description of the modern monk, I have stressed the element of swimming against the current, of taking part and yet having a different attitude, of belonging to the fifth and seventh group and yet not accepting the rules of the game. It is this nonviolent, holistic, and all-embracing attitude that makes of the monk precisely someone who does not accept the trends of the times, the *mundus* as it goes—that is, the System. So, in this context, the *fuga mundi* would not be an antisystem or a countersystem—that is, a dialectical opposition to the System—but the monk's nonacceptance of the ways in which the problems are posed.

If by *mundus* we mean the System, then we can still find, nowadays, a sense in the *fuga mundi* of the monastic vocation. The monk is simply the person who does not play that game. This is a very traditional attitude, at least inasmuch as the monk does not adjust himself to the rules of that world. The change may be expressed better in the second part of what I said: not abiding by the rules, and nevertheless playing the game. Here is the difference. You do not escape from the world, although you withdraw from it and struggle against it, and strive for a better alternative.

You may retort that the rules *are* the game, so that if I do not follow the rules I cannot play the game. I disagree. This would only be the case if our relation to the world were a dialectical one. But that is precisely what I contest, on the basis of the *madhyamamārga*, the middle way of the Buddha, and of the sentence "in the world but not of the world" by Jesus. You are "in the world" playing the game, but not "of the world." And, further, the game is in the playing, and by doing this you may be able to lay down another set of rules different from those imposed by the authorities. Without rules there can be no game, but the imposed or accepted rules should not be the only ones. And here, again, is the difference. Some will say: Let us upset the game by a violent revolution, let's seize power and impose our own set of rules. The monk, I submit, playfully plays the game, and in playing he changes some of the rules—at the risk of his life, obviously. For by changing the rules he will eventually change the game, and this will not be tolerated. Civil resistance, for instance, is an example of playing the game, accepting the framework of that society, not just shooting it down or substituting another model; but at the same time not abiding by the rules, resisting rules felt to be unjust or inhuman, and being ready to become victims, martyrs, and be pushed aside.

I hear echoes of the Old Testament in some of the things you say: There is a notion of tragedy, of loss, of sorrow, connected to barrenness, to having no children, to a body that does not bear fruit. It always struck me as somewhat sad and ironic when, in a monastery, they chant the psalm saying, "Your wife, like a fruitful vine at the heart of your house," being meanwhile surrounded by men whom I knew would be very good fathers, men who were kind and gentle, and whom I could see having beautiful children. Hence my question: What happens, I wonder, to Man's genetic pool, since the people who are interested in religious life do not have descendants—and this has been the case for centuries—while "those of the world" keep on multiplying? Let's deal a bit more thoroughly with the subject "barrenness and religious life."

As to your first question, it is important to realize that celibacy is not a universal feature within the monastic tradition. It is mainly found in those traditions that link a notion of individual salvation with a very peculiar mode of temporal consciousness, so that *individual destiny* is emphasized, though in many different ways. Traditions that stress celibacy seem to stress the salvation or destiny of the individual human being. Buddhism would not use such terms, but it comes to the same: "Work on your salvation with diligence," said the Enlightened One. By contrast, Judaism and many of the African religions seem to think of salvation collectively, as a people. I say this to properly set the issue of celibacy, which should be distinguished from that of sexuality and has, on the other hand, a great deal to do with nonattachment.

For the Jewish people, and for most African peoples, salvation and the entire human pilgrimage is a collective matter, a people marching toward an end; so, the barrenness of the celibate life would appear as a kind of cosmic pessimism, and it could not be accepted. Celibacy, in this instance, proves not to be a universal category, but a particular way of seeing, a way of realizing the perfection of the individual, under certain conditions. These conditions are, first, the emphasis on the individual (but the word "individual" is a little misleading here), and second, a peculiar ahistorical sense of time. The spiral conception of reality—the karmic, kalpic, and Christian ones—vouches that nothing is lost if you have no children. For the Hindus, not to have children, especially male children, was a calamity. Hindus insist that, as far as possible, you should have children before you embark on your *saṃnyāsa*. In other instances, when the *group*, the *tribe*, the chosen people, the race, and so forth, are the most important category, celibacy would be totally out of place. So I think we should shift the reflection on celibacy from the sexual basis, on which it is generally put nowadays, to another, more cross-cultural—and, in my opinion, deeper—series of reflections.

I fully understand the feeling of sadness when listening to the chanting of psalms of the Jewish tradition in a congregation of unmarried males. On the other hand, as to the genetic manipulation of humankind, I would not admit that kind of premise, because it is methodologically, ontologically, epistemologically wrong to treat human beings like so many peanuts. I do not think that, even if the genetic laws are indeed laws, they apply here. Certainly, one can manipulate the genes, but I do not feel that we can reduce everything to genetic laws. So genetics is neither an argument for nor an argument against monastic celibacy. I could be sarcastic and say that it is a blessing that "overreligious" people do not reproduce: their offspring would likely be bigoted either in favor of or against religion... just joking, of course.

In the quest for wholeness in monasticism, and not perfection, the trend seems throughout the centuries to have been Apollonian. What about the Dionysian side? And also, in your opinion, how does a monk integrate his own feminine dimension, and a nun the masculine?

As to the first question, I would say that the Dionysiac, by definition, has no blueprint or preprogrammed plan, or else it would be Apollonian. It has to be holy (or unholy) spontaneity, an orgy, or whatever: something is really Dionysiac when it surprises you as much as everyone else taking part in it. The only thing to be said would be: *Do not stifle the spirit*, especially for the development of the Dionysiac aspect of life. To the monks I would like to say just that: let us not stifle the spirit. Now, of course, this implies and requires a real purification of the heart, so that true spontaneity does not lead to the slavery of a bacchanal.

As to the second question—how the monk integrates the feminine, and the nun the masculine—let me say, first, that I think this integration is a totally healthy and necessary one. If we delve into the Christian monastic tradition a little, we will discover an extraordinary number of friendships between people of different sexes—paradigmatic examples, many well known, many others less well known, of extraordinarily intimate relationships, which must certainly be considered as sexual relationships. Not that they had gone to bed together, which would be unthink- able... perhaps because the whole beauty and dance and play of communication and mutual excitement and mutual inspiration would fade away the moment one particular aspect of sexuality had imposed itself on the whole interplay.

The sexual encompasses the body, the spirit, the eyes, the hands, the gestures—everything, any connection, any friendship, any relationship. The bare fact that you are a different living being is something that puts not only my mind but everything into play. We seem sometimes to think in black-and-white: here is the male and there is the female. But the whole thing is a gamut, and normality consists of interaction, both within myself and with every living being. When I speak to another person, I am all the more sexually conditioned the less I think that the other person is a man or a woman. Experience shows that the less conscious you are that your partner in the dialogue or conversation is male or female, the more genuinely your sexuality is brought into play—understanding by sexuality this polarity, this yin/yang of the human being.

In the Vedic ritual of marriage—just before the two go and discover the Pole star as the center round which everything turns—there is a step in which the bridegroom says, "I am He," and the bride says, "I am She." I am *the* He, I am *the* She. I embody and represent one pole of the polarity, and not just this individuation of a nice girl or a young bridegroom. This integration is achieved by conqueringyour internal and external freedom. I call this the new innocence, which permeates our spirit, our thoughts, our intentions, and everything else. The moment I want to possess, I fall into concupiscence, which is a sin, both in marriage and out of marriage. This is *parigraha* (grasping) and doing violence to personal relationships, which are not in the order of having, but of being. The really free and spontaneous action is not conscious that it is free and spontaneous, just as meditation is really thoughtless when it is not worried by the thought of thoughtlessness. These relations, in the Christian tradition, between pairs of holy men and holy women are extremely revealing : those people's lives were not sexually atrophied. And yet they had neither children nor that sort of make-believe that modern films and literature suppose sexuality consists of. I think we are in one of those moments in which things are in flux and new avenues are opening up. We must only hope that these avenues will be followed in a creative way, that is, without preplanned thoughts and preconceived ideas, since creation happens out of nothing.

Now, about "how does the male monk integrate the feminine and how does the nun integrate the masculine?" I am not precisely proposing a greater friendship between monks and nuns, but rather, a greater openness of the nun toward the *animus* and of the monk toward the *anima*, assuming that these Jungian notions are valid. The important thing is to have no fear or, in the traditional language, to have purity of heart.

Could you more precisely state the role of the monk in politics?

Let me make a general statement: *Thinking leads to knowledge.* And that is one approach—you think about something, and finally you may understand. Contrari- wise, *contemplation leads to action.* If I think that so many people are starving, and so on, I may finally find the causes of it and be able to explain this whole thing. But if I contemplate the very same case, I cannot leave it unchanged. I will have to do something. I will have to get my hands dirty and plunge into action. The real criterion of true contemplation is that it leads to action, even if that action consists only in transforming one's own life and immediate environment. If this is the case, the monk has the strictest moral obligation to denounce, to cry out, to speak up, and to act. And this action ought not to be just a *re*action—like throwing a bomb, or writing a letter to a newspaper—but something more effective. Contemplation is a dangerous activity. Nor is it an exclusive prerogative of the monk, which is what leads me to warn against overcompartmentalization. I spoke of the archetype of monkhood, and this cuts both ways; the person who is a canonical monk may also be many other things.

Yet I think the monk today is spurred into action by his very vocation, with all the dangers this implies. If we do nothing, then we are in the same boat as the French bishops blessing cannons while the German bishops blessed the fighters so as to let their peoples wage war against each other. If we do nothing, we bless and condone the status quo, which is already a political decision.

How can we distinguish between synthesis and syncretism?

Syncretism is an external juxtaposition; synthesis is a living assimilation. Syncretism is a accumulation; synthesis is a living organism. A symbol of synthesis is the Eucharist. You eat and you assimilate, and what happens is not that you are converted into Christ, but that Christ is converted into you. It is not that you become the consecrated bread, but the consecrated bread becomes part of your proteins. And that is synthesis.

Synthesis is produced by the way in which we assimilate; it reveals the metabolic aspect of the entire reality. You grow, and religions themselves grow by this positive metabolism, not by mere juxtaposition. Syncretism, on the other hand, is a kind of indigestion we have to be wary of today, when we too optimistically suppose we can eat everything that is put in front of us. And when we meet, and when the religions of East and West meet, I would certainly want to forewarn you against the possibility of indigestions that would not lead to a synthesis.

The secret is to keep the balance. Some people would just like to eat everything they are offered, and other people use all sorts of spiritual and intellectual preservatives that may stifle the openness of the spirit. At the present moment, I think we are at a crossroads where *viveka*, discernment, and patience are needed in order to discover the signs of the times. The challenge of modern monasticism is that it finds itself at the crossroads, and on the deepest level of very many traditions. It is not by imitating a few externals that I become a Hindū, or whatever.

The gist of my presentation is not so much to supply a solution or an answer, but rather to evoke in all of us this sense of uneasiness, which is perhaps one of the best translations of the Buddhist *duḥkha*, which is the human condition itself—a creative uneasiness, in that it makes us aware of the enormous responsibilities we have. And it makes us aware that our trusting God—which is a very normal, natural thing—today implies the tremendous challenge of trusting *ourselves*, both personally and collectively. A small group of people can do enormous things. I think the monk should overcome that sort of inferiority complex toward the political situation suggesting that we can do nothing because we do not have the means. I think that the most effective way of destroying the power of the powerful is by not being impressed by their power—to render them powerless by simply ignoring that they are so powerful. It is a question of continuing calmly alongyour route when the guns are leveled at you. Of course, it is easier said than done.... Perhaps we should not even say these things, but just do them. And we do them when we have integrated our doing and our being.

9
Synthesis

A synthesis is neither a systematic overview, nor a summary. I will try to put together three different groups of problems, followed by a fourth, more general reflection.

The first group of problems would come under the cross-cultural pattern guiding our overall approach. The second would frame the sociological challenge, the third would be to sketch some anthropological problems, while the fourth will try to bring a provisional close to the dilemma of the "two spiritualities."

Cross-Cultural Pattern

I presented nine *sūtras.* They are a challenge. They invite a further understanding, or perhaps herald a new mutation in monastic life, or else they demand rejection altogether, so that monastic spirituality is kept uncontaminated by secularity. I draw your attention to the fact that during the days at the symposium we shared four liturgies, which indicate to me at once the way in and the way out. If the solution is not in some sense liturgical, I do not think it will endure. But liturgy, as you know, means "the work of the people," *leit-ourgia...* so we still have much work to do.

To speak of a synthesis requires a certain explanation of the ground on which one has built the intellectual construction of what has been said.

We all know that monotheism is not essential to monkhood. Christian monks are generally theistic, Buddhist and Jainas are certainly nontheistic, and Hindūs by and large neither one nor the other.

I cannot now elaborate the proper background for a synthesis. I shall only sketch my Trinitarian hypothesis over against the backdrop of a scientific model and a Judeo-Christian paradigm.

According to a condensed assessment of the scientific option, there is a starting point here—that is matter, which is the cosmos—and that there is a temporal and linear evolution which passes through vegetative and animal life, then through human life, ultimately gets to the divine, and continues. This scientific view embraces, in a certain sense, the entire reality: from primal matter, through 4 billion years of evolution, up to Men and then the divine. This is the mystery of reality. One may refine this view, or say that it is one of many possible scientific paradigms, but at any rate it can serve as a model for the scientific worldview.

We could draw it like this:

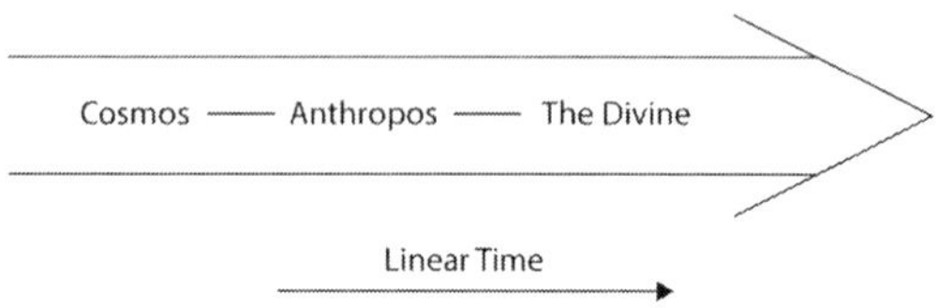

Figure 1

It is clear that the word "divine" as it has been used by Paolo Soleri will be contested by other scientists. We can as well call it the Superhuman, the Future, the Unknown—but deciding which is not relevant for our purposes. The monk collaborates here in the unfolding of the universe toward the divine by being rooted in the past and open to the future.

Another option is a certain Christian view—and I only say "Christian" to make it a little simpler—which admits this line of evolution, but emphasizes that the divine is also a *theos* outside the whole concatenation. This *theos* has a triple function. At the beginning there is God, the divine impulse, who or which starts the whole show, gives the "kick-off," as it were. So it begins here. Obviously, the "kick-off " is divine, and this God is already at work so that evolution may take place. A typical example of this view would be Teilhard de Chardin. Now, such a God has three main points of contact with the world. At the beginning : creation, the first arrow, the starting point, the kick-off. Then, lo! When human beings appear—whether Abel or Christ or whoever—a second descent of the divine takes place. The Christian word for this is Incarnation: the second eruption of the divine into the temporal reality. And finally there is a third line, distinguished from these two (though I won't now enter into all the subtleties of the theologians), the one marking the last encounter. Here we have a two-way traffic. On the one hand, this event is called *parousia*, the Second Coming. On the other hand, Peter calls it *apokatastasis pant¯on* (the restoration of all things), and Paul calls it *anakephalai¯osis* (the recapitulation) of all things in Christ. This last contact reabsorbs the whole of creation in the way it all began. And that's the end of the story. God and Man live together happily ever after,...

We could combine the two schemes like this:

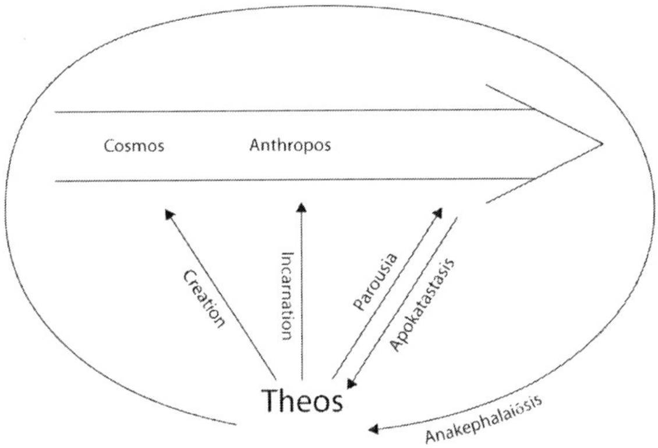

Figure 2

Now, if scientific time is linear, monotheistic temporality certainly does not need to be so. The Christian monk here is rooted in the mystery of the First Coming of Christ and stands as an eschatological sign of the Second Coming, as a witness that only the one thing is needful.

We could obviously refine this scheme and consider the passage from *cosmos* to *anthropos* as a more complex process of evolving forms of life and consciousness. So, under *cosmos* we would have inorganic and organic matter, vegetal and animal beings, and so on. Under *anthropos* we could also include the different kinds of bodies (the gross, the subtle, etc.) and of conscious beings (demons and spirits of all sorts, including the Gods). We could equally assume that this scheme, once it has come all the way round to an end, repeats itself, be this in identically the same way (circular view), be this on different planes (spiral view), and so forth and so on.

I would like to present a third scheme, which offers a cross-cultural pattern. We have at the very beginning a dimensionless triangle, a still point, in which the material element, the factor of consciousness, and the unfathomable freedom I call divine are all three already there. Then this triangle evolves: a spherical wave unfolding globally in all directions. There is a kind of rhythm, or breathing—the systole and diastole of reality—and these pulsations are what constitute Time.

We would then have the following mandala:

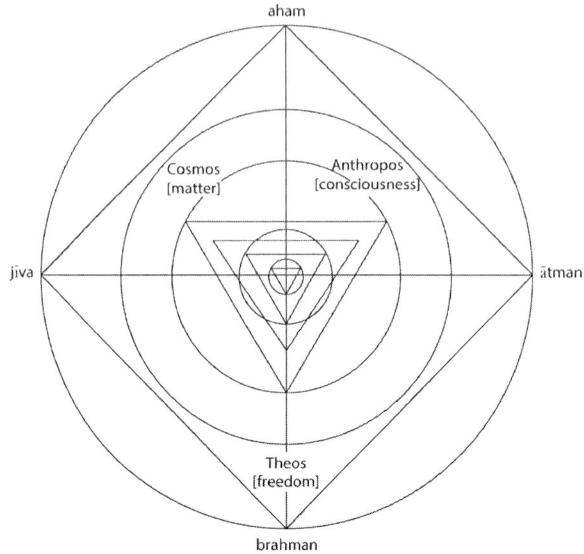

Figure 3

The mandala helps us visualize the center, which is not always easy. That center, at once immanent and transcendent, is at the very core of the three constitutive dimensions of reality, each of which is present and effective in the unfolding of everything that is real: the *Cosmos* (or matter and energy), *Man* (or consciousness and will), and the *Theos* (or freedom and absolute love).

I shall not develop now what I call the *quaternitas perfecta* represented by the four Sanskrit words *jīva*, *aham*, ā*tman*, *brahman* (soul, I, self, ground). The concentration of these four—that is, letting the four centers coalesce into one—would amount to realization.

Monkhood would represent here the quest for the center, under the assumption that this center is totally simple. We do not know anything about the center except by approaching it in a more or less perfect way. But the activity by which one reaches the center depends on how we imagine, surmise, believe, experience... the center to be. By and large, the thrust of the monastic tradition has been to reach that center by *simplification*—implying that the center is simple. The modern monk, as I have said, would like to get at it through *integration*—implying that the center is complex. This does not deny, of course, that before you can embark on a proper integration, you have to purify your being and simplify your life; only then is integration even possible. Inasmuch as to look for truth, to create beauty, or even to earn one's livelihood or organize society or increase wealth or produce instruments is related to that activity of centering, of concentrating, of striving toward that very center, we are cultivating the monastic dimension of life.

And how do we become centered? The answer differs according to culture(s), religion(s), and time(s). We have already given the one example of Hindū and Christian monasticism.

The scientific model is part of the Western approach, in which the transcendent seems less transcendent and more futuristic. It is indeed the *futuristic* center: here transcendence is not outside time, but in the future. Perhaps the greatest tribute to this modern scientific archetype is that no less a theologian than Karl Rahner speaks of God as *die absolute Zukunft*, the Absolute Future. In the scientific model, this futuristic center is attained by means of measurable knowledge. There is also another path within the Western system, the Marxist one. It is equally futuristic, but oriented toward the perfect classless society. A main difference is that the means is not measureable knowledge but politico-economic action. Still, these are all considered means to attain the center.

The monk, then, can exist in different cultures, ideologies, and worldviews. In all these lifestyles, however, the monk seems to have a kind of anticipation of that very center, which spurs him on in the quest. In sum, this quest for the center depends greatly on the different conditions and assumed beliefs about where that center lies, or what constitutes it.

The Sociological Challenge

And now we leave behind these grand scenarios of cosmology and metaphysics in order to enter into modern Western society, but in a way that our reflections are also applicable, with qualifications, to the societies on the way to modernization. In spite of other theoretical possibilities, today modernization and Westernization are de facto almost synonyms. The dream of modernizing without Westernizing is just that—a pious and naïve dream, but one that is not incarnated in reality. But this is a different topic.

What, then, is the sociological challenge? It is that in this modern Western society, the system is breaking down. I use this simply as a codeword: *the System*—that is, the social, political, economic, and religious order—seems to be collapsing. To many people the system seems merely imperfect and unsatisfying. But I dare say that it is unjust and even inhuman. It cannot just be reformed. It has to be redeemed. It represents the shift of the center from God, or Man, or Cosmos into one particular corner of reality with pretensions of universality. I called it "technocracy" or "technocentrism." I suggest that this system is falling apart because it has tried to resolve the global human predicament by and with the means and insights of one particular culture or religion. And here lies the seriousness of cross-cultural studies, which imply a good deal more than patchwork or cosmetics to beautify or whitewash the existing system. I repeat that, ultimately, the reason for the collapse appears to be not that the system as such is so bad, but that in today's context it amounts to an abortive attempt to solve global human problems within the structures and strictures of a single culture. Thus the system is "de-centrated," off-kilter, distorted; it has lost (or never found) its center.

To be sure, there has never been a spotless and ideal human system. But all the systems of the past were partial empires. The empires of China, Assyria, Rome, Christendom, Spain, Britain, and so on, did indeed collapse, but there were always other heirs and other victors to learn the lessons or to repeat the mistakes. The modern technologico-economic system is not the North American or the Russian empire, for instance; it permeates in a protean way most cultures of the planet; it is multinational and even multi-ideological. To want to impose the Roman vision of the world, or the British rule—this may be good for Rome or for Britain; it may even be, in some ways, beneficial for the people thereby "civilized," that is, subjugated. But none of these former imperialisms could claim to be universal in the sense of the present-day system, which offers neither heirs nor beneficiaries nor alternatives on the same level as the system. When this system crumbles, it is the end of history!—that is, of the historical myth of humankind.

The task of the monk is to concentrate on and in the quest for the center. But today, as we have been at pains to describe, many no longer envision this center in another world, in time above or ahead. When the center was believed to be God (you recall St. Benedict saying, "*Si revera Deum quaerit*" [if one *truly* seeks God...]), and in this search one seeks God and God alone, then that effort would center you and the entire universe as well. Secularity may be telling us that the center itself is not to be found solely in a transcendent, atemporal God disconnected from the world—so that we would reach the center only once history is over and the world finished, in the *parousia*, at the very end, the Last Judgment, when God will be all in all and the arrow of evolution will have reached its target—but that this center is equally material and human, that is, *cosmotheandric*. This is the ultimate challenge of secularity to the monastic dimension of Man: looking for God and God alone in a disincarnated and utterly transcendent way may not be of much help to us if we are to find the very center of reality, and thus center ourselves and the universe on ultimate truth.

It goes without saying that we should not make a caricature of the symbol God, but neither can we deny that the whole problem today requires a deeper and enlarged experience.

The task, then, is the quest for this center, along with a search for the factors that have "de-centered" the universe of our experience. I may use a single traditional word here, but we shall have to translate it in an existential way. The traditional word would be *hamartia*, sin, *avidyā*, ignorance, but the translation will have to explicitate the *results* of this severance—that is, hatred, or whatever: hunger, injustice, wars of every imaginable variety, inequities and iniquities of all sorts, and so on. I submit that today's most urgent monastic task involves a search for God in the direction of politics, society, economics, science, and culture; and not in perpetuating a suprasocietal, apolitical institution sublimely unconcerned with economic affairs, sovereignly above scientific disputes and exquisitely unconnected with culture. Such a God would be an abstraction, not a living God and not, certainly (to take an example from the Judeo-Christian-Islamic tradition), the partisan God of Abraham, Isaac, and Jacob.

Concrete Concerns

Three very concrete concerns appear to me to issue from the sociological challenge outlined above.

- First, a need for *formation*. But the first step toward this is genuine *in*-formation.

  Monastic traditions are not in general sufficiently aware of the state of the world, which worsens and sickens day by day. By this I do not mean being supplied with mass media information, or newspapers, the latest idea or an instant replay of what happened somewhere in the world yesterday—all of which may indeed only distort the real vision and genuine perspective that is needed in order to lead reality on the way to its center, toward its destiny, however we may interpret this. But there is a tremendous lack of information nonetheless. That sovereign nonchalance, unconcern, or disinterest in worldly affairs today can in fact only appear as the most *un*-monastic of virtues, since it fosters the cruelty of indifference, callousness, and guilty ignorance. Many anchorites of ancient times became cenobites for the sake of edifying the brethren. Perhaps the new monasteries should again be centers where the real "building up" of the world is studied and cultivated.
- Second, a *contemplative study* or approach to these very problems, so that they are not viewed as merely technical affairs of data and information, science and logistics. Today's global human dilemmas are not subject to immediate or technical solutions. All that we have

been saying here about contemplation should have a direct bearing on the very ways we tackle the urgent human problems of everyday life: society, politics, science, culture. A sui generis methodology should emerge that integrates the activity of contemplation and the life of contemplative action. I would like to not be misunderstood to be saying that such a study should reduce itself to sociological issues only. A knowledge in depth of one's own tradition, for instance, is equally imperative. Moreover, we can no longer rightly know ourselves if we do not also know our neighbors—and their opinions about us. The knowledge of other spiritual traditions is a monastic imperative as well.

- Third, a call to *action*. For monasticism, a call to action does not mean activism or mere "politicking." We could perhaps reinterpret those words by St. Paul: *Conversatio nostra in caelis est.* Our *politeuma* is in heaven. And *on earth, too*, says the modern monk, because heaven is not only merited here on earth but also incarnated here below. Our polity, our *conversatio*, our activity, our field of action, our lifestyle, our commonwealth, our state, our concern is on earth. Heavenly citizens we may be, but living here on earth. We must dirty our hands, says the modern monk. Our *politeuma* is in the *polis* of this world, and this, too, has become a monastic imperative: *action*, a call to action for the new polity, the new political incarnation—not, I repeat, in the minimized sense of the word "politics" in common language.

Traditional monasticism converted the monasteries into a *politeuma*, a model of commonwealth in symbiosis with the environing world. But what was once a symbiosis can become parasitism if communication, and even communion, is not reestablished. It may be retorted that this is a very lofty and idealistic view of the monk. I was encouraged to read in the Supplement to the *New Catholic Encyclopedia* (1979) that "the monastic institution is prophetic." Without wanting to identify the two charisms, it cannot be denied that the new monk is no longer satisfied with a *fuga mundi* and tries to accept a *consecratio mundi* in a very special way.

Anthropological Problems

The third way in which I would synthesize all that we have been discussing would come under the heading of *anthropological problems.* I say "problems" because we are not really prepared to face the fact that our underlying anthropology simply does not have all the answers, and this amounts to a cultural scandal. That science changes is not a scandal under the assumptions of the worldview prevalent in the West today; it belongs to the very natures of both science and the human mind. Pure natural science can have the freedom and the beauty of changing every five minutes, like the weather in Vermont, because science does not claim to offer an anchor for human life, only an explanation of how things happen. But that we try to found our lives and direct our own existence on the basis of something that is "A" today and "B" tomorrow, and changes again to "A" the day after tomorrow : that is a scandal. That something can be a sin one day and a virtue the next shows an anthropological instability and uneasiness that is the sorry outcome of very many cultural factors.

In other words, the scandal inherent in holding fast to the scientific view of Man is that this view claims to be rational, and because the human being is assumed to be a rational animal, Man is supposed to follow the findings of modern science. And yet this very science changes constantly, not to mention the many divergent opinions represented by acknowledged scientists. It is closely akin to the scandal felt so acutely by Descartes, but this time leaning in another, almost contrary, direction. Descartes was taken aback by the many disparate theological opinions of his time, which could obviously no longer pretend to direct human life. He made a tabula rasa of all of them and tried to found an indubitable—and this meant to him a rational—method. Today we have not so much a profusion of conflicting theologies as a proliferation of many mutually incompatible rational systems, which thus defeat their own purpose of rationally directing human life.

I am not proposing that we go back to unproved theological beliefs or fall into irrationality, or into the democratic intellectualism that operates as if the vote of the majority were the only criterion of truth. I am, however, endeavoring to rediscover the place and function of *myth* in human life, and to situate rationality in the total human—and cosmotheandric—context.

Anyway, it does not help to say we have no anthropology to meet the challenges of our day. At least we may be coming to grips with the problematic. And to be aware that the problematic is unresolved is already the beginning of something. That "something" may be, to begin with, precisely that we cannot rely on scientific paradigms, as also we cannot rely utterly and blindly on any of our own conceptions of the human being. That we cannot rely completely on the *logos*, that we cannot rely fully on orthodoxy, that we need both wings to fly with the wind and a deeper ground that does not depend on our ideas, conceptions, or ideologies—it is a daring proposition. It would mean the end of the Platonic period of civilization; the *eidos* would cease to be the final criterion. This is what I mean by *the new innocence*, which is not a "second" innocence.

I hear already the objection that I am contradicting myself by establishing the doctrine that we cannot rely on doctrines. This is not so, on at least two counts. First, because I am not saying that we should not rely on doctrines. I am affirming that this reliance is shaky. We are perfectly free to rely on any doctrine we like. Then we ourselves at a later stage, and also probably others around us, will contest our own doctrine. We can then say that our doctrine is good for us. Period. Without extrapolating. Or we may say that all the others are wrong and don't see the issue. Then we will engage in a doctrinal debate. Neither case presents major difficulties regarding our question. We have a plurality of conflicting doctrines, and so doctrine is no criterion for supraindividual truth.

But second, I am not contradicting myself because I am not contending that the rational aspect of Man should not be rational. I am affirming that rationality and even the *logos* are not the only aspects of the human being that constitute its "essence": what Man is. Man is also spirit, and the spirit is not subordinated to the *logos*; Man is also myth, and the myth is irreducible to the *logos*; Man is also body, and the body is not reducible to the mind. I am further affirming that these elements cannot exist one without the other, so that I am not propounding the preponderance of the myth over the *logos* or vice versa. Nor am I advocating any kind of materialism. Theologically speaking, I recall that very early on, the Christian church had already condemned "subordinationism" as a heresy: The Spirit is not subordinate to the *Logos*. *Pneuma* and *Logos* are knit together by the abyss or silence or nonbeing of the Father, *fons et origo totius divinitatis* (source and origin of the entire Godhead), to speak with the Councils. But I should revert to our synthesis.

After focusing on some of the problems, I would like to deal with this problematic in very concrete terms now. By looking for a definition of the monastic dimension, we have probably found three types of monk. We should carefully distinguish them now, so as not to induce confusion. Monk Number 1: The archetype, that central dimension that exists in the human being. As I have said time and again, if we hold up Monk Number 1 as a model for the *humanum*, then the trouble begins. It is only one dimension. Then, Monk Number 2: People and groups that strive to cultivate the dimension of Monk Number 1. And Monk Number 3: Institutionalized or traditional forms of monasticism.

We may now reach some clarity if we address ourselves to two groups of problems: practical issues and theoretical questions.

Practical Issues

I would like to stress that most *practical* issues we face today are linked with the double relations of contemporary monk N. 2 to traditional monk N. 3—that is, how the emerging and proliferating contemplative groups (monk N. 2) can relate constructively to the institutionalized forms of monastic life (monk N. 3). With this we touch on problems of temporary monasticism, of monastic spirituality *in concreto*, of active life, of mixed communities of men and women, of transcultural lifestyles, of multireligious monasteries, and so on. It is the privilege and burden of monk N. 3 in the traditional monasteries to understand, foster, advise, and help to develop further the new groups of monk N. 2 so that a healthy pluralism might be attained, or at least sought. Many a modern monk N. 2 may not at present be willing to look to monk N. 3 as a source of inspiration, and yet this needs to happen, for without it the link with tradition may easily be broken and both groups will be the poorer for it. And if monk N. 3, in the traditional monasteries, does not open up, or descend a little, monk N. 2 will not be able to climb up. The meeting place may very well be in between, but precisely in the land of Man, not in no-man's-land.

And how is the traditional, classical monasticism of monk N. 3 going to open itself up? How is monk N. 2 going to climb up and purify the many tentative and experimental paths into a new pattern of monasticism? These are primary issues with which we can only begin to deal effectively if a healthy dialogue is fostered between monks N. 2 and monks N. 3. All over the world there begin to be some essays toward such a dialogue, and it continues to need encouragement from both sides.

I would also like just to mention four types of issues with regard to monastic lifestyles: poverty, marriage, involvement in the world, and sexuality.

- *Poverty* needs fundamental reconsideration. Interestingly enough, in societies where the economy was not the dominant value, poverty was not seen as a concept that could be reduced to the economic aspect. To be a beggar could be a decent way of life. This is what the word *bhikṣu* means, incidentally. And the Christian West has also its mendicant orders. Poverty later became a primarily economy-based value, and monks began defending economic poverty. Now we find ourselves confused because, in a pan-economic world, economic poverty cannot be defended at all; it would amount to sponsoring starvation and injustice. And yet the name still perhaps conveys more than just an economic value: "Blessed are [you] the poor *in spirit*...."

- A problem that I would not like to see closed off a priori is that of *married monks.* The question of married monks must be considered not only from the monk's point of view but also with respect to the change it would imply in the very conception of marriage. Married monks will change our perceptions of marriage at least as much as they will change our notions of monasticism.

There are practical problems in the present setting of monks N. 3, indeed. But I am addressing myself to the more fundamental question of whether celibacy belongs to the essence of monasticism. If my distinctions are valid, we will agree that monk N. 1 as the archetype of monkhood is perfectly compatible with marriage, that the contemporary experiences of monks N. 2 have not yet sufficiently crystallized to offer us a pattern, and that the immense majority of monks N. 3 are vowed to celibacy.

No need for me to stress again that I find great value in and valid justification for celibacy, although always a posteriori. The point here is different. It is double.

The first point is whether it is of the essence of monasticism to be unmarried. In light of both the theories and the praxis of other religions, I shall have to answer in the negative; I know that a certain legalistic view refuses to call "monk" a married man or woman, but, *de nominibus non est disputandum*. Besides, we must take note of some contemporary essays of monk N. 2.

The reasons why the greatest proportion of monastic institutions have opted for celibacy might be summed up in three fundamental points. The first is the sociological context in which monasticism has grown and matured. It would have been practically impossible to institutionalize a monasticism of married people. The second reason is the conception of marriage and married life prevalent until our own times—whether as a consequence of the praxis or the result of a theory does not make much difference for our case. Not only women, but married life on the whole was considered practically secondary to the primary concern of human perfection. If the monk was seen as the paradigm of perfection, it seemed but natural that married life was not fitting for a monk. Women also have monastic vocations, but we know all too well from the Jaina *sādhvīs* onward the subordinate role of female monasticism throughout the ages. I also have the same suspicion about the traditional married monks. I say this as the fruit of simple observation, as well as with reference to what we know about the subordinate position of married women in most of those societies. This suspicion is enhanced if one considers the role of the Greek *paredra* and the Hindū śakti. Everything has been geared to the perfection of the male, or at least the paradigm is male-dominated. Nor can we say that the *virgines subintroductae* and the *agapetes* will solve the problem. Such a model will most certainly neither suit nor serve our present-day sensitivities. The third reason would be the underlying model of monasticism as *vita angelica*, life on the *pāramārthika* level. The monastic ideal claims to be "supernatural," on a higher plane—not *laukika*, worldly.

I am not implying for my argument here that males and females are merely equal or that celibacy is superior. I am only saying that the moment that monasticism is not seen as *the* perfect life, *even if* these two hypotheses were correct, the impossibility of married monks does not follow.

The second point is the difficult practicability and feasibility of having married monks within the major monastic institutions of most religions. And I leave it at that.

- *Personal involvement in the world.* That a Salesian or a Sister of Charity does something out of his or her personal charism, forgetting that there is a collective charism of that particular religious congregation, is understandable insofar as each person has a special vocation, but we may say that such a person acts only *in obliquo* as a member of that religious community. I would not say the same for a monk. Christian monks during the last few centuries have been more or less influenced by this kind of collective ideal, instead of discovering the heart of their personal calling. Perhaps the Jesuits could be said to represent an adaptation of the monastic ideal to the new mentality of their times.

  My point is the following. The monk's involvement in the world is not an institutionalized activity on a collective basis, like schools and hospitals and so forth, but the personal concern of the monk with that part of the world that is near to him. And here another set of problems opens up: personal idiosyncrasy vis-à-vis hierarchical authority. Along this line I may say that the cenobitic and hermitic styles of life need reshuffling. And I would recall the "networks of the heart" currently being created. If such networks among monks could be established, they may indeed have the opportunity to create a new state of affairs and a further degree of consciousness. This is true mainly because, as we have already pointed out, involvement in the world can no longer consist in a purely individualistic initiative.
- *Sexuality.* Traditional monasticism, as we noted earlier, has considered the monk an asexual being : the sexual needs are for the sake of the species, says Christian Scholasticism, not for the

fulfillment of the individual human being. So the monk has simply to overcome and at best sublimate the sexual urges, and the more he ignores sexuality the better. Today's Western sensibility is certainly different, and this can be neither bypassed nor ignored. There are five areas here that should be considered, and I shall simply enunciate them.

The *body*, an issue we have already developed.

Sex, in the sense of sexuality, not just the "sex needs" of mammals. Human beings have sexuality, which implies the whole interplay of human relationships. In this sense I would say that the play, the pleasure of the polarity between human beings, can be a highly contemplative activity.

Friendship is a chapter in itself that needs a clear distinction from the two extreme positions of seeing in friendship a disguised—and often unhealthy—sexuality, or considering friendship as a totally asexual relation. I still believe one can live without a spouse, but I doubt very strongly that one could really live without a friend.

Genital sexuality should be distinguished from the constitutive sexuality of human intercourse in the more general sense I have elucidated. The genital aspect has very often been exaggerated—out of a sense of repression, perhaps?—but it is a problem that has to be considered.

Celibacy is again an important aspect that should be considered.

Theoretical Questions

Time and again since the very beginning, although always in a subdued voice, I have been putting the question whether monk N. 1 is only *what* we detect and discover in the best monks, or whether there is something else to it that might have been more or less latent in olden times and that is now more forcefully emerging. Is the new monk I have sketched simply a variation of monk N. 3, one that still fits into monk N. 1, or is it another archetype altogether?

This question also contains the practical implication that an answer to it may well provide the space to deal with the relations between monk N. 2 and monk N. 3 as we discussed them a moment ago.

Monk N. 3 as archetype gives us an entrance into the archetype of the monk—that is, monk N. 1. But through monk N. 2 we have also gained access to monk N. 1. Now, does what we have found—the vectors we have detected and the force factors we have discovered—allow us to say that we are speaking of the same archetype, or should we recognize a *novum* here? In other words, are the old monk and the new monk radically incompatible? Is it a reformation or a mutation?

This question seems to me so central as to require a chapter of its own.

This, then, would be my provisional synthesis, which in no way claims to be the final word. And so, I close it with a sense of imperfection and inadequacy.

The path before us remains open, but I shall pause here to invite you to embark on it with me.

Discussion

We spoke of the first and the third world, and we connoted the second world exclusively in a Western sense. And yet 95 percent of people in the second world would not understand this language, simply because they are surrounded by a different ideology. How can we overcome this gap? Are we really speaking a universal language?

"We are not universal." Indeed, and thank God, there is no *lingua universalis.* We have to be humble and concrete. I do make a distinction between being provincial and particular (which is over against general and abstract), and being concrete and alive, which is not in opposition to being universal. There is no *lingua universalis.*

We have to be convinced, first of all, that we have constitutive limitations—thanks to which we exist. But we also have to have an open eye and an attentive ear, to see and to hear and to understand that there are other tunes and other dances and other languages and other rhythms... which are real, even if we do not understand them. Perhaps there is one thing I would call universal, and this is a kind of loving madness, which has to do with the *ānanda* of Śiva. But that is another question.

When we use the word "monk" or "monastic life" to describe the essence of human existence, the goal of the final integration toward which every human being should be moving, are we not perhaps stretching the term too far? Is there such an objectifiable essence to monasticism? Do not the words "monk" and "monastic" lose any concrete meaning?

I think that this is a very important question, but I feel an internal contradiction in it. On the one hand we say, "Monasticism is not objectifiable. So, why are we objectifying it?" And here I would say, "Certainly, I fully agree, it is not objectifiable." If I used the word "archetype," I did it because an archetype is—by definition—not objectifiable, given that it is always a function of the consciousness you have of it. The archetype is not an object sitting quietly somewhere: its true nature is made up of the whole of our relationships, from the more or less amorphous depths of collective humanness.

On the other hand, some say, "Our way of life *is* objective, clear-cut, and you should not introduce confusion. If we also call married people monks, we are unduly stretching the words. Monastic life has clear-cut boundaries that should not be crossed." I may agree or disagree, but that is secondary. I would like to present this internal contradiction as a paradox. Is monasticism a way of life that has to be kept as it is, without altering its features?

I would respond that we have a semantic problem here. What is "monasticism"? Is it the particular and objective way of life as it has been for the most part understood, or is it one particular and culture-bound expression of a more universal archetype that I have called "monkhood"? And yet I accept the warning in the question: "Beware, even with the best intentions! Don't introduce any useless confusion." We should not stretch the meaning of words to the point of meaninglessness, certainly, but is it not also true that certain types of cultural patterns have very often monopolized the meanings of words?

There is something most revealing in the life and history of the words. I think that this life of words cannot be put into a computer, and I express this idea with the example of the rainbow. Certainly I know what blue is, and what violet is, but there are very many shades in between that produce perhaps the most beautiful colors... and so I do not know if what I see is blue or violet or blue-green or both the colors at the same time.

A Note on Thinking and Speaking

I would like to make a couple of preliminary statements. The last twenty-six centuries of Western self-understanding, culturally speaking, are based on that dogma—assumed and accepted dogma from Parmenides to Husserl, with few exceptions—that paradigm first formulated by Parmenides, which states that the two fundamental pillars on which we have to rely in order to be human, and to have a human orientation in the world, are *thinking* and *being*—namely, *nous* and *on*. The whole history of Western thinking is founded on the assumption that the *nous*, the mind, is the guardian shepherd of the *on*, the being, and that being can only be expressed as what the mind tells us that being is. We have, of course, all the possible variations: *being* and *thinking* are two, they are one, they are related, and so on. The whole of modern science implies that it is precisely the *nous*, the thinking attitude, the mathematics, the calculation, that will tell us how being is, how being will behave. By utilizing Riemannian geometry, the "-1" and negative squares and all the rest, we think, and thanks to our thinking we build skyscrapers, bridges... and they *do* stand.

In short, thinking discovers but also conditions being. Now such thinking exacts a great price. Thinking that leads to intelligibility cannot violate the principle of noncontradiction. If I think the being, if I think *this*, then I cannot think *non-this*, and *this* has to remain the same as long as my thinking activity lasts. Otherwise, if *this* does not remain the same, I would not know what I am thinking about. If you think, "Two tulips and two roses are four flowers," after five minutes two tulips and two roses must still be tulips and roses in order to be four flowers. Thinking—to say it briefly—*freezes* being. The tulips must remain tulips. Thinking assumes being to be what it thinks it is. All the laws and all ethics follow as a consequence, precisely because thinking tells me what being is, and what truth is. Being is really molded and, in a certain sense, fixed by thinking. If being is not the prisoner of thinking, because it may be "thought" to be prior to thinking, it yet has to abide by the rules of thinking, which become the rules of being. The rules of being are postulated by the rules of thinking. And most philosophies, Eastern and Western, proceed from this assumption.

But this paradigm is not universal. It is not assumed or taken for granted in India, for instance. In India, the ultimate polarity—the yin/yang, so to speak, of the Indic effort at human orientation in reality—is not thinking and being, but *being* and *wording*. Or rather, *being* and *speaking*; being and letting being be; being and letting being escape. That means being and letting being express itself, without the reflection of self-consciousness, without going back to the being from which you have departed. It is a kind of total spontaneity. Being explodes itself into being, into word, into the expression of that being, into something that goes its own way, like an expanding universe that nothing and nobody—and certainly no being, no thinking, no lack of contradiction, no logic or logistics, no anything—can control or guide. Blissful spontaneity, yes, because what is most important is the process, the dance, the total expanding of being.... Who could control it? And who would control the controller? Who would think the thinker? Who would know the knower? You cannot know the knower, as the *Upani@ad* says. There is no way to control the flow of reality. Thinking is not the ultimate parameter. Being is just... explosion! And this would explain the monastic concentration on purifying the heart, the source of our being, and allowing the Spirit, which is Freedom, to direct and inspire us.

The Challenge of Secularity

Life does not need to be logical, but it destroys itself if it is antilogical. The two paradigms of simplicity and complexity that we have encountered seem to be, in the long run, mutually incompatible. Meanwhile—that is, in between, while life lasts—they create a healthy polarity, if maintained within limits. Furthermore, *blessed* simplicity will not allow real fragments of reality and of human life to be stripped away on the pretext of helping somebody to reach perfection. The remedy would be worse than the malady. Complexity as such is not necessarily positive either. It has to be a *harmonious* complexity, which takes into account the *cum* (together) of the *plexus* (folds of reality) in order to reach a true embrace (*amplexus*).

Can there be a marriage between simplicity and complexity? Is the archetype of the monk lost if simplicity is given up? Here we have not really dedicated equal time to the archetype of secularity. This was not our direct topic. But a few observations may be pertinent at this juncture. First, a sociological observation; second, an anthropological remark; and third, a metaphysical one.

- *Sociologically* speaking, in a world menaced by increasing technological complications, to have people stressing simplicity is more than an outlet for freedom, health, and humanness. Even if we are condemned to complexity, not everybody can adapt to it. We need respites, exceptions. There is also the fact that the beginning of every new technological "progress" generates innumerable victims due, as previously mentioned, to the fact that there are different human rhythms and varying degrees of adaptability, but also because the first technological essays in any given field are imperfect and often exact a high price in human substance. There is something very appealing in looking to monasteries as high places of human relaxation and temples of simplicity.

Moreover, besides complexity there is complication. People tend to complicate their lives. Industrialization may well mean consumerism, and many today are becoming aware of the dangers and antinatural effects of the technological world. A call for blessed simplicity is needed, and urgently so. If the old monks give up, new monks will emerge and perform this vital function of reminding the world by their example that only a very few things are necessary for a full and happy human life, much less to reach "eternal life"—which does not, of course, need to be postponed into the future.

But simplification of a complicated life and lifestyle is one thing, and utter simplicity taken to its final consequences quite another. Total simplicity—that is, a specialization in simplicity—may lead to inhuman practices or fall into the most traditional monastic temptation of "acosmism" or *vita angelica* (angelic life).

This means that blessed simplicity cannot be the *only* principle governing human life, for if it is, it will destroy that very life. Now if this is the case, either blessed simplicity can no longer be the monastic principle, or monkhood cannot be the total paradigm for human life, but only a dimension of that life that must be combined with the principle of harmonious complexity. Here is the ultimate locus for my statement about the impossibility of totally institutionalizing monkhood. It would amount to absolutizing that which is properly only a single dimension of human life.

This leads to a delicate sociological remark. We witness today a certain questionable relationship between monastic institutions all over the world and the larger religious bodies to which they are more often than not attached. I am referring to the tendency, be it organized as in Roman Catholic canon law, be it in the minds of the people and directives of the authorities concerned, of keeping the old monastic institutions as museum pieces and preventing their evolution—which by the same token is considered a betrayal of their ancient and authentic calling. I am referring to the desire, mainly on the part of outsiders, to see the monks preserve badly needed values. You have to live in Rome, Bangkok, Rishikesh, or the Kangra Valley to realize this trend of "authorities" wanting to preserve the old institutions in their pristine purity, uncontaminated by the air of modernity. There is a valid point to this, but it becomes problematic and ultimately defeats its own purpose if it is done from the exterior, as a result of more or less subtle pressures. "People expect you to be like this. You are supposed to behave this way and to say these things..." are the kinds of sentences we hear all too often. And this brings us immediately to the second observation.

- *Anthropologically* speaking, the question is how to integrate these two principles in our lives. Specifically for our purposes, how can the modern monk or nun handle the traditional pull toward simplicity and his or her own (not just societal) push toward a harmonious integration of one's being ? The *quid hoc ad aeternitatem* (what use is this for eternity?) can have devastating effects if eternity is seen as just the salvation of the pure soul in an afterlife. The obsession with the *sarvam duḥkham* (all is suffering) can equally lead to a real castration of the human personality.

We are not discussing here which anthropology is the more valid—that is, that which sees human perfection in an eschatological life on a higher *nirvanic* or "paramarthic" plane, or that which believes that the harmony of the human personality requires one to integrate all the *possible* human values in one single being. We are not forgetting the warning that to want to achieve an ideal that is too high or inappropriate leads to total deception and fiasco. Nor am I pleading for sheer humanism. I am simply stating how our contemporaries chart a course to their own perfection and the meaning of their lives. What matters here is the anthropological image that Man has of himself.

It probably comes to this: Has the *humanum* only one dimension, or is it pluridimensional? To avoid this question would cheapen traditional monastic spirituality. The monk does not want to be everything. He has renounced many things, eventually everything. But one ideal or aim he sticks to: the Absolute, *nirvāṇa*, *mokṣa*, *sotēria*, salvation, the glory of God. He stakes everything on that, and not necessarily in an exclusively individualistic way. On the contrary, the ideal of the *bodhisattva* is a monastic one; the ideal of being a living victim for the salvation of the whole world and the vocation of the vicarious representation of the whole of humankind is central to monasticism. The question is how this goal is reached—by attaining that simple core of everything, by simplicity at the end of a thoroughgoing process of utter simplification, or by attempting to bring about the harmonious complexity and integration of all possible values in the "melting pot" of that particular person?

To overlook this double underlying anthropology would do an injustice not only to the theoretical problem of the New Monk but much more so to that particular person who is now, as it were, seething in the twin fires that we have called simplicity and complexity. The monk here suffers in this particular form the more general tension between tradition and secularity. If the second paradigm is found to be more valid than the first one of simplicity, the structural changes in traditional monasticism will have to be radical. And there is no point in blurring the dichotomy, although the conduct of practical affairs may demand prudence, patience, and great discernment of spirit. But the individual monk or nun may be caught in the dilemma and have to face the practical problem of whether he or she will better serve the cause of monkhood by transforming the old structures or by beginning new ones. Do we really have here the case of the new wine and the old wineskins? I cannot push the question much further right now. We may briefly consider the last dilemma.

- *Metaphysically* speaking, we detect immediately two radically different conceptions of reality. The problematic has already emerged from time to time. For the purpose of these considerations, I would also like to bring the different cosmological assumptions under this same heading of metaphysics.

The ideal of *simplicity* assumes that all of reality is, in its ultimate character, *simple.* Now neither space nor time, nor history, nor the body are simple, or even simplifiable past certain limits. Only the "soul," consciousness, *cit*, is reducible to a point without dimensions. Consciousness has this remarkable power of embracing multiplicity in the simplicity of a single intuition. No wonder the monk is more interested in the interiority of consciousness than in the exteriority of the plurality of things.

The ideal of *complexity*, on the other hand, assumes that reality is ultimately *pluralistic*, not reducible to any single principle, and thus that realization is not a jump into a simple Absolute, but rather a process by which the complexity of our being is brought harmoniously to its completion.

No monk needs to be a metaphysician, but the ultimate metaphysical paradigm is ever present in any of the moves he will make. Ultimately, the hypothesis of the Absolute is at stake here. We might even say: monotheism versus "polytheism," although I strongly object to the common use of the last word in this sense. No polytheist has ever said that what the monotheist affirms to be one is many. But many theists would also be unhappy just to stick the *monos* before their theism, since their God is neither one nor many. But we should not linger much longer over this chasm that seems to be obvious, despite the fact that words do not convey the whole issue, and much less so as we try to articulate the problem in a cross-cultural context.

I may now attempt to formulate a synthesis from a Trinitarian perspective, first, and in an advaitic language immediately thereafter. It is all related to what I have called the *cosmotheandric* intuition and sacred secularity.

In the final analysis, *simplicity and complexity are not dialectically opposed*, because the ultimate structure of the universe does not need to be conceived as dialectical. Their relation is dialogical. They have meaning not in opposing and contradicting each other so as to generate some "higher" synthetic amalgam, but as a mutually constitutive relation, so that the one does not make sense without the other and each mutually supports the other.

Simplicity is more than the absence of complexity. It is merely "monoplexity," I would say, if the word were allowed. The folds have been folded again, but not obliterated or destroyed—although, qua folds, they no longer exist. A certain transformation, as we have seen, is certainly required. On the other hand, complexity is not just an accumulation of folds, of layers of reality one upon the other, but the display of the many folds in one coherent—that is, joined and fitting—pattern, which is one in its manifoldness. Now this oneness is not plurality, but it certainly is pluralistic; that is, it forms a manifold pattern.

The oneness, we are saying, is pluralistic because there is only the oneness of the manifold that nobody can encompass, as nobody can be outside reality. If the color green could see the colored world, it would see all the other colors as green or as the result of their composition with green. It could not speak of a plurality of colors, but only of a pluralism that could be expressed by the generic name "color" without really differentiating each color in its own light. Plurality is only grasped from the exterior. Only a mind above and outside the world of color can embrace the plurality of colors. Monism is the view from the interior. Although the green-mind may perceive some differences, if it is powerful enough and concentrates on its self it will affirm that ultimately all is green. Pluralism is not a view such as would be seen from the inside and the outside at the same time. It sees all as predominantly green, but also hears other witnesses speaking of other colors and believes that reality is multicolored. Inasmuch as it sees, it is monistic (everything is green); inasmuch as it hears, it defends plurality (it hears it said that other colors do exist); and inasmuch as it believes, it is pluralistic (it believes that in its green vision the shades of other colors are included). Pluralism does not reduce everything to intelligibility.

The Trinitarian language would go like this: the Trinity, we have to clarify at the outset, is neither a monopoly of Christianity nor, for our purposes, of the divinity. Every bit of reality has this Trinitarian imprint. And thus human perfection does not consist in becoming one with the Son, or with the Father, or with the Spirit, but in fully entering into the life of that very Trinity without eliminating any of its constituents.

The Trinity is neither one nor three, that is, neither simplicity nor complexity. Seen from the interior, as it were, it looks like simplicity: each "person" voids itself totally in order that the other may "be." The Father sees only the Son. He does not see the Father, but only the Son (who is all that the Father *is*). He does not see his *seeing* (the Spirit), but only the Son. And I could similarly elaborate on the other two "persons"—utilizing here the Christian nomenclature. Personhood is sheer relationship. There is nothing outside these relationships. If there were a kind of substantial "knot" independent from the "net," we would have tritheism or, in the universe, plurality. The law of the Cross—that is, of sacrifice as pure immolation—I would say reigns also in the Trinity. This voiding of each person is complete. Seen from the interior each person is totally void, empty. If we were to look at that person we would see nothing, as each person has already given oneself up to the other. In point of fact, person is neither singular nor plural. The Father "gives" everything he is and has to the Son; he begets a Son identical to him. The Son is equally exhausted in his gift (the Spirit) to the Father—which the Father has precisely "inspired" through the Son. The

Spirit in itself is nothing, no-thing (the "thing," *res*, Word, is the Son, the *Logos*); it is pure gift, which is only such in the actual giving.

Now from the exterior, as it were, in and by the very act of speaking about all this and trying to unfold it for our minds, it is complexity. It is even the maximum of complexity, since all the riches of reality are encompassed in the Trinitarian dynamism. This is the meaning of the Incarnation: that the world shares in the ultimate Trinitarian adventure, although it unfolds in the strictures of space and time. Seen from the outside, the whole process is the com-plexity of the entire reality: Father, Christ, and Spirit, in Christian language.

We can speak about the ineffable only as unspeakable—that is, unspeakability is an attribute of the speakable; everybody realizes in and through the experience that no word of ours says all that it "wants," "desires," "purports"—or even means—to say. We hear, "I mean to say," constantly in conversations. Why? Because we can never fully "say what we mean," and the partner has to "get it" in the spirit. We speak then about the ineffable by opening up, pointing out, letting ourselves be *somehow* aware of the silent component of the word, of the unspeakable side of the spoken. Without words, there would be no silence—just as there is no real word without silence. All is Trinitarian relation.

In *advaitic* parlance I would say that reality is neither one nor two, and so neither we nor the world can be brought under the total sway of the one or the two. God and the world are, likewise, neither one (it goes against common sense) nor two (two what?—it would contradict the very conception of God). *Advaita*, a-dualism, is not monism. It would be monism if God had so absorbed the world (since they cannot be two) as to rob it of its ultimate reality. It is not dualism either. The world is not *another* reality facing God, or the One, or Brahman. They are not two "aspects" of one and the same reality, because they are not "aspects" at all—that is, perspectives, epistemological devices, or facets of a monolithic reality. Reality is not to be encompassed by the mind: *cit*, *buddhi*, *jñāna*. Reality is also *sat* and ānanda, being and bliss. And if we can speak of it this is not because they are reducible to *vāc*, to word, to intelligibility, but because they are inseparable and yet not the "same." There is ultimately nothing that is the same, because the mind to which this "sameness" seems the "same" is not outside of it. This a-dualistic conception also demands the maximum complexity. If there were only one thing, there would be no complexity at all; monism would be quite sufficient and *advaita* not required. But if simplicity were not also a dimension of the real, dualism would in its turn be a plausible enough hypothesis. Complexity and simplicity embrace in *advaita*, as well as in the Trinity.

Where is the monk in all of this? I may venture now, perhaps, my hypothesis—and *epektasis*, in the sense of hope. I shall expose it in its bare essentials.

Let us call the *humanum* the symbol for human perfection over, above, and besides the distinction between the natural and the supernatural. The belief that this *humanum* is utterly simple would constitute the archetype of monkhood. The *humanum* has thus a center, simple without dimensions, a core that in an eminent and, for us, rather incomprehensible way encompasses all of what I *really* am. This *humanum* is not only invisible, it is also not realized here on earth. It needs a transcendent existence, be it in time (the future), in space (paradise), or altogether beyond (*nirvāṇa*, Brahman, God). The realization of the *humanum* is an eschatological task. You have to discover it, either in hope or with an intuition (*anubhāva*) that transcends space and time, by realizing that you are "already there." This is the way of simplicity, and traditional monks have followed this path.

The belief that this *humanum* is complex and that it can be realized only if the different elements are integrated could still be accepted by some monks. Where the divergence arises is when this integration is considered irreducible to one single "thing," when the ultimate "stuff " of the real is in itself manifold, complex. This archetype I would call secularity. The *humanum* has no single center. It has two or more centers. Space and time are definitive and not to be whisked away as something alien to the *humanum.* Even if they are ephemeral, it is this very provisionality that gives them reality for Man in his ultimate concern. Realization is a personal task that cannot be postponed, and cannot be gained by eliminating elements of reality as if they were not there, or were not real.

Is there any way of bringing these two archetypes together? The very manner of putting the question is obviously biased. Simplicity cannot tolerate a second at its side. Is there but the possibility of a Oneness without a second that still does not fall into a simplistic monism? Or, from the other perspective, is it possible to give due credit to all the ingredients of reality without falling into the indiscriminate atomistic anarchy of sheer plurality?

While the asceticism of interiority or the monastic ideal works on the perfection of Man, the asceticism of action or the secular ideal of complexity works on the perfection of the world. The synthesis can be approached if these two activities are seen—and performed—as two aspects of one and the same ontological dynamism of the person, so to speak.

The asceticism of interiority reminds us that our first and primordial task is to be engaged in the perfection, fulfillment, or liberation of that aspect of reality which is ourselves. Be it a *jīva* or soul that one has to extricate from all the entanglements of matter and *karman*, as in many spiritual traditions; be it the *ātman* or self that one has to realize in its perfect Oneness, as other schools will defend; be it the person that has to be fully integrated, passively and actively, into the Whole to which it belongs; be it the blowing up of all particularities, individualities, or even of all being in order to transcend all contingency or illusion; be it performing the allotted tasks for the time being, because we are only beings in time; be all these as they may, this human aspiration to work within oneself and with oneself is as delicate, subtle, and even as difficult and long as the other asceticism of externality. To be engaged in one's selfperfection in this sense is not egoism, but the fullest realization of the human being.

At the same time, the asceticism of exteriority reminds us that we are not isolated monads or purely spiritual substances, but part of a higher and wider reality in which not only are other fellow-beings sharing, co-dividing and influencing our destiny, but in which other dimensions of reality are also involved in the same ultimate adventure. The ideal of secularity reminds us that to work for the betterment of the world and the transformation of the external structures of reality is as delicate, subtle, and even as difficult and long as the inner striving for perfection. The authentic scientific spirit is precisely this. To be engaged in the perfection of the cosmos is not vanity, but the fullest realization of the person.

The crisis of our contemporary human period, and at the same moment its great opportunity and vocation, is to realize that the human microcosm and the material macrocosm are not two separate worlds, but one and the same cosmotheandric reality, in which precisely the third "divine" dimension is the unifying link between the other two dimensions of reality. Otherwise, to withdraw into the business of saving one's soul becomes sheer egoism or cowardice, and to fling oneself into the task of saving the world sheer vanity or presumption.

Now, in order to realize the synthesis, we have to become increasingly aware not only of the correlation between the inner and outer, human and cosmic aspects of reality, but of their *in*-relatedness, so that ultimately it is one and the same concern. From the pre-Socratics speaking about harmony, through the *Ṛg-veda*, whose last word is concord, to Sri Aurobindo affirming that "all problems of existence are essentially problems of harmony," there is a constant thread in the human quest for sacred secularity.

If the overinstitutionalization of monasticism has produced world-denying specialists and had a harmful influence upon people, often even turning religion into an alienating factor in human life, the overinstitutionalization of secularization has produced, and is still in alarming proportion producing, a deleterious impact upon the peoples of the earth, turning them into quasi-robots, mechanizing human existence and converting the new religions of Marxism, humanism, secularism, scientism, and the like into life-denying ideologies.

Is the synthesis possible? Ontology, once upon a time, was the field that encompassed anthropology, cosmology, and theology; the integral system of theories regarding Man, the World, and the Divine. In our contemporary time we do not have such an ontology, and many doubt whether it would even be able to fulfill such a task. What is certain is that anthropocentrism is as insufficient as cosmocentrism or theocentrism. A new awareness is called for. But this awareness can only come out of an experience born of an integral praxis. Here also a new asceticism is required: a new praxis of plunging into the depths of the human psyche, as much as soaring into the heights of the cosmic spaces and sensing the immanent-transcendent throbbings of the Divine.

It may perhaps be said that this is ultimately what not only the best monks, but also the most profound secularists, have always been seeking. This could well be the case—and then it would only confirm my hypothesis. But perhaps one was not sufficiently aware of the radical and ultimate divergences in their respective conceptions of reality. My assumption here is not that we have lost the key to open the puzzle of the universe, but that there is no key, either epistemological or ontological, because the *logos* is not all that there is, and even being is "only" all that there *is*. But this "only" may not exhaust reality.

Will the new monk be able to integrate these two dimensions of human life? The academic or the scientist experiments with his ideas. The monk does so with his life. Experimenting with ideas is generally called thinking. It is the region of the "mental." Generously, it may perhaps be called "comprehension," but it would not properly be called "knowledge"—that is, the human fact of being born together with the very thing thus known. It requires real humility—as the monastic traditions will stress—to understand, that is, to stand under the spell of whatever is understood. You are vulnerable when you so understand. The monk understands with his *hara*, his middle, as the Japanese would put it. The true gnostic of the Christian tradition is not the "intellectual," but the contemplative. Contemplation leads to action, because the contemplative understanding is the total realization of the "thing" understood—so that it catches you, it dominates you, it has power over you. In sum, intellectuals experiment with ideas, but monks experiment with their lives. It is an experience of life and death.

*Appendix: Letter to a Young Monk**

I understand your predicament. Not long ago you were a novice. You are a professed monk, but have not yet taken your perpetual and solemn vows. You have not yet spent enough time in the monastery to feel so at your ease that you think you have no other option than to continue in the routine you criticize in the older monks, and from which you would like to escape. You feel that you still have a chance to fulfill the ideals of your life, but you do not know in which direction you should go.

You are not alone in this dilemma. I have found it all over the world, and not only among Christian monks. The crisis of monkhood seems to be universal. Perhaps it is a normal process dating from the origins of monasticism. The crisis may even belong to the human condition, and not only to the present situation. You start with the novice's zeal and you slowly mature in a way that often you cannot distinguish between wisdom and inertia, maturity and laziness. But there is a difference, it seems to me, with those classical times in which the foundations were not shaken. In those times we could speak of a primarily personal crisis. But today it is both personal and institutional. Even more, today it is also societal. There is no point in hiding it. Not all your uneasiness can be attributed to your lack of holiness. It is the fabric itself of the institutions that is in crisis. No wonder you are disoriented. Perhaps we are all without an Orient.

However, this is not an excuse, neither for you nor for me, for not striving to find a solution to the predicament. Let me repeat some of my thoughts, which I have often expressed before.

My intention is to write words not only expressing conditions but also laden with action. "*Spiritus substantia est sermonis et sermo operatio Spiritus*," writes Tertullian, echoing the *Dhammapada* (IV.9): "The Spirit is the strength (the essence, the substance) of the word and the word is the representation (the activity, the praxis) of the Spirit" (*Adv. Prax.* 26.4).

The monastic institution, by and large, has become not only part of the Establishment, but even one of its main pillars. Preaching patience,

* Written to a North American monk at the beginning of the 1980s.

and sometimes being blind to injustice, devoting itself to the—so-called—education of the young, especially those who come from the wealthy classes (even when the poor are educated so that they can be assimilated into the current customs of this unjust society of ours), singing old psalms as if nothing had happened, in this way it becomes an obstacle to the radical change that almost every perceptive thinker sees as necessary.

But I am writing a letter now and not a treatise on the situation of the world or monastic institutions. Both problems are implied in your more personal question, but I should not concentrate now on such large problems lest the individual dimension is swallowed up by this ocean. What can you do? What can I do? To save the world sounds naive. To reform your own monastery seems unwise. We have grown used to obedience as trust in and submission to a superior. We are never sure enough of ourselves to be able to face freely and without fear a venerable and ancient community or institution. Slamming the door and leaving is no solution either. Experience teaches that you are then swallowed by a much bigger monster: the modern technocratic complex. To go on as usual is not satisfactory. So what is to be done? I see only one way out.

What gives weight to my answer is that I suggest following the way of Nature: replanting. The branch from the old tree goes back to the nurturing soil and grows independently—and yet with the strength and encoded wisdom from the old one. More than speaking of a new seed, I prefer here the metaphor of the planting of an already developed branch, a new "foundation" of the old monastery.

Let me spell it out a little more.

I am sure that amongyou there are a handful of other monks, or friends, who feel the same. Why not "conquer" your own freedom by winning, first of all, the confidence of the "elders" and presenting, second, a workable plan of an initially "dependent" but autonomous new "foundation," a new branch of the old tree, which slowly may develop even into another separate and different institution? The metaphor of the branch may be misleading if we think of it too deterministically as a mere repetition or imitation of the old model. If the soil is different and the new plant takes its nurture from Mother Earth, the result may be very different. The concept may be better expressed by the image of the *nova et vetera* (new and old things) of the gospel.

The *vetera* are the traditional principles of contemplation, the quest for the absolute, freedom of spirit, the balance between human, cosmic and divine rhythms, and so on.

The *nova* are more direct (and yet not superficial) concerns for people, greater sensitivity for politics, greater openness to the characteristics of the new monk—to which I have referred in this text.

May I add that there would be no *vetera*, no venerable monks, no old monasteries, not even roots and tradition, if there were not also the *nova*—that is, the impulse of youth, the innovation of imagination, the urgency of change, and the desire to overcome the old. And vice versa, there would be no *nova*, new things, without the *vetera*, the old habits. Birds could not fly if the air did not offer them resistance. We all need one another. *O felix culpa!*

What I am saying is that a break with tradition is not necessary. We need roots. And, at the same time, a mere imitation of tradition would be sterile: it would yield neither fruits nor flowers. Tradition is there in order to be handed down. I would prefer to say "taken up." In any case it is there in order to be passed on by way of transplantation or planting, by transformation in the very act of handing it over, because although the sun, the water, and the air are the same, the soil, the sap of the new generations, and the spirit of the times are different. In this mood I have to add that it should not be the work of only one person, but of a small group, although the initiative and the leadership may spring from one person alone.

You will ask me what the nature of such a group should be. Here I cannot give a concrete answer. First because there can be no "blueprint" for such an enterprise, and second also because each group can be and—I would add—must be different.

My plea to the superiors is that they should allow such a freedom; I would ask them to trust in the Spirit and not break the communion, even if the juridical links will have to be loosened due to the rigid legal structure of the present-day status quo. I would like to convince them not only of the need to revitalize present-day monastic life, but that they should take on the responsibility of sponsoring movements of which they do not completely approve, or do not fully understand. If they cut the umbilical cord too early the child will die. But if they say, "Do as you like, but leave," they will be jointly responsible for a possible failure. If you let them go totally, if you call them "charismatic" movements, they will not last long or they will degenerate. Monasticism should have a greater role in the present world and on a large scale, but neither a mere continuation of the old forms, nor little attempts springing up like mushrooms, exposed to the acid rain of particular catastrophes (or individual crises) will render this possible. In olden times they created oblates, third orders, pious unions, congregations, and the like. This movement has to be continued, but in new forms. It is not a question of reintroducing firstand second-class monks, thus transplanting the social class struggle into the monastery. I know that one of the main obstacles is fear and/or concern that the new venture may turn sour and even tarnish the prestige of the "motherhouse" or create tensions with higher authorities. The evangelical prudence of the serpent may help here. You bless, you encourage, you give support, but you do not consider yourself morally responsible or having to approve what you do not need to. Establish a kind of thomistic "*relation rationis.*" They are linked to you, they may feel fellowship, even protection, sympathy (very important), and most of all freedom, but do not feel compromised, responsible, and accountable for their possible failures or even their possible successes. The union of the Mystical Body is not broken so easily. Let them fly. Is not the mystery of maternity the fact of having courage in the face of the unknown? How will that life develop to which the mother is giving birth? If parents do not fear that children may one day become drug addicts or be born with defects or bad inclinations, should "abbots" and "masters" have less confidence? I am simply stressing the most traditional understanding of the title that superiors have had in the religious tradition of Christianity: that of being fathers and mothers. They could probably learn, like the biological parents of our time, that they are not proprietors, nor ultimately responsible for the destinies of their children. Parents, says St. Paul, do not sadden the spirit!

My plea to young monks (and obviously nuns, and also not-so-young people—it is not a question of gender or age) is that you should have confidence in yourselves, that you should think (I say think and not just fantasize) with profound conviction that for God no "word," that is, action, is impossible; that the energy you feel within yourselves has historical significance; that where the Spirit is, there is freedom; that real love dispels fear; that as soon as you step out of mediocrity you will be safe, that the possibilities are enormous and the world is thirsty for such steps. That you should not just imitate, but listen and study; that many of those who observe from outside are waiting for a first brave step... Courage means putting one's own heart into action. I insist that you are in a privileged position, you are the link with the past and, at the same time, the seeds of the future. But seeds must blow in the wind, that is, go with the Spirit, in order to fall on other, unknown ground, and yield fruit. "judge for yourselves what is upright" (Lk 12:57).

Dear friend, you will tell me that I am speaking too much in the abstract. I know it. Your situation is different from many others, I know that, too. Each case is unique. In certain cases the change should be radical. In others not. One charism should not be confused with another. My main concern is to avoid that so many ideals and healthy human ambitions be paralyzed by false prudence and psychological fears. Elsewhere I have explained at length that the theological virtues of faith, hope, and charity have, first of all, to be cosmological virtues: faith in oneself, hope in one's ideals, and love for one's fellow-travelers in the pilgrimage of life.

My concern is, of course, that we take the monastic vocation seriously, that we have this ardent aspiration to holiness, to reach the full stature of Christ, that is, of the human Spirit, that we renounce all that is trivial, and that we literally concentrate on the only necessary thing, which implies both physical and spiritual concentration: growing in density until we reach the center of ourselves, and thus center it with the center(s) of reality. I advise you not to be superficial, to shun banality, and not to fall prey to melancholy or fits of anger. I am convinced that every one of us is not only of divine nature, but also forms a single body with all humankind or, to express it better, with the whole cosmos. We are not isolated individuals, nor a pile of sand lost in the ocean of reality, but a reflection of totality, not a part of a mechanical universe, not one of the many pipes and screws of the modern megamachine that can be easily substituted, but a unique microcosm in which the destiny of the entire reality is at stake. I hope you have not been brainwashed by the mechanistic ideology that is so pervasive in our current world. You are not a part. You are unique. And you can only trust in God if you have confidence in yourself.

I will add no more now. I am convinced of the importance of the challenge and the urgency of the moment. Any way in which I can offer my help will be a joy for me.

In festivitate
Maternitatis Beatae Mariae Virginis

Part Two

The Hindū Monk

10
*The Monk According to Hindū Scriptures**

Breaking Down Barriers (Saṃnyāsa)

Inspired sages called *saµnyāsa*
the actual abandonment of interested actions
Erudite people define "renunciation" [*tyāga*]
the abandonment of the fruits of any type of action.

—*BG* XVIII.2

The price of a perfect sacrifice cannot be less than that of one's own life. The only way to let the sacrifice develop perfectly and fulfill all its potential is to cast aside all the obstacles that could impede the release of the secret force it carries with it. These obstacles can come both from the object of the sacrifice and from what can upset it. If Man wishes to accomplish the perfect sacrifice that enables the universe to reach its climax, he must offer his personality, he must renounce and transcend himself. Renunciation is the pinnacle of sacrifice.

Anyone who has had the personal experience and discovered that true sacrifice is the sacrifice of one's own deepest being in the only reality that can receive this immolation, or in other words, the one who is brought by the Spirit, to the Spirit in the Spirit; the one who has discovered that the subject and the object of the sacrifice—*ātman* and *brahman*—coincide, ceases to desire sacrifice. For him, the interior and exterior actions of sacrifice no longer have sense because his "I," his personality in society, ceases to exist. Not only does he renounce everything, but also his own I and the renunciation itself. It is for this reason that, although the traditional *āsramas* indicate two phases to renunciation, some holy men, and other traditions, speak of a

* Original edition: Le moine selon les écritures saintes de l'hindouisme, in Les Moines chrétiens face aux religions d'Asie (Bangalore: AMC, 1973), 80–91.

"phase which is not such," in addition to the two previous ones: *atyāsrama* (cf. *SU* VI.21). In the end, in fact, it is not that one renounces something, because what one renounces is not something; it is not renunciation if not to nothingness.

The ideal is total transparency, but history and experience teach us that the road is long and that there are no shortcuts to avoid the bends and curves of the road leading to the end, to the ultimate reality. And so there arises in us the intuition whereby he who renounces has become the bottomless conscience, where the sacrifice in which life is given takes place.

This is not only true at the simple level of human existence, it is also true in the field of thought. So many misunderstandings and accusations of monism and pantheism would disappear very quickly if the texts that speak of the omnipresence of God and the unity of the world were considered in their true context, that is, that of the ultimate spiritual experience that has now eliminated the personality of the individual as a spectator or actor of the sacrifice. This sacrifice, indeed, not only leads to the immolation of the victim; it is also, as we have already mentioned, the holocaust of the one who accomplishes it, including one's faculty of thinking.

In the religious mentality of India, the holy ascetic does not exclusively represent an ideal of renunciation. Indeed, very often this aspect is not regarded as essential. He is rather an example of a pure life stripped of everything. His body is no longer the instrument and the wrapping of (his own) life, but exists in the pureness of the *ātman*, in the transparency of the *brahman*, in the surprising Presence of which the witnesses of the life of the holy man are more or less aware (depending on the degree of zeal achieved).

After having said that the road is long and that we must resist the great temptation of the "holy men," which is the subtle idolatry of considering themselves as people who have achieved "fulfillment," I would like to describe some characteristics of this road.

A deep dissatisfaction is part of human life. Even if we have really done everything within our power, we have nevertheless neglected other actions which it would have been possible to do. In the Indic tradition, dis-illusion is the starting point of philosophy. It could also be said that the transcendence of the human condition begins here. The ancient and famous *ā*sramic tradition of India was very balanced. It allowed the husband, and at times the wife, to withdraw into the forest after having performed their duties in society. They then dedicated themselves to a life of renunciation in search of the Absolute: it seems, indeed, that this Absolute cannot be attained in domestic life. There is a whole philosophy on this theme of the third *āsrama*: the *vānaprastha*, or state of the forest-dweller (cf. *Manu* VI.2).

Some, however, did not feel the need to pass through all these stages. It was believed possible to arrive more directly by becoming monks, entering the state of the *saṃnyāsin*, that is of the renouncers: their desire is to immerse themselves in the Only One. They aspire to total liberation from the temporal and spatial parameters of the human condition. They abandon their own body, they neglect it, or rather, they cease to think of it.

Much literature has flourished regarding this theme. It has been considered at various times as the jewel or the disgrace of Indic culture. Whatever one may think of it, three principal elements can be noticed in renunciation as it is considered by the spirituality of the *Veda*. One can even say that each of these corresponds to one of the three periods of the Scriptures: the Vedic era, the intuition of the *Upaniṣads*, and the interpretation given by the *Gītā*.

In the first period we notice a certain absence of ascetic spirituality. Asceticism is simply tolerated, probably because it already existed and was considered a particular form of experience that some members of the community could freely undertake. But it would be a mistake to depict Vedic revelation as ascetic spirituality.

We may summarize the second period with the famous words of Yājñavalkya to his beloved bride Maitreyī before embracing the life of a hermit in the forest (*vānaprastha*). He tells her that the ultimate object of our desire and our love is not the object immediately attained by our senses, but the *ātman*, the underlying *ātman*, ever-present and effective: "It is rather for love of the *ātman* that all beings are so dear to us" (*BU* II.4–5). All this means that renunciation is considered a means, a way therefore to reach the supreme goal, not for evasion or for escape, but for internalization and passing beyond: the husband, the wife, and everything else are certainly loved, and justly loved, but the profound reason of this love and its ultimate object lie beyond the external appearance of things.

This aspect has been developed in the third period, which can be considered the cornerstone of asceticism as we find it in Vedic revelation. There are two ways to understand renunciation. It can be the abandonment of a positive value in favor of another that is deemed higher. Or one can abandon this value because one discovers that in fact it has no value. In this case, renunciation exists only for he who considers it from the outside. For the *tyāgin*, that is, for the person who renounces, there is not in fact any renunciation. The renunciation is therefore not true but to the extent that it does not appear to be a renunciation. As long as we aspire to something, we should not renounce it. It is only when the desire disappears that we can renounce it. This can explain the need to insist on the correct vision of things, and on the exact perspective from which we have to consider them in order to see them as they actually are.

It is only "by knowing it [*brahman*] that it is possible to become an ascetic." We cannot truly renounce something until we have discovered that for us this "thing" is none other than a "pseudo-value," an appearance of a positive thing. Otherwise we would do better not to incur the risks that can arise from such exclusion. The ultimate reason does not only consist in the psychological fact that the desire of something—be it, for example, renunciation itself—only subjugates us even more; it is rather the theological fact that Man's ultimate goal cannot be attained by "human" means. Indeed, only the calling of the Absolute can lead us there (*MU* III.2.3; *KathU* II.23). Yet others would affirm that it is not possible to overcome desire because of an ontological reason. Only by drying up the source, not by suppressing the object, is it possible to overcome desire. Indeed, desires are a projection of an inner "thirst" (cf. *BU* III.5.1). One is not yet really a *saµnyāsin* until one has discovered that there is nothing left to renounce: not because there is nothing outside us, but because one understands that neither things nor us are absolutely "a thing"... or, borrowing the conciseness of an *Upani@ad* (*Yada ahar eva vīrajet, tad ahar eva pravrajet*):

> On the day you are totally disillusioned,
> on that day you will become renouncers.
>
> —*JabU* 4

which we have already quoted and will quote again in a slightly different translation.

The Keśin—Muni

The famous hymn of *Ṛg-veda* X.136[1] deserves a comment, even without any Indological apparatus. The comments on this hymn are many, but perhaps with the exception of those of Jeanine Miller and Karel Werner, the dozen commentators I know interpret it with the condescendence of the conventional thinkers faced with the excesses of the orgiastic. I believe instead that there we can see the monastic archetype in his most pristine purity, without the complement of harmonious complexity. The hymn does not deal with blessed simplicity, but with absolute simplicity.

A posteriori, from a historical point of view, the monastic ideal presents a double paradigm. On the one hand, *the monk as the perfect Man*, the fulfilled one, who has attained peace, equanimity, and freedom; the fulfilled Christian, the greatest embodiment of the *humanum*, the *jīvanmukta*, that

1 See the text above, in the chapter titled "The Canon of the Disciple."

is he who has saved his own soul. Chinese wisdom is probably the supreme expression of this, with its model of the gentleman, the superior man, the nobleman. This is the idea that has prevailed in the world in general, and in the West in particular. It is the idea that has also dominated our description, although the other dimension was always present in ever y line of the text. Perhaps one can reach such an iconoclastic conception as we find in this hymn only at the end of a long journey, like that of the *saṃnyāsin* who renounces all worldly life after having lived it (*Manu* VI.33).

But in our hymn another paradigm is also expressed, which is fairly present throughout our study, too. *The monk as a rebel*, as a nonconformist, as the one who breaks all the rules of the game and aspires to be totally free; the one whose characteristic is conscious madness. It is not a pretend madness, it is real, the madness of a man with shining eyes (cf. the Greek *glaukos*, although the word could also come from the Arabic *iwaq*, fool).

This most lively hymn of the *Ṛg-veda* probably describes a Jaina monk, he "who is dressed by the wind." This ascetic has acquired powers of the highest order, although his way of living does not correspond to any of the officially recognized conditions of life (*āśramas*). His function consists in collaborating directly with the Gods: he is their partner. His outward appearance reveals his vocation and the sincerity of his life. He lives anywhere, he feels at home in the East and the West, he is a universal man; but the price of all of this is that he probably ceases to be a normal person. He is the *keśin*, the man with long hair, the *muni*, the silent one.[2] If he does not speak, it is not because he forces himself not to declare the many things he has to say (that would be hypocrisy), but simply because he has nothing to say. He does not cut his hair, he is instead busy "forging" his thoughts and unraveling the knots of time and space. Will he succeed?

These madmen, these long-haired ascetics, are well aware of being mad, and besides they want to be and seem it. Their madness is their weapon and their identity. Therefore this monk does not hide in his cave, or withdraw from the world, but enters the public arena and scolds the people, upsetting all their habits. The tragedy of Don Quixote was that, when he was lucid, it was thought he was mad, and when he was mad it was thought that he was lucid. The tragedy of Nietzsche lies perhaps in the fact that he plays at being mad without being so, and ends by being mad without wanting to.

2 Modern scholars debate whether the word *muni* comes from the root *man* (or *men*): "to think," or rather if it relates to the Greek *mania* and *mentir*. Be that as it may, *muni* already appears in *RV* VII.5.6–8 and VIII.17.14, with the meaning of breath and ardor; thus *mū* means inspired, seized by an inner enthusiasm. Hence it comes to mean a saint, an ascetic, a monk, and above all he who has taken a vow of silence. In *AV* VII.74.1 a *muni-deva* (*muni* God) is mentioned, who has special powers as a healer.

The *keśin* knows he is mad and wants to be so. It is his only weapon to combat the senselessness of reason and the hypocrisy of civilization. Imitating St. Isidore of Seville, one could say that he wants to be and knows he is mad because he thinks that men have lost their *locus*, that they do not keep in their proper place, that a humanity separated from the Gods, the winds, the earth, and animals is a *dis-locata*, removed and mad humanity, because it has artificially constructed a *locus* to live in; it is the world of its reason that imprisons it and with the passing of time is destroying it.

There are many ways to "translate" this hymn for our current situation. Socrates and the Cynics already knew something about it, but the majority of institutionalized monks seem to have forgotten the example of Milarepa, the call to *enthousiasmos*, and even more the radical protest against a *humanum* meant as anthropological perfection disjointed from the earth and heaven. One is a *jīvanmukta* not because one is a saved soul, but because one is freed from every soul. But one cannot make a simple theory out of all this without immediately involving rationality as the supreme judge. It must be his life, his example, his existence that provokes the challenge. When all is said and done, what this monk denies is history, evolution, and the ultimate rationality of things. He has been able to glimpse that he lives in the *antarikṣa*, the intermediate region between heaven and earth—the world that acts as a mediator, according to another hymn (*AV* I.32)—whence springs forth the energy of the entire universe, because it is the link of the whole of reality. But this monk does not speculate; he lives, he considers, he drinks, he dances, he puts his own life in danger, he is everyone's and everything's friend, he does not worry about either making or rattling off speeches, he certainly does not write books nor does

he defend himself. He is silent because, as we have already seen, he has nothing to say. His simplicity is extreme.

He does not want anyone to imitate him, because he does not imitate anyone; he does not present himself as a model, because he has no models. And this is fundamental. It is pure spontaneity, maximum freedom. His life is not a walk along a path, but a flight through the air, where there are no roads. There are no moral laws, because there are not even physical laws. The monk is the explosion of freedom that rational mortals have tried to dominate and channel toward an Omega point, a God, an *eschaton*, or an entropic death of the universe. But this monk is not even an anarchist who destroys others and sparks revolutions. It is he himself who drinks the cup of poison, who takes the cross, and who will probably lose his own life. But utilitarians do not understand this, although they define themselves as spiritual realists. When the "madness of the cross" is put forward as an argument—therefore a rational one—in order to defend a position, madness does lose its energy, like salt that has lost its flavor. We have already said that monasticism hides a mystery. The *muni* is silent because he cannot find a way to translate his intuition. He cannot only clothe himself in words. It is he that collaborates with the divinity: he who does good, *saukṛtya*, the *ergon agathīn* of Christian scripture.

Probably the description of this hymn is that of the spiritual hero, and our intention was not to present the monk as a spiritual giant, but as a human archetype. The *keśin*, with his long hair, certainly stands out from others, but it is not that these ascetics have grown their hair long; they simply have not cut it, they have let it grow naturally. Could it not be that in every Man there is a hero, a unique being ? Could it not be that our culture, behind the protection of democracy and equality, wants to reduce us to a common denominator and even to a number, if that were possible? Could it not be that the monastic archetype is the seed of what is unique and heroic in each of us? How is it possible to believe in an infinite and free God, if there is not in us the same seed of infiniteness and freedom? The same happens with nudity. The *muni* does not go about adorned with costly and sophisticated clothes; he has simplified himself but, as we have already said, he does not go around naked. He goes around clothed by the wind and protected by it, by the "spirit."

The *keśin* is the monastic archetype, although man does not live with archetypes alone. But without this we would grow weak.

Without Desire and Without Identity—Vairāgya

The movement of interiorization that begins with the *Upani@ads* will later lead to a stripping and a sharp abandonment of all the veils with which reality is covered. Two currents are mixed in the idea of the *saμnyāsin*, the monk, the acosmic ascetic who has renounced everything.

The first is the moral perfection of the one who always tells the truth, who has perfect control of his own passions and desires, who is full of compassion and love....

Whatever human ideal we may come to conceive, this saint embodies it. The second is the total overcoming and transcendence of the human condition: the *sādhu*, the man who immediately goes to the goal and who finds himself beyond all the limits imposed on other people, be they in the moral, social, physical, or intellectual field. He is no longer a citizen of this world: he already lives on the other side. He bears his witness to the end by reminding humankind that it is still a prisoner in the grip of the *saṃsāra*, the world of appearances. The balance between these elements is not always maintained, but certainly both are deeply present in the *Upaniṣads*.

Perhaps one of the most amazing expressions of this balance is found in the famous sentence of the *Īśā-upaniṣad* 1: "Find joy through renunciation" (*tene tyaktena bhuñjīthāḥ*). Authentic ascesis does not consist in narcissistic satisfaction: it is instead the discovery that freedom from the ties of desire permits us to savor things without being obsessed with the fear of losing them, or the sadness of not having them. The ascetic is totally free.

Some sources:

BU III.5

Those who have reached the knowledge of *ātman* overcome the desire for children, the desire for riches, the desire for the goods of this world, and live as begging ascetics. For desire for children is desire for wealth, and desire for wealth is desire for earthly goods; all this is nothing but desire. Therefore, let the brahman go beyond knowledge and lead the life of a child. When he has gone beyond both knowledge and childlike life, then he becomes a silent ascetic. Only when he goes beyond ascetism and nonascetism does he became truly a knower of *brahman*. So, what can a true brahman do? That through which he becomes such! All the rest is insignificant.

BU IV.5.1–3

1. Now Yājñavalkya had two wives, Maitreyī and Kātyāyanī. Of these two, Maitreyī had understanding of *brahman*, whereas Kātyāyanī possessed only the common knowledge of women. Now Yājñavalkya wished to prepare for another way of life.
2. And he said: "Maitreyī, I am about to leave this way of life. Now I must take some decision about you and Kātyāyanī."
3. Maitreyī replied to him: "If even the whole earth were mine, would I become immortal by this?" "[Certainly] not," replied Yājñavalkya. "Your life would be just like that of wealthy people, but in riches there is no hope of immortality."

MahanarU 505–17; 530–38

505. "The Ultimate is Truth, and Truth is the Ultimate!" Thanks to Truth, you will never fall from the heavenly world, because Truth belongs to the righteous. This is why there is such joy in Truth.

506. Some say: "The Ultimate is Ardor." But there is no higher ardor than fasting, because the ultimate Ardor is difficult to attain to the end! This is why there is such joy in Ardor.

507. "The Ultimate is the Complete Self-Control," say the brahman-students constantly. This is why there is such joy in the Complete Self-Control.

508. "The Ultimate is Peace," say the hermits in the forests. This is why there is such joy in Peace.

509. "The Ultimate is in giving [to others]," all people so often proclaim; nothing is more difficult than giving. This is why there is such joy in giving [alms].

510. "The Ultimate is Duty": everything in this world is under the influence of Duty. This is why there is such joy in Duty.

511. "The Ultimate is Procreation," most people think; so that so many children are born. This is why so many people rejoice in Procreation.

512. "The Ultimate are the [three] Fires of sacrifice," they say. This is why the Fires of sacrifice are to be established.

513. "The Ultimate is the *agnihotra*," they say. This is why there is such joy in the *agnihotra*.

514. "The Ultimate is Sacrifice," they say, for by means of sacrifice the Gods have attained heaven. This is why there is such joy in celebrating Sacrifice.

515. "The Ultimate is the mental worship," say those who know. This is why, in truth, those who know rejoice in the mental worship.

516–17. "The Ultimate is Renunciation," says the brahmanic priest, for *brahman* is the Ultimate, and the Ultimate is *brahman*! "In truth, renunciation transcends all the ultimate things we mentioned, because they are inferior to it," teaches he who knows. This is the secret teaching. [...]

530. "Renunciation": this is how those who reflect call *brahman*.

531. And *brahman* is the universe, the supreme bliss; it is the Self-Existing Being. This is why it has been said: "The year is Prajāpati."

537. [...] Having recognized *brahman* in this way, with your spirit, with your heart, you will no longer move on the path of death, because you will know!

538. This is why it was possible to say that renunciation surpasses any other ardor.

MaitU VI.28

And, furthermore, it has been said: having passed beyond the experience of the elements, the senses, and their objects; and having next seized the bow whose string is the life of renunciation, and whose stick is steadfastness, he pierces with the arrow of unselfishness—through the door of *brahman*—the guardian at the gate, he who wears delusion as his crown, greed and envy as his earrings, whose staff consists of impurity and sin, and who, dominated by self-love, wields the bow whose string is anger and whose stick is lust, thus killing the people with the arrows of desire. Having done away with him, he crosses over in the boat of the syllable *OM* to the other shore of the space within the heart. He enters slowly, even as a miner in search of minerals, the inner space that is thus revealed [to him]. Thus he enters the hall of *brahman*, thrusting away the fourfold sheath (of soul), according to the instructions of the Master. So he becomes pure, purified, empty, peaceful, breathless, selfless, infinite, indestructible, stable, eternal, unborn, free; he is established in his own glory. Having seen what [the Ultimate Reality] dwells in his own glory, he looks upon the wheel of life as a wheel that rolls on. Thus it has been said:

> If for six months one practices *yoga*,
> eternally liberated, one achieves the infinite *yoga*,
> the highest, the most mysterious, the most perfect *yoga*.
> But a man who is full of passion and inertia,
> though he may have received other enlightenments otherwise,
> if he is attached to son, wife, or family,
> he will never achieve it, never at all!

JabU 4, 6

4. Janaka, King of Videha, once paid a visit to Yājñavalkya, and said, "Master, teach me, I pray, about renunciation."

Yājñavalkya replied, "After completing the life of a student, a man becomes a householder. After completing the life of a householder, he becomes a forest dweller, and renounces all things. Or he may renounce all things directly, either as a student, or as a householder, or as a forest dweller. Whether one has completed the vows or not, whether one is a student or not, even if one has not completed the [initiation] rites, on the very day when one becomes indifferent [to the world], on the same day should one leave and become an ascetic."

6. [...] Unencumbered as at birth, with no ties or possessions, they set foot resolutely on the path of *brahman*. At prescribed times they go out for alms, just in order to maintain life, in purity of spirit, with no other vessel than their stomachs; they keep their spirits in peace, whether they get something or nothing. They may inhabit a deserted house, a temple, a bush, or an anthill, the root of a tree, a potter's hut, a crematorium, or by the

sandbank of a river, a hill, a cave, the hollow of a tree, a waterfall, or simply on the ground without a home of any sort. Without regard for themselves, without desires nor urges, absorbed in contemplation and established in *ātman*, they bravely suppress their own evil deeds and master they own bodies by renunciation. Such is a *paramahaṃsa*; such indeed is a *paramahaṃsa*

PaingU IV.9

[...] What is the use of the study of the *Vedas* for those who have seen the *ātman*? For the *yogin* who is filled with the nectar of knowledge there is nothing left to be achieved. If there still remains something, then he is not a man who has existentially understood the truth. He remains alone, but not alone; in the body, but not in the body; his inmost self (*ātman*) becomes the all-pervading. Having purified and perfectly fulfilled his thinking, the *yogin* sees: I am the Whole, the highest bliss (*param sukham*).

KaivU 2–6

2. He knows *brahman* by the practice of faith, love, and concentration. Not through actions, not through offspring or wealth, but only by renunciation does one attain life eternal.

3. The ascetics enter into this shining shrine of the cave of the heart, and of what lies beyond the heavens.

4. The ascetics who have well understood the end of the *Vedas* have become pure by the practice of renunciation. At the end of time they dwell in the world of *brahman* and, having overcome death, they are liberated.

5. Having reached the last stage of life, one should sit in a solitary place, in a relaxed posture, with pure heart, with head, neck, and body straight, controlling all the sense organs, after bowing with devotion to the master.

6. Meditating on the heart-lotus, in the center which is free from passion, pure, inconceivable, beyond sorrow, unthinkable, unmanifest, of eternal form, benevolent, peaceful, immortal, the source of Brahmā.

The True Yogin—Vairāgya

We will not enter into the details of the debate about polarity and tension between action and contemplation, work and renunciation, commitment and retreat from the world, which absorb the attention of post-Vedic spirituality. Nevertheless, from the era of the *Gītā* we find all the elements of this fundamental problem at quite a mature stage.

The *Bhagavad-gītā* strives to present a synthesis that states absolutely that pure inaction is not possible (cf. *BG* III.8, etc.); that any action, whose core is not contemplation, is useless (cf. *BG* III.27, etc.); and therefore that every activity must be performed as if it were a sacrifice (cf. *BG* III.9; IV.23, etc.). The very acts of the spirit must be intellectual sacrifices (cf. *BG* IV.33, etc.).

The true *yogin* is not the one who does not act, but he who acts with real detachment, that is, without seeking a result of his action: not only at a moral level, but also at an ontological level (cf. *BG* II.47; III.4; III.17; IV.20, etc.). The true ascetic not only keeps perfect self-control and total equanimity of the soul (cf. *BG* VI.9, etc.), but at the same time he has also freed himself of every type of desire. He sees the Lord everywhere, and at the same time all things in Him (cf. *BG* VI.30, etc.); he is ready to act when it is necessary, and he deems it his duty to do so (cf. *BG* III.20; XVIII.73, etc.).

The message of the *Bhagavad-gītā* is fundamentally identical to that of the *Upaniṣads*, and yet it introduces new melodies. The *Gītā* reestablishes the balance, totally correcting excessive interpretations. The authentic *yogin*, the complete Man, is not the acosmic monk who tends to an ideal of inaction and "un-tie," which proves absolutely impossible. Certainly the *Gītā* teaches detachment from works and their fruits (cf. *BG* III.19), but this detachment should not be confused with the fact of "not [being] bound," both in an ontological sense (as if values could exist in isolation) and in a psychological sense (as if each commitment was bad in itself). The *Gītā* recognizes that there are actions that must be done, and not doing them would be an omission. The complete Man is simultaneously *yukta*, connected to entire reality, committed in the network of human relationships, and *vimukta*, free, freed of everything. He is committed but dominates, he is detached but not "unbound"; he is involved in action, but he does not remain entangled in its net. From this derives his "holy indifference," his serenity, his peace: not the peace of someone who has taken refuge in an ivory tower or in an inaccessible place, but that of someone who has installed himself in the very heart of reality.

Some sources:

BG V.2–3

2. Both renunciation and the *yoga* of works
lead to the salvation of the soul,
but, of these, the *yoga* of works surpasses the renunciation to works.
3. You must see as a *saμnyāsin*
the one who neither hates nor desires;
because, freed from all dualities,
he easily and joyfully got rid of bondage.

BG VI.1–23

1. He who acts as he should,
yet is unconcerned for the fruits of his action
is the *saṃnyāsin* and the *yogin*,
not the one who does light the fire of sacrifice
but does not carry out the acts.

2. What is called renunciation (*saṃnyāsa*)—
know it, O *Paṇḍāva*—is in truth *yoga*;
for no one can become a *yogin*
without renouncing all will to desire in his mind.

3. To the sage climbing toward *yoga*
action is a means;
for the same sage, after reaching the peak of *yoga*,
serenity is the means.
[...]

6. The Self [*ātman*] is a friend to Man,
to him whose "I" has been conquered by the Self;
but to him who does not own his own Self
the "I" is a foe, and it acts as such.

7. In the one who has conquered his self
and attained, in peace, the control
and perfect mastery of himself,
then the Supreme Self has a base and balance
in heat or cold, joy or pain, honor or disgrace.

8. The *yogin* who is satisfied with his own self-knowledge,
who has wisely understood his own balance,
who is the master of his own senses,
who regards the mud clod and the gold stone alike—
such is said to dwell in *yoga*.

9. He whose heart is impartial
to foes and friends,
to the neutral and indifferent, to the sinner and saint—
such is the "excellent" one. [...]

14. Tranquil and free from all fears,
observing the vow of *brahmacarya*,
his whole mental being kept under control and looking at Me,
he needs to stand fast in yoga, giving himself wholly to Me.

15. Remaining thus in *yoga*
by controlling his own mind,
the *yogin* reaches the supreme peace of *nirvāṇa*
and abides in Me. [...]

18. When the whole mental consciousness
is perfectly disciplined and freed from desire,
and it quietly abides in the *ātman*,
then you can say: "He stays in *yoga*." [...]

20. The mind becomes silent and tranquil
by the practice of *yoga*,
thus the Self is seen inwardly,
in the Self and for the Self,
so that the soul is content.
[...]

23. The actual consciousness of this inalienable bliss is *yoga*.

11
Parivrājaka
*The Tradition of the Monk in India**

nyāsa ity ahur manīṣiṇo brahmāṇam

—*MahanarU* 530[1]

The centuries-old history of Indic traditions offers us a dual paradigm of the universal archetype of the monk.[2] Very often they are not distinct states, and this has created confusion as these two archetypes are very different and at times also contradictory. It is rather like the contemporary model of the Catholic priest (a model, in fact): he must simultaneously be a monk, a prophet, a liturgist, a spiritual guide, an administrator, and a bureaucrat.

In the world of Christian monasticism, this dual archetype was represented, long before St. Benedict, on the one hand by the first two and, on the other, by the last two species of the quaternary division of the famous *Rule of the Master* (chapter 1). This makes a caricature and a criticism of the wandering monks and of those who are called sarabaites, and praises the anchorites (hermits) and the cenobites. The *Rule of St. Benedict* (chapter 1) deals with it in the same way; it repeats the execrations against the first two species, respects hermits and sympathizes with the cenobites. This severe, and often justified, judgment will be decisive for the Christian West: order is maintained even at the risk of suffocating the spirit. Perhaps this is a tendency belonging to the West, particularly in these times.

* From *Parivrajāka: la tradition du moine aux Indes* published for the first time in the Italian version translated from French in *Alle Sorgenti del Gange. Pellegrinaggio spirituale* (Milan: CENS, 1994), 155–67.

1 "Renunciation, this is what those who think call Brahman." Cf. also J. Varenne's translation, verse 516: "'L'Ultime, c'est le Renoncement,' dit le prêtre brahman; car le *brahman* c'est l'Ultime, et l'Ultime c'est le *brahman*."

2 Cf. the previous part, "Blessed Simplicity: The Challenge of Being a Monk."

The spiritual world of India, on the other hand, will permit the coexistence of four classes.[3] For greater simplicity, we will reduce them here to two, not guided by an ethical or sociological judgment, but by what I would prefer to call the dual archetype of monastic spirituality.

On the one hand, we find the *monk as the perfect Man*. He is the fulfilled person, he has attained peace, equanimity, sweetness, freedom; he is the highest incarnation of the *humanum*. It is without doubt Chinese wisdom, represented primarily by Master Kung and the Confucians, that offers us the most complete model of it: the gentleman, the superior man, the nobleman. This ideal of the monk can be found in the Christian tradition as well: the monk is the perfect Christian, the perfect Man filled with all virtues.

Monasticism, as well as the whole culture of India, is paradoxical. On the one hand it emphasizes this perfection, this accomplishment of Man. The *jīvanmukta* is the one who has freed his soul, who has washed every stain away from it and burned all its *karmans*. In India, Vedic culture was oriented toward earthly well-being. The ideal was that of the pursuit of a human life lived in fullness. The good things of this world, prosperity and longevity, were sought after. The first *Veda* only speak exceptionally of renunciation.

But the *Upaniṣads*, at the end of the Vedic era, sing its praises and elaborate its theory, destined to ascetics. Some embraced this life as young men; others after having performed all their social and familial duties and after having lived as hermits in the forest. They are also called *saṃnyāsin*, those who have renounced everything. Often we see a combination of this ideal of the monk as the perfect Man who always tells the truth, who is full of compassion and love, who exercises perfect control over his passions and his desires, and the second type that we will now describe.

There is in fact also a second current: the ideal of the overcoming and the total transcendence of the human condition. This current is older; it is pre-Vedic. It represents a primordial human archetype that has often been suffocated (or overcome?) by the Man who defines himself civilized, the city-dweller, where total freedom is no longer possible (or desirable?). In the *Upaniṣads* the two currents mix. Christian monasticism seeks a *middle way* between angelism and humanism. The *Upaniṣads* prefer to speak of a *higher way*: the divine way, that of the āt*man*, the realization of *brahman*.

The *saṃnyāsin* is the Man who goes directly to the goal, who is beyond the limits imposed on other humans, in the moral, social, physical, and

3 Cf. R. Panikkar, *Contribution du monachisme chrétien d'Asie* à *l'Eglise universelle*, in *Les moines chrétiens face aux religions d'Asie* (Vanves: Secrétariat AIM, 1974), 342–53.

intellectual fields. He is the one who is no longer of this world, who already lives on the other side, on the other bank of the river. Dual paradigm, we say. But let us first of all see some texts.[4]

Life has its rhythms:

When a householder sees his skin wrinkled, and his hair white, and the sons of his sons around him, then he may resort to the forest.[5]

—*Manu* VI.2

But there is still an *atyāśrama*, a state without a state, beyond everything

Having passed the third part of his life as a hermit in the forest, he may live—by abandoning every kind of attachment—as an ascetic during the fourth part of his existence.

—*Manu* VI.33

The monk is indifferent. He has overcome all dualities (*dvandva*):

Let him not desire to die, let him not desire to live; let him wait for his (appointed) time [...]

—*Manu* VI.45

He is the perfect Man:

Let him patiently bear hard words, let him not insult anybody, and let him not become anybody's enemy for the sake of his body.

Against an angry man let him not in return show anger, let him bless when he is cursed, and let him not utter untrue words [...].

—*Manu* VI.47–48

Renouncers achieve immortality:

Those who in ascesis and faith dwell in the forest, peaceful and wise, living a mendicant's life, free from passion, go through the door of the sun, to the place of the immortal *ātman* [...]

—*MundU* I.2.11

4 Cf. the previous chapter. Our choice here must be very limited. In my book *The Vedic Experience: Mantramañjarī*, 1st ed. (Berkeley: DLT, 1977; reedited, Delhi: Motilal Banarsidass, 2001), there are numerous Vedic texts. The literature and the case history on renunciation are immense. See, for example, P. Olivelle, ed., *Vāsudevāśrama Yatidharmaprakāśa: A Treatise on World Renunciation*, 2 vols. (Vienna: Gerold, 1976–77). An important text is that of L. Dumont, "World Renunciation in Indian Religion," *Contribution to Indian Sociology* 4 (1960): 33–62.

5 See *JabU* 4 for a classical description of *saṃnyāsa*.

Know *brahman* by the practice of faith, devotion, and concentration. Not through actions, not through offspring or wealth, but only by renunciation does one attain life eternal.

—*KaivU* 2

But the journey is total divestment since, as St. John of the Cross will later echo, the uncreated cannot come out of the creation.

A brahman contemplating the worlds that have been built up (by works) will have to reach indifference, because the unmade cannot be attained through what is made....[6]

—*MundU* I.2.12

He [*ātman brahman*] cannot be reached by the word nor by the mind nor by sight. How, then, can he be grasped, except by exclaiming, "He is"?

—*KathU* VI.12

One must act promptly. Grace does not wait:

On the very day one is freed from (the world) illusion, on the same day one leaves everything and becomes an ascetic.[7]

—*JabU* 4

To summarize:

Those who have reached awareness of the ātman overcome the desire to have children, the desire for wealth, the desire for things of this world, and lead a life as begging ascetics. In effect, the desire to have children is a desire for wealth, and the desire for wealth is the desire for things of this world: all this is nothing but desire. May the brahman [priest] therefore go beyond knowing and lead a child's life. When he is beyond both knowing and that state of childhood, he becomes a silent ascetic. It is only when he has reached beyond asceticism and nonasceticism that he truly knows the *brahman*. [...]

Let us pass now to the second paradigm. There is, indeed, another type of monk, fairly present, too, in the texts we have just cited. He is the *monk as a rebel.* He is no longer the perfect and fulfilled person, who has burned all his *karman*; he is the rebel, the madman, the nonconformist, he who breaks all the rules of the game and aspires to be totally free; he who joyfully does not care about the world, as well as about his fellows men; he who the moral majority will treat as a madman and whose characteristic is precisely conscious madness. Not a pretend madness, but a real one. Still, the madman

6 *Nāsty akṛta kṛena.*

7 *Yad ahar eva virajet, tad ahar era pravrajet*: a literal translation would be quite difficult.

we are speaking about knows he is and wants to be mad... and as such does he appear. His madness is his weapon and his identity. For this reason, instead of withdrawing into a cave to dedicate himself to meditation, he goes into the public square, shouting and gesticulating, insulting and swearing, denouncing the madness of reason and the hypocrisy of civilization, playing havoc with men's serious "game." Also the Christian West used to have its "madmen of Christ" and wandering monks. St. Paul himself had written on "the madness of the cross" while denigrating "philosophy." In any event, our monk breaks all conventions.

Here the *jīvanmukta* is no longer the one who has freed his soul from all attachments, but he who has freed himself from his soul, he who no longer has a soul.

There is a crucial point in the classical definition of the renouncer: he is the person who has abandoned all rites.[8] We need to understand well what this represents for the brahmanic tradition. To abandon worship means letting the world crumble: if in the morning the priest does not celebrate the *agnihotra* (the offering of fire), the sun will not rise that day.[9] Worship is essential for the life of the universe.[10] Well, the monk laughs at it! The acosmism is total.[11] Here we discover an inner tragedy: the exigency, the need (also logical) of acosmism and its impossibility. Whoever becomes aware of it perishes in his turn. Here, as elsewhere, only a constant new innocence can save.

One could also appeal to the etymology of *saṃnyāsa*. *Nyāsa* (*ny-as*, *-asati*) means throwing down, dropping, abandoning, depositing on the ground, therefore renouncing. The *saṃnyāsin* will be not only he who renounces for himself or himself, but also he who drops the world, who lets the universe crumble—obviously because he has discovered something more, the truth of truth, whether it be called void, nothingness, or otherwise. He is the *keśin*, the long-haired ascetic, the *muni*, the silent one.

The hymn X.136,[12] unique in the corpus of the *Ṛg-veda*, speaks to us of an ascetic tradition precedent to the Vedic tradition. The Jaina tradition in any event already knew it. It is not appropriate to make an "indological"

---

8 Cf. Olivelle, *Vāsudevāśrama Yatidharmaprakāśa*, 2:30, who writes that this is the only explicit formal definition of renunciation.

9 Cf. *SB* III.3.1–5 and my comment in Panikkar, *Vedic Experience*, 360ff.

10 Cf. R. Panikkar, *Le Mystère du culte dans l'hindouisme et le Christianisme* (Paris: Cerf, 1970).

11 See ṅ's (Henry Le Saux's) defense, which I would define as majestic and tragic, in *The Further Shore* (Delhi: ISPCK, 1975).

12 See above, "Canon of the Disciple."

comment now.[13] It is sufficient to indicate that both Sāyaṇa's classic interpretation, who sees a solar myth there (*Agni, Vāyu, Sūrya*), and the majority of the most modern commentators, who link it to certain shamanic practices like the ritual use of drugs, err in general in an excess of rationality, when there is not a sort of condescendence of the moral majority toward the excesses of those who have broken the bounds of what is "reasonable."

Without neglecting the part of truth in each of these interpretations, I would like to insist on an aspect that seems to me at the same time more central and more topical: the conscious challenge of these monks to the historical culture of their time, and ours. I see there the most profound part of the monastic archetype, too often "tamed" by the first archetype.

Socrates and the Cynics knew something about this, while the majority of the "installed" monks seem to have forgotten Milarepa's example, this call to *enthousiasmos* and, still more, to the radical protest against a *humanum* intended as an anthropological perfection detached from earth and heaven. The earth has its storms and cataclysms, and heaven has no laws. He, the *ke'sin*, has not forgotten it; but he does not build a theory on it. It is his very life, his example, his existence, and not his ideas, his writings, or his words that present the challenge. What he denies, at bottom, is history, evolution, the ultimate rationality of things. But he does not speculate: he lives, loves, drinks, dances, puts his life in danger; he is the friend of everything and everyone; he does not draft speeches; he does not write books; he does not defend himself. He is the silent one, he who has nothing to say. He does not want to be imitated by anyone, as he himself has no model. Here is an aspect that seems fundamental to me. His attitude is pure spontaneity and freedom. His life does not consist in walking along a path, but in riding the winds, the nonpath. For him, the world is the explosion of freedom, which reasonable mortals want to subjugate and lead toward an Omega point, toward a God, toward an *eschaton* or an entropic end. But this monk is not even the anarchist who provokes revolution and destroys others. On the contrary, he becomes a collaborator of the divine: he is *saukṛtya*, maker of good (cf. the *ergon agathon* of Christian Scripture); he has discovered that he lives in the *antarikṣa*, the intermediate region between heaven and earth, the mediator world whence universal energy proceeds and that is the link of all reality; this *antarikṣa*, which, as the *Atharva-veda* says (I.32), reminds us that "the universe is fresh each day, like the currents of the sea."

In the last instance, it is he who drinks the cup of poison, the chalice

13 Cf. K. Werner's analysis, "Yoga and the Ṛg-Veda: An Interpretation of the Keśin Hymn," in *Religious Studies* 13 (1977): 289–302.

of the cross, and who perhaps loses his life. But no utilitarian, even if he declares himself a "spiritual realist," will ever be able to understand him.

It is here that the difference appears between Western culture, particularly modern Western culture, which marginalizes this monk, and traditional Indic culture, which opens a space to him that is much greater than that once granted in the West to the village madman. The monk then finds himself in a sort of symbiosis above all with the people, but also with the powerful, who see in him what they themselves are unable to realize. Could it be that this hymn was able to recognize that there is also a monk in every man, a unique (*monachos*) and therefore incomparable being, irreducible to any pattern? Could it not be that contemporary technocratic culture, instead, behind the façade of an egalitarian democracy and an order that can be dictated by computers, wants to reduce us to a common denominator, and consider us as simple numbers? Could it not be, rather, that this very monastic archetype is the seed of the only heroism still present in each of us? Whatever the answer that is given to these questions, it is certain that the strength of these monks, of these *keśin*, these *muni*, these *saµnyāsin* is a constant challenge and an example that continues to inspire *los pocos sabios que en el mundo han sido* (the few wise men ever existed in the world [Fray Luis de Leon]): renunciation has surpassed the ardors, *tapas* (*MahanarU* 568).

Can a synthesis be traced, on the one hand, between the two models of monk and, on the other, between the monastic paradigm and so-called modern life? The strength of the *Bhagavad-gītā* resides, it seems to me, in the effort to reach the first synthesis: *yukta-vimukta* could be its formula—that is, being in communion with the universe, being aware of keeping cosmic order, remaining unattached to anything and performing one's work without trying to justify it through its results.[14]

As regards the second synthesis, the one that should be a combination of traditional spirituality, which I would call the one of blessed simplicity, and the modern ideal of harmonious complexity, it appears to be the task and the challenge of our age.

Tavertet, August 15, 1991,
Feast of the Assumption of the Body into the Divinity

14 Cf. *BG* II.47; III.4ff.; IV.20; V.2–3; VI.1–5; XVIII.3; etc., a comment on which could clear up this point.

12
Letter to Abhiṣiktānanda on Eastern and Western Monasticism

Abyssus abyssum invocat!
"Deep calls to deep at the voice of the cataracts"

—Ps 42:7

The West calls the East
and they meet in the cataracts of the Word:
dabar, vāc, lógos

Vārāṇasī, December 7, 1975
(second anniversary of your Great Departure)

Dear Abhiṣiktānanda,

Do you remember? Some years ago I suggested that a "tribute book" should be published for your sixtieth birthday. At the time you mocked the idea, so I did not insist. Now I take my "revenge," though it will not be about one single book, but a series of texts from all over the world; showing that your forty-year-long dream will soon be fulfilled, confirming once more the parable of the grain of corn that needs to fall on the earth and die to be fruitful.

"An hour awaited for fifteen years!" You wrote to your family when, on the morning of August 15, 1948 (on the first anniversary of the Independence of India, although you did not seem to be struck by the coincidence), you reached the port of Colombo and went straight to Madras, enteringyour Promised Land, which you were never to abandon. Throughout the years you remained faithful to your calling, overcoming all the trials that India held in store for you. As early as 1947, you had written from your monastery of St. Anne de Kergonan to Father J. Monchanin in India about the possibility of joining him, or, anyway, cooperating with him in the spiritual bridge-buildingyou both envisaged.

"Her call fills me with anguish," you said in a letter,[1] referring to the fascination that India had for you. This "anguish" indeed, is one of the words that appears most frequently in your personal journals throughout the years.

Dear Svāmījī, this is not a fictitious letter I am writing to you; it is real and genuine, a continuation of our long correspondence and a follow-up to the letter you wrote after decidingyou would spend at least a month with me in Varanasi. How I regret that we later had to cancel our plans because you were very tired "and still very weak"[2] with no strength to undertake the journey. Two months later, in fact, you had passed beyond all earthly limitations, and my last letter to you arrived when you were no longer with us, in this time and this space.

We had planned to speak at length about so many common concerns—the Church, Christianity, Hinduism, the new generation of theologians, etc.—and there were so many problems that your spirit, lively and attentive as ever, wanted to share with some of your friends here, in the holy city of Vārāṇasī, this side of the River. Now you have crossed to the other shore, but precisely because we both believe that there flows the same River, I can write you a real letter, not a literary fiction or some sort of "supernatural" communication. Although an intimate letter addressed to you, it is also an open letter to all those who, directly or indirectly, know and love you. You have broken down the boundaries!

I am still greatly moved by the reading of most of your personal journals. I only regret that those written after 1965 were destroyed, so that, except for some excerpts that have been saved, every reference to those years is a secondhand one. Doubtless it was a well-meant decision taken out of zeal, in order to protect your own privacy, and maybe somebody else's; however, I am all the more sorry because it was done by a *saṃnyāsin* (a renouncer) who nevertheless thought he had a property "right" over those manuscripts, therefore a right to do what he liked best with them, namely to throw them into the Ganges. Why should we be afraid of our nakedness, hiding the dark sides of our existence? Or, on the contrary, the bright sides? Anyway, what remains of your private writings is rich enough to give material for study, and for a possible book.

I will use your journals only to support what I want to express through this letter, which is in no way intended to be a study of your thought, nor

1 Letter of August 18, 1947, in Jean-Michel Le Saux, Raimundo Panikkar, and the Abhishiktananda Society, *La Montée au fond du coeur : le journal intime du moine chrétiensannyāsī hindou, 1948-1973* (Paris: Oeil, 1986).

2 Ibid., October 6, 1973.

will it try to follow your inner pilgrimage by analyzingyour private papers. I know very well that those notes you used to write down were of use to you, and that you often played the role of the *pūrvapakṣin* (devil's advocate) with the sole intention of expressing a momentary mood. I hope that future studies will interpret those pages for what they actually are, in the light of your whole life and works. Most of the quotations I use here were inserted after the first edition of my letter, after having read your journals, as a confirmation to what I had already written. The two quotations from Monchanin have been taken from his last book.[3] All the rest is based on my personal memories.

The Experience in India

We are grateful to you, dear Svāmījī. You were one of the most authentic "Western" spirits ever to sail to our coasts in order to expose himself to the genuine "Indian" experience. You had a truly Western character and a profound Western formation. Only a man equipped with all the traditional Western resources could have done what you did, endured the discouragements you met, and overcome the internal and external obstacles that stood in your way. I would like to emphasize this. Immediately before writing this letter, I went through your manuscript, *Amour et Sagesse*, written in 1942 for your mother. It is a moving confession of your traditional Catholic faith, in the best sense of the phrase. It shows a command of scripture, tradition, and a deeply assimilated knowledge of theology that many a highly placed professor might well envy, and, at the same time, a mature fer vor that only a true contemplative can communicate. He alone, who has assimilated tradition at its best, can go beyond it. Everything else is just amateur fantasies, with catastrophic consequences for both sides in the dialogue, as we have experienced so often: all those superficial "enthusiasts" hurt more than help both the Western tradition they come from, and the Eastern tradition they claim to imitate. But I imagine you would interrupt this digression of mine by wavingyour hand as you used to, a happy symbiosis between the Indian *mudrā* conveying indifference and patience, and the French gesture meaning "let it go."

As late as 1970 you were still saying, "The problem of Advaita-Christianity appears only on the notional level,"[4] and, except perhaps for the last year of your life, you always faced this problem most intensely. We are grateful to you, because not only did you live your life *with* us, giving it away so beautifully, but you also lived your experience *for* us. The

3 J. Monchanin, *Mystique de l'Inde, mystère chrétien* (Paris: Fayard, 1974).

4 Letter of November 27, 1970, in *La Montée au fond du cœur*.

internal contradictions and rending conflicts ("déchirements," you called them) that beset you for decades helped us to see and to discern far more than any cheap synthesis or stubborn refusal could possibly have done. You became one of us; you lived for us a life that Indians alone might never have experienced in all its tensions and polarities. How often duringyour years of prayer, solitude, and meditation you used to complain that what you saw and suffered did not seem to be felt in its excruciating polarity, either by ordinary Christians or by the great majority of Vedāntins and even *sādhus* (monks); for all of whom you coined the epithet *nāmarūpins*, those who restrict themselves to the names and shapes of things, to appearances!

Your distrust of concepts, of the mental, of entanglement in the *nāmarūpa*, the name and form, your frontal attacks on theologians, philosophers, and all those you called *vivartavādins* (those who share the limited idea of a world as an illusory transformation of Brahman)—all this is well known to those who knew you. You were a man of orthopraxis, rather than orthodoxy. Our gratitude is for your life more than for anything else.

Only a few months after your arrival in India to take up residence in Kulitalai, Father Monchanin, whom you had joined, wrote:

> As the days pass in his company, I admire more and more the scarcely believable *convergences* of his views with my own aspirations. And this is all the more *striking* because on the humanist plane... we differ so much.[5]

Indeed, a certain estrangement became inevitable. It was your same holy fellow Monchanin, or to call him by his Indian name, Parama Arūbi Ānanda, who, when you had lived a few years together, in late 1955, could write,

> I experience a growing horror for the forms of muddled thinking in this "beyond-thought" which more often proves to be only "staying on this side," where everything drowns.[6]

The Saṃsāric River

Your entire life, Abhiṣikta, was a desperate effort to cross this *saµsāric* river (cosmic flow), which, for you, carried not so much the monsoon mud of matter, but the cold wintry waters of the mind. Many feared you would capsize in the crossing; now most concede that, in spite of whirlpools and storms, you did at the end really cross over and reach the land of nonreturn—because the only ones who return are those who do not attain the other shore,

5 Ibid., September 10, 1948.

6 Ibid., December 17, 1955.

the *at°ta* or Beyond, about which Monchanin wrote, in 1955, in the Preface to your book *Guhāntara*, which had to wait so many years before being published. You were fully aware of the difficulties. Years after Monchanin's death you wrote in a private letter that he "became more and more skeptical about the possibility of harmonizing Vedānta and Christianity."[7] But you added in your typical way in the same letter: "*and yet it moves!* or rather this will remain unshakable like Arunāchala!"

But let us go back to your orthopraxis. Many people were put off by your sweeping statements, oversimplifications, and your judgments of others. They listened only to *what* you were saying; they did not understand you. They dissociated your words from the man you were and interpreted your utterances within a "learned" framework, which was not in fact your context. They were attentive only to the *what*, disregarding the *who*. Some call this "objectivity," the "scientific attitude." I well understand your dismay and irritation. You felt you were being reduced to lifeless "notions." For years you suffered from being regarded with suspicion by those who questioned your orthodoxy, always blind to your magnificent orthopraxis.

Do you remember, dear Brother, what happened on the morning of July 31, 1955, when you had already been to Arunāchala and experienced the impact of *advaita*, and when you had already said and written so many daring ideas? Do you remember your distress in Bombay, in the house of a man who at the time tremendously influenced your life and used to insist on your "liberation" from Christian or any other kind of worship, when, while unpackingyour things, you saw with dismay that the "ara," the heavy stone that serves as the altar, was slightly broken and that therefore you did not dare to say Mass? You went to confession and there learned of the privilege of the "antemensium."[8]

Your *doxa* may have been in turmoil, but your *praxis* was of the strictest. Your asceticism, moreover, is not open to question. How often had I to say to all those "skeptics" in the fifties: You go and live the same kind of life, and then we shall speak.

Over a year later, when you were performingyour marvelous *tapas* (ascetic practices) in total solitude, you could still write so candidly:

> This afternoon the hosts were damp, heated, stuck together, solidified, etc.... [We perceive your disappointment, but we wonder why you did not think about using the plain bread from the village.] I had to write at once to Âāntivanam to get some

7 Ibid., December 23, 1970.

8 A cloth in which a holy relic was inserted. The missionaries could use it instead of the "ara."

> others. Strange how the perspective of having to do without my Mass, should they not arrive in time, upset me.

Then you are unfair to yourself by adding :

> I believed myself much freer of the Mass than I really was. There lies deep within me a Christian *adhiṣṭh*āna (substratum) which is difficult to overcome.[9]

Or, as you wrote three years before your death: "[I have] a visceral attachment to the Christian myth."[10]

I do not want simply to recount anecdotes. What I want to say goes much deeper; it concerns what I believe to be your weakness *and* your greatness. Permit me to say aloud what we often discussed together alone.

I say, "weakness," because what really worried you was orthodoxy and its proper formulation, whereas the experiential realm that you strove to expound is tainted the very moment you try to explain it. The innocence and therefore also the sincerity of thought is lost, since you cannot combine the two: the reflective preoccupation with orthodoxy and total spontaneity of heart. Besides, what you had at heart was inexpressible; and the fact that you wanted to express it in words, and others also wanted you to, just made the matter more obscure. Not only is a silence proclaimed as silence ipso facto distorted, but even a felt silence is no longer a silence. You wanted to make the *logos* (word) subservient to the *pneuma* (spirit), unlike most Westerners, who have been attempting for centuries to encapsulate the spirit in the intellect. Deep was your distrust of "ideas" and "words," no less than your suspicion about the current christological statements, though you yourself were a man of Christospiritual depth as well as remarkably talented in writing, both in English and French.

Am I too bold in bringing Trinitarian subordinationism into the picture? The ancient subordinationists meant to subdue the Spirit to the *Logos*; you, exactly the opposite. Once at Ȃāntivanam, your āśram, when Monchanin was still there, I vaguely recall feeling, but not daring to say, that the Saccidānanda āśram was not only named after the Holy Trinity in heaven, but also represented it on earth, Monchanin being the *logos* and you the *pneuma*—both springing from the same mysterious source, the Father—whether the *pneuma* was to be intended according to Latin or Greek theology (*Filioque*, or *per Filium*). In any event, a crypto-subordinationism was at work in either case. Were not the tensions in the *ashram* a reflection of that same old Trinitarian controversy? They were not merely psychological

9 Letter of November 22, 1956, in *La Montée au fond du coeur.*

10 Ibid., September 7, 1970.

divergences: both of you were too deep and too genuine for that. They were theological polarities or, at least, options.

Were you to live in the more radical Hindu way, as the Spirit prompted you, or were you to accommodate yourself to the exigencies of the Logos, as Father Monchanin wished? An extraordinary challenge, and a striking paradox, for your Indian name refers to Christ (the Logos) and Monchanin's to the Spirit (*pneuma*): *complementum oppositorum!*

The Experience of Being

As this is my last letter to you, you will—I know—excuse these personal reminiscences, but I must not lose the thread of my discourse. Your most vulnerable point, it seems to me, was in the field of the *logos*, of doctrine, formulation, expression, word, language. You suffered from it and were distressed when, while you were still at Kulitalai, your manuscripts were negatively criticized and probably misunderstood by those considered to be great authorities on the matter. How could they understand your writings without *standing under* your own experiences? I must say, you reacted in a wonderfully humble way. The best evidence of it is that most of your writings did not see the light of day until late in your pilgrimage. Now they face the world as clear denials of what I termed your "weakness"—a weakness that you in fact overcame.

It was edifying to me (not without a certain joy in seeingyou a bit less acosmic) to notice how carefully you chose the right words for your publications. You learned during the last ten years of your life that we write for others and to be understood by them. You took pains in correcting and revisingyour work again and again. I remember your telling me that you had to relearn French. Your published writings achieved a very precise expression; you had the tenacity of a Breton.

I named this tension "your greatness," and it *was* so, first of all because of its spontaneity and genuineness. There was within you, and in spite of you, an *elan*, an urge, a life, a spirit (either with small or with capital S, as you shrewdly pointed out). It was not so much to do this or that as a thirst to be, as you wrote in your journal: "To do? To do what? I am not here to do anything but to be." This was your greatness, because you were not aware of it. But the tension inside you was, too: a tremendous, unquenchable thirst to be. You did not let this "being" take care of itself; you *wanted* to be, you incorporated in yourself the best dynamism of the West, your being could exist only *by being*. The will to be was so lively in you, and that's why you did not give up; you held out to the end. You insisted that one had to overcome the mental, and your very emphasis on this seemed a contradiction. You overcame the mental not with words, not by talking about it, but by your life, your true orthopraxis.

"To be, from God's point of view, is prayer,"[11] you wrote in your *mauna mandir* (silent retreat). All that you wrote and said was validated by the witness of your life, and it was an expression of your being. That's why these expressions should not be divided from your being. They are not independent theological documents, nor isolated spiritual teachings. This, of course, is valid for every writer, and no text is completely independent of its own context, but it fits you particularly: you need to know the writer if you want to understand the written texts. There are some texts that, despite their dependence on a given context, try to express something that goes far beyond the actual milieu they come from. Most of your words were cries, interjections, and prayers coming from experience and aimed at experience, being repeated in the greatest range of tones. One of your last writings, published posthumously, put all the "blame" for this on the *Upaniṣads*. You wrote,

> Teaching of the *Upaniṣads* is not a matter of formulations—notions and proposition—which could be transmitted, that is, taught or received as such. Upaniṣadic formulations have no further function than to lead to an experience.[12]

You had suffered so much from "microdoxic" interpretations that you hardly listened when I argued that the same could be said of any living tradition and sacred text, including the Christian tenets and even dogmas, which are means, channels, *media quibus*. I remember how we once searched for a passage in St. Thomas Aquinas where he affirms that the "peaks" of sacred doctrine should not be imparted to everybody—an exact parallel to the word *Upaniṣad*, commonly interpreted as "secret doctrine." It was only much later that I found the passage quoted in a pamphlet by Svāmī Acyutānanda Sarasvatī, one of the few Western Christian monks ever to have received an orthodox and traditional Hindū initiation while remaining a Carmelite. I wish that his life were known to the world, and his example studied and followed.[13]

---

11 Ibid., November 26, 1956.

12 *Clergy Monthly* (1974): 474.

13 Karel Soetaert, born in Belgium in 1912, became Father Lambert of the Mother of God when he took his first Carmelite vows in 1931 and Svami Acyutānanda Saraswati (with the distinction of Adyātma Svārupi bestowed upon him later) when, in 1967, after twenty-eight years in India (during which time he acquired Indian citizenship), he was initiated into the *samnyāsa* order of the Saraswati Dasanamis without ceasing to be an obedient and exemplary Roman Catholic Carmelite monk until his death in Alwaye (Kerala) in 1968.

Two people could not be more different than you were—a clear example of the manifold ways in which the Spirit works among humankind.

A year before your death, your *samādhi*, you applied this idea to Christianity:

> Christianity is first *upaniṣad*, correlation, non-direct teaching. Direct teaching only produces *nāma-rūpa*. Correlation sets the spark of *anubhava* (experience); only this fulfills.[14]

Your writings were so sincere, your insights so genuine, your discoveries so true, that you found it difficult to think that other people could have reached the same type of conviction:

> The inner mystery calls me with excruciating force, and no outside being can help me penetrate it and *there, for myself*, discover the secret of my origin and destiny.[15]

And you continued in the same tone for several pages. Your sentences always bore the mark of personal epiphanies. That is the reason why it was easy to misunderstand them by ignoring their link with you, and you knew it all too well:

> There is always a risk of taking ersatz experience for experience. The way of *kevala* (solitude, unity...) is terrifying in its nakedness.... The danger is to take the idea of *kevala* for *kevala* itself.[16]

You wrote that same day.

Let me deal a bit more with this dimension in your life of which you knew only the "other side," the negative one, without seeing its true greatness. To put it otherwise: Your meeting with Nothingness, Svām°j°, did not happen in the often easy, shallow way of so many Westerners who, dissatisfied with their own heritage and enthusiastic about Eastern glimmerings, swallow anything exotic and believe themselves to have already realized the supreme mystic experience just because they have foretasted the limits of their individual faculties. No; you offered all the resistance of a "Breton" soul to an ultimate intuition that would blur any final distinction between good and bad, God and world, being and Non-Being. To engage seriously in such an enterprise, requesting us to sink into the realm of nonreturn, it is not the same as trying some *yoga*, *advaita* or tantrism. I am not questioning the sincerity of so many people following that kind of experience. I am just stressing the seriousness and pioneering character of your life, a total and absolute consecration to a life that, as

14 May 28, 1972, in *La Montée au fond du cœur*.

15 Ibid., April 19, 1956.

16 Ibid. (published in "*Esseulemen*," in *Intériorité et Révélation*, 130).

you knew, would demand a real death—as the only, paradoxical condition for a true resurrection. If we die with the "hope" of rising, this is not a real death. Without the *lama sabachtani* (the words of Jesus on the cross, "My God, why have you forsaken me?"), there is no real death, hence no true resurrection. But this is not my point here. My point is best made by recalling two episodes in your life, both of which gave you a great deal of suffering and uncertainty, since at that time you were not conscious of the deep reasons coming into play in your spontaneous reactions, as always happens with any sincere attitude.

The first was a proposal made to you of a journey to the West to attend a conference—a serious one. A course was to be given on Indic spirituality, especially yoga, and you were asked to preside as an "expert," even a "guru" (master). You could not deny the gravity of the invitation nor the possible good you might do. Moreover, you agreed with me that a visit to the West, the very first after your arrival in India, would give you not only insight into a changed Occident but a new perspective on India and her spiritual message. Yet you refused. I vividly remember our conversations and letters we exchanged on the subject. You felt in your heart of hearts that it would betray the plunge you had taken into an experience allowing of no return; instinctively you understood that you could not play with your own life and that, once you were dead to anything in space and time, you should no longer withdraw, going back to temporal "missions." Let me thank you, Svāmījī, all the more because my role of devil's advocate at the time was a strong one. You were right, you resisted playing the *jīvanmukta*, the accomplished saint, who can act in the *l°lā*, or play, of this world as a *bodhisattva*, the enlightened man who stays in this world in order to save all the other beings. You did not accept to play such a role, and you were right, beloved friend. All of us now bless you for your "stubbornness."

The second incident was when you heard that some dear friends were planning to "abandon" India and plant their tent elsewhere. Hardly anybody understood your burst of indignation and, again, it was my privilege to be your confidant and the outlet for your anger. You considered their leaving India a betrayal, a defeat, and even cowardice on their part. You were projectingyour own calling onto other people. For you, that *would* have been a betrayal, because of the depth and uniqueness of your life-and-death venture with Hindu spirituality.

You were not simply experimenting; you were totally committed. You could only leave India as you left it, by dying, to arise in the hearts and minds of those who, either directly or indirectly, will know about you. You yourself did stress, in fact, that your calling was unique, it could not be generalized. Proof of it was your total reconciliation with those same friends, the minute you sensed they were simply fulfilling another task, according to the mysterious laws by which life reveals itself in this *saṃsāra*.

Your greatness, Svāmījī, lay in your purity of heart, which led you to an uncompromising position. You did not spare even your best friends when they departed from what you thought—alas, "thought" (without the agreement of the party concerned, sometimes)—the right and proper way. A few months before your death, you wrote to me after refusing to attend a monastic meeting in India:

> It is not by way of verbiage and discussion that reform will come. Benedict, like Anthony, went to the desert and Francis to the crossroads without gathering in "congresso" the monks of the area.[17]

You yourself were a gesture, a cry, a symbol. Now that you can no longer reply, except by sweetly inspiring us to study the meaning of your life in depth, I dare draw (if imperfectly) some outlines of your Self, that Self which for so many years you were unsure whether to consider *ahaṃkāra* (ego) or *aham* ("I"). Imperfect as it may be, this sketch will perhaps encourage the publishing of better perspectives and more reliable portraits by those who are maybe already working on it, but they currently have neither the time nor the wish to take part in an enterprise that must await its proper time.

Two Loves

Shortly after your arrival in India, you had commented,

> I felt with joy the French atmosphere of Pondicherry. But now I have found myself "at home" again at Rue Dupleix, the Indian sector! I have two loves.[18]

Yes, you had two loves; and those two loves—for the Christian *mārga* (way) and the Hindu *dharma* (religion)—struggled within you during the entire twenty-five years of your life in India. Only at the very end, after your heart attack, or as you put it, "the Adventure of the Great Week,"[19] did the two seem to come into harmony. You wrote, then, of the flash that was the culmination of your life-quest:

> After a few days there came over me something like the marvelous solution of an equation: I had discovered the Holy Grail. And this I say to whoever can capture the image. The quest for the Grail

17 Ibid., May 25, 1973.

18 Ibid., February 20, 1949.

19

is fundamentally none other than the quest for Self. Unique quest signified under every myth and symbol.[20]

Two months later you had drained the whole Cup. Do you know, Svāmījī, that *the* dream that C. G. Jung had during his only stay in India was of the Grail? Is this perhaps evidence of the integration of which I am speaking, the fact that, at the very end of your life, you too had recourse to that myth Jung himself called a "primordial European dream" (*ureuropäischer Traum*)?

For a quarter of a century you were haunted by the call of the abyss, by the *advaitic* experience that you sensed gave all the answers, because it eliminated both question and questioner. It was "the call of the higher abyss"[21]—as you effectively put it, playing on the paradox. Yet you resisted; you did not dare take the final plunge, as you yourself wrote on several occasions. You preached it to others, you presented it as the "solution," and yet you doubted, you felt it to be a betrayal of your other love, not only externally, as far as Western culture was concerned, but, more deeply, concerning the loyalty to that Christ whom you called *Sadguru*, true Master (as you still remarked on March 23, 1970), although you could not dissociate Him from his geographical and historical milieu. You spoke of creation as "the fission of the One"[22] (for you felt creatureliness precisely as a fissioned particle) and you remarked, "Heaven exists for whoever desires it and Hell for whoever fears it."[23]

Did you see that, as tradition requires, I preceded this letter with some words from the Holy Scripture: *Abyssus abyssum invocat*, as you used to sing at least once a week in the chorus or pray silently? The unfathomable deep of the Judeo-Christian tradition is crying out to the no less bottomless depth of the Indic wisdom. What these words convey is the abyssal nature of the encounter. You sensed so well that the fruitful *maithuna*, union, the only livable symbiosis, was not ultimately dependent on problems of technology, science, sociology, or philosophy, but on a mystical embrace in the depth of the abyss. Already it can be heard: the roar of cataracts, of living, of divine waters—the *āpo divyāh* of the two traditions. For you, the struggle was not just dialectical or academic; your entire existence was at stake.

Like St. Paul, you were convinced that if Christ did not rise from the dead we were the most wretched of all living beings. You wrote,

---

20 Ibid., September 11, 1973.

21 Ibid., July 21, 1956.

22 Ibid., April 7, 1955.

23 Ibid., August 2, 1954.

> By committing myself totally to *advaita*, I risk, if Christianity is true, to stray onto the wrong track for all eternity.[24]

Years later you were still repeating the same anguished cry:

> Therefore I am full of fear, plunged in an ocean of anguish whichever way I turn.... And I fear risking my eternity for a delusion. And yet you are no delusion, oh Arunāchala![25]

If *advaita* is true, you thought your entire life, and, what is more, all efforts and achievements of twenty centuries of Christian tradition to have been nothing but a bad, even pernicious dream. Your quest was for life and death on a cosmic level. Those who do not understand that the struggle is an ultimate one have no idea what the contemplative life means, what the fight against the devil means in the old monastic tradition: they have understood nothing about the life of the spirit. No need, Swāmījī, to defend you from all the dilettantes and *nāmarūpins* who wanted merely clear-cut standpoints, or exact formulas, at least.

The Mystical Poet

You were a poet, Svāmījī, and you knew it. Do you remember when I teased you, because in one of your books you referred to me as an artist "also"? In October 1956 you composed a beautiful hymn to Arunāchala after the manner of the Song of Songs. But your inspiration reached a peak in the absolutely sincere poem that you composed from the *mauna mandir* some days later:

> You ravished me, O Arunāchala,
> as a virgin to whom one speaks words of love
> and you left me there, like that before you.
> ...
> And I remain naked, lying right there,
> and I have no more strength to rise.
> I am clothed in shame,
> I dare not look at myself
> for all this is your work, O Arunāchala,
> and I will no more think of you.[26]

---

24 Ibid., September 25, 1953

25 Ibid., November 27, 1956.

26 "Tu m'a viole, o Arunāchala,
comme une vierge a qui on dit des mots d'amour
et tu m'as laisse la, comme ca devant toi.

"Et je reste la nu, gisant, comme ca,
je n' ai plus la force de me relever

You could not resist any more "the sundering call of my deepest being"[27] while on that same day you confessed once again your passionate love for Christ of over forty years, declaring in touching terms that you have been faithful to Him in an uncompromising and unflinching way. We should not, and do not, minimize your dark night and your subsequent purification, my dear brother.

It took years, however, to incorporate into yourself the advaitic experience. Sometimes it seemed that you *had* undergone it, and that your will was resisting it, but you knew that the true experience is irresistible and that you had not yet undergone it, since doubts were still creeping into your... what? Was it not the *mind* that was responsible for all this delusion? You used to retort, when you felt that I was making it too simple: Would not the entire structure of Christianity collapse? Or, at least, would it not lead to "the explosion of dogmatic, cultural, and sociological Christianity?"[28] "So what?" was my immediate, exasperated reaction. The fact that we were aware of such dilemmas showed that we were not on the right path, and that neither a "yes" nor a "no" has any bearing on the real problem. A long story, Svāmījī.

The fascinating aspect of your growth is that it was not an academic or intellectual process, but a vital one. It was not a quandary of your mind but an aporia of your life. I argued that there exists also an intellectual experience and that we cannot throw away the mental without discarding what sustains it; that the great obstacle here is not so much the intellect as the will. This is where you were in truth a great Westerner. "*Wollen ist Ursein*," the will is the primordial Being, said Schelling summing up the Western experience. This, however, is where you won. To undergo the advaitic experience in the Indian context had been done time and again (your cherished example was Ramana Maharshi), but to reenact the same experience with another type of "material"—that is to say, not with a different type of consciousness, since every mental construction is surpassed, but with another anthropological makeup—this was your contribution. What I dared call your weakness was, in fact, your real greatness. You needed to break with centuries-old mental and spiritual habits that lay heavily on your psyche. You had to do violence to yourself. That led me to see your uncertainty as a false problem and,

---

je suis couvert de honte
je n' ose plus me regarder
car tout cela est ton oeuvre, o Arunāchala,
et je ne veux plus penser a toi."
Ibid., November 15, 1956.

27 Ibid., November 24, 1956.

28 Ibid., July 14, 1956.

as such, the cause of a useless struggle. Anyway, without passing through all these troubles, you would not have been able to help so many of your contemporaries.

Connections

To unite the Western tradition with the advaitic experience, it was not enough to undergo the experience; it was necessary that this experience consumed all Western *upādhis*, or limiting adjuncts, that it transformed the traditional Western approach to reality and exhausted it within this same advaitic intuition. I was tempted to make this too easy, perhaps because the Indic spirit had already cleared the trail, or because the Westerner already foretastes it, or already has an intellectual gleam of it. A mediator, not an intermediary, was needed, a person really at home in the two worlds. You yourself liked to quote, though in a higher sense, that famous verse of the tenth *mandala* (book) of the *Ṛg-veda*: that the *keśin*, the long-haired ascetic, "bears the two worlds." You were such a *keśin*; you were really led by the Spirit, and this is what, fortunately, you did not know.

We agreed that the central cosmological dogma of Christianity was generally relegated to the very end of the *credo* as an appendix: the resurrection of the flesh. We all know the possible Iranian origin of this tenet. Nevertheless, it is this ultimately divine destiny of matter that makes it more difficult to reconcile the Christian belief with an unqualified *advaita*, which would not allow for any pollution of the total purity and spiritual transparency of the *pāramārthika*, the ultimate level. You suffered the antinomy and refused to solve it by watering down the Christian tenet or by diluting the advaitic doctrine. I remember that, during our conversations, you would not accept my harmonizing explanations, lest you be disloyal to *advaita*, and at the same time you would not give up a certain belief in resurrection. You were never satisfied with merely intellectual answers. Unless you experienced, you would continue in your struggle. I know that toward the end this tension disappeared. Do not regret that you have written no theory on this, Svām°j°. Others will do it in your wake.

In 1956 you wrote of the "ever stated and never solved problem of the relation between the mystical experience of the Christian and that of the Advaitin."[29]

But three days later you wrote for yourself,

29 Ibid., February 6, 1956.

> It is false, absolutely false, to oppose Christianity and Advaita. Yet truth does not reside in an impossible synthesis of both but in a surpassing where both remain totally themselves.[30]

From then on you were directed toward that "dépassement," that "going beyond." The search led you down many mazes, such as that of considering Christianity to be only at the level of appearance, or *vyāvahārika*, and not at the ultimate level of the *pāramārthika.* This made you suffer deeply, for you were tremendously loyal to yourself. You considered that as long as you wanted to get rid of Christian cultic practices, you were not liberated from them and hence should not give them up. You did not take things superficially.

The Christian Eucharist was not for you another form of *pūjā* (cult). You wrote of it, "The Eucharist puts at my disposal the total Incarnation,"[31] and later, "The Eucharist is the fulfillment of the universe in God."[32] This, however, did not deter you from saying,

> The Incarnation, supreme myth, manifestation in the cosmos of that interior mystery each Man carries in his very depths. Supreme sacrament, plenitude of all magic, of all theurgy, through communion in which Man reaches the depths of self. Christ, in truth, is the cosmic and social expression of what every Man carries buried in him.[33]

It was probably on the same day that, in a long meditation on *advaita*, you first hinted at a solution, an over-coming; but then you came back to your existential anxiety:

> There are two faces to Christ, the historic face and the meta-historic face. Christians celebrate the historic face. India and all cosmic religions the metahistoric one. Are these two not necessary in this world so that the praise and knowledge of Christ be complete? These two faces, anyway, are not opposed to one another. The historic face is the expression of the other one. And the *kevalin advaita* is the plenitude of Christian worship.[34]

Were you on the right track? A few days later, after an attack of influenza you wrote,

---

30 Ibid., February 9, 1956.

31 Ibid., June 12, 1952.

32 Ibid., April 15, 1956.

33 Ibid., February 1956.

34 Ibid.

> Why not go beyond everything and remain plunged in the sovereign peace of *advaita*? However, Christianity clamors that *advaita* is not compatible with it. And, in truth, true *advaita* makes the institutionalized Vatican Church blow up. What then? These ties that one has not the *right—or* perhaps the *courage*—to break and that are my anguish and kill my body more than any deficiency of diet, climate, etc.... This essential anguish at never being able to take rest or joy in all that used to be my rest and joy... Whoever once has felt on his tongue the taste of *advaita*, what nectar is left for him to desire? But from now on he must renounce nectar, whoever proffers it. From the two cups he cannot drink. This is the price of *śānti* (peace) and *ānanda* (joy).[35]

And yet with the ruthless honesty of a journal written only for yourself, you wrote in that same entry when you were examining the old, torturing problems as to whether fidelity to yourself obliges you to abandon the Church:

> As long as "desire" to leave the Church is in me, it will be the sign that the time has not yet come. This goes also for Sāntivanam. Desire is *rajas*. All is so natural in *sattva*. Can there really be a desire to be?[36]

Freedom

I wonder if you had in mind that *sūtra* of Patañjali that affirms that freedom (*kaivalya*) resides in the identification between *sattva* and the *puruṣa* (primordial Man)? That is, that total purity, perfect solitude, absolute genuineness, can be attained only when our being succeeds in identifying our essence and our existence, as it were, or our humanity and our cosmo-psycho-somatic side. Only then can we act naturally and spontaneously, that is, perfectly freely. How far you are here from the puritanical attitude of those who abandon their native soil because they do not find it pure enough for the flower they expect to produce!

It would be fascinating to follow the internal travail of your life and find the milestones of your synthesis and harmony. You accepted with complete earnestness both your advaitic Hindu experience and your existential Christian commitment.

35 Ibid., February 17, 1956.

36 Ibid., November 22, 1956.

> As long as I call somebody brother here on earth, for whatever reason, I have the right to call Father the extreme depths of the *guhā* (*cave*).[37]

you wrote in moving self-defense. It was on this same date that you could write,

> The Christian experience is truly the *advaitic* experience lived in the human communion.[38]

I can hear you accusing me of succumbing to the theologians' temptation and protesting that you are not interested in theory. I never believed you in this—and you were grateful for my disbelief.

Let me now try another approach that may serve to explain your innate distrust of entering into any philosophical inquiry.

The Inner Struggle

May I venture, dear Abhiṣikta, a comment on your inner struggle? Please do not misunderstand me. This is neither psychological analysis nor philosophical investigation. It is the tentative reflection of a friend.

Your struggle was not on the mental plane; it was not primarily intellectual. You used to say that you could not care less about philosophy. You wanted "to live the Gospel without theologizing."[39]

I used to retort that this was already a philosophical statement. You smiled at me, made your typical gesture of "what to do?" and we left it at that. Certainly your suffering did not spring from merely intellectual anxiety.

Nor was it a theological scruple. In the early days of your stay in India this might have been the case, but your inner freedom soon overcame any fear of "coups de Denzinger" (the famous collection of Catholic dogmas). Your fidelity to yourself and the Church had deeper roots than fear or concern about appearances.

I believe that your struggle was a monastic struggle, specifically, a Christian monastic combat, *advaita* supplying only the outer garb, the terminology, and the occasion. Do you remember our long discussions on the way up to, and down from, Gangotrī? You described them beautifully in your book *Une messe aux sources du Gange*,[40] but did not mention the

37 Ibid., March 8, 1972.

38 Ibid.

39 Ibid.

40 Paris: Seuil, 1967.

ultimate consequences that had emerged from our conversations. You perceived them as a threat to your ideas, and you preferred to accuse your own lack of courage, but that of course was not the case.

I argued that, taken to its ultimate conclusions, *absolute* monasticism was not human and certainly not Christian. Not human, because monasticism has an inbuilt claim to, and an irresistible tendency toward, absolute acosmism. Monasticism seeks to break all boundaries, the limitations of the body, matter, and mind, as well as of the spirit: it aspires to transcend the human condition and attain the angelic one, under the guise of "divinization" in Christianity, "realization" in Hinduism, and *nirvāṇa* in Buddhism. It is not Christian because such "perfect," completely logical and coherent monasticism stands in clear opposition to the Incarnation. Incarnation clearly stands for the divinization of the concrete, the limited, and even of matter and the body (since the *logos* became not only "flesh" but body), but without the destruction of the latter, of the human, even of the corporeal. On the other hand, "the *keśin*, the radical monk, has no *pratiṣṭhā* (support),[41] which is more than just not to have a pillow upon which to rest the head.

I suggested further that the "trouble" did not lie in choosing either a radical or a mitigated acosmism, but stemmed rather from a lopsided insight, viz., a vision of reality as being only *nirguṇa-brahman* (Brahman without attributes) to the exclusion of the cosmos. You did not question the nature of the Advaitic Absolute, which leaves no room for the world, nor did we discuss in detail what I call the "cosmotheandric" intuition (a vision of reality as a constituent interaction among the Divine—infinity, freedom; the Human—conscience, will; the Cosmic—spatiotemporal matter).

In fact, we did not pursue the matter further. You knew, of course, that I was not against the monastic dimension in human life, but only against a certain absolutistic interpretation of monasticism. But I should not press my point here.

Monachos

In any case, *advaita* enabled you to make explicit the ultimate attitudes of this internal dilemma of monasticism. Your last disciple recalled, to both of us, your shock when, in Gangotrī, after listening to your eulogy of the acosmic life of total renunciation, the life led by the naked Hindu ascetic who remains there all the year round in total silence, I almost instinctively cried out, "Then why not *you*, here and now ?" You felt sad, and so did I. You felt it a lack of courage on your part not to live as he did, considering

41 May 4, 1973, in *La Montée au fond du cœur.*

the garb you wore and the vow you had made. I, for my part, felt I had been wrong in being too "logical."

When discussing with Hindus or Christians at a theoretical level, you could defend, and brilliantly, both *advaita* and the acosmic ideal of the monk. When alone and faced with realizing it in your own life, you felt the pain of being unable to live up to your ideal. This inability made you unhappy, humble, and distressed by the thought that you were not heroic enough to "take the last step." At the same time, I am sure you were convinced deep within yourself that by abandoning everythingyou would be abandoning reality as well, an act that, though logically justified, might be existentially destructive. In order to go beyond everything, you would need to leave reality behind you.

What people could not understand, what you yourself could not grasp, nor I formulate, was the inner struggle between the *ahaṃkāra*, the "old Man," and the *aham*, the "new Man." We toyed with phrases like "renouncing renunciation," "letting the ego disappear," "dying totally to ourselves," but you were not fooled by wishful thinking and mere mental flashes. Until and unless all of this had become part of your life, until it was "embodied" or "transcended" (strange, how these two words, at this deep level, are equivalent—does not the mystery of the Eucharist mean to eat Transcendence?), you could not rest, at peace, with the joy you had felt at Aru...ācala. That joy disappeared the moment you discovered yourself a Christian, who must accept not only the concrete in himself but the limitations of history, which for you meant Church, Vatican, Organization, and so on. Your journals are sometimes pathetic in this regard and reveal you on the verge of a breakdown. And to make it worse, "I am alone, terribly alone."[42]

What made you suffer was the radical existential dualism of the *advaitic* distinction between *vyāvahārika* (the level of appearance) and *pāramārthikn* (the level of reality and truth). On that latter level nothing of the first could enter. In the same way, a certain traditional monastic spirituality so stresses the transcendence or otherness of God that it demands from you, in order that you may reach the Absolute, a total dereliction of the relative, a complete annihilation of all that you are and can be, of all your creatureliness. We were constantly passing from a Hindū terminology to a Christian one and vice versa. This reminds me of your remark:

> Whoever possesses several mental (or religious or spiritual) languages is unable to absolutize any formulation whatever it be—

42 Ibid., August 26, 1955.

evangelical, upaniṣadic, Buddhist, etc.... He can only testify to an experience—stammering it out....[43]

This in turn reminds me of the expression *in excessu mentis stare et videre* (to find oneself in mental ecstasy and [then] see), and *quidquid Deus non est: nihil est* (whatever is not God is nothing)—observations that do not come from Himalayan *ṛṣi*, bold mystics, or profound philosophers, but from the sober Thomas à Kempis. Because you felt that in the Christian tradition this attitude, whether for theological reasons or for lack of fervor (*tapas*) or spiritual courage, was dying out or had become sociologically impossible, you turned to India as the land in which monastic experience had been lived to the full. It is not for me, now, to speculate on historical influences, Jaina ascetics, Hindu *saṃnyāsin* (renouncers), and Christian monks, or to debate whether monasticism has its roots in human nature or culture. Suffice it to say that you felt the call of India not because you were Christian, but because you were a monk and wanted to be one completely and to the end. Am I right? Did you not write that *saṃnyāsa* "carries in itself its own death"?

For reasons that are perhaps too autobiographical to be expressed, I think, Svāmījī, that I can understand the center of your life: it was your monastic vocation, your being a monk. You were tortured—as you often said—by the apparent incompatibility between Christianity and Advaita. Experientially and existentially committed to both, you could not solve the tension between the two, except perhaps at the very end of your life. Central to you was your monastic commitment. You wondered whether, out of loyalty to yourself, you should leave the Church; you hesitated to give yourself fully to *advaita*, but you never for a moment questioned your monastic consecration, includingyour way of life. This was the core.

In retrospect one sees the amount of egolessness that such a struggle implies. The tensions and polarities of two religions and civilizations, at the deepest level of their respective worldviews, were going on within you. Your support was your life of a monk, your commitment to the ultimate search, which led you to renounce anything else and overcome any obstacle. Many will find in you all the weaknesses of a mortal creature (how wonderful!), but we must pay tribute to that pure and clear gift of your existence which allowed you to become a *kurukṣetra* (a battlefield) where the outcome of the war was still totally undecided.

Do you remember the preface to your *Guhāntara* where Monchanin, your Christian *guru*, tries to defend you by saying that your intuitions are not of an indological or philosophical or even theological nature? He goes on to state that the three traditional ways of Western Christian spirituality

43 Ibid., April 30, 1973

(affirmation, negation, and eminence) offer guidelines for the understanding of your insights. He goes on discreetly to suggest that the way of eminence, though often almost a reversion to the first kataphatic or affirmative way, is not subject to its limitations. He writes,

> The way of eminence is not a turning back, not an infinitization of the finitudes of the intellect. The way of eminence is a surmounting of the second degree, without ever denying it. What is negated, is irrevocably negated.[44]

It is here, dear Svāmījī, that we can situate the existential gesture of your whole life. Your struggle, as I have said, was not a struggle of the mind, nor of the heart. Your mind was far too alert and clear not to know its own limits, your heart too pure and unselfish to worry about itself. Your *askesis*, in the classical sense of the word, your struggle, took place in the "*palestra*," in the arena of being, of life, of your own total existence. This is why we all are indebted to you: you lived that struggle for us.

A Unique Path

You did not remain at Gangotrī, and I did not, for that, deem you a coward. You did not remain in constant solitude either, and we are glad you did not. Nor did you solve the problem on the intellectual plane, and for this also we are thankful. It means that in this "space-between," in this *antarikṣa* where we live, we can still move and be, because life has not been identified with the consciousness of it or even with its intellectual or spiritual dimension. The real question and its answer reside on a deeper plane than any mentioned.

I should not use these pages to express my point of view about the monastic vocation, which is a constitutive dimension that every human being is called upon to realize to some extent. I should not reply to your objection that the absolute cannot be conjoined with the relative, that the *pāramārthika* has nothing to do with the *vyāvahārika*—the real with the appearance. We would run the risk of getting involved in a merely scholastic debate. You yourself "lived" the contradiction within yourself too thoroughly and too well, to resort to other kinds of argumentation. You were far from acosmic, and this humanness of yours was by no means an imperfection or a fault. For it was this very warmth of your being and of your life that provided a solution, even after the recrudescence of your *saµnyāsa* ideal. Let me explain it a little better.

A question keeps on echoing in me, Abhiṣikta, though I am not sure whether to put it to you, now that you can no longer answer. Anyway here

44 Cf. Preface, *Guhântara*.

it is, hopefully helping us to get a better understanding of you. After so much Freud, Jung, psychological analyses, critical approaches to religion, and—last but not least—the destruction of your last journals, the question gets even more embarrassing. So, excuse me if I express it candidly.

You wanted to found a monastery; you did not. You wanted to open an *āśrama*; you could not. You dreamed of Christian monks and solitaries in the deserts and mountains of Bharat, but the deserts remained uninhabited and the mountain caves untenanted. You desired to be a Hindu monk; you felt unworthy. You aspired to be a *saṃnyāsin*; you remained an aspirant in your own eyes. Now it is not about "re-evaluating" all these statements, and discovering the "providential" way in which you succeeded, any apparent failure notwithstanding. It is not the point, here. I think that in the last period of your life you found an equilibrium between incarnation and transcendence, the *vyāvahārika* and the *pāramārthika*: a balance between extreme historicity (time is an indispensable factor of eternity if not "the real thing" itself) and extreme acosmism (time, space, matter, body are only obstacles, nonentities in the superior realm of the spirit). What you achieved is, to me, genuine *advaita*: the dynamic overcoming of all *dvandvas* (dualisms) without falling into monism, the existential overcoming of separation (sin) without pantheistic reductionism; in other words: authentic redemption. You acquired a deep human quality and a poise that radiated through the ecclesial milieu of India.

At the end of your life, you found a *śiṣya*, a true disciple. This reawakened your ideals, caused you to revert to the "fervor" of the acosmic monk; it reawakened in you your almost vanished dream, once so intensely felt, to live according to the strictest standards of the *saṃnyāsa*. In the last article you published, dealing precisely with the *saṃnyāsa*, you wrote, "The *saµnyāsin* is essentially acosmic, as were the original Christian monks."[45] Your responsibility toward your *cela* (disciple) made you more strict, more critical of any compromise with the world. Can you remember your sarcastic comments regarding the Asian Monastic Convention at Bangalore in 1973, the year of your death, an event in which you refused to participate? Yet—and here is the core of my question, here where all our categories collapse—you had just discovered a fundamental human dimension: fatherhood. The strictness of your abstract ideal softened in the love and warmth of that concrete encounter. Thus your fulfillment as a person was not reached through the fellowship of the brethren, nor through communion with new friends who understood and loved you, but in the

45 This is the text currently published in book form as *The Further Shore*, 13. Originally you wrote, "The *sādhu* is essentially acosmic, as was also the case of primitive Christian monasticism" (text of the article published in *The Divine Life*, September 1973).

depths of your own concrete, even corporeal, self. Paradoxically, on the one hand you became sterner as to your ideal, even dreaming that your spiritual son would be able to achieve what you failed to; you become, once more, theoretically stricter, defending the purity of that ideal which was, perhaps, a projection of a psychological desire. On the other hand, on an existential level, you became "father," that is one of the most common experiences, and this time paternity made you more human, more concretely loving, with a love that had both *nāma* and *rūpa* (name and shape). You were full of care, and even anxiety, for this child, and your acosmic ideal collapsed before the experience of being a father, rather than a master: "A human relation that reaches deep down to the most intimate depths of paternity,"[46] you wrote in a private letter. Here your theories collapsed. How wonderful is *Bhagavān* (the Lord) in all his works! Was not this the continuation of your destiny or rather the culmination of your life? It is also, maybe, a paradigm for our times regarding the excruciating issue as to where absolute perfection lies. Who wants a *mokṣa* (liberation) that is only escapism? Who wants narcissistic models of individual perfection? We shun caricatures of traditional types of sanctity, yet feel that holiness may well be the supreme value. But where is it? In what does it consist? You reached realization by becoming father. You came to India to make Christ known to Hindūs, and were yourself converted to the supreme experience of Indic wisdom-*advaita*:

> I had come to make You known to my Hindū brothers. And it is You who made yourself known to me through their mediation, under the disturbing features of Arunāchala.[47]

You became not a Christian *sādhu*, but a *saṃnyāsin* who found in Christ a living symbol, in as much as a *saṃnyāsin* can still operate on the symbolic level. You wanted to transcend all boundaries, and you believed that the ideal of *saṃnyāsa* was the only appropriate way. After years of doubts, internal ordeals, and purifications, you had yielded to a more human conception of it. And now you discovered a disciple who reminded you of your own words, who took you so seriously that, ashamed of your "laxness," you returned to an uncompromising theoretical acosmism. By then, however, it was too late for your weakened body and impossible for your loving heart, because your disciple was dear to you in the way of the *bhakti* (devotion), which, so far, you had believed to be incompatible with the hardness and adamantine transparence of the *jñānin* (wise men).

You came to India as a monk, to find in India the ideal of the monk, and there, without ceasing to be one, you begot a son. You became not "abbot"

46 November 3, 1970, in *La Montée au fond du cœur*.

47 Ibid., November 14, 1956.

of many but father of one, and though on a spiritual level, it was indeed a true paternity. What happened, Svāmījī? Did Arunāchala play a trick on you once again? You became a loving father, you had fathered your own child. Everyone who visited you in the last months of your life can testify to the fact that you were another man—transfigured. We will not try to penetrate this last mystery of a human being.

I can only end as I began, expressing our gratitude for having come among us and our commitment to keep the flame, the *agni*, alive, the flame that devours everything, to the summit of Arunāchala.

Allow me to finish in the traditional Indic way, Svāmījī. Our greetings are always warm and exuberant; but we never express a wish to see each other again, saying good-bye or *au revoir*. It would be like killing a friendship, denying the reality of an encounter, saying that the meeting had not been worth it so it was necessary to repeat it, since anything repeatable is not authentic.

Let me then discreetly disappear from the visible plain, as you did, and without saying anything enter the invisible sphere, where communion subsists and love does not require duality.

P.S.: The Example

This letter requires a *post scriptum*, which I would like to show you, Abhiṣiktānandajī, as you can still help us to put things right. It has to do with the paradigmatic value of your life. Or, more simply, it concerns a question: What value does your life have as an example for us? There is a methodological objection: isn't it too early for this reflection? Isn't it sufficient to honor the friend, the monk, and let people know his writings before trying to talk about your message?

I think the objection is valid. We should not hasten the rhythm of history. I will therefore not try to answer such an ambitious question. Nevertheless, the very fact that we do not think that it is enough to duplicate your manuscripts and circulate them among a few friends proves that, in one way or another, we do not only think of you as an odd fellow, who stops children playing and makes adults' heads turn, but that your impact goes beyond the influence of just some books or an inspiring memory for a very small group of dear friends. Yet the only thing that I can attempt here is to sketch some of the vectors to be checked by others and proved or disap proved by history.

Having had the privilege of being present at the birth or the consolidation of so many wonderful ventures in this country and elsewhere,

I would like to formulate some hypotheses, although I may risk provoking critical reactions. Let me once again act as *pūrvapakṣin*, a sort of "devil's advocate," which was so often my role during our conversations: nowadays, who cares about monasticism?

A small élite may find your life interesting, even stimulating, but the majority of Christians will be indifferent. As far as the Hindūs are concerned, what will be the impact on them of your life, your ideas and your works? Hinduism is so rich in saints and *sādhus*! The fact that someone coming from another country and another tradition has followed their ancient way seems strange and a little anachronistic to a young India, which is rapidly growing away from the religious inflation of the past. Can we consider you a model to be imitated?

It is easy to give an antipragmatic answer or assume an "aristocratic" position, stating that we are not concerned with immediate results or tangible effects, but with truth and authenticity. It is too simple to neglect the importance of the social dimension and the ecclesial aspects, because it is from its fruits that we will recognize the value of a human phenomenon; recognition has a public aspect.

Briefly and frankly: are *svāmīs* and *sādhus* still needed today? And does your life represent a model for India in general, for the Church in particular, or for some Hindū *sampradāya* (tradition), or is it perhaps something to admire but not to be imitated? More than once you told me that it is important that there be inaccessible snowy peaks. But the problem is precisely this: Are they inspiring heights, radiating beauty, or dark valleys of obscurantism? Is the *saµnyāsin* an ideal to be imitated or an anachronistic figure to overcome? You felt the problem acutely and you knew well that not all are called to this life (whatever it can mean at this depth). It is not a way for all. This is certain. The problem is not so much to know if few or many are called to follow this path, as whether in our time this path is intrinsically valid—that is, if the human being, following it, can arrive at true fulfillment.

Neither you nor I are prepared to admit that human beings can be considered part of a mega-machine and "sacrificed" to a sort of castration of the person for the good of the community. The law of the cross does not consist in suffering, sacrifice, and asceticism as ends in themselves, but it indicates the way to enter the kingdom, to attain the fullness of life. In the same way, *vairāgya* (renunciation) is not a synonym of masochism, but it aims at the disintegration of all chains, obstacles, so that *mokṣa* (liberation) can shine in all its splendor.

In simpler words: Either the life of a traditional *saṃnyāsin* is valid in itself, or it has no reason to exist, and therefore it should be transformed without considering the stimulating effect that such an institution can have on the mind. Human manipulation should not paralyze the full development of a person for love of the community.

Furthermore, we cannot be satisfied with the purely subjective answer that some people seem to be very happy with their acosmic vocation. We are not questioning the right of the individual to follow what he thinks best. We are pondering on the pragmatic value of the traditional *saµnyāsin* that you preached to us, Svāmījī.

Before continuing, we need to clarify a point to avoid the most dangerous misunderstandings for the life of a social group, something that would lead to a devitalization both of your "message" and of the creative tensions within the church, which I presume is still the main location of your example. I am referring to that pious "hypocrisy" that so often corrodes the spirit of a religious or nonreligious group and paralyzes the best enterprises.

It leads to this type of reaction: we try to tame Svāmījī, we adopt him in part, but only to the extent that he does not upset the thought patterns that are familiar to us, just as we accept revolutionaries in the social field only when they have been subjugated and put into the straitjackets of "microdoxy." We put a bit more devo tion into our life (it does not disturb us) and also a bit more social interest (which can only be useful), but let us not take the prophetic cries too seriously, for fear that they convert us, completely upsetting our life.

We "interpret" the exaggerations of the saints so much so that we build monuments in memory of them, thus calming our conscience while we go about our business as usual. What would become of the church, if everybody was an acosmic *sādhu*? What would become of the country, if everybody was a radical social reformer? And of the world, if we were all uncontrollable saints? Thank God, we are on the right side, given that the Holy Spirit seems to do everything to avoid that hypothesis.

And so we continue happily to serve two masters. Will we not render a better service to the men of present and future generations, according to the two disciplines that you have lived—as a monk and as a *saṃnyāsin*—declaring without hesitation that your life is an example of what should not be done, rather than exalting in words your greatness and even admiringyou as an inimitable model and limiting ourselves to that?

No! We should listen to your call to sanctity and consider your example of uncompromising faithfulness to your convictions, your behavior of total sacrifice. We should also learn from your inner conflicts and from your external battles. We should be moved by your life and not grow proud in your name, but sincerely humble ourselves in our name. All your limits, all your idiosyncrasies serve only to bringyou closer to us and render you more human, less acosmic. I begyou not to take it badly, dear Abhiṣiktajī, if someone does not swear by your "ideas" and your vision of the human, Hindū, or Christian ideal. You did not simply limit yourself to communicating "ideas"; you tried to create the conditions for the spontaneous creation of an experience. And it cannot be denied that that experience exists!

This is not the moment to continue to discuss your conviction of the essential acosmicness of monks. We will consent to consider it as *questio disputata*—and *disputanda*—open to debate. Would you admit with me that the acosmicness of monks is only valid if the Absolute is acosmic? But an Absolute that is not all-embracing is somewhat problematic! What is really important, however, is this total openness to the Absolute, this obedience to the Spirit, this inebriating awareness of the "*a Patre*," whose experience you lived so deeply.

As you wrote back in 1955,

> I am but in three Persons [. . .], yet subsisting in the second.[48]

48 Ibid., May 5, 1955.

SECTION III

THE DWELLING PLACE OF WISDOM*

* This Section is based on the following texts: *Der Weisheit eine Wohnung bereiten* (Munich: Kösel, 1991), from a conference delivered in the church of St. Ursula, Munich, March 14, 1990, and *Quaternitas perfecta*, from a series of conferences during a spiritual retreat in the Domicilium House, in Weyarn, Upper Bavaria, March 16–18, 1990.

Prologue

Gaudens gaudebo in Vita,
quia in corde hominis iucundam
sibi Sapientia mansionem paravit.
[I shall fully rejoice in Life
because Wisdom has prepared a happy
dwelling place for itself in the human heart.]

Wisdom Is the Art of Life

This could be a simple description of the primordial human experience, expressed by peoples in almost all cultures. Wisdom is a *savoir vivre*, whereby *savoir* does not mean knowledge *about* life, but simply intellectual experience *of* life.

No one can live without wisdom. The wise sustain the world, according to almost all religions. But the modern world would hardly admit to that and, as a result, is obsessed with the need for security. The subject matter of this book, however, is not a criticism of modern times, but an invitation to wisdom. Nor will we find here advice about ways to become wise; just an invitation to take the challenge of rejoicing in the profound meaning of life, and it is this that all traditions understood as wisdom. To live an experience in which there is no division between knowledge and love, soul and body, spirit and matter, time and eternity, the divine and the human, male and female... to experience the harmony among all the polarities in our existence.

It is a personal invitation that we very often do not dare to believe in. Faith is not a doctrine, but rather openness to this risk.

In many traditions, wisdom is represented as a lady, sometimes a queen, who presents herself in a mysterious triad that makes for the fullness of human life, which the Christian Scholastics would call *esse-scire-posse*, or *unitas-veritas-bonitas*, or something like that. Indian tradition speaks of *karma-bhakti-jñāna* (action, devotion, knowledge), or *artha-kāma-dharma* (richness, love, order), or even *sat-cit-ānanda* (being, consciousness, joy), or thinking, speaking, and acting; the Chinese tradition speaks of Man, the heavens, and the earth.

Experts in both East and West have claimed this lady, named wisdom, as their own. Be they theologians, brahmans, philosophers, mandarins, priests, or doctors—all have claimed to rule over wisdom and to have access to a special entry gate to wisdom's dwelling place. Once in a while these groups have condescended to inform the common people what wisdom had revealed to them. At times these groups have prescribed what science was to examine and what its teachings had to be. Although the imprisoned fine lady was celebrated as the queen of science, she was in a tighter spot than any constitutional queen. She could only put her signature on what was presented to her.

Noble figures such as Socrates, Buddha, Lao-tzu, and Jesus tried to liberate wisdom and to provide access to it; however, chief inquisitors of all kinds thought they knew better what the masses needed. Yet these eminent figures continue to exercise an inexplicable attraction. They may no longer have power, but they still have an undiminished authority. The sage is not a professional, such as a king, a priest, or a scientist; the sage has no power, such as of the state, God, or science; the sage's authority, which could turn him or her into an advisor, has a much different origin.

I could have situated these reflections on wisdom in the history of thought, but then the rather existential character of this book might have been lost. My interpretation tries in general to avoid theological and cosmological controversies, because this is not a purely academic work. Becoming familiar with wisdom is more than theoretical reflection on it.

The subject of this book is the wisdom of life. In most religions the idea of "wisdom as the seat of freedom" is well known. Wisdom provides us with happiness and joy. It is the dwelling place where we can be at home, where we can be ourselves, and that means blessed. The criterion for wisdom, its first fruit, is joy: *ānanda*, *charis*, *beatitudo*, blessedness. We are responsible for this joy. Although the *bodhisattva* has renounced his *nirvāṇa*, he is full of joy. Such an experience probably cannot be explained by reason alone. There is suffering in the world that concerns me and is my suffering also; yet I am not overcome by sadness. Why joy and sorrow can be experienced at the same time cannot be explained rationally.

Why are we responsible for our joy? Metaphysical anthropology would provide this simple answer: the goal of human nature, indeed of any nature, is blessedness. If we do not reach this goal, it means that we are not walking in the right direction.

The kingdom of wisdom, paradoxically, can be entered by all because it transcends the world of the senses and the intellect; its place is the mystical. To use the language of Indic cultures, primarily the Buddhist one, we might say that the kingdom of wisdom (*jñāna*) is already present where morality (*shila*) and the peace of the soul (*dhyāna*) have been reached: wisdom penetrates both.

Wisdom has always been the wealth of the common people.

Even today, it is present in the sayings, parables, and narratives of the various peoples, be it in Africa, Asia, or elsewhere. Wisdom resides in the spoken rather than in the written word. Wisdom books are, by and large, collections of oral tradition that have been intensified and refined by the sieve of time.

Note Concerning Language

Modern languages are marked by patriarchalism. It is high time to overcome this: our time is in desperate need of regaining the feminine dimension of life, and that women, in particular, regain their rights. But neither a matriarchalism (as much as we might long for it at times) nor a dualism between males and females is a satisfactory solution.

The Latin word *homo* signifies neither male nor female but the totality of Man where there are polarities but no divisions. Sex, gender, and polarity—the biological gender, the grammatical gender, and the polar structure of reality—are three different things. Feminine and masculine are not the same as woman and man. Even though the gender of the German words "sun" and "nose" is feminine and "river" and "stomach" are masculine, these things are not, biologically speaking, either feminine or masculine. *Yin* and *yang*, warm and cold, light and darkness are polarities that belong to reality as a whole and cannot be reduced to either "male" or "female" since the biological gender is just one of many polarities.

I would call this reduction sexomorphism, or the sexomorphization of reality— our modern urge to squeeze all diversity into the paradigm of one differentiation, viewing reality only in the image of the human being (anthropomorphous) and the human being only in the image of gender (sexomorphous). The grammatical gender of the German word *Mensch* (Man) is masculine: "he" means gender, not sex. For decades I have been pleading for a new gender, not for the neuter (neither/nor, hence castration) but for the *utrum* (both/and), hence in all of reality, therefore also with reference to the divine, the human, and the cosmic. Meanwhile, I use "he" without overemphasizing the masculine, and, on the other hand, without wanting to proliferate the fragmentation of reality by means of plurals and repetitions (human beings, he/she, God/Goddess, etc.).

The fact that I am familiar with several languages yet cannot command one in particular makes me concentrate on the listening, and hence obeying (*obaudire*), task in spoken language. For that reason, I pay close attention to the etymology of words and their relations, and I am convinced of the impossibility of a singular universal language. That is why I cite in this book foreign sayings in the original— simply to teach us that neither are we alone in our undertaking nor can we reduce everything to a single expression or language. Language—much like wisdom—has many dwelling places.

Kodaikkanal, 1990
Tavertet, 1991

13
Preparing a Dwelling Place for Wisdom

Sapientia aedificavit sibi domum.
Wisdom has prepared a dwelling place for itself.[1]

Since the 1930s the theme of this book has been a mantra to me, a music of words, which has accompanied me and with whose rhythm I have tried to live. Not only music can resound in us but also thoughts. The ear is not the only part that hears; the mind also does, and the whole body, all of one's being. The language of wisdom is able to unite the ear, the body, and the mind.

We are accustomed to reading words. We have almost stopped "eating" words, and we are even less used to letting words become flesh and embodying them. That is so even though both similes originate in the Christian Holy Scriptures.

Preparing a dwelling place for wisdom—It is an invitation to build a happy home in the heart of Man. How can we incarnate these words? I would like to contribute to the practice of true spirituality with some reflections on wisdom. In this simple phrase are contained three basic insights on human existence. We shall reflect on our *mantra* and perceive its meaning in the here and now without any rush, preconceived notions, or expectations.

Wisdom

1. All human traditions have praised wisdom in various forms and words and with varying emphases. Philosophy is one of the forms. Wisdom's ideal seems to be a human invariant. Every person and every people try to reach something that can be called by that name. But the notion of wisdom today is somewhat distorted in contrast to its traditional forms: if it has always

1 Pr 9:1.

been easily forgotten, nowadays it has been discredited, which is probably an exception in the history of mankind. It has been distorted through the technocracy of this age and replaced by the great success of the scientific worldview, disfigured by what we call modern life. Today's lifestyle provides us with a plethora of information as well as with many conveniences without which we seem unable to live. Modern wisdom appears as a rich, beautiful, educated lady, who doles out gifts, accommodates us in a comfortable and hospitable fashion, relays information, and makes us rich. The price of such advantages is the complication of our existence.

Nevertheless, this is not the traditional face of the lady. We have to rediscover, unveil, and look at this lady anew, since her face is now hidden under the veil of her makeup.[2] Whether scientists, businesspeople, politicians, or even experts on religion—few of them are any longer striving to be sages. Instead, they equate wisdom with a kind of practical prudence, if with anything. "I, wisdom, dwell with prudence,"[3] wisdom says, but I am not identical to the latter.[4] Wisdom demands insight, skill, and intelligence, but it goes further and reaches another level of reality, another depth.

Those at home in the biblical tradition are familiar with the wisdom books and the wisdom-related statements of the Jewish tradition.[5] These old texts, with an Egyptian background, tell what wisdom is like in a clearer fashion than I can describe here. I do not need to repeat these texts; instead I invite the reader to a personal reflection. I presuppose here a certain familiarity with this kind of wisdom literature; however, my intention is not to present a treatise about the past but a presentation by which we may experience wisdom.[6] I would like to play a little with wisdom, because I know it likes to be played with.[7]

The word "wisdom" is etymologically related to *vidyā*, *veda*, *idein*, *videre*, vision, knowledge. The Greek word *sophia* and the Latin word

---

2 Jb 28:21.

3 Pr 8:12.

4 "The Wisdom of Solomon" and its predecessors—for example, the work of the Egyptian Amenope (who lived at least one thousand years earlier)—could be viewed as sacred forms of this prudence. YHWH says to Job that "to fear the Lord is wisdom and to avoid evil is prudence" (Jb 28:28), which correlates with Pr 1:7.

5 Thomas Schipflingen, *Sophia-Maria* (Munich: Verlag Neue Stadt, 1988).

6 For a good introduction to the old problem, see the essays on *sophia* in *Theologisches Wörterbuch zum Neuen Testament*, ed. G. Kittel and G. Friedrich (Stuttgart: Kohlhammer, 1957–73). As for the Jewish Bible, see the same entry in *Theologisches Wörterbuch zum Alten Testament*, ed. G. Botterweck and H. Ringgren (Stuttgart: Kohlhammer, 1970–2000).

7 Pr 8:30ff.

sapientia point to experience, skilfulness, and taste. Although the word "wisdom" points to different contexts in other languages, the two aspects—knowledge and taste—seem to be always kept together. St. Bonaventure clarifies that by deducing *sapientia* from *sapor* and *sapere*, from taste and knowledge.[8] Thereby he attests to an affective, sense-related, tasterelated side and to an intellectual, cognitive, scientific side of wisdom. Wisdom is both *technê* and *epistêmê*, action and knowledge, practice and theory. "Wisdom is piety," the Bible says, Augustine comments, and Bonaventure repeats, that is a filial relationship with the source of all being.[9]

Heraclitus said that *sôphronein*, healthy thinking, is the greatest virtue; wisdom, *sophia*, consists of speaking that which is true and of acting according to nature while listening to the latter.[10] "Only one thing is wise," he says in a different place, namely, "to recognize the insight that directs everything through everything."[11] This statement reminds of the *pratītyasamutpāda*, the "basic interrelatedness of all things" in Buddhism,[12] as well as the *sarvam sarvātmakam*, the "all-in-all connection" in Âivaism,[13] and the doctrine of the "mystic" body of Christ in its cosmic dimension. Wisdom is the vision of the whole as the whole. Periandros, one of the Seven Sages of ancient Greece, said, *meletê to pan*, that is "take care of all." This is the same yearning expressed in the *Upaniṣads*, as we will see.

Our first step, therefore, leads us to the insight that wisdom is a kind of integrated experience that shapes our life.

2. Rather than describing in further detail the various aspects of wisdom, we shall now focus on what is "unwise" and learn by its opposite what wisdom demands of us today. The opposite of wisdom is not clumsiness and ignorance, since wisdom has its place not only in action and knowledge. Further, the opposite of wisdom is not foolishness. Many times it is the fool or the idiot who is the sage, even in Western literature. Etymology makes it clear that dumb (foolish) and dumb (mute) are interrelated, as are the

8 Bonaventure, II *Sent.*, d.4, dub.2.

9 Jb 28:28 (see note 24). The Vulgate translates, "*Ecce timor ipsa Domini est sapientia, et recedere a malo intelligentia.*" Augustine (*De Trinitate* 14:1) distinguishes between *eusebeia* and *theosebeia*, summarizing both concepts as *Dei cultus.* He translates, "*Ecce pietas est sapientia; abstinere autem a malis, scientia.*" For Bonaventure, cf. III *Sent.*, d.35, a.u., q.1.

10 Heraclitus, fragment 112: "Thinking in a healthy fashion is the greatest perfection, and wisdom consists in speaking the truth and acting according to nature by listening to the latter."

11 Heraclitus, fragment 41: Diels translates: "Only one thing is wise, understanding the thought, which knows how to steer everything in its own way."

12 See my book *The Silence of God* (Maryknoll, NY: Orbis Books, 1989).

13 As, for example, Abhinavagupta, *Parātrīśhikā-vivaraṇa*, passim.

respective German words *dumm* and *stumm*. According to the words' stems (see *Dummheit*), foolishness is related to stammering, stumbling, staggering. Often the sage is silent. It is enlightening and important for our time to hear what Heraclitus formulated in the best spirit of the Western tradition: The opposite of wisdom is knowing it all, *polymathia*. To be precise, to want to know it all is true "nonwisdom." It is a result of the urge to know many things. This urge, in turn—Buddha would add—is the source of all suffering. One should not repress it when it appears; still, knowing it all does not, according to Heraclitus, produce understanding or procure wisdom.[14]

Heraclitus's remark had a polemic character already in its own time, during the fifth century BC. Heraclitus had directed it at Xenophanes and Pythagoras. The remark criticized instances where the method of specialization was used to gain wisdom. This basic polemic is all the more radical in light of philosophy's modern development. In what might be called a proleptic vision directed at Descartes, Heraclitus emphasized that genuine wisdom was impossible wherever knowledge has to be compartmentalized in order to know something about the world and its constituent parts. Heraclitus spoke out against the fragmentation of knowledge, against analysis as a necessary means for understanding.[15] This is so topical! It is perverse how we are bombarded by information as if we needed the latter to live humanly. Whatever we call scientific progress is nothing other than the expansion of specialized sciences that divide themselves more and more in order to enlighten us less and less. The real problem, however, is that this method has become a serious requirement for us, and we now regard its analytical path as "natural." We say research, but we mean a (more or less violent) intervention in nature.

Whatever modern science may be, and whatever its advantages for the elite groups, the kind of knowledge that can be chopped to pieces, whose development forces a continued chopping process once one has started that way, is not wisdom at all. We find ever more subdivisions, make more discoveries, and come to more interesting and attractive results. In the end, however, we are unable to put things together—like a child who has taken apart a toy. We are no longer able to play because we are too occupied by the analysis of the various parts into which we have dissected reality.

The holistic attitude has been lost because the person has been reduced to reason, reason to intellect, and intellect to the ability to classify and to

14 Heraclitus, fragment 40: "Knowing it all [*polymathia*] does not teach reason [*nous*]" (Diels). In another place, Diels translates *nous* as "mental force" (*Paideia*, 242).

15 "Buddhism therefore rejects thought by distinctions and opposites; that is the analytical way of thinking," writes Fumi Sakaguchi in his enlightening book *Der Begriff der Weisheit in den Hauptwerken Bonaventuras* (Munich: Pustet, 1968), 77.

formulate laws about how things work. This kind of knowledge no doubt has its place in life and is even useful. The problem is not knowledge itself but our urge to take this analytical direction, thus forgetting the totality of things. We call it the oblivion of the self, the *ātman*, the forgetfulness of the whole whose center goes through us. (In order to avoid entanglement in philosophical discussions at this point, I do not mention the oblivion of being, though I assume that Heidegger has seen this problem, too.) Simplicity of wisdom is not an artificial simplification of life (reductionism) but the discovery that I am at the core of the entire reality, and I can approach and conceive of reality, if I do not forget myself, and if I do not objectify reality, thereby turning myself into a severed subject. An integrated experience takes place only when theory and practice meet, when my need for knowledge is not independent of my existence, when my heart preserves its purity. Many traditions say that seeking knowledge, the knowledge of good and evil, was the original sin of humankind.[16]

Sin means here the rejection of, and separation from, the *interindependency* of all being. I say "inter-in-dependency" because every being has its degree of freedom.

Thus, the second step of this reflection takes us closer to ourselves. It shows us that wisdom, as a basic attitude, is dependent on the transparency of our selves and the genuineness of our lives. Wisdom is personal harmony with reality, unity with Being, Tao, heaven, God, nothingness....

3. Neither wisdom nor truth is exclusively a basic intellectual value. As already indicated, wisdom is an attitude stemming from experience and, therefore, presupposing both understanding and action, *sapere* and *sapor*. Not even the knowledge of wisdom is a merely rational action but, moreover, a touching of reality, a realization, that compares with a not-knowing. Both Eastern and Western traditions remind us of this fact continually. The Western tradition of apophatism, of learned not-knowing (*docta ignorantia*) or the "cloud of unknowing," is more than twenty-five hundred years old. "The person who is truly in connection with God in this life, is united to God as to someone totally unknown" (*unitur ei sicut omnino ignoto*), Dionysius Areopagita says.[17] Thomas Aquinas agreed with him on this statement,[18] saying that ultimate human knowledge of God lies primarily in knowing that we do not know God as God.[19] And Evagrius Ponticus

16 Gn 2:17.

17 Dionysius Areopagita, *De mystica Theologia* I.3 (*PG* 3:1001).

18 *Sum. theol.* I, q.13, a.13, ad 1.

19 "*Illud est ultimum cognitionis humanae de Deo quod sciat se Deum nescire in quantum cognoscit illud quod Deus est*" (*De potentia* VII.5, ad 14).

exclaimed, "Blessed is he who has reached an infinite ignorance" (*agnôsia*).[20]

The wisdom of the *Upaniṣads* tells us that we should strive not for multiplicity but for that by which, when discovered, we can understand everything.[21] Is there such a thing? How could I understand that which causes all understanding to occur, which allows for understanding everything? Many traditions (if not almost all) have emphasized the active and transforming character of understanding : one becomes what one understands—at the same time understanding only that which one is ready to become. Medieval Scholastics put it this way: one understands only what one loves. The most important thing is this "becoming," which creates our communion with reality.

Since truth shares this same existential character, both wisdom and truth belong together.[22] The *Rāmāyana* says, "In fact, the old sages and the Gods respected the truth (*satyam*): Whosoever speaks the truth in this world enters the highest of dwelling places."[23] Another passage reads, "Wisdom (*satyam*) is God in the world. It is on wisdom that justice always is built. It is in wisdom that everything is rooted. There is no higher level above that."[24] "On wisdom (*satyam*) the earth rests, because of wisdom the sun shines, due to wisdom the wind blows: Everything depends on wisdom."[25] A passage of the *Mahābhārata* puts it this way: "Through wisdom the law (*dharma*) is preserved; through diligence and practice knowledge (*vidyā*) is preserved; through cleanliness beauty is preserved."[26] Christian Scholasticism states quite plainly that one "should set out by intellect and arrive at wisdom."[27] Truth leads to wisdom, but not automatically or by itself.

The human longing for wisdom is found everywhere, and it seems to be the most specific human longing. Plants love the light; animals want to be happy; human beings want happiness, too, but in a much deeper and more intense fashion. Man is Man because he or she is able to gain wisdom and

20 Evagrius Ponticus, *Kephalaia Gnostica*, *centuria* III.88.

21 *BU* II.4.14: "That by which everything is understood, how can one understand it? How can one understand that which understands?" (*yena-idam sarvam vijānāti, tam kena vijānīyāt, vijñātāram are kena vijānīyāt*).

22 See my essay "Die existentielle Phänomenologie der Wahrheit," *Philosophisches Jahrbuch der Görresgesellschaft* 64 (1956): 27–54.

23 II.109.11.

24 II.109.13.

25 Cf. *Vṛddha-cāṇakya* V.19 and also 18, quoted in O. Böhtlingk, *Indische Sprüche* (St. Petersburg : n.p., 1870–73; Wiesbaden: n.p., 1966), proverb 6741.

26 V.1132.

27 "*Ab intellectu inchoandum est, et perveniendum ad sapientiam*" (Bonaventure, *Hexaemeron*, col. 3, n. 1.

longs for it. The third eye, salvation, enlightenment, *satori*, resurrection—all are symbols of wisdom. We can truly say that, in this sense, wisdom is a human invariant.

Wisdom is attained not by *knowing many things* but by *not knowing*. One has to go right through the intellect, thus not negating but transcending it. Only then is knowledge not an obstacle to living. The *Kena-Upaniṣad* tells us very incisively: "It is not understood by those who (think they) know it; it is understood by those who do not (know they) know it."[28] This statement goes beyond even what Socrates said. It tells us that those who know do not understand. Those who know that they do not know are still on the knowing side (they know that they do not know), therefore they do not really understand, either. Paul would call them "the sages of this world." They are the academicians, the professors, and all other self-declared "sages" who know that they do not know. But if they know that they do not know, they cannot be happy. Only those are sages who are so not-knowing that they are not even aware of this fact. There is absolutely no room for pretense here.

This statement is not a paradox but a deep human experience that can be felt by anyone. It is the total negation of any elitist concept concerning wisdom. Accordingly, the Hebrew Bible states that anyone is allowed to go to wisdom and be satiated.[29]

Paul, however, introduced a dichotomy in the thought of Christianity that contrasts with many other traditions in the history of religions. Paul speaks of two kinds of wisdom: the *sophia* of the world or of the flesh, and the *sophia* of God, the divine wisdom that is hidden in the mystery.[30] Paul's distinction resulted in a dualism in Christian tradition from which many Christians have not yet completely recovered. Maybe this distinction was realistic and beneficial in Paul's situation, but it gave rise to a special development in religious history whereby the basic traits of wisdom became obscured by time, with far-reaching consequences.

Our third step is even more unequivocal: "Those who know, do not talk; and those who talk, do not know," says the *Tao-te Ching*.[31] Whoever presumes to have "arrived" should be careful not to stumble, Paul warns. The street robber, the sinner, the slave... will be saved in the end, while the monk, the ascetic, the (apparent) saint will be lost, according to legends from all over the world. It is not the person who wills but the one who is

28 II.3. See also *RV* I.164.32.

29 Pr 9:3 and Si 24:18.

30 See 1 Co 1:19–23, 26–30; 2:4–7; 3:18–20; 4:10; Col 2:8; Rom 12:2; etc.

31 N. 56, cf. also 81.

"chosen," according to the *Upaniṣads*, Âivaism, and Christianity. Hence, this third step leads us to pure grace, against which our will remains powerless.

Dwelling Place

1. A dwelling place is not a garment, it is not an individual affair, not a kind of private salvation. It is not *for me.* I cannot simply own, manipulate, and enjoy wisdom. I cannot simply use it, consume it, misuse it, not even for some beneficial cause; nor can I use it up or abuse it. Intellect can be manipulated and used as a weapon; one can wrestle with intellect and win; one can overpower and persuade the less informed. The same is true for reason.[32] But it would be contrary to wisdom's nature to use it as a weapon, as a tool for a specific purpose. Wisdom is not even useful. It is good for nothing. It is not a ser vant. It is completely superfluous. It exists only where there is abundance, only where wisdom is allowed to overflow out of its plenitude. One cannot adorn oneself with wisdom; one cannot attain wisdom; one cannot conquer, capture, and comprehend wisdom and then perhaps use it for a good cause. In short, no sort of individualism will ever locate wisdom.

The term "dwelling place," *oikos* in the Septuagint, does not at all mean what one might take it for nowadays: a more or less comfortable garage, which "defends" us—etymologically speaking—and which contains all necessary amenities for our well-being so that our lives will be comfortable and, to a certain degree, joyful. "Preparing a dwelling place for wisdom" does not mean predisposing a garage. It is a sign of this modern culture, obsessed with quantity, that in almost all cities, houses (and also streets) have lost their names or never had them in the first place; instead, houses are distinguished by numbers. "Preparing a dwelling place" does not mean overcoming some kind of homelessness the moment I know I have a private property for which I own seven keys, and where I can enjoy the dividends of "wisdom." The oft-decried homelessness of the modern person results from the fact that scientific cosmology is not able to offer a human dwelling place. The scientific world is no dwelling place. The person is lost in the quantitative desert of an "expanding" universe and the chain of millions of years, reaching back to our animal ancestors. The person is homeless because the scientific worldview has lost the human dimension, and even more so because this worldview's dwelling place has not been erected by wisdom but by an extrapolating calculation. In such a universe, it is impossible for the person to feel at home. Little wonder that mobility has become a characteristic of modern society. Millions of tourists are only roaming

32 See my essay "La dialéctica de la razón armada," Concordia 9 (1986): 68–69.

about, taking tours; U.S. citizens change their addresses once every four years on average. A home that has not been built by wisdom is not a home.

Hence, the first dimension of a dwelling place is the world as our homeland. The world is a dwelling place for all—for the homeless, the poor, the people. Bonaventure speaks, in true Franciscan manner, of wisdom as multifaceted so that it can be experienced in many ways and become nebulous to the proud and plain to the lowly.[33] Wisdom is not complicated; it is not the sum total of many facets of knowledge, not even of multitudinous experiences. One cannot pile up and accumulate wisdom. There can never be a capitalization of wisdom. Rather, the dwelling place is a caravansary, with courts under open sky for each pilgrim in this world. May I interpret Meister Eckhart's "seclusion" (*Abgescheidenheit*) as an exclusion from every kind of exclusivism?[34]

Man resides in an inhabited and habitable world. One cannot experience wisdom unless one regards the whole world as one's own homeland. This is more difficult for modern Man though at times less dangerous than for former generations, since the average modern Man lives in a world devoid of angels, ghosts, Gods, spirits, and other such beings. The city dweller does not live with animals in forests. Hence, we are unable to experience the world as a dwelling place by regarding ourselves solely as isolated atoms in a quantitative universe. We can no longer experience what astrology taught and Gregory the Great once proudly commented on: "Man is not made for the stars, but the stars for Man."[35] Thomas Aquinas enforces this view by maintaining, in line with the astrologists, "The wise person rules even over the stars."[36] Thus, both men acknowledge the premise of astrology, namely, that the person is connected with the stars, they just reject the subjection of the person to the constellations.

In a word, the primary dwelling place of wisdom is our universe, our world, and still more concrete, our Mother Earth. In this way, maybe, a path is opened to "ecosophy," which has to be clearly distinguished from ecology.

Here is not the place to criticize the urge of this culture to leave this planet, an urge modern technology allows us to imagine as a certain possibility. One might interpret it as a *fuga mundi* (flight from the world);

33 "*Haec igitur sapientia dicitur multiformis, quia multi sunt modi experimendi,... ut etiam veletur superbis, aperiatur humilibus*" (Bonaventure, *Hexaemeron*, col. 2, n. 12. The biblical connotations are here apparent: cf. Lk 1:51–53; 10:21; Mt 11:25; etc.

34 See Meister Eckhart, *Von Abgeschiendenheit*, *Deutsche Werke*, vol. 5, ed. J. Quint (Stuttgart: Kohlhammer, 1963), 377–458 (text, 400–437; translation, 539–457).

35 "*Neque enim propter stellas homo, sed stellae propter hominem factae sunt*" (Gregory the Great, *Homilia X in Evang.*, commenting on Mt 2:1–12).

36 *Sapiens homo dominatur [et] astris* (*Sum. Theol.* I, q.115, a.4, ad 3; cf. also I-II, q.77, a.1).

however, such a trip would not be a departure from earth but an escape from ourselves. This syndrome contains a basic idea that is relevant to our topic: If one does not feel comfortable on earth, if earth is not a dwelling place for wisdom, then it is not surprising to dream of interstellar travels and to imagine leaving our planet. Then earth is only some sort of blanket on which we "gravitate" because of Newton's law of gravity or on which we "sit"; it is something to which we have no inner relationship. The shaman is concerned with something totally different when leaving the physical body in order to commence the trip to heaven. The shaman leaves earth with the purpose of returning to it and of bringing back something of the hidden wisdom in order to help his fellow humans. Such a trip is not an escape from earth, because earth is still the dwelling place. Modern space trips, on the other hand, are an anthropological alienation, not to be compared with the urge of the Argonauts.

2. "Dwelling place" also means "house"; it is a building to be constructed. The Bible does not speak of a "habitat." It talks about the activity of building a temple, a house, a dwelling place—*oikodomeô*, *aedificare*; *oikia*, *aedes*. One might translate it as "to make a dwelling place liveable." An uninhabitable or an actually uninhabited dwelling is no dwelling place at all, just as an unsung song is no song. But we are concerned here with the political and meta-political aspect of the activity of dwelling. (Politics means here the public activity of the person [*politeuma*], the human activity in the *polis*, and not the specific job of the politician.)

Our text calls it a "dwelling place," not a cave, and certainly not a hell, not a hidden place, nor an esoteric mystery. The real mystery is open and accessible; true wisdom is simple and therefore perhaps hard to locate, but it certainly is not elitist.[37] "Nothing is hidden, except in order to shine forth."[38] Truly esoteric teaching is not another doctrine, but the invisible side of exoteric teaching; it remains invisible to those who have eyes but cannot see.[39] "The big secret is that there is no secret," a "mysterious" text of Âivaism from Kashmir says.[40] "The secrets of the heart that the person wants to hide become conspicuous to all," the *Chung Jung* says (I.1.3).

37 This is emphasized, and justly so, by M. Machovec, *Die Rückkehr zur Weisheit: Philosophie angesichts des Abgrundes* (Stuttgart: Kreuz, 1988), 87ff.

38 Mk 4:22.

39 Cf. Is 6:9ff.; Mt 13:13; Mk 4:12; Jn 12:40, etc.

40 *"Etad guhyam mahāguhyam"* in *Paratrīshikā* 2, by Abhinavagupta, *Paratrīshikāvivarana*, trans. J. Singh, ed. B. Bäumer (Delhi:, 1988), 18; cf. also 53ff. The word is translated by Abhinavagupta either as "this secret, big secret," or as "this secret, a nonsecret." The stem *guh* means literally "concealing," "covering," "keeping secret"; *guha* means "hidden space," "cave," "ditch." *Guha* is understood as hidden space and as a symbol for something secret (cf. also *BG* IX.1–2, where it talks about *guhyātamam* and *rāhaguhyam*).

Christianity's greatest subversion of its Jewish sources lies in describing wisdom no longer as a privilege of the scholars, the aristocrats, the chosen ones, "the pious," the just—not even the "sages." Salvation is for all, and wisdom can be attained by prostitutes, Samaritan women, tax collectors, the uncircumcised, and primarily the common, poor people, the *anawim*.[41] This fact may explain why Paul introduced a double meaning of wisdom.[42] Wisdom has a visible dwelling place: "One does not light a lamp and put it under a pitcher but on top of the lamp-stand; thus, it gives light to everyone in the house."[43] A dwelling place is neither a cave for the "perfect" nor a castle for the privileged; it is a home for all.[44] According to St. Bonaventure, "Our soul can be inhabited by divine wisdom as if it were a temple."[45] He adds that wisdom thereby becomes "the daughter of God, God's bride, and God's girlfriend."

Therefore, a dwelling place is not only the earth, not this secret refuge as we still might say, but a house, a true homestead. It is a place to stay where we can settle down, a home where we can be ourselves, where we can have a human relationship with things.

We do not need to hide this wisdom; neither do we have to protect or defend it. Just as a free person manages daily affairs without weapons, a true dwelling place in a truly human culture does not need electronic or other defense systems. True wisdom does not need a bodyguard, nor even a copyright.

3. Sacred writings tell us that wisdom has a double dwelling place. On the one hand, it is the human heart (Hebrew *leb*);[46] here the heart symbolizes the totality of the person.[47] The heart is understood in an intellectual, spiritual, and physical sense; it follows the rhythm of nature, being at the same time in contact and symbiosis with other hearts. On the other hand,

---

41 Mt 11:25, to cite just one passage.

42 See n. 33 above.

43 Mt 5:15; cf. Mk 4:21; Lk 8:16; 11:23.

44 Jn 4:2. There is a play here on the words oikia and monê: one house, many dwellings, many homesteads.

45 "Mens nostra... a divina sapientia tamquam domus Dei inhabitur" (Bonaventure, Itinerarium mentis in Deum IV.8). For Bonaventure it is clear that "in any thing perceived or known, Gods hides within" (in omni re, quae sentitur sive quae cognoscitur, interius lateat ipse Deus) (De reductione artium ad theologiam 26).

46 Pr 2:10.

47 See Die Lehre von Amenope III.9–18. The entire chapter says that one should preserve and digest wisdom in the heart; cf. also A. Marzal, La enseñanza de Amenope (Madrid: Marova, 1956), 85ff.

it is the entire earth that is a dwelling place of wisdom.[48] Hence, a dwelling place is neither just a small house nor a certain community or civilization but the human heart and the earth at large. "In the good heart of Man (lies) wisdom," the Bible says,[49] and the earth is its dwelling place.[50]

The *Ṛg-veda* sings, "By carefully pondering within their hearts, the sages found the connection between being and nonbeing."[51] An *Upaniṣad* says it even more precisely: "Truth (wisdom) is understood with the heart; because, certainly, truth (wisdom) makes its home (has its basis, roots) in the heart."[52]

The Chinese, the Indic, and the Christian traditions speak of the heart of the world and discover a close correlation with the human heart: "Just as big as the universal space (*ākāśa*) is the space in the heart (*antar-hṛdaya ākāśa*). In the heart lie heaven and earth, fire and wind, sun and moon, lightnings and stars, what is (among us) and what is not (among us); everything is contained in it."[53]

Another *Upaniṣad* repeats what later became a common conviction: "The heart is truly *brahman*.... The heart is its dwelling place (*āyatana*—where one enters and remains), the space (*ākāśa*), its basis (*pratiṣṭhā*) which one has to recognize in order to be stable.... The heart is the dwelling place of all being, the basis of all being; all beings rely on the heart."[54]

It is well known among Semitic peoples that the heart (Hebrew *leb*; Akkadian *libbu*) is also connected with *rûach* (the personal human spirit), *nefesh* (soul, life), *neshamah* (breath), kidneys, and flesh. The same seems to apply to African cultures. In a word, the heart is the center of the person and as such is the seat of wisdom. The center has the same distance from every point of the circle. The wise one is even-tempered, fair, and unbiased, as Chinese classical literature emphasizes. In sum, wisdom is not an area of specialization.

Wisdom without its dwelling place is not wisdom but simply an abstraction, a term. Wisdom has to be incarnate; it has to be rooted. There cannot be a dwelling place without foundations! Without personal experience, without dwelling place, wisdom is nothing. Inhabiting and

---

48 Pr 8:22–31.

49 Pr 14:33.

50 Pr 8:2ff.

51 RV X.129.4.

52 BU III.9.23: "Hridayena hi satyam jānāti—hridaye hy eva satyam pratishthiam bhavati—iti." I have already said that satyam is the unfolding state of being being (sat), hence truth and wisdom.

53 *CU* VIII.1.3.

54 *BU* IV.1.7.

being are even etymologically connected. Inhabiting is the way of being to wisdom. One inhabits as one makes a sojourn, as one discovers a place. One does not simply live anywhere but in or at a certain *where*. This *where* is the earth, the home, and the human heart. Wisdom is always only a guest. For good reason, hospitality was the first of people's duties toward their neighbors. One should receive wisdom as a mother would conceive a child. But we cannot give birth to wisdom on our own accord, just as that is not possible for a woman alone.

Every conception needs a womb. The dwelling place is wisdom's womb. Wisdom lives in us in the same way that the Incarnation has been experienced by Christian mystics: "And He lived among us,"[55] pitching His tent (*eskênôsen*), when we found His dwelling place in our hearts.

Hugh of St. Victor in the Western tradition of the twelfth century offers a short formula of what since Augustine was a common view. There are, he says, three houses: the whole world, human society, and the personal soul. All three are dwelling places of the divinity, the "houses of God." The divine, the human, and the cosmic, we could translate, share the same dwelling.[56]

Preparing

1. A dwelling place does not present itself already prepared. It is not something that nature provides; it is something that culture provides. We have already said that one has to inhabit a dwelling place. An empty home is no home. A purely theoretical wisdom is no wisdom. Wisdom does not enter an uninhabited dwelling place. But before moving into a home—or, perhaps at the same time—one has to construct, build, and furnish it: One has to prepare it.

Some biblical texts say that it is the woman who builds a dwelling place for wisdom.[57] In similar fashion, Indic texts say that the woman preserves the home, just as the *dharma* preserves well-being (riches).[58] Thus, building a home is not the job of engineers but rather resembles the process of giving birth. The *Atharva-veda* says that the home is formed by ritual and built by the sages.[59] How can one prepare a home?

---

55 Jn 1:14.

56 "*Domus Dei totus est mundus, domus Dei ecclesia catholica est, domus Dei etiam est quaelibet, fidelis anima*," Hugh of St. Victor, *De arca Noe morali* I.1 (*PL* 176:721A).

57 Pr 14:1.

58 See Böhtlingk, *Indische Sprüche*, prov. 6074.

59 IX.3.19.

One should never go out looking for wisdom. One can only begin by preparing a dwelling place for wisdom. The adage "Seek wisdom!" cannot mean that one should chase after wisdom as if it were an object, a thing one could hunt for. Wisdom is not the end of a long pilgrimage.

According to the biblical passages, wisdom outdoes the pearls of beauty.[60] In the Chinese tradition, Chuang-tzu says that this magic pearl can only be found by means of unintentionality. Each kind of search for beauty would leave fingerprints and take away its glamour, as if one were to touch the wings of a butterfly. One has to become surprised by beauty, become transformed by it. No violence of reasoning, no effort, no search leads to this end. The search for wisdom would stain wisdom's independence and soil its sovereign liberty. There are two possibilities: either I want to be the ruler of wisdom and treat her as my servant (demanding this and that, wanting knowledge, power, and pleasure), or I allow myself to become penetrated, enlightened, and inhabited by wisdom. In the latter case, the initiative lies with wisdom, and that belongs to nature's proper order, so that everything I could find besides would no longer be true wisdom to me. "Whoever finds me, finds life."[61]

Hence it is not wisdom that is to be found, but life; not some retrieved object, but one's own true life. Wisdom is not an object. One cannot set out searching for it.

It is appropriate that when, standing before wisdom, we hold no power. After all, wisdom itself is without power. Wisdom is only bestowed authority by those who allow themselves to be visited by it spontaneously. Wisdom is neither an object of the intellect nor of the will. This statement was one of the main doctrines of the Buddha: each kind of craving, even the desire for *nirvāṇa*, destroys both the one who searches and what is being searched. At this point, a linguistic differentiation between spontaneous aspiration (the "spiration," the very breath of the spirit: *Betrachtung*; cf. *tractare*, *tracten*, aspire) and conscious desire might be helpful.

2. Hence, preparing is not a pursuit after wisdom; it means being ready. Strictly speaking, we are not talking about a kind of preparation in view of what is to come. Wisdom cannot be manipulated, not even in expectation's subtle ways. Hope does not relate to the future; it relates to the invisible dimensions of reality and not to somethingyet to come.

Our text does not tell us that it is sufficient to be prepared for the arrival of wisdom, and it will appear automatically as soon as we are ready.

60 Pr 3.15; Ws 7.29–30; Jb 28:18; and Pr 31:10.

61 Pr 8:35.

Instead it tells us that wisdom itself will prepare a dwelling place. We must not interfere. Any kind of egocentric spirituality steered by our own will is suspicious. The preparation on our part consists of placing trust in wisdom, which means that we acquire confidence in reality, an attitude described by the classics as, for example, *rita*, *dharma*, *kosmos*, *taxis*, *ordo*.

Such preparedness requires a purity of the heart that might be illustrated by the seclusiveness (*Abgeschiedenheit*) of the mystics of the Rhineland and the *śūnyatā* of the Buddhist *prajñāpāramitā* tradition. We should not use force on wisdom, not expect positive results from our deeds. That is what the *Bhagavad-gītā*[62] and other wisdom doctrines teach. The *Gītā* says—possibly in reference to Buddhist teachings[63]—that the person is wise (*buddhimāna*) when standing above her deeds. One does not prepare oneself for wisdom. One lives as one wants to, has to, can live; one lives as one does, regardless of merits and possible advantages based on one's deeds. One might mention here the beautiful Zen narratives stating that the master eats when eating and sleeps when sleeping and does nothing else besides, or that for the enlightened one rivers are once again rivers, mountains are mountains, and the marketplace the marketplace.

Wisdom is free; it is a present, a pure gift. Our readiness for wisdom is an end in itself, not a means by which to acquire wisdom. We must simply give "her" the chance to seek us, or, to be more precise, we only have to care about not putting any obstacles in the way. And, to be even more precise: we have to act so as to let wisdom be—be itself—whether she comes looking for us or not. Is wisdom not meant to be free? Do we want to lock her up in the cage of expectations? It has become difficult for us, the descendants of a patriarchal civilization, to take the middle road between passivity and activity. Did we not find out that the means that helped us gain selfcontrol, acquire certain virtues, or reach a degree of perfection (to speak with the words of the old schools) could also become the biggest obstacles in our attempt to live life authentically? Being quite simply means *being*, letting the "being" be, not disturbing it by means of violence, activities, thoughts; leaving being's activities alone. It would be totally wrong to view such an attitude as quietism, even though the danger of a certain quietist rigidity might be present. But where there is life, there is danger.

We are talking here about the art of trusting, of experiencing, of observing, and of respecting being. When choosing to experiment with things, we end up using violence on them and become impatient. We become impatient because we are not in harmony with the rhythms of

---

62 *BG* III.4; IV.18–21; XVIII.49.

63 Cf. *Dīghanikāya* III.275.

being, because these rhythms are not enough for us. We do not let the being be because we ourselves do not want to be. In this impatience, our longing for death becomes apparent—*thanatos*, death, pulling us to an unconscious death drive. Being is not static; it has its own inner rhythm, which we must learn to perceive. Preparing means being able to wait—which does not exclude intervening when necessary.

3. But what can this kind of *preparing* look like? Preparing does not mean conquering, studying, or prearranging. It deals with the feminine attitude of preparedness, the art of good faith, of being quiet. Preparing means neither overpowering wisdom by searching for it nor preparing ourselves in the secret hope that wisdom might visit us. In order for wisdom to build a dwelling place for itself, it needs freedom. This freedom has a name, which has been bestowed by many wisdom traditions, although it has suffered from a bad reputation in some circles. The name is grace.

One cannot *dole out* grace. No one can distribute it; that would be unfair (here the distortion starts that finds expression in the power and might of God's executives and their idea of a monarchic God). Yet one can *receive* grace. This attitude is foreign to us, since mere receiving does not match up with the servile attitude of the subordinated. Fear is not a virtue in this case. Only love allows us to receive, and it produces fruit from what has been received. We want to fight for peace, but we rarely are ready to simply receive it. We want to pay the price for every single item, for each measure, and we call that justice, but we are hardly able to accept something offered to us for free. We want to find a cause, even a reason, for everything; but we are hardly ready to receive something given out of mere grace. In one word, we want this and that, but we do not want to give up our will. Perhaps we no longer are able to do so. Our not wanting still equals a wanting. The kingdom of grace lies outside of all we want and do not want. Wisdom is pure grace.

The *Tao-te Ching* says,

> There is one thing, which is indiscriminately perfect. Even before the heavens and the earth came into being, it was present. So calm, so alone. It stands by itself and never changes. It circles yet does not change position. One could call it: mother of the world. But I really do not know its name. I simply call it the *tao*.... The man finds orientation through the earth, the earth through the heavens, the heavens through the *tao*, the *tao* through itself.[64]

We must stop somewhere in our reflections, and it is there that the

64 *Daodejing* 25.

kingdom of wisdom starts. The preparation of a dwelling place appears now almost as a vicious circle: If I want to construct a dwelling place, I will destroy it; if I do not want to, nothing will get done either. If I allow wisdom to prepare a dwelling place for itself, I will be somewhat aware that it will do so eventually and we will be dwelling together. How can I not wish for that? Yet because of such a wish, how can I avoid reducing wisdom to my own expectations, thus limiting its freedom? The art lies in transforming this *circulus vitiosus*, this short circuit, into a *circulus vitalis*, a living circle. Everything depends on the source, the reason for one's searching, the source of one's questioning, one's spontaneity in living. Jesus was asked, "Where do you live?"[65] Those asking the question were most likely familiar with the questions of wisdom tradition: "But where does one locate wisdom?" "Where does wisdom come from?" "Where is her home?" "Where does she live?"[66] Yet the question the people asked Jesus was not a repetition of this; instead it already constituted an answer, namely, an embarrassed one. After all, Jesus had asked them, "What are you looking for?" But they did not know what they wanted. They had only been attracted by his radiating figure. Jesus's answer was not noetic.[67] "Come and see," Jesus said.[68]

Hence, both practice and experience matter; there are no quick recipes for wisdom.

But how can we build a dwelling place for this wisdom without being able to recognize it first, without knowing anything of it? I do not know ahead of time whether it is wisdom that is coming or a ghost, an impostor, a liar, a thief, an unwelcome guest. Our hospitality is genuine only when we do not know the guest ahead of time, when we do not select; it is not real when we only accept the sages, the believers, the members of our own social caste. But hospitality is real when we accept the guest, regardless of standing or appearance and without any form of discrimination. Not even Abraham knew for sure who was visiting him[69]—three angels or three thieves, he could not tell. Hospitality with conditions attached is not hospitality but only a business—tourism, for example.

Such guests of old have been a king's daughter, an angel, the devil, a lion, Christ himself. All traditions tell us that when we invite the stranger, the unknown, the unsightly, and the unintelligible, the room where revelation can take place will form. This kind of hospitality is a form of surrender, a risk.

65 Jn 1:38.

66 Jb 28:12–20.

67 See the angel's reply in Lk 1:34ff.

68 Jn 1:39.

69 Gn 18.

It could get dangerous when opening up a dwelling place for everybody and everything without any criteria and differentiations. Here is where danger lurks. It is easy to say that we will prepare a dwelling place for wisdom, that we like accommodating wisdom and giving everything for it, that we like opening our hearts to wisdom so that it can reform and transform us. But we do not know what wisdom looks like, what it is, and where it has lived before. This is the risk, the step in the open, freedom itself. Our "alchemic" activity here is to transform the guest, who might not have been wisdom, to begin with.

When we take this step, receiving becomes a genuine conceiving. Then preparing a dwelling place for wisdom means receiving the stranger, the unknown, that which plainly seems threatening; and making him bud, blossom, develop, and be born. It is an activity for which the simile of biological childbirth is not even strong enough. It has to be a *theandric* activity. It is a wrestling with the guest, with what could be transformed into wisdom, with God, with the angel, with the You. All in all, it is about polarity at large—not about two individually developed characters that are opposed to each other but about a genuine polarity that has grown out of itself and from which everything else draws its existence. Wisdom is unknown until we, the I and the You, encounter each other. It is not wisdom until I have received it. It cannot be received by me and impregnate me as long as I am not wrestling with, absorbing, and somehow beginning an intimate interchange with it: In this polarity rests the transforming power of receiving. This is the metamorphosis, the transformation of the vicious circle into a living circle. It goes without saying that we cannot conceive a child by willpower alone. Another person must be part of it—and love as well.

We have said earlier that there is no proof on our part and no identification card on the other. Everything remains open, and the possibility of a mistake is always present. The wrestling for wisdom is always open-minded and humble. There is, however, an internal experience by which we can recognize wisdom as such. Its name is peace, joy, and freedom. Hence, by its fruits we will recognize it.[70] Wisdom also has an external mark. Thus, Chuang-tzu (IV.1) says of the sage, "He needs his inner eye, his inner ear in order to penetrate things and does not need reasoning of the intellect." And he continues, "Such a person is visited by those invisible, so they can *prepare a dwelling place in him*; how much more will he be visited by other people then. In this way, the world can be transformed."[71]

70 Mt 7:16–20.

71 *Zhuangzi* IV.1 (trans. R. Wilhelm).

Preparing a dwelling place for wisdom: We are talking here about a basic attitude, needed today more than ever. It means, in a negative sense, that we should not squander our time with all kinds of things—although they may be important and pleasant—which do not constitute wisdom, do not bring salvation, and do not allow for joy to appear. All of us have known about this truth for a long time. One does not need to add anything new, only to recall the old. After all, we know all about this truth, but we have no time for it....

An Islamic legend recounts that when Allah saw and recognized the sad condition of the people, how they were treating the earth, he decided to once again send Archangel Gabriel among them. In a way, Allah thought, the Qur'an is too difficult and too long, Gabriel will have to state it again in very simple terms. It will reverse the ecological catastrophe and make believers more straightforward, their faith more effective, and fundamentalism unnecessary. So Gabriel set out with this simple, plain wisdom message. He travelled everywhere, used all aides of the heavenly hosts, and finally, after a long time, returned to heaven. His wings were totally soiled, and he was completely exhausted. Allah asked him how he, Gabriel, had fared, whether he had delivered the message. "Oh, sure," Gabriel said. "But people did not have time to listen!"

The solution is very simple, but we can find it only in quietude....

14
Quaternitas Perfecta
The Fourfold Nature of Man

This is its magnificence
[that is the immortal spheres]
but even greater is Man:
one fourth of Him are all living things,
three fourths are the immortals in heaven.[1]

Introduction

In the following pages we will observe more closely what the human dwelling place of wisdom looks like. It requires that we meditate on our true self. We are not talking here about a certain picture of Man, as generated by the various human cultures of the world in both theory and practice in their respectively distinct ways. We are talking here about something that *preceded* these developments and interpretations and therefore finds expression in most peoples through their particular traditions.

In order to describe this original insight, we cannot limit ourselves to a single tradition's language and thought. This would mean equating the world of this one tradition with the universe at large, thereby making its "cosmovision" a blueprint for all others. Yet at the same time we must avoid an artificial dilution of the various traditions that attempts, for unity's sake, to impose a common denominator. Such a dilution would have to omit all the elements of each tradition that could not be made to agree with the others, so that in the end only common platitudes devoid of life would be left. A third difficulty is that many people today are no longer familiar with the tradition of their ancestors. Modern life itself has already caused a certain impoverishment of the past, perhaps not in its most profound archetypes but certainly in the kind of superficial existence most people live today. This

1 Cf. the *Puruṣa-sūkta* in *RV* X.90.3.

is the case not only in the West, that is, in the Christian countries, but also in similar fashion in Africa, India, Japan, and in most other parts of the world and in their religions. To be sure, there are groups everywhere wanting to counter the impending secularism and syncretism by means of a revival and a stabilization of their own respective traditions. But this dilution has already taken place, and an artificial fundamentalism cannot become the spine of a living body, regardless of whether one calls it humanity, "Body of Christ," "*dharmakāya*," or something else.

How can we create a language that is not exclusive but still concrete, that is simple to understand but still thorough? It would have to respect the various traditions as such and *also* avoid stumbling over the obstacles we have mentioned. If there is such a language, it must be found in the basic human condition as we see it in a large part of humanity: what characterizes us? What makes us human? This is the most general but at the same time the most concrete question we should discuss and ponder here.

Elsewhere I have dealt with this subject from the viewpoints of traditional anthropologies, thereby developing the concept of a *quaternitas perfecta*, a fourfold image of the human being. I may recall here the famous verse 25 of *The Golden Verses of Pythagoras*:

> I swear it by the One who in our hearts engraved
> The sacred Tetrad, symbol immense and pure,
> Source of Nature and model of the Gods.[2]

Each of these traditions sometimes uses a set of symbols and terms: for example, in Greek antiquity the words *sôma*, *psychê*, *polis*, and *aiôn*; in India the words *jīva*, *altam*, *ātman*, and *brahman*; and in many archaic traditions (of which we are also reminded by Western esoterics) *earth*, *water*, *fire*, and *air*. With the help of these symbols, we will speak of four centers, thereby placing basic human traits in their midst. We will assign to each of these centers certain symbols: an element in Nature, a word from the Greek or Indic anthropology, a human possibility, a philosophical side, a state of consciousness, and an anthropological area. The symbols proper to each center are not simply interchangeable; *sôma* is not *jīva*, and *aiôn* is not *brahman*. The *quaternitas* as a whole constitutes a *homeomorphic* structure, a unified system that has in each of the examined traditions its respective function and meaning. This structure will be depicted in the chart at the end of the chapter.

---

2 The translation is from Naiàn Louise Redfield, who rendered into English *The Golden Verses of Pythagoras*, explained and translated into French by Fabre d'Olivet, 2nd ed. (London: Putnam's Sons, 1925). This *quaternitas* was well known by the Scholastics. See, e.g., Hugh of St. Victor, *Didascalicon* I.11.

We are primarily concerned with the basic dignity of Man, because the person is a microcosm, a representation of the whole, a spark of the never-ceasing fire. This cross-cultural image of Man could enable us to overcome the split of reality that so painfully tortures and threatens modernity. This image could transform the various dualities (*dvandva*)—resulting from a destructive break between Man and the earth, the subject and the object, understanding and love, arts and sciences, masculine and feminine—into creative polarities. This would be true also for the final break of reality, the one between Man and God, time and eternity, or Creator and creation. The *quaternitas perfecta* gives us a chance to discover an adequate human spirituality; it is the basis for a new spiritual attitude of the person to self, to the other, to the environment, and also to the all-embracing reality called God in many traditions.

What should we do? How should we act? How should we apply ourselves and behave?

Not just since Kant, but also since the beginnings of philosophical meditation, certain ethical questions have emerged in both Western and Eastern traditions. Humanity is seeking a solution to these questions when giving different, but ultimately homeomorphic answers. Yet even more basic are the questions: Why should I *have to*? Why should I ask for an *ought*? Why should I ask myself at all what to do? A danger lies hidden here. Life is filled with dangers, and we have to face up to them, not circumvent them or avoid them. The danger here is called quietism, fatalism, regress into irrational behavior. We must not forget that, in human life, both nature and culture are intimately related. Not only nature is involved in Man; human nature is also culture, or better, cultural. One must emphasize that. But at the same time one should not lose joy and spontaneity when trying to overcome danger. To begin with, we should try to embrace the whole as the whole; or, to say it differently, we should try to experience the nakedness of life. We must discover the center, which so often has been covered up by all kinds of activities.

One could try to overcome the question of why we should be concerned with the *ought* by taking a third step: Why should I do something ? Why should I have to? Why should I even have to ask this second why?—One could go on like this forever. When innocence has been lost at one point, when the "why" has popped up, the further questions cannot be repressed. This, however, does not solve the problem.

If we want to solve the problem, we must face it from a different standpoint. There is a human attitude for that, which I call the *new* (not the second) *innocence*, rooted in a basic ground so that any further question become unnecessary.[3] With our anthropological *quaternitas* I hope to have touched on the primeval foundation for our time.

The *quaternitas*, the fourfoldness, represents this wholeness of which we have already spoken. First we will concentrate on one center of this fourfoldness and then on the other centers. The reason for this *concentration*, this focusing in, is to bring together under the one aspect the entire manifoldness of the world, and to retrace these conditions each time to One center without any forms of reductionism. This process will take place for each of the four centers, so that we experience them all in a *concentric* fashion. Thus, a human life would be able to overcome the ruptures, the schizophrenia, the tensions, and the painful torments by which it so often is marked. Wise is the one who, in a concentric way, experiences and lives out these four centers. The circles around each of the centers are not identical since the body is not the soul nor all of reality. But both body and soul are concentric, so that the center of the world goes right through the middle of my soul as well as my body.

Speaking without any introductory explanations about such fundamental, difficult questions may not be appropriate; perhaps I have been influenced by the Western need for acceleration. But if anything is worth doing, it may be worth doing in an imperfect manner, too.

Thus I dare to take on the *quaternitas perfecta* since it is something that affects us all as both human beings and creatures and since it is an essential ingredient of reality.

There are some difficulties here: first, the difficulties of my own language; second, the particular difficulties of today's languages in trying, especially here, to express the relevant conditions and experiences; third, the difficulty of language at large. Furthermore, I cannot do justice to this integrated anthropology, since not all symbols are thoroughly discussed. Our intent is to point distinctly to the seat of wisdom, where, according to Christian tradition, Mary is seated (*sedes sapientiae*). This seat is a symbol of the unmarred basic human nature. Mary's calling is the destiny of Man in general. Otherwise, there would not have been a revolution among the angels in heaven. But Man, who plays a role there, too, is supposed to be fully human, *Adam*, *puruṣa*. We are dealing with full humanness here—that is, the divine and cosmic one—on a par with the human side, not with its specific particularity. The essence of something—according to Indic philosophy—is not its specific difference.

---

3 See R. Panikkar, *La nuova innocenza* (Sotto il Monte-Bergamo: Servitium, 2003; new ed. 2005).

First Center: Earth and Body

The first dimension is represented by various symbols: earth, *sôma* (body), *śarīra* (body, individuality), *karman* (action), *bonum* (good), being awake, and the area of morality.

Sôma and śarīra: We are body; we do not simply *have* a body. We are individuals; we do not only have individuality. We are active individuals; we not only exercise certain activities. We are earth; we not only are gravitating on a planet, not only are living in a country, not only are standing on this earth as if it were just a platform. As long as we do not overcome our separateness from matter and are not healing this break, as long as we regard bodily activity or *yoga* simply as a technical exercise and the body in one extreme as an enemy and in the other as a ruler, we will not have lived to the fullest potential as human beings. We will remain torn. Eventually it all will take vengeance, not only in terms of health or activity but also in terms of inner dissatisfaction and restlessness.

Our meditation could also be called *practical introduction to spirituality.* The word "spirituality" has both good and bad connotations—good, as it circumvents aspects of doctrine usually connected with the word "religion." Spirituality is not yet too much marred by dogmatic differentiations and intellectual subtleties. Furthermore, the word has the advantage that it ignores the view that the various religions are self-enclosed, as if separated by fixed, old boundaries. There is, for example, a spirituality of love or of political involvement that pours through all the various religions. At the same time, however, the word "spirituality" has a negative connotation, since it seems to deal with the "spirit," as if we could neglect everything else. But this would be the wrong kind of spirituality; it would have lost its relatedness to matter, to the earth.

We are primarily body, individual, earth. Connected with this relatedness to body and earth are activity, action (*karman*). We *are* these individuals, these bodily beings, these active subjects; the state of being awake is essentially part of what we are. Only because of that are we able to feel, to sense, and to experience.

Earth: "Earth" means matter; it could be a stone, a tree, a mountain, a house, my finger—going further, perhaps also a machine, a car, an airplane. We must not draw back from earth. One might refer in a probably poor exegetical exercise to the Bible, for example, Genesis 1:28, "making the earth subject to us." But if we do so in a sovereign, elitist way (thus making ourselves the generous kings), presuming to dominate the earth intellectually and believing that we understand it better, our human vanity may be satisfied for a time. Ultimately, however, this is not enough—for our human need for wholeness, for the fulfillment of the earth's destiny and the destiny of the universe. As urgent and as necessary as short-term solutions may be, the basic problems require a much more in-depth treatment. We must start with the realization that the break between the "it" and the "we" has to be mended; we, too, are earth.

As long as I do not regard every piece of mere earth as my own body, I not only disregard the earth but also misunderstand my body. Understanding begins at this point! All scientific and anthropological inventions (and imaginations) about the human being have arrived only later—proteins, chromosomes, alpha waves, and so on.

For thousands of years, people have not been schizophrenic, have had full awareness of their personalities without fathoming any of our physiology, biology, and chemistry. All of these may be necessary, nice, and useful today, but, anthropologically speaking, these findings are simply accidental paraphernalia, something dispensable for reaching the fullness of human existence. Modern sciences might even become hindrances after a certain time; certainly they are unnecessary for enjoying and attaining the fullness of human nature. Concerning humanness, we moderns are in no way exceptional just by being Westerners, first-class passengers on this planet. Useful as it may be, technology is no absolute value.

Earth, body: Having a normal state of consciousness, an awareness of our individuality—all these are essentially human. We are real only when we *are* all the above. If I have to take a dance class to learn the turning of my body or the art of motion, then something of my humanness is missing. If I have to consult a book to tell me that the trees are pretty and only then look out the window to confirm that, then I am not yet fully human. (This is not to criticize books or dance classes; what matters is the way we use them and our body.) We must return and develop an attitude where true human (not just animal-like) spontaneity becomes possible, where we can again learn, talk, see, and enjoy from within.

One can hardly assume that flowers think of, reflect on, and imagine how beautiful they are. And we are more than flowers, as the Gospel states (Mt 6:30). If we want human beauty to become a reality to us, we have to learn from the bud bringing forth the flower—without strain or force, in the proper rhythm, and in its own time. The Gospel says that we should *look at* the lilies of the field and at the birds in the sky and not ponder over them or take them home to see them better. Our culture should be at least as natural as the nature of a flower. Violence sets in only when our cultures are unnatural. Struggle is a natural state, but not war. Hunting may belong to human nature, but not what modern societies are doing : They are artificially accumulating food and turning it into a weapon. In fact, we should not need laws to tell us that the production of arms is against human rights. But our idea of the human being and our ethical thinking concerning arms have not gone as far as they have concerning cannibalism, which our sensitivity perceives as a transgression against humanness.

Karman, *bonum*, *morality*, *individual action, and external activity*: We are that, too, though not exclusively. A Western master—someone from the Rhineland, Meister Eckhart—speaks of three veils that are hiding reality from us as the coat hides the body. He mentions these veils in an exposition of Romans 8:18 (*LW* IV.11.2).[4] The biblical passage speaks of *revelatio*, revelation (which really means an "unveiling") of glory, of splendor. The first veil is the "*velamen boni*," the veil of the good, the moral. It is a thick veil: everything on earth is protected by the veil of the good and threatened by evil. Everything is evaluated under the categories of good and evil. Whatever it is we want to accomplish, we want it *sub specie boni*, under the aspect of good. I do something *because* it is good! I want it *because* its purpose is good—whatever its good may be. We become active because we envision a good goal. "*Voluntas videtur quasi mercenaria*," the will appears mercenary, Eckhart says, contrary to Western dogma.

The good not only moves human beings, but every living being. Man is not simply attracted by something material: it may be splendor, a piece of truth, a revelation of beauty, something we envision, something we have to, or want to, accomplish. Good is very powerful, but ultimately it is only a veil.

The veil of good has to do with the will. Only under this veil's protection, so says Eckhart, is the will able to "comprehend" (Reality). Revelation is the unveiling of this splendor; it is the removing of the veil that covers everything governed by good (and evil, as its counterpart) and, therefore, belongs to the kingdom of the will. Schelling has said, "The will is the primordial being."[5] Here we find the opposite: the will is only an appearance of being. Humanity, having believed in this will to power and the power of the will, has accomplished great things through this belief. The will is the engine, the power that moves us. Modern pedagogy tells us that we have to have a goal and a strong will, and that we have to use the will for reaching the goal. Yet we have produced a worship of the will as a result. The will has become our biggest commodity; we are no longer able to imagine life without goal, purpose, and will. Often we even reach

4 Meister Eckhart, *Die Lateinischen Werke*, *Sermones*, ed. Joseph Koch et al. (Stuttgart: Kohlhammer, 1956).

5 F. Schelling, Werke (Stuttgart: Augsburg, 1856ff.), II.1.338.

these goals and meet our plans. All great empires of history and all great human accomplishments are wonderful testimonies to the fruit of the will of a person or a people. Surveying thousands of years of human experience, however, we see that such glamour also has its dark side, that the price to be paid for such testimonies of our culture is the exploitation and subjection of other peoples and even of other parts of our own personality. The flower is without a "why," as Angelus Silesius says.

The will is usually directed toward action, the *karman*, activity. The will's field is morality, the moral life. The will "wills" to dominate human reality. It reigns in the areas of the individual, the bodily, and the earthly; among the four seasons, it corresponds to summer. The will pushes us toward a goal, and if we do not reach it, we feel frustrated. But if we want to overcome one-sidedness, we must team *concentration*, by which we shall reach a center in this incredibly complicated territory of the will. Our journey there cannot be through resentment, repression, that is, an even stricter will or an even stronger unwillingness. We must find our true center and root ourselves there. One cannot go against the will without being taken again by the power of the will. Wisdom cannot be a fruit of the will, as we have already seen. Only by being centered is the will placed where it belongs.

Harmony of action: There is one criterion for this center. I could mention many witnesses from the most varied religious traditions to make my case. According to St. Ignatius of Loyola, this criterion is the *indifferentia sancta*, the "blessed indifference," a certain calmness, a sovereign composure toward things.[6] Expressing it in our words, the characteristic of the center, of the central point, is its equidistance from all points on the circumference. This is the kind of indifference we are concerned with; it was called "equanimity" by the ancients, and the Buddhist tradition calls it *upekṣā* (*upekkhā*).

It would be the wrong kind of indifference—though one that is found quite frequently—if it did not allow me to become enthusiastic, excited, if it did not permit me to get involved in something my heart aspires toward and to take steps against something I consider bad or inhumane. But it means, on the other hand, a loss of the middle, an absolutizing that slips into fanaticism when I worship this emotion, this movement of the mind and self, to the point that everything depends only on winning the battle. When I am "centered," I do not lose the center—which cannot be lost anyway. It is then that I attain equanimity, a balance and an inner strength that permit

6 This expression does not appear literally in either Ignatius's *Exercises* or in the *Constitutions*, although the adjective "indifferent" appears twice in the former and eight times in the latter. However, Ignatius's later years and the original spirituality of the Jesuits in general are filled with this "indifference."

me to risk my life without making everything dependent on the victory of my efforts: there is much more in human life than victories!

But here, too, lurks a vice into which equanimity can slip. This vice is sluggishness, the lack of enthusiasm, of interest, of engagement, and of vitality. As always, true wisdom consists of the proper balance; one can reach this balance by means of contemplation. Of course, it takes a certain adroitness, and at this point I introduce the word "harmony." The search for the center is not a crusade. Harmony can develop only when emerging by itself. One cannot force its evolution. Nowhere should a sign of violence be present, especially not inner violence. The Confucian tradition teaches that when a gong is well forged, whatever way it is hit the sound issuing from it will always remain pure and harmonic. It is the kind of harmony that does not depend on externals but simply is; it has no need of being provoked.

The reality of nature, and especially of human nature, is like a net, a great wealth of distinct influences that in the end come together in one whole—we are *śarīra*, individual creatures. Therefore, we need to identify ourselves with our bodies, with our "earth." Alchemy and the traditional teachings of the elements had their source in such a form of identification, not in a physical curiosity about how the earth rotated, about how heavy or dense something was, or things like that. Even without Newton's law of gravity, it is possible to discover that one's body and a stone are related to weight and are similar in this respect.

The veil of good: How can I make it transparent in such a delicate way as not to tear it, and so as to let me catch a glimpse of both good and evil? How can I recognize it as a veil, leaving it the way it is, as a tool of revelation, of an "unveiling"? Meister Eckhart writes, "Not by adding, but by subtracting, God is found in the soul... because God is innermost in the soul, and the creature can only contribute by means of one's own cleansing and preparing" (*LW* IV.11.2). The answer lies not in denying good and evil, but in realizing that both good and evil are only external veils that do not touch the naked creature or pure reality. In the Indic tradition, the lotus is the symbol of this untouched state of cleanness.

Indra is a Vedic God who—as a scandal to some Indologists—stands beyond good and evil, not because he commits moral crimes (then he would not be beyond evil) but because he has torn the veil. Certainly, this is highly dangerous and discomforting ! But when actions are simply patterned after a certain model, they cannot be free. Perhaps only a God can afford to do without the model—or a new human innocence can. Perhaps this is what Christians called *theôsis*, deification.

In this center are united *equidistance* and simultaneous participation in all things. The question is how to allow my identity to grow to the point where I can identify with both my body and the entire earth; at the same time I will remain distant from everything and will not absolutize it. I need to experience my own body, headaches included, or something much worse than that, which however should not lead me to despair. I will discover that, though I *am* what I experience, I am not *solely* that, because what I am is *my* own being, and this being is what constitutes my identity. Being is a verb and cannot be turned into a subject, let alone into an object. When we allow "our" being to penetrate our body and the "earth," we can then enjoy its freedom in us, which would mean that we have overcome the "ought." But I cannot go on without breaking the harmony of our description.

I began this chapter with the questions, What should I do? What should I think? This overcoming of the "ought" can be sincere only when we simultaneously overcome the subject in the classic formulation: What should *I* do and think? This leads us to the second center of our *quaternitas*: the overcoming of the I, which means, paradoxically, the overcoming of any identification of the I. This can happen only when complexity is not repressed but is assimilated and embodied in such a way as to leave room for further assimilation and embodiment. "The sage acts without making decisions," Chuang-tzu says (II.9).[7]

Second Center: Water and Self

The second dimension in which we exist—which allows us to exist, without which our life would fade away—has once again various symbols, described differently in the various traditions. Each of these symbols focuses on one of this dimension's aspects: water, *psychê* (soul), *aham* (I), *jñāna* (knowledge, understanding, reason), *verum* (truth), dreaming, the psychological aspect in the deepest sense of the word. Just as we are *śarīra*, *sôma*, earth, so we are all the above.

We will examine now four of these symbols. We may suspect the importance of *water* comes from the fact that our bodies consist of more than 70 percent water. But we are "water" also in another sense. In the same way, we not only have but also are *knowledge*, *understanding*, *reason*. This is not meant in an abstract sense. After all, we are *aham*, "I." And we are *truth* inasmuch as we are looking for it. All these symbols are pointing directly to *the other*, to this otherness (of ourselves), to the *alter*, the *altera pars* of ourselves, and not only to the *aliud*, to the "alien," to the Non-I. There is

7 Richard Wilhelm translates it as, "The sage is innocent [and] simple" (*Der Berufene ist einfältig schlicht*).

no I without a You; there is no isolated and individually existing soul in the least respect, no individual life. Water and understanding are symbols of relationship. We exist and live in a web of relationships. We become aware of our own I by becoming aware of the I of others.

This second dimension of the *quaternitas* has something to do with patience. As the Gospel of Luke says: We will only live and gain our lives in patience (Lk 21:19). Patience is synonymous with tolerance—at least, this is the case with the Greek word *hypomonê* in this Gospel (Lk 8:15). We can recognize this also in the symbol of water: water is tolerance; any sort of container is sufficient, big or small, it does not matter. Water adjusts, endures everything, has no special preference, is not edgy, not solid; it always gives in. One can jump into water from a height of many feet, and the water recovers its smoothness, every time.

Water: The symbolic power of water lies, first of all, in the fact that it flows, that it refreshes, that it makes life possible, and that it can trickle away. But something else exists, in addition, of which we have lost sight (here various wisdom traditions of Africa become important). Water is not only the source of life but is life itself. Water *is* life. Therefore, such phrases as "the water of life" or "the water of eternal life" (see Jn 4:14) should not be understood in a figurative sense only. The fact that we cannot exist without water is more than a mere game of ideas.

Even the polarity between the water's dynamics and flowing, on the one hand, and its stillness, on the other, does not yet exhaust the symbol. (In some traditions water symbolizes the spiritual pilgrimage: flowing, bubbling water means *life*, while water quiet as a mirror becomes a symbol of self-discovery.) Water is life; thus, its characteristics are those of life itself.

On the Tuesday after Easter, people sang in the Latin liturgy: "The water of wisdom he gave them," in reference to Sirach 15:3. The *Atharva-veda* sings, "Why do the waters, flowing toward truth, never stop flowing?" (X.7.37). According to many traditions, including the Jewish one, the primordial waters were not created (Gn 1:2). Water is "the medicinal drink for immortality" (*SB* IV.4.3.15) and the lap of God (*SB* VI.8.2.4). Water is the source of man. The Chinese word *ch'üan* consists of the signs "pure" and "water"; similarly, the Latin word *fons* (spring) means origin.

Jñāna: Understanding means intellectual understanding of what is given, of what is present. "All that is understood, is understood by something already present."[8]

8 Bonaventure, *Sententiarum* II, d.23, a.2, q.2: "*Omne enim quod cognoscitur, cognoscitur per aliquid praesens.*"

With this sentence Bonaventure sums up in his own Occidental language what many traditions hold. Be it in the *parousia* of the Greek, the *pramā...a* of Indic philosophy, or the distinctions of the present (whether *prae-sensu*, *prae-sens*, *prae-essentia*...) and present reality, *présence* and *trace*, all of them point out the *in-between*. Christ said, "The kingdom of God is *between* you" ("in the midst of," *entos*, Lk 16:21); or, as the *Gospel of Thomas* says, "The kingdom is inside of you and outside of you" (*logion* 3). Man is a being for whom reality is present as a totality. Therefore, Man is also knowledge and understanding.

Knowledge is not only knowledge *about* something; understanding does not simply mean to be familiar with something (or being able to do something, being in command of something or having power over it). When viewing knowledge solely as a refined hunt for information, for laws, for some sort of objects, we are, in reality, still thinking in a very unrefined manner. Not only do women not want to be objects for men—and vice versa; things in general have begun protesting against being treated as mere "objects of understanding." We are slowly learning to regard animals seriously as sensing creatures. Thus, the protest arises against cold-blooded experimenting on animals in research laboratories. But the point goes further: As brutal as animal testing is, even things are crying out: Stop treating us as mere objects (of exploitation, or resources). Respect for life entails respect for *all* beings. This is *ecosophy*.

The need for manipulative experiments for the sake of gaining insight and under the pretense of utility is, culturally speaking, a pathological need. Certainly one can extricate many insights from nature that way, just as one can squeeze out confessions by torturing someone—which is always done by the dominating party. But one should not seek comfort in the thought that frogs or amoebas are suffering less because of a little anaesthesia. Theoretical Puritanism is not the point here; the basic attitude underlying it is. Native Americans used to ask trees for forgiveness before cutting them down. Alchemists tried to trace the deeper relationships of the various elements with each other and the dynamics of God's creation. Astrology used to investigate—in spite of many aberrations—the interrelatedness of all occurrences in the cosmos. All these preserved a deep respect for creation. Today it is different. Yet we cannot simply revert to these traditions; rather, we are dealing here with a "return," which—as almost all traditions suggest—begins with a turning inward.

Here it is especially important to critique the most relevant method of today's sciences, the experiment. The experiment is not a path to wisdom; it presupposes, on the contrary, a distorted image of Man. We do not want to discuss here the so-called problem of knowing in Western philosophy (or what Indic philosophy calls *pramā...a*)—the means, that is, of true knowing, such as conclusion, attestation, cognition, and the like. Nor are we criticizing each human intervention in nature, but the very idea of understanding as an intervention in the enclosure of being. In order to do so, we have to distinguish the experiment from experience and observation.

Understanding through experience, observation, and experiment: Experience means allowing something to directly affect and penetrate me. It means absorbing it so that I can identify with what I have come to understand. The person's ability of understanding is nothing but the ability of identification—the fact that we can become *everything.* In the Western tradition, Aristotle said, "The soul *is* everything, so to speak" (*De anima* III.8; 431b.21), primarily because the soul is able to know everything. This sentence was also one of the pillars of medieval ontology until epistemology became severed from the former. Similarly, the *Upaniṣad* say, "One becomes what one understands"; "whoever understands *brahman*, becomes *brahman*" (*MundU* III.2.9.3B).

Experience is full of risk. Only what has been experienced in ourselves can be interpreted and known; only then can one understand it. Only what has penetrated me and then springs out of me in a spontaneous fashion has life, power, and authority. One might explain this more precisely in philosophical language. Buddhist logic even says that the principle of identity is not poignant enough for upholding true understanding, because the identity between the one who understands and what has been understood is greater than the identity of the logical principle of identity. Even Thomas Aquinas would agree with this affirmation.

But one could also explain it differently: during the 1920s or early 1930s a simple woman came to see Mahātma Gandhi in his *āśram* in Ahmadabad, asking him, "Mah*ā*tma, would you, please, tell my child not to eat so many sweets! Please, tell her that it is bad for her teeth!" Gandhi remained silent and did not say a word. The mother looked down. She thought she had said something inappropriate and retreated in embarrassment. A few months later, she came back to the *āśram*, and there was the opportunity for a follow-up—perhaps more out of curiosity than motherly love. This time, Gandhi accepted her request; then she asked him why he had not answered before. "You know, my daughter," said Gandhi, "at that time I liked eating sweets myself too much. My words would not have had any impact on your daughter!"

Sermons not lived out and loved and completely internalized and words not stemming from one's personal life cannot be powerful. How can I tell the little girl, "Don't eat sweets!" if I eat sweets myself ? How can I dare say a word if I have not created, lived, endured, discovered it earlier myself ? Every person understands this logic. Experience as a path to understanding, as an identification with what has been understood, is a sacramental intertwining of the person with the things one understands. This way we grow, mature, live.

In the case of experience, identity is complete: I am what I understand. But we do not understand *everything* in life by means of experience. For example, a smoker theoretically knows but does not understand the harmfulness of smoking by experience. One can get information from others, know of statistics on lung cancer, and so forth. But as soon as I experience that smoking is not beneficial to my body, I quit—unless I want to harm my body intentionally.

There is a second way of understanding, which differs from experience since it presupposes a certain distinction between the one who understands and what has been understood. It is called *observation.* In the case of experience, everything penetrates me; perhaps I cannot stand that and would collapse under the force, the intensity, the power of experience. Observation is different; it is a paradoxical thing. For one, it can be described as a "passive activity," requiring attention and consideration; for another it can be described as a consent to be influenced, to be reached by the outside, even to be attacked at times. Understanding in the form of observation is not yet identical with what is, in a stricter sense, meant by understanding in most Western languages: recognizing, realizing, comprehending. There is a possible wordplay in English: to understand means to "stand under." One does not stand above, as we commonly might see it; instead one is subdued by the matter one understands. That is observation.

In order to be able to observe, one does not need to identify with the matter or the thing observed. One need not become a fish, a bird. One simply has to be present and wait until the (un)expected appears. But one must not expect too intensely, or else one becomes nervous and disturbs the observation. One need only wait. When the animal comes, the revelation arrives, one waits, anticipates, observes, remains passive, leaves initiative up to the thing, the other (not the *obiectum* one can "thrust forward"). It is then that one learns and understands. It takes time, because one is subject to a thing's moods; one is dependent on the freedom of reality on whose rhythms one must not impinge. Actually, observation (*observatio*) means preserving (*servare*) a situation the way it is. A more philosophical name for this conscious acceptance of a present situation would be *perception*: we perceive what is facing us.

In this way, by means of experience and observation, each person gains understanding. Children have experiences the moment they are born. As we grow, our ability to observe increases continually. Experience can become dangerous, observation disappointing; experience requires an open mind, observation patience.

Modern science prefers a third method of understanding. It is the *experiment.* It consists in altering, in a more or less artificial way, at least one variable in an observable system and then assessing the alteration of the system at large. The experiment makes possible the calculation of variation and variables and is at the same time built on this calculation. One can list the various steps of this calculation; one can plan ahead. Experience requires long preparation, observation an empathic adaptation to the rhythms of nature. But the experiment is supposedly more practical and gains quicker results than the other two. Experience penetrates me; in observation I have to participate—but the experiment runs "on the side"; I just have to check once in a while what has happened.

Francis Bacon, who in this modern sense is called the father of the experiment, speaks explicitly of the aim of controlling nature (*Novum Organum* I.70ff.). Before his time, the word "experiment" had almost the same meaning as *experientia*, experience. Strictly speaking, one would have to distinguish between experiments and measurements, but both are closely related.

I suggest that this third kind of understanding is an abnormal kind: one does not really come to understand the thing itself, one simply gets to know a certain reaction of a certain matter within determined parameters. The experiment is primarily an opportunity for controlling, for calculating, sometimes for previewing and influencing. Ultimately, it only offers information concerning a certain course of events, but it does not say much about the nature of things, about reality, about our own nature. Even a child explores this method of understanding when experimenting with toys—but after that, one cannot play with these toys again in the same way because the experiment has turned the toy into pieces; it has altered the nature of things. By this kind of method, one might gain power, prestige, money... perhaps even contentedness—fascinating things, without doubt. But understanding in its true sense cannot be gained this way. One fits reality into a system of thought, not the other way around.

The distinctions between experience, observation, and experiment should not be understood as separations. All three methods of understanding are often intertwined and even show some hierarchical structure. Ultimately, the experiment needs observation, which has to turn into a certain experience so that we can gain understanding. There is no pure experiment but also no pure experience.

This reflection has a very important corollary: knowledge by experience is impossible without love. Modern science can know without loving; so can analytical philosophy, but traditional philosophy cannot be divided from loving knowledge, or better, cognitive love.

Aham: An intimate relationship exists between the I and the You. German idealism could turn itself inside out, if it were to introduce a dialogue between the I and the You, rather than maintaining its dialectic between the I and the Non-I. Idealism is certainly correct in saying that the Non-I is not the I, but rather its opposite. Based on that, one can logically divide reality into the spheres of the I and the Non-I, a split that consequently leads to absolute idealism. But the relationship between the You and the I is neither the dialectic relationship between the Non-I and the I nor a relationship between the I and itself. This is nothing culturally specific, but a common human experience, very evident in children. Unfortunately, modern languages have completely lost the dual (as opposed to the plural, which exemplifies this twofoldness in terms of grammar). In Sanskrit, Arabic, and Greek, on the other hand, it is preserved.

In this context, I dare make a more general comment: I am under the impression that we are practicing language genocide. Not only do we kill trees but also human languages. In this century alone, over one thousand languages have disappeared. If that continues, it will take less than one century for the majority of today's five thousand languages to become extinct. Languages are not only tools, but each language constitutes a world—not only a worldview. Each language is a wealth of human life. Not only animal species are rendered extinct; hundreds of human heroic characters and myths are also disappearing or are close to extinction. The reason for their waning is that we have assaulted the languages as if they were simply means of information, like satellites or radios.

We come back now to the singular, dual, and plural. One and many, I and all of them... in our language, there is no grammatical form expressing the I-and-you (singular). The dual has great power; it is not the plural but presupposes a You, thus forming a more complex entity. This fact has been quite impressively described by Ferdinand Ebner, Martin Buber, and others.[9] The You constitutes the addressability of the person, Ebner says. The "in-

9 Cf. F. Ebner, Fragmente, Aufsätze, Aphorismen (Munich: Kösel, 1963), especially Fragment 2 ("Einsamkeit: Ich und Du"), 87–95, and "Die Entdeckung des Ich und Du," 800–819; M. Buber, Das Dialogische Prinzip (Heidelburg : L. Scheider, 1962), especially "Ich und Du," 7–136.

between" person (*Zwischenmensch*) is the true person, Buber says. "If there is no [any] other person (or thing), there is no I," one can hear already Chuang-tzu say (II.2).[10] The in-between is the dual, that which overcomes the "you-lessness" (Ebner) of the I.

The dual reflects the discovery that the I needs a You, which is different in nature from a third, the It, and from all others. The dual is an experience, and its disappearance is a revealing example of the change of human behavior. Whether or not we call each other by first names (because we have become a little familiar) has very little to do with it. It has to do with something else, namely, with the experience of the I, impossible without the experience of the You. And this You needs not be only the "beloved You of my heart"; it can also be something threatening. But it is a part of me without which I am unable to live. It is something that can challenge, endanger, love, somehow change me, and which rescues me from my proud loneliness. Many a person's rescue may be found in owning a cat or a dog. It is better than nothing, but certainly cannot be a model for this I-You relationship. For one's reflecting on self, for being oneself, *aham*, the You without which there is no I, is needed.

The You is not something I choose. Indian sociologists are very proud of the fact that the Indian custom of arranged marriages is, despite its "primitivity," proving apparently more successful than the Western range of marriage options and choices. In India, the discovery of the You is not a question of individual choice and decision. "I marry the woman I love"— "I love the woman I marry": this is the usual formula for differentiating the two patterns. Certainly, it also depends on one's faith or superstition, one's tradition or routine. Here in the West, it would be objectionable if we wanted to introduce such a (at least nowadays) foreign system. This is not my intention. I am only attempting to understand the differences, because ultimately we are talking about the bare experience of life—an experience, standing apart from such cultural or historical differences, but still not separated from them.

Psychê, *dreaming, and verum*: speaking of *psychê*, I could mention the Zen meditation, which—starting from the fact that the psyche cannot be an object of knowledge, since its true being transcends consciousness—can help us lead it to stillness and quietude. Mentioning it might be enough at this point. Concerning the symbol of dreaming (in the truest sense of the word), one would have to discuss depth psychology, but also the *Mā...fūkya-upaniṣad*, which stresses that the dream world is more real than what we call waking consciousness.

10 R. Wilhelm translates, "Without this something, there is no I" (Ohne jenes Etwas gibt es kein ich).

If the danger in the first dimension is sluggishness, here it is intellectualism, the urge to examine things by means of experiments and not to understand them by observation and experience.

If, according to Meister Eckhart, the temptation and, simultaneously, the task of the first dimension is the *velamen boni*, the "veil of the good," the temptation of the second is the *velamen veri*, the "veil of the true." Just as the will can only function under the veil of the good, the intellect can only function under the veil of the true. If the first dimension carries with it the danger of placing everything under the will, the second holds the danger of using the intellect solely. One should insert an observation here parallel to our remarks concerning the first center: one must not neglect reason; one must not forget truth—but reality cannot be reduced to intelligibility, to "thinkability." Reality is not *only* truth. In reference to Dionysius, Bonaventure says, "The highest form of reality is called darkness because the intellect does not comprehend it."[11]

History seems to show that people committed the most horrid acts in the name of truth. One could argue on phenomenological grounds that truth is always what one is *looking for*. But one cannot argue that what one *finds* is always truth. What one is looking for may very well be truth, but what one finds may *not* be truth. When insisting on knowing the truth, one has already destroyed truth in one's soul, since wisdom no longer resides in it. As Thomas Aquinas teaches, it is a contradiction in terms to insist on holding the truth; it can, at the most, hold us. Truth is always only a veil, and that means ultimately that we cannot identify truth with reality at large. As soon as we touch truth, it becomes infected by all our shortcomings; thereby the truth that is supposed to set us free becomes our captive. How could it set us free then?

This does not mean that we cannot rely on truth. It only means that truth itself is merely a cover for reality, necessary so that being can become visible to us. Truth is the visibility of being (*Esse*), as far as being is intelligible. But the person must move toward this revelation, must be able to remove this veil, and be prepared to live on in this bottomless "abyss" of mystery. *Ungrund*, says Meister Eckhart (*DW* III.36, etc.).

Third Center: Fire and Being

For the first dimension of the *quaternitas* I have chosen the name "waking"; for the second "dreaming." The third dimension is connected with "sleeping" in the classical sense of Indic philosophy (*suṣupti*). If the first dimension

11 Bonaventure, *Hexaemeron*, col. 2, n. 32: "*Dicitur tenebrae, quia intellecuts non capit.*"

is called *śarīra* and the second *aham*, then the third is called *ātman*. If in the first we are speaking of *sôma* and in the second of *psychê*, then we are speaking here in the third of *polis*. If the symbol of the first is the earth and of the second the water, then in the third it is fire. And if the first level is *karman* and the second *jñāna*, then the third is *bhakti*. If the center of the first dimension is the moral and of the second the psychological, then the center of the third is the ontic. We are fire, *polis* (city), *ātman* (self), *bhakti* (devotion), *ens* (being), which all correspond to the state of sleeping and the area of the ontic.

The danger of the first dimension is sluggishness, of the second intellectualism. In the third, we have to recognize a certain sentimentality (the heart, feeling, all that has its place here but also its dangers). The veil of the first dimension is the will, which makes us look at everything under the aspect of good and evil—what to strive for and what to avoid. The veil of the second dimension is the truth, which we can see by means of reason and will. The veil of the third dimension is even more difficult to describe; it is connected here with the symbol of fire. Meister Eckhart calls it *velamen entis*, "the veil of being," of being at large.

Ens: I want to explain the problem we are dealing with here with an example from the history of religion: The historic misunderstanding between Christianity and Buddhism has its essential origin in the fact that from an *ātmavada* position—from the viewpoint, that is, that there exists a firm substance, a firm central point of being, a "soul," in the person—one cannot understand the *anātmavādin* (the follower of the *ānatman* teachings). Between *ātman* and *ānatman* one cannot mediate on a doctrinal level, because the substantialization of being on the one hand, which makes the highest level of reality the ultimate of being, and on the other the conviction of an essential impossibility of substantialization of reality, which makes the "highest level of reality," *śūnyatā*, *nirvāṇa*, emptiness, are primordial, incompatible views that cannot be reduced to a common denominator. Despite this, there are certain bridges in intellectual history, where both sides have not refused to enter dialogue.

Likewise, in the Christian (as well as in the Jewish and Islamic) tradition, one can find several authors who hold that being and reality are not identical.

Meister Eckhart connects this third veil with Romans 8:18, which was mentioned above. Eckhart is talking here about the glory, the *doxa*—that is, the splendor of the true life. Revelation removes all veils. Revelation pulls away all that is covering up glory: the veil of the good, the veil of the true, and also the veil of being itself. This process occurs "in us," as Eckhart emphasizes in reference to the Latin text of the biblical passage. Since "the nature of the soul is far from the kingdom of this world, the soul's nature resides in another world above the soul's capacity, above intellect and will.... But the nature of the soul is never intruded upon by creation, and by God only without any covers" (*LW* IV.11.2).

We are not dealing at this point with intellectual dogmas. We must understand what Meister Eckhart has said from his special point of view; this has been said also by many Buddhist traditions in their larger contexts—each tradition in its own language—by a part of the Indic tradition, and by some branches of mysticism at various times. It is basically the insight that reality cannot be broken up and that therefore a separate self-awareness does not represent the order of reality. Reduced to a simple formula, one might say in reference to this Hindu version: *brahman* is so much pure consciousness that it is not even consciousness *of something*. Therefore *brahman* is not even aware of itself, *brahman* does not know it is *brahman*. *Brahman* does not know *anything*! Īśvara, on the other hand, knows that it is *brahman*—and, by knowing it, it is *brahman*.

Polis: Continuing our previous parallelism of words, one might say, "I am *ātman*, I am *polis*, I am *fire*, I am *bhakti*." *Bhakti* is devotion and love. *Polis* means city, tribe, political community. We are not talking about a community coming into existence as the result of high spiritual goals and ideals, but through the links of the tribe, of the natural community, which is natural because its members live in one another's neighborhood, because one knows the other, because they go into battle together and are, in a sense, blood-related. Telephones and television sets are only substitutes for real neighborly relations. I do not mean that in an exclusive sense but in a true, down-to-earth, bodily, political, communal sense, in contrast to any utopian community. The human being not only lives in a community, not only belongs to a certain society. Man is community, is *polis*.

Concerning the Western tradition of this symbol, one would completely misunderstand the Greek *polis* if one regarded it as a purely technical thing, a democracy only formed for assessing the rules of people's behavior. A *polis* is a *mesocosm*, a field where microand macrocosm encounter each other. A *polis* cannot be imagined without its temples, its Gods, its vertical dimension. All these are part of it, as water is part of a swimming pool. Where else but in the *polis*, in political life, does one perfect the self, reaching one's contentment, allowing all the possibilities of one's personality to flourish? Where else is one deified, cured, saved? (Political life is in this sense, of course, more than a parliamentary dabbling with laws.) The fullness of the person becomes reality only in communion with the Gods, the neighbors, the things, the animals—with all creatures, that is, constituting a *polis*. Without all the above, a *polis*, a *civitas*, could never offer such fullness to the human being.

It was Augustine who destroyed this comprehensive meaning of *polis* in the Christian tradition—primarily in order to help the people of his time rescue political life—by distinguishing between *civitas Dei* and *civitas terrena*, the city of God and the city of the world. Augustine lived during a time when both Greek and Roman ideals were disintegrating. The natural community of the *polis* was practically destroyed. The majority of people could not reach the ideal of becoming perfected in the city, in the political life. The old Gods were banished, their sacred things defaced.

During Augustine's time, followers of the old Gods were already persecuted. The Christian God had been introduced by Constantine for a political reason—a fact we criticize all too easily, though it cannot be denied that its consequences were terrible in later Christianity. But the old political order of the Roman Empire, though in the midst of decay, was the only order imaginable at that time.

Augustine maintained the unity of heaven and earth, and wanted to rescue the unity of human life, which reached its perfection in the *polis*. But he knew well—as difficult as it may be to understand from our post-Enlightenment position—that it was an unrealizable dream of the human being to reach salvation in one single *polis*. There were too many slaves, women, children—too many people who did not take part in this perfecting process. So Augustine opens a window and presents to people a divine city (not simply some vague heaven in which everyone believed anyway) by telling them: Since it is impossible for people to realize human life here and live it out, they have this city of God as a real *polis*, as another chance. This is a great thought as a pastoral theme, but historically speaking it is the beginning of a dichotomy of heaven and earth, one that has henceforth characterized Christianity. Perhaps there is a possibility today of bringing about a reconciliation between the two poles. This is one of the main duties Christians have in the Western world nowadays.

Ātman: I *am* community. The person cannot realize one's life, realize one's nature, without being something other than this individual, singular ego. The person cannot simply be concerned with controlling one's body, decorating one's soul, and cultivating a good relationship with the other. The wealth of Man goes much further. I am not simply individual. This is what the word *ātman* indicates. This word cannot really be translated. The common equivalent "self" is just as enlightening as it is deceptive. The fact that I am *ātman* or, better, the fact that I am the *ātman*, too, constitutes the discovery of the third dimension of being. However, this third dimension cannot be the discovery of reason. The *ātman* knows everything.

I would like to describe briefly this basic experience by referring to today's scientific-technological world in which most of us live. The Chinese people of the thirteenth century saw something similar with even greater clarity, and also the *Upaniṣads* of the sixth century BC give us a hint of it. We, too, are beginning to feel its consequences: It is the impossibility of mastering all areas of knowledge. I cannot know everything. The more I know, the more I know that I do not know. Thus, an inflation of knowledge develops, which is just as bad as our population explosion. Literature today is so vast and complex that no one can read everything, not even in one's special field. I rely on excerpts from excerpts of a certain kind of literature. But how can I understand anything when trying to get to know *everything* (in a quantitative sense)? Can I do any more than simply understand this or that singular aspect? Then I begin to understand that even if I assumed that I could know everything, this knowledge will not give me true understanding.

Such was Heraclitus's complaint against the followers of Pythagoras. The Indic tradition is also familiar with this problem:

> Where there is such a thing as duality, there one sees the other; one smells the other; one tastes the other; one talks to the other; one listens to the other; one thinks of the other; one touches the other; one understands the other. But when everything has already become *ātman* to me, with what and with whom could one see; could one smell; could one taste; could one talk; could one listen; could one think; could one touch; could one understand? It is that by which one can understand the whole of reality: how can one understand this thing ? It is not like this or that (*neti-neti*). It is incomprehensible because it cannot be comprehended; indestructible because it cannot be destroyed; independent because it cannot be tied down; it is free, cannot be upset, cannot be harmed: How could one understand the Understander? (*BU* IV.5.15)

The proper question then is, "How can I understand what understands everything ?" (*BU* II.4.14).

What is necessary here is a radical reversal of our civilization's direction: it is either geared toward the production of things (technocracy) or toward the perfection of subjects (humanism). Both are basic orientations, mutually exclusive in their goals. In our time, technocracy rules humanism. When gaining power is at stake, some can—but always only a minority!—be quite easily successful by means of technocracy. When it is a matter of dominating, changing (or destroying) this world, we are quick to act these days. But becoming personally fulfilled depends on completely different factors. Some people reach this goal; others do not. Yet this is the point: to attain personal fulfillment in life and personal participation in life's fullness. (I would call the *humanum* in the *quaternitas perfecta* "humanism," which does not denote the common anthropological image of Man, as I have explained already in *Humanismo y Cruz* [1963].) To say it in words of the Christian tradition, we are dealing with the glory, *exousia*, and *doxa*, the splendor of what is real. What is life for? What is the one thing that makes us not only move but *be*?

We are dealing here with a basic orientation of communal, not individual, nature: whether the individual is happy or not may be an individual question. But whether the priorities of our civilization are directed toward happiness or toward power or not, only the community can determine. We can start to glimpse that here it is not only about morality but about the very *destiny* of the *polis*, where Man is in the hands of a superior destiny, however he may call it. Man has always had a certain confidence in Reality, because he cannot do otherwise. Philosophically said, we must let the Being be, therefore we must set the Being free, since we find out that the Being itself is in jeopardy as soon as our thought and our will meddle. On the other hand, we cannot remain passive; we have to intervene. Among human beings, however, there is no consensus.

Here the breach of Augustine's split becomes apparent: my salvation, my wholesome health—that is, my realization as a human being—no longer takes place in the realm of the here and now, of present existence, but in the kingdom of having-it-alllater in the *civitas Dei* (not *hominum*). Thereby one practically loses the validity of the request: "As in heaven, so on earth" (Mt 6:10). Hope vanishes.

Fire and bhakti: At this point, the symbolism of fire, as viewed by many human traditions, is important. Fire devours, rages, and destroys. It turns things to ashes, which the wind scatters. Fire can only be fire as long as there is something to burn. As soon as something turns into fire, what made the fire possible disappears. Fire feeds on what enables it to live. It is not like earth. In Hinduism, *agni* is what destroys itself, what gives itself power to live, a power only realized when surrendering in self-sacrifice. In Buddhism, *nirvāṇa* is, literally interpreted, the extinction (of fire). When nothing is left of the candle, the flame dies out by itself, because it was nothing but wax not yet become fire.

The Christian tradition speaks of two books, the book of life (Holy Scripture, which the sages read and which requires a certain amount of preliminary knowledge) and the book of nature, which *everyone* can read. Augustine says that Holy Scripture is elitist, only directed to a few; the book of nature is for everyone, even—to translate it literally—for the "idiots" (*idiotae* literally means "laypersons," "common uneducated people"). In the former body of writings only the scholars read, but in the world and in nature even the uninitiated can read. Augustine says, "Let God's page [that is, Holy Scripture] be a book to you so you will hear [one 'hears' the book!]; let the whole world be a book to you so you will see." Augustine knows that, according to Paul, faith comes from hearing, but understanding from seeing. One can "hear" the book, perhaps glean some meaning for oneself from it, but one can "see" the world. The codices are made for the scholars, but the entire world is made for the ignorant. Bonaventure teaches that after the Fall "the book of the world died and was destroyed."[12] Through mercy, however, the things of the world were once again "as a book, in which the creating (*fabricatrix*) Trinity reflected, presented itself, and could become legible."[13]

Such is human wisdom grown out of traditions. It frees and removes us from the successes of our post-Enlightenment world, so that perhaps we will be enabled to gain a more universal human experience without remaining entangled in the hermeneutic net of the past three or four centuries. How can we dare to have fellowship with people—let alone having fellowship with the earth—when we are the *only* enlightened people in the world? We can never reach fellowship that way. We have to start learning to read all over again, this time not the books made of paper but the book of nature, which not only contains forests and rivers but a direct view of the world in which we live. Everyone can see—not only as an elitist "listener" of a book (which used to be read aloud in former days), but as a direct onlooker upon reality. This view has an ultimate, essential characteristic: Seeing is not reflecting on what has been seen, but it is simply a sighting, a viewing by which one is infected by what one sees. It is not solely like a perusing of a pretty picture album, which might reawaken so many memories. In order to see, I must forget that I am seeing. Otherwise, I am only *thinking* that I see, I am only imagining that I see a beautiful landscape. True seeing is unmediated. And that is a universal analogy. It has nothing to do with some optical phenomenon; it is not thinking that I see; it is not enjoying what I see; it is simply seeing. That which is seen is something never seen before, unexplored: *ātman*, *polis*, fire, *bhakti*. *Bhakti* means here "love" and denotes the centrifugal power to come out of oneself and consume oneself, just as fire does.

If we cannot find a meaning in these symbols and pictures, we might assume that we have lost a fundamental part of our humanness. In order

12 Bonaventure, *Hexaemeron*, col. 13, n. 12: "*Iste liber, scilicet mundus, quasi emortuus et deletus erat.*"

13 Bonaventure, *Breviloquium*, q.2, c.12.

to discover ourselves, to know ourselves in the depth of humanness given to us, we must truly live. This insight is expressed by the three dimensions discussed, the first triad of the *quaternitas perfecta.*

Man is Man only when humanly living.

We made what may look like digressions just as a comment on the fullness of the human condition, as was indicated in the title of this second part. Man is the priest of Nature, the intermediary between heaven and earth, as so many traditions teach.

Fourth Center: Air and Spirit

In the 1930s, during a campaign of the Non-Cooperation Movement in Bihar, North India, Gandhi met a former classmate he had not seen in many years. The latter walked up to Gandhi to greet him. He did not wear handmade clothes, which was the sign of Gandhi's movement for independence, but "English" clothes. The two surveyed each other and recognized the situation very quickly. The friend explained, "I have to live somehow! Five children, mother-in-law..." Gandhi replied, "I don't see the necessity." And he walked off with his people. Either—or. It is hard having to feed many hungry mouths. The man was working for the government service; if they saw him associating with those half-naked fellows, he would lose his job. He had to make money, do good, provide for his family.... Gandhi had other priorities and walked off.

This is an illustration of the spiritual life. One risks everything : "If your hand or foot gives you trouble, chop it off and throw it away from you" (Mt 18:8); "Whoever wants to save one's life, will lose it" (Mt 16:25). Just as uncompromising is Śaṅkara's *Vivekachūdāmani* (21, 79, 164, 299, 508, and many other passages). We either accept the spiritual life with all our heart by thrusting ourselves into it with intensity and passion or we view it only as a new luxury article to be consumed. Everyone will have to experience this dilemma at least once in life. Life is in our hands. We forge our destiny ourselves, although external forces may influence us and play their part. Life does not exclude coincidence or providence. As a writer, I may have to wait for inspiration coming from the outside: "The spirit blows where it wills" (Jn 3:8). But if the Holy Spirit does not find me with pen in hand, inspiration will pass me by and remain useless.

The fourth dimension is air (breath, spirit), *kosmos* (*ākāśa*, ether, the open space), *brahman*, *tūṣnīm* (being silent), *nihil* (nothing, emptiness), *turīya* (the "fourth state," which transcends waking, dreaming, and sleeping), the realm of the mystical. One cannot see this one, only guess it; sometimes it even rips apart trees, carrying with it a mighty force. There is no veil here because there is nothing to hide. There is nothing to hide, no *velamen*, because there *is simply nothing*: it is nothing and does not say anything. Meaningless words, to those who do not experience it anyway.

We have a primordial experience that can help us describe this dimension. It is the experience of *freedom*—not the concept of freedom itself or the idea, but the experience. Certainly freedom does not mean here being able to choose at the supermarket between two kinds of tea. When life consists only of choosing between things given, we do not really live. We only live when risking this life over and over, when allowing life to live.

If we do not succeed in doing so in a natural way, the bold ones in society and the young generation will teach us in their own ways that life wants to be lived by means of risking it. But there are also mad drivers, drug addicts, people who are doing something that gives them at least the impression of living because they put their lives at stake. When many people of a society can experience life only by means of such foolish things, it is proof we are not living life at all. I consider those activities a perversion but not a negation of life. If we are not, in both word and deed and by our convictions, truly lived by life itself, if we are only experimenting with what is safe and pleasant and does not appear dangerous, then we are not living. A life not lived takes vengeance through death. Life wants to live, but repressed life seeks death. The tragic events of our century, which—out of the midst of a modern civilization of order and security—have led to modern warfare, should be a warning to us.

The experience of life and the experience of our actual situation belong together— and that even in the area of knowledge. This view contradicts, of course, Descartes's philosophy, whose concern for certainty has enticed us, with our consent, into having a certainty and security complex. Bonaventure, a contemporary of Thomas Aquinas, says in amazingly severe words, "Concerning the theory that some kind of science is all the more valuable (noble), the greater its certainty, one will have to say that this science does not contain any truth."[14] And the ingenuous Augustine formulated an earlier version of the Cartesian *cogito ergo sum*: *Si enim fallor, sum*: "Even if [I am] mistaken, I [still] am" (*De civitate Dei* XI.26).

Nihil: We have to probe yet deeper. True experience of life carries with it the experience of contingency, the touching (*tangere*) upon the nothing. "If someone upon seeing God knew what he saw, he has not truly seen God," Dionysius Areopagita says.[15] A text of Âivaism from Kashmir says,

14 Bonaventura, *Sententiarum* III, d.23, a.1, q.4, ad 5.

15 Dionysus, *Epist.* I (*Caio monacho*), *PG* 3:1065a. The traditional translation says, "*Et si quis, viso Deo, cognovit id quod vidit, nequaquam ipsum vidit.*"

"The biggest secret is that there is no secret."[16] Evagrius Ponticus says, "Blessed is the one who has reached infinite ignorance."[17] Ignorance, *agnosia*, *ignorantia*—yet it needs to be infinite!

But I am also this: *Brahman*, which does not even know it is *brahman*; ether; the empty space (which has little to do with the empty space of science); the wind; breath. We are all of that. When limiting the ego to our small person, to the community, or to our social relationships, we have only little regard for ourselves. What we need most is to be convinced of our dignity. "Above all, respect thyself," say the Pythagorean *Golden Verses* (8).[18] We need the experience of our own infinity; self-confidence; the awareness that we are not just a particle in the universe—that would be distressing, especially by viewing the universe in terms of sheer quantity. No, we are a mirror of all of reality (to use an old metaphor). It is a very special mirror, where reality shines in such a way that the differences disappear. It is what antiquity already called the microcosm. Yet at the same time this mirror contains also the entire macrocosm. Both microcosm and macrocosm belong essentially together. They are not two worlds: they are concentric, when we are (con)centrated.

Silence: At this point, the word "contemplation" is appropriate. It has very little to do with such words as "reflection," "meditation," or "theory." Contemplation is not a synthesis of *actio* and *theôria*, of practice and theory, but it is the very ground where both practice and theory originate. Contemplation has both an intellectual and a practical aspect; thinking leads to a certain clarity, practice to a certain change of affairs. Contemplation is not a mixture of both; nor is it a synthesis; but it is this basic attitude where both knowledge and action have not yet been separated. The ancients used to say, *Operari sequitur esse* (action follows being). Later, people viewed it the other way around: *Esse sequitur operari.* Though both action and knowledge may be distinguished as different ideas, we only *are* when both action and knowledge are not separated. This is certainly the true, human experience.[19] Contemplative life is neither pure meditation nor pure action; instead, it is contemplative action and active contemplation, the undivided life. Its name is wisdom.

We have to emphasize here that Man is not an isolated being on whom external relationships have been heaped as a supplement. These relationships

16 See Chapter 13, note 40.

17 See Chapter 13, note 20.

18 *Pantôn de malista aischuneo sauton.* One could also translate this as "honor thyself," if honor, like *aischunê*, conveys both modesty (shame) and honor. See above.

19 See R. Panikkar, *El concepto de naturaleza*, 2nd ed. (Madrid: C.S.I.C., 1972), esp. 197–232.

would then be only circumstantial. Instead, Man is constituted by the totality of those relationships that form, by nature, Man as a whole. I stress once again that the anthropological thought of today's dominant civilization is much too narrow in defining the human being. When animals are simply viewed as machines, as the West has practically done following Descartes, then the human being becomes in the modern view a "rational machine" following Aristotle's definition of Man as *animal rationale.* Such a view is of very little use for our *quaternitas.*

Here lies the existential core of our discussion: the correlation between *karman*, *jñāna*, and *bhakti* (action, understanding, and love) is complete. Therefore, one might choose the word *tūṣnīm*, quietude, silence, calm, for the fourth dimension in order to round out the *quaternitas.* Other traditions have chosen, for example, *sigê*, *silentium*, *sosiego*, *Abgeschiedenheit.* This kind of quietude does not refer to a quietude of thought, which would be *yoga*; not to a quietude of action, which would not be human; not to a quietude of the heart, which could be fatal. We are here dealing with transcendence in immanence.

Instead, this silence is something the old Chinese called *wu wei*; Chuang-tzu describes it as an unintentionality that is the necessary prerequisite for every authentic action: "The not-acting is the law of the sage" (XIII.3). The *Tao-te Ching* says, "The sage is effective without acting, teaches without talking" (2), mainly because this not-doing is also a part of Man. Christian mariologists would call it "the fullness of grace"—as Mary heard from the angel (Lk 1:28). This way, the elements of nature, culture, and grace are in full harmony and union. There is nothing artificial; nor is it mere passivity, not quietism, because it is part of Man's dignity of being commissioned to bring the universe to perfection. Perhaps one could call it the cosmic rhythm that enters and penetrates us and is transformed by us at the same time that we adapt to it. The rhythm of being is not predetermined; harmony is creative and, at the same time, has to be created.

The Mystical: If the first center constitutes the area of the moral, the second the psychological, and the third the ontic, we have to speak here of the mysticism. But one must be careful with the word "mystical," because there is danger of turning it, first, into "mist" (fog) and then into "schism" (split). The highest and most noble things in this world are precisely those that can more easily be corrupted. True mysticism, however, is part of this harmonious not-knowing, of this inner peace, of this unquenchable joy that so easily turns into cynicism, indifference, inhumanness.

What could the word "mystical" mean? One might employ here the analogy of the "third eye." Since Plato, the Greek tradition says that the reality can be known by means of the empirical, through the five senses of seeing, touching, tasting, smelling, hearing. The *aisthesis*, the perception through the senses, is a human feature and is indispensable for all spiritual practices. If it is overlooked, it will have negative consequences. Sensuousness is not only essentially human; it is also an essential ingredient of reality. In sensuousness, in the aesthetic, beauty resides. *Kosmos* means both jewel and world. The Greek Orthodox tradition of Christianity, which is close to pre-Christian philosophy, says that the first attribute of God is beauty.

If one loses the ability to perceive through one's senses, one is lost. But one has to penetrate sensuousness—not simply supplement it—by the intellect, by the *nous*, by the rational, by reasoning, by our intellectual consciousness. Thanks to this, we will be able to develop our sensuousness, our will, and our reasoning. Man is a sensuous but also a rational being. We must not neglect the intellectual dimension of the person: Reason has its rights, and it would be suicidal to contest them.

Nevertheless, it appears that in some cultures the image of Man and the concept of reality have been reduced to these two dimensions. This is the great danger inherent in all exclusively technocratic civilizations. People of all times, even those of cultures thinking highly dualistically, remind us that there is still a third eye that opens up to us a third facet of reality. Along with Plato, one might call the first dimension *ta aisthêta*, the second *ta noêta*, and the third *ta mystika*: the mystical.

We have a third "organ" that helps us get in touch with reality just as the other sense organs do. The senses correspond to the material and space-time dimensions of reality. The intellect, the *nous*, corresponds to the intellectual dimension of reality, which is just as real as the physical. When we say, for example, "justice" and "truth," we mean a physical force, too, a reality-creating force. But there is still this third, additional sense indicative of an otherwise invisible dimension of reality. That is the mystical, the unpronounceable, which cannot be named, so that, when still needing a word for it, one might call it "nothing" or "the nothing."

The relationship of this third dimension to the second is analogous to the relationship between the third and the first. The person cannot have purely sense-related perception; it is always somehow related to the intellect or to consciousness. In a similar fashion, one cannot have intellectual perception without the presence of the third dimension. This third dimension comes into play in such a way that it allows us to "sense" intellectual insight; to "see" that there "is more" than the intellect can convey to us. By means of the intellect the person fathoms that reality, in any of its forms, is of infinite depth. Likewise, one fathoms that reality might also be different. Both infinity and freedom are basic human experiences that presuppose reason yet transcend reason at the same time.

Our three "organs," windows, sense potentials for reality, are inseparably connected. When I am thinking, my brain is involved. When I am sensing, my intellectual awareness is also involved. Similarly, this third "organ" is always present. Reality cannot be reduced to two dimensions. The role of the third "organ" is to deepen the two others. Its nature is to penetrate them in such a way that the third organ itself remains invisible, unpronounceable, undetected. Whenever people attempted to turn mysticism into a special field, severed from other dimensions of life, mysticism earned a bad reputation, and justly so.

The assumption of being able to speak of this third dimension without including the other two is contradictory. As soon as one imagines that this third eye, this revelation of the highest, this special place of the heart could remain single and independent from the senses and intellect, the corruption so often connected with the word "religion" begins. Only by opening up to the sense-related, the material, and the intellectual dimensions of reality do we experience that these alone are not sufficient. Thereby, either slowly or quickly, we realize the third dimension. But at the same time we cannot dispute the fact that especially those peoples of the world who call themselves "developed" are in general spiritually underdeveloped and suffering from a cultural atrophy of their third organ.

Teresa of Avila was cured of this pride in the mystical life during her first years in the convent. A new mother superior was to be elected—in those days there still existed a kind of democracy in the convents. In her state of spiritual rapture, Teresa heard a supernatural voice, which assured her that it was the will of God for her to become mother superior. So she was smiling to herself about all the others, the little politicians, who even in convents were busy working and staging an "election campaign" of sorts. Then the election came, and Teresa did not win. Crestfallen, she walked up to the crucifix and complained with him, given the good relationships they maintained. Teresa was smart enough not to expect a special kind of revelation. Nevertheless, she could hear all of a sudden very clearly the answer amid her tears: "Well, Teresa, *I* certainly wanted you to become mother superior, but the nuns did not!" God did want one thing, but if the nuns did not.... Mysticism gives no privileges.

The mystical without the intellectual is a ghost. The mystical without the sensuous is nonhuman. But likewise, the sensuous without the intellectual and the mystical is crippled and banal. Thoughts by themselves, without that atmosphere that makes them understandable, are simply arms of intellectual violence. The three are essentially one.

But there is one difference: the sensuous can be cultivated by discipline and asceticism. The intellectual can also be cultivated, though this discipline is much more refined. But the will cannot be commanded: the will's act of wanting does not depend on the will itself. Therefore, freedom is more than a matter of the will. One has to cultivate the will in a very gentle manner. The intellect cannot be forced, but it can be trained. The mystical is given for free; it has no price; it is within everyone's reach. Our modern world, however, is not accustomed to gratuitousness: everything has a price. The mystical is not for sale; it is a gift—but we must have our arms open and our hearts unburdened to receive it.

In the case of the mystical, things are even more subtle: again, one has to cultivate it, but in contrast to the sensuous and the intellectual, one cannot either force it or train it; it is not a matter of training nor of the will. It is primarily the craving for *nirvāṇa* that is the great obstacle to reaching *nirvāṇa*. The will for holiness leads to hypocrisy or pride. The desire to become a spiritual personality or a spiritual person in order to have a little more peace, a little less sorrow, a better mood, or whatever, is exactly what leads to frustration. This urge is ultimately responsible for the epidemic of depression in our modern era. Depression simply means that there exists some pressure against another "pressure." Depression is an illness of the will: I aim high, and then something interferes by opposing my will. Voluntarism is a cultural illness.

The mystical cannot be trained or cultivated; however, it can be loved—a simple giving of oneself. One cannot love on command. Love is creative, real, without a why (*sunder Warumbe* [Eckhart]). Only purity of the heart puts us in a position where this third dimension of the quiet, of the invisible, complements the other two. The "commandment of love" is a contradiction. Christianity, or *Christiania*, I would say (that is, the Christic experience), cannot be a religion of the commandments. Aristotle had already realized it, when he said that God, as the Supreme Good, moves all beings ōs *erōmenon*, "insofar as He is loved" by them.

It means that the "will as primordial being" does not have the final say. The way to spirituality is ultimately not a way. Still, we cannot be satisfied by mere faith, simply because we have to use also the intellect and the senses. We cannot rely on the fact that everything is grace, a divine gift that we simply and passively receive. Though everything is grace, the process will have to start over and over again—and never without us. As long as we live, we will never see the end of this process. The new innocence is an innocence that perpetually renews itself.

Kosmos: At this point, we must explain what we mean by freedom. Freedom has very little to do with freedom of choice. Choosing only means deciding—dividing, that is, between "A" and "B"—thus making a cut through reality. Freedom cannot result in separation. Solomon knew that when pronouncing his famous verdict. There are no half children; the mother will not allow the child to be torn in half, even if the judge may not place it in her custody (1 Kg 3:16–28). To choose means to be concerned, and do violence to what is discarded, but that is not freedom, though it may well be a need.

How do I experience being free? What do I experience in being free? First, I have to experience that I am free from fear; that is the prerequisite: to be free from the fear of life, of death, of success, of failure, of love, of disdain, of suffering, of the truth, of myself. Fear has to disappear in all its stages. It is absent not because there are no longer any frightening objects around—there is also fear of the nothing—but because the subject that should have fear is no longer present. It is not true that there are no longer any ghosts, any threatening power figures, or whatever; instead, my ego, which is supposed to hold fear, no longer exists.

It is understandable that complete absence of fear is not possible as long as the person is not free, as long as there is still the ego. As long as the ego exists, fear may even be beneficial. It is what is called "prudence" or "wisdom of this world" (see 1 Co 1:19–20), then. Without a certain amount of fear, human life would turn into chaos. Hence, we do not mean that every kind of fear is despicable; we are simply saying that every kind of fear stifles freedom.

Second, when I am free of fear and, in this sense, free of inhibitions, then I am detached from all kinds of limitations. I do not mean by that the borderlines or parameters that are part of my personal nature. These simply determine me, thereby enabling me to embrace reality. (This may be said against every kind of individualism that misunderstands freedom as limitlessness.) Instead, freedom is a much deeper dimension of existence, a radical indeterminateness at the basis of everything I do and am. Freedom in this sense is not a question of my parents' and grandparents' chromosomes, of culture and language, of social relationships and other circumstances. Instead, freedom is where I am experiencing, metaphysically speaking, nothingness (which is an experience without content, an experience of nothing in particular). This experience cannot be described; one can only radiate it. Without this experience, life has not yet been lived. To live it does not depend on highway directions, business orders, or some other externals. Instead, it is dependent on *nothing*. As a result of such an experience, I will certainly not commit suicide; that would be proof of my imprisonment, of my attachment to externals of which I want to rid myself. Freedom does not need to be set free.

Freedom is the experience of infinity, of the fact that no one else has ever been what I am. At its beginning is the experience of my uniqueness (I start to realize it). There is something inside me that makes *me* capable of overcoming what in me, sometimes, craves for things, goods, and people; wants to enjoy, to possess. It is something inside me that I try covering up with all this greed. And this something is unique, untransferable; speaking in a paradox, it has been *entrusted to me.* It is I who am that central point of reality that is determined by nothing else: a divine core. The experience of this freedom lies in the fact that something is entrusted to me that is irreplaceable, and this something is my true I. The whole universe exists, but I exist, too, with the constant possibility of not being.

What we are talking about could be best illustrated by the now-unpopular belief in hell. The seriousness of the belief in hell is the experience, on the one hand, that there is something inside me which wants to grow and be but which, on the other, can be lost in a sort of abortion process. I am not a spare part that can be exchanged. If I do not enact what I am, no one else will. Here no one else can help me out, no one can replace me, since it is not a matter of doing a certain job, of having a certain function. It is a matter of being, not having. The point is that something within me is ultimate and cannot be reversed. Job speaks of the path that cannot be retraced (Jb 16:22). Such is the experience of freedom, the supreme human dignity.

Thomas Aquinas says, "Sinners, as far as they are sinners, do not exist" (*Sum. theol.* I, q.20, a.2, ad 4). "*Inquantum vero peccatores sunt, non sunt, sed ab esse deficiunt.*" Something that could have been born into eternal life has not been born. There will be forever a hole in its place. There will not be any I ever. I have lost my reality: that is hell. Thus, we understand the Christian tradition in those verses by Dante: "Justice moved my high Maker: The divine power made me, the highest wisdom, and the primal love" (*Inferno* III.4–6):

> *Giustizia mosse il mio alto fattore:*
> *fecemi la divina potestate,*
> *la somma sapïenza e 'l primo amore.*

Hell is the work of divine justice. It means I am unique, irreplaceable, not a replica of some other model. It also means that I should not imitate anyone else. That does not imply that I am particularly important or will enjoy extended longevity in the cosmos, which may be suggested by the idea of hell. I once comforted an anguished lady concerning her fear of hell and told her that this eternity, which is hell, will not even last a minute. Eternity has no duration.

The way to find spirituality is not a way, as Abhinavagupta (*upayā*n*upaya*) and also John of the Cross state: "At the peak of the mountain there is no path.... At the peak of the mountain: nothing." It is a paradox: an introduction to true spirituality is to experience a reality that has not been created yet, which is not dependent on a ready-made image of Man or an a priori worldview. Rather, it is the experience of a reality just now newly created by us. Since there is no way or path, we do not have the fear of losing it, of becoming lost. The point is to awaken in us a genuine vitality, which I have tried to suggest above. Only when arriving at this in-depth level where we are truly open, where central reality opens up to us in form of the experience of grace or of one's inner condition, where the I is nothing more than a receiver; only then will we, paradoxically, experience the freedom that sets us free from every kind of fear and the feeling of self-sufficiency. Then we will experience the uniqueness of our lives, which mirrors, each individually, the entire universe.

This is the mystery of Man, a *quaternitas* that is, on the one hand, reflected in each one of us, and which, on the other hand, allows us by means of its mirror effect to remain ourselves.

The following table illustrates what has been said:

I	II	III	IV
earth	water	fire	air
sôma	*psychê*	*polis*	*kosmos*
śarīra	*aham*	*ātman*	*brahman*
karman	*jñāna*	*bhakti*	*tūṣṇīm*
bonum	*verum*	*ens*	*nihil*
waking	dreaming	sleeping	being silent
the Moral	the Psychological	the Ontic	The Mystica

Glossary

abba (Aramaic): Father; as Jesus called God.

Abgeschiedenheit (German): "detachment"; an expression coined by Eckhart in his treatise *On Detachment*; represents one of the central points of his mystical conception, implying both an active and a passive attitude.

abhavyatva (Sanskrit): the inability to attain liberation; used in Buddhism and Jainism.

abhimāna (Sanskrit): vanity, presumption, deceit, attachment.

Abhinavagupta (*Abhinavaguptācārya*) (Sanskrit): a tenth-century Śivaite mystic.

*Abhiṣiktā*nanda (Sanskrit): monastic name of Henri Le Saux (1910–1973), a Hindu-Christian monk who sought to synthesize both traditions in his work and his life.

ācārya (Sanskrit): teacher of *Veda*, spiritual guide who imparts initiation. The term is anterior to *guru*.

acosmism: doctrine that denies reality and/or the value and ultimate sense of the world (*cosmos*).

actio (Latin): activity, action.

adam (Hebrew): man, the first man, as prototype, according to the Bible. Only later it became a man's name. Etymologically related to "red" and "earth," "ground."

ad-extra (Latin): outward.

ad-intra (Latin): inward.

advaita (Sanskrit): nondualism (*a-dvaita*). Spiritual intuition that sees ultimate reality as neither monistic nor dualistic. The recognition that the merely quantitative problem of the one and the many in dialectical reasoning does not apply to the realm of ultimate reality. The latter, in fact, possesses polarities that cannot be divided into multiple separate units; not to be confused with *monism*.

advaitin (Sanskrit): followers of *advaita*, who profess *ātman-brahman* nonduality.

agapē (Greek): love.

Agni (Sanskrit): the sacrificial fire and the Divine Fire, one of the most important

Gods or divine manifestations, the mediator or priest for Men and Gods.

agnihotra (Sanskrit): the daily fire sacrifice performed morning and evening in all homes of the high castes, which consists of an oblation of milk sprinkled on the fire.

agnostic: a recently coined philosophical position that claims that there is no such thing as certain knowledge, especially with regard to God and ultimate questions.

agōn (Greek): fight, struggle, battle; the agonic sense of life.

agora (Greek): public square where the townsfolk gathered and held meetings in ancient Greece.

aham (Sanskrit): "I"; first person pronoun. *Aham* as ontological principle of existence is generally distinguished from *ahaṃkāra* as a psychological principle.

aham asmi (Sanskrit): "I am"; a formula of spiritual creation or *mahāvākya*, deriving from the *Bṛhadāraṇyaka-upaniṣad*.

ahaṃkāra (Sanskrit): the sense of the ego.

ahiṃsā (Sanskrit): "nonviolence," respect for life, not killing and not wounding, not desiring to carry out violence against reality. A moral and philosophical principle based on ultimate universal harmony. The root *hiṃs* from *han*means "to wound," "to kill." This is not exactly a Vedic notion; it appears only a few times in the *Upaniṣad*; it was developed in Jainism and Buddhism.

Ahriman (Persian): principle of darkness and evil, according to Mazdaism; a noun deriving from Angra Mainyu (evil spirit), used by Zoroaster.

aiōn (Greek): cosmic time, eternity; also a period of life.

aisthēsis (Greek): perception, sensitivity, sense, knowledge.

ākāśa (Sanskrit): air, sky, space, ether, the fifth of the primordial elements (*mahābhūtāni*), which is the element of sound. It is all-pervading and infinite, and therefore often identified with Brahman.

aliud (Latin): the other, neutral. *alius* (Latin): the other (other I). *amerimnia* (Greek): absence of anxiety.

'am ha'aretz (Aramaic): "people of the earth," lower classes, the disinherited, the poor, the untouchable, the ignorant, those who do not know the *Torah*.

amplexus (Latin): embrace.

amṛta (Sanskrit): immortal, imperishable (*a-mṛta*); refers mainly to the Gods; noun, neutral: immortality, absence of death, and nectar of immortality, *soma*, the sacred drink (ambrosia).

anakephalaiōsis (Greek): summary of all things (in Christ); used by St. Paul.

ānanda (Sanskrit): joy, bliss (cf. *sukha*), the delights of love, and especially the highest spiritual bliss; *sat*, *cit*, and *ānanda* represent three possible attempts at defining *brahman* or absolute reality.

anātman (Sanskrit): absence of *ātman*, of the substantiality of an individual ontological Self.

anātmavāda, *nairātmyavāda* (Sanskrit): mainly Buddhist doctrine of the insubstantiality of the *ātman* or Self.

anātmavādin (Sanskrit): follower of the doctrine of *anātman*.

anima mundi (Latin): soul of the world; as an analogy of man, the earth is conceived as the body of expression of a planetary Consciousness or Soul.

animus-anima (Latin): masculine (in the woman) and feminine (in the man) image or characteristic, as psychologically thematized by C. G. Jung.

anitya (Sanskrit): impermanence.

antarikṣa (Sanskrit): that which is "between," the space of air between the sky and the earth, atmosphere, intermediate space (cf. *dyu* and *pṛthivī* as two other terms for *triloka*).

anthrōpos (Greek): man, in a general sense.

anubhava (Sanskrit): direct experience, knowledge deriving from immediate spiritual intuition.

apatheia (Greek): impassibility, indifference, calm, imperturbability (complete liberation from all emotional stress produced by the events of life).

apokatastasis pantōn (Greek): restoration of all things at the end of the world, or of a period of time, according to Christian Scripture.

aporia (Greek): difficulty that prevents one from going beyond reason, dead end.

arhat (Sanskrit): ascetic, saint, the highest and most noble figure of Theravada Buddhism.

asat (Sanskrit): nonbeing; denial of being; as opposed to *sat*, being.

asparśayoga (Sanskrit): yoga without intermediary, without mental content, stopping of the mind, "nonmind."

āśrama (Sanskrit): state of life, the four traditional periods in the life of the "twiceborn": student (*brahmacārin*), head of family (*gṛhastha*), inhabitant of the forest (*vānaprastha*), and itinerant ascetic (*saṃnyāsin*). Also the hermitage of a monk and, therefore, the title of an ascetic. Also indicates a spiritual community, generally under the direction of a *guru* or spiritual teacher. Also refers to a stage in human life.

asura (Sanskrit): spiritual, incorporeal, divine. In *Ṛg-veda* the highest spirit, God (from *asu*, life, spiritual life). Varuṇa is considered an *asura*. Later the meaning changes completely and *asura* (now analyzed as *a-sura*, or "nonGod") takes on the meaning of demon or evil spirit constantly opposed to the *deva* (*Brāhmaṇa*).

atha (Sanskrit): here, now, furthermore; particle translated according to context.

ātman (Sanskrit): principle of life, breath, the body, the Self (from the root *an*, to breathe). Refers to the whole, undivided person and also to the innermost center of man, his incorruptible nucleus, which in the *Upaniṣad* is shown to be identical to Brahman. The Self or inner essence of the universe and man. Ontological center in Hinduism, which is negated in Buddhism.

ātmānātma-vastuviveka (Sanskrit): discernment between real and unreal.

ātmavāda (Sanskrit): doctrine that accepts the existence of the Self, the *ātman,* as the essential, incorruptible center of being.

ātmavādin (Sanskrit): follower of the *ātman* doctrine.

ātmavid (Sanskrit): he who knows the Self (*ātman*), who has fulfilled his innermost being.

atyāśrama (Sanskrit): the state beyond the four traditional states of a man's spiritual being (cf. *āśrama*), which transcends them in complete spiritual freedom.

Aum (Sanskrit): cf. Oṃ.

autarkeia (Greek): self-sufficient.

avatāra (Sanskrit): "descent" of the divine (from *ava-tṛ*, descend), the "incarnations" of Viṣṇu in various animal and human forms. Traditionally, there are ten *avatāra*: *matsya* (the fish), *kūrma* (the tortoise), *varāha* (the wild boar), *narasiṃha* (the lion-man), *vāmana* (the dwarf), Paraśurāma (Rāma with the axe), Rāma, Kṛṣṇa, Buddha, and Kalkin at the end of time. In general, any personal manifestation of the Divinity, descended into this world in human form; descent as antonomasia.

avidyā (Sanskrit): ignorance, nescience, absence of true and liberating knowledge, often identified with *māyā* and a cause of illusion and delusion.

āyus (Sanskrit): vital force, vitality, life, temporal existence, the length of life granted to man. Cf. Greek *aiōn*, aeons.

bandhu (Sanskrit): bond, connection, relation, friendship, friend.

Bhagavad-gītā (Sanskrit): The "Song of the Glorious Lord," the "Song of the Sublime One"; a famous ancient Indian didactic poem included in the *Mahābhārata* (often called the "New Testament of Hinduism"), the most well-known sacred book in India.

bhakti (Sanskrit): devotion, submission, love for God, personal relationship with God, devotional mysticism. One of the paths of salvation through union with the divinity.

bhakti-mārga (Sanskrit): the path of love and devotion, one of the three classical spiritual paths (cf. *karma-mārga*, *jñāna-mārga*).

bhārata-nāṭyam (Sanskrit): divine dance.

bhāṣya (Sanskrit): commentary.

bhikṣu (Sanskrit): he who begs for food and leaves home, the monk.

bios (Greek): existence, biological life, length of life.

bodhisattva (Sanskrit): the enlightened one. In particular, in Mahāyāna Buddhism, he who, having attained liberation on earth, makes a vow to help all other beings attain liberation before they enter *nirvāṇa*.

Brahmā (Sanskrit): the creator God (cf. the "Trinity," later Brahmā, Viṣṇu, Śiva).

It is not important in the *Veda* but in later periods it inherits many of the characteristics of Prajāpati.

brahmacārin (Sanskrit): student of Brahman, i.e. of *Veda*; novice who lives a life of chastity and purity. He who lives in the first of the four *āśrama*.

brahmacarya (Sanskrit): life of a student of Brahman, also of the chastity and education of Brahman. The first of the four *āśrama* (cf. *gṛhastha*, *vānaprastha*, *saṃnyāsa*).

brahman (Sanskrit): prayer, sacrifice, the inherent power in sacrifice; the Absolute, the ultimate reason underlying all things; in the *Upaniṣad* it is identified with the immanent Self (*ātman*). Also, one of the four priests who perform the sacrifice or the clergy in general.

Brahma-sūtra (Sanskrit): traditional Hindu text; one of the bases of the Vedānta. *Bṛhadāraṇyaka-upaniṣad* (Sanskrit): one of the most ancient and important *Upaniṣad*. *buddhakāya* (Sanskrit): lit. "body of Buddha," universal solidarity, the behavior of the Buddha.

buddhi (Sanskrit): the highest faculty of the intellect, also comprehension, thought, meditation.

cakra (Sanskrit): center of energy in the subtle body of man (related, perhaps, to each plexus); lit. "wheel."

capax Dei (Latin): capacity of the soul to perceive and receive God.

cela (Sanskrit): disciple.

cenobitic: relating to the monastery (*cenobium*).

Chāndogya-upaniṣad (Sanskrit): one of the most ancient of the *Upaniṣad*, which deals with the mystic value of sound, song and the identity of *ātman-brahman*.

chara (Greek): grace, joy, cheerfulness.

circulus vitiosus (Latin): "vicious circle," bad reasoning, which states what is still to be proven.

circumincessio (Latin): compenetration of the three Persons of the Trinity. Corresponds to the Greek *perichōresis*.

cit (Sanskrit): root noun (from the root *cit-*, to perceive, to comprehend, etc.), meaning "consciousness, intelligence." One of the three "characteristics" of Brahman (cf. *sat*, *ānanda*).

civitas Dei and *civitas terrena* (Latin): "city of God" and "earthly city"; theory formulated by Augustine (354–430), according to which there are two citizenships or "states."

cogito (ergo) sum (Latin): "I think (therefore) I am." *coincidentia oppositorum* (Latin): coincidence of the opposites. *colloquium salutis* (Latin): dialogue of salvation.

complexio omnium (Latin): integration of all things.

comprehensor (Latin): one who truly comprehends; one who already possesses the beatific vision, the fulfilled man.

compunctio cordis (Latin): repentance, heartfelt sorrow, the essential attitude of monastic spirituality.

consecratio mundi (Latin): consecration or sanctification of the world; the secular is sacralized, contemplated in its sacred dimension.

contemptus saeculi (Latin): contempt for all that is temporal and worldly.

conversatio (Latin): dialogue, conversation between the members of a community; the human relationship, especially political, based on words.

conversio (Latin): change or transformation, generally religious; one of the translations of *metanoia*.

conversio morum (Latin): change in customs, way of living.

cosmotheandric: the nonseparation between World, God, and Man.

creatio continua (Latin): "continuous creation"; doctrine of the continuous creative force of God in the sense of the preservation of the universe and universal government.

Christianity: religiosity based on the experience of Christ.

darśana (Sanskrit): from the root *dṛś*, to see, to observe; hence vision, sight; philosophy, *Weltanschauung*. In a religious context it means the vision of a saint or God, hence also meeting, audience, visit.

Dasein (German): being here; real, existing man; a term used mainly by M. Heidegger; human existence.

deva (Sanskrit): connected with *div*, sky, light (Latin *divus*, *deus*), celestial, divine. Also God, divinity, heavenly being, cosmic power. The *deva* are not on the same level as the one God (sometimes called also *deva*, in the singular, or *īśvara*) or the absolute (Brahman). They are powers that have different functions in the cosmos. Subsequently, the human sensory faculties are also called *deva* in the *Upaniṣad*.

Dhammapāda (Pāli): collection of 426 Buddhist verses of the Pāli canon.

dharma (Sanskrit): cosmic order, justice, duty, religious law, religious and social observances transmitted by tradition; "religion" as a collection of practices and laws. That which holds the world together. One of the four "human purposes" (cf. *puruṣāsartha*).

dharmakāya (Sanskrit): mystical body of *dharma* in Mahāyāna Buddhism.

dhyāna (Sanskrit): meditation, contemplation. *diachronic*: that which extends through time. *diakonia tou logou* (Greek): ministry of the word. *diatopic:* that which extends through space.

digambara (Sanskrit): ascetic of the Jain religion who walks naked as a symbol of detachment and purity.

dīkṣā (Sanskrit): initiation; the preliminary rites; consecration of one who performs the sacrifice, such as that celebrated, for example, at the beginning of the *soma* and leads to a "new birth." Out of the context of sacrifice *dīkṣā* is the initiation of the disciple by the *guru* into *saṃnyāsa*, the life of the errant monk.

dipsychos (Greek): one who has a double soul.

discretio (Latin): discernment, discretion, prudence.

docta ignorantia: classic term used by Nicolaus Cusanus to denote supreme innocence, ignorance of one's own knowledge.

doxa (Greek): glory.

dualism: vision of a basic split within the being into two principles, each irreducible to the other, particularly spirit and matter, soul and body.

duḥkha (Sanskrit): disquieted, uneasy, distress, pain, suffering, anguish (lit. "having a poor axle hole," i.e., that which does not turn smoothly), a basic concept in Buddhism and Hinduism. Opposite of *sukha*.

Dulosigkeit (German): absence of all reference to any "you."

dvandva (Sanskrit): pair of opposites, e.g., cold and heat, pleasure and pain.

dvija (Sanskrit): one who is born a second time into the life of the spirit, the initiated.

dynamis (Greek): power, energy, capacity.

ecclesia (Latin): church, assembly, reunion. *eidetic*: relating to knowledge; from *eidos*, idea. *eidos* (Greek): idea, form, appearance.

ekāgratā (Sanskrit): concentration in one spot; hence simplicity and purity.

ekam (Sanskrit): one; generally the primordial oneness, the origin of all, later identified with Brahman.

enstasis (Greek): entering fully into one's self: through concentration and meditation one attains a state of absolute identification (absorption) with the contemplated object, with the Self.

epektasis (Greek): dilatation, expansion, extension; man's trust in his divine destiny, according to St. Gregory of Nyssa. Hope.

epistēmē (Greek): science.

erōs (Latin): love.

eschatology: from the Greek *eschaton*, which refers to the ultimate, both in relation to time (the last things that will happen, the end of this life), and in ontological importance (the ultimate reality).

exclusivism, *inclusivism*, *pluralism*: terms indicating an attitude toward non-Christian religions, which (a) considers the latter as being excluded from the salvation of Christ, (b) absolutizes the salvation of Christ by granting a place to nonChristian religions, and (c) recognizes that the different visions of the world are mutually irreducible.

esse sequitur operari (Latin): being follows action.

extasis (Greek): ecstasy, "outside of itself."

extra ecclesiam nulla salus (Latin): "outside the church there is no salvation."

fanum (Latin): temple, sanctuary. Cf. *pro-fanum*.

fides quaerens intellectum (Latin): "faith seeking understanding."

fuga mundi (Latin): escape from the world; an attitude indicating a departure from the things of this world to focus on a world beyond that is considered the "true" world.

Gautama (Sanskrit): family name of prince Siddhartha, who became the Buddha.

Gītā (Sanskrit): cf. *Bhagavad-gītā*.

gnōsis (Greek): saving knowledge, liberating wisdom. Cf. *jñāna*, *prajñā*.

gopī (Sanskrit): shepherdess full of love and devotion for Kṛṣṇa; symbol of the soul united with the divine being.

guhā (Sanskrit): cave, grotto, secret place (human heart).

guṇa (Sanskrit): the three qualities or attributes of being : *tamas*, darkness; *rajas*, desire; *sattva*, being.

guru (Sanskrit): cf. *ācārya*; usually refers to one who has attained fulfillment.

hamartia (Greek): sin.

haplotēs (Greek): simplicity, naïveté; *h. kardias*: simplicity of heart.

hara (Jap.): center, place of vital energy in man; area of the belly.

hen (Greek): one, unit.

hermeneutics, *hermeneutic*: "the art of interpretation"; the theory and method of understanding and interpreting writings.

hiraṇyagarbha (Sanskrit): "the golden germ," a cosmological principle in the *Veda*, later identified with the creator (*Brahmā*).

holistic: that which considers reality in its entirety.

homeomorphic: that which performs a similar function.

homeomorphism: theory used in comparative religion to discover functional equivalence in two or more religions.

humanum (Latin): the basic human; that which is specific to all humanity.

hypomonê (Greek): patience, perseverance.

*ihā*mu*trārthaphala-bhoga-virāga* (Sanskrit): renouncement of the reward for good deeds done.

inclusivism: cf. *exclusivism*.

Indra (Sanskrit): the great divine warrior who wins all battles in favor of his worshippers, both against opposing clans (*dasyu* or *dāsa*) and against demons such as Vṛtra and Vala. His virile power is irresistible and is the *soma* that provides him with the energy needed for his mighty exploits. He is the liberator of the compelling forces; he releases the waters and the light. His weapon is the *vajra*, the lightning bolt.

Īś*ā-upaniṣad* (Sanskrit): one of the shortest of the *Upaniṣad*, which deals with the presence of the divine in all things.

Īś*a*, Īś*vara* (Sanskrit): the Lord, from the root īś-, to be lord, to guide, to possess. Although a generic term for Lord, in posterior religious systems it is more often used for Śiva than for Viṣṇu. In the Vedānta it is the manifested, qualified (*saguṇa*) aspect of Bṛahman.

itivuttaka (Pāli): "so I have heard"; traditional form of passing on the teachings of Buddha and the heading of a text in Buddhist writings.

Jainism: post-Vedic ascetic tradition organized by Mahāvīra (fifth to fourth centuries BC), path of purification emphasizing the importance of *ahiṃsā* (nonviolence). Religion slightly anterior to Buddhism.

jīva (Sanskrit): living being (from *jīv-*, to live); the soul in its individuality, as opposed to *ātman*, the universal soul. There are as many *jīva* as individual living beings.

jīvanmukta (Sanskrit): "liberated while alive and embodied," the highest category of the holy or fulfilled person who has reached the destination in this life and, therefore, in the human body; he who has fulfilled his *ātman-braham* ontological identity; he who has reached his own being, becoming totally integrated.

jñāna (Sanskrit): knowledge (from the root *jñā-*, to know), intuition, wisdom; frequently the highest intuitive comprehension, the attaining of *ātman* or *brahman*. *Jñāna* is the result of meditation or revelation. Cf. *jñāna-mārga*.

jñāna-mārga (Sanskrit): the path of knowledge, contemplation, and intuitive vision; one of the three classic paths of spiritual experience, generally considered superior to those of *karman* and *bhakti*, although many *bhakta* regard *jñāna* as merely as form of *bhakti*.

jñānavādin (Sanskrit): person who claims that supreme knowledge (*jñāna*) is in itself sufficient for liberation. Actions barely count.

kaivalya (Sanskrit): isolation, solitude, detachment; one of the spiritual states of supreme freedom.

kalpa (Sanskrit): a period of the world, a cosmic time of variable length.

kāma (Sanskrit): the creative power of desire, personified as the God of love; one of the *puruṣārtha*.

kāraṇa (Sanskrit): cause.

karma, *karman* (Sanskrit): lit. "act, deed, action"; from the root *kṛ*, to act, to do; originally the sacred action, sacrifice, rite, later also moral act. The result of all actions and deeds according to the law of *karman* that regulates actions and their results in the universe. Later also connected with rebirth, it indicates the link between the actions carried out by a subject and his destiny in the cycle of deaths and rebirths.

karmakāṇḍin (Sanskrit): refers to those who emphasize the importance of the action, in occasions of ritual, for salvation/liberation.

karma-mārga (Sanskrit): the path of action; one of the three classic paths of spirituality (cf. *bhakti*, *jñāna*). In the *Veda* it refers to sacrificial actions viewed as the way to salvation; later includes also moral actions, or all actions that are performed in a spirit of sacrifice.

katachronism: interpretation of a reality or doctrine with categories that are extraneous or posterior.

kāya (Sanskrit): body.

kāyotsarga (Sanskrit): the abandoning of all bodily activity; spiritual exercise in which even the possession of one's body is renounced.

kenōsis (Greek): annihilation, emptying of oneself, overcoming of one's ego. *keśin* (Sanskrit): "long-haired" (*keśa*), he who has long hair, ascetic, monk. *kleśa* (Sanskrit): affliction, impurity of the soul.

koinōnia (Greek): community, communion.*kosmos* (Greek): order, the ordered universe, the wholeness of the world.

Kṛṣṇa (Sanskrit): *avatāra* of Viṣṇu (lit. "the black one") and one of the most popular Gods. He does not appear in the *Veda*, but he is the revealer of the *Bhagavad-gītā*. He is the divine child and the shepherd God of Vṛndāvana, the incarnation of love and the playful God *par excellence*.

kṣetra (Sanskrit): "field," both in a metaphorical and literal sense. Knowledge begins with the distinction between the field and he who knows the field, i.e., between the world (as the object) and the knowing subject.

kunamnama (Sanskrit): rigid, inflexible; the feminine form *kunamnamā* also indicates a feminine divinity.

kurukṣetra (Sanskrit): the battlefield where the war of the *Mahābhārata* was fought and where Kṛṣṇa revealed the *Bhagavad-gītā* to Arjuna.

lama: head of Tibetan Buddhism.

laukika (Sanskrit): natural, worldly, temporal.

leit-ourgia (Greek): activity of the people, liturgy.

līlā (Sanskrit): divine game, the world as the amusement of God. This concept is not Vedic but Purāṇic.

liṅga (Sanskrit): characteristic feature of Śiva; phallus.

lingua universalis (Latin): universal language.

locus theologicus (Latin): the proper and legitimate place of theological activity.

logos (Greek): word, thought, judgment, reason. In the New Testament Christ as the word of God (Jn 1).

loka (Sanskrit): "world," open space, place, kingdom. Cf. *triloka*.

lokasaṃgraha (Sanskrit): the "keeping together, maintaining of the world" by the wise man and the saint through the sacred or liturgical action (concept of *Bhagavad-gītā*).

madhyama (Sanskrit): central position, middle.

madhyamamārga (Sanskrit): the middle path taught by Buddha.

Mahābhārata (Sanskrit): epic poem that tells the legendary story of the Indian people and expounds its prescriptive values.

mahātma (Sanskrit): "great soul." Name of the founder of the Jain religion (fifth to fourth century BC).

mahāvākya (Sanskrit): "great saying." Refers to great expressions of the *Upaniṣad* that express very concisely the content of the experience of the Absolute.

Mahāyāna: "great vehicle." Branch of Buddhism established in India two thousand years ago.

maithuna, *mithuna* (Sanskrit): union, mating, copulation both in a sexual and metaphorical sense.

Maitreyī (Sanskrit): wife of the sage Yājñavalkya. Was considered a "knower of Brahman."

manas (Sanskrit): mind in its broadest sense, heart, intellect, the internal organ that is the seat of thought, comprehension, feeling, imagination, and will. In Upaniṣadic anthropology *manas* is one of the three constituent principles of man (cf. *vāc*, *prāṇa*).

maṇḍala (Sanskrit): lit. "circle." Mystic representation of all reality; a pictorial illustration of the homology between the microcosm (man) and the macrocosm (the universe). Also a book of the *Ṛg-veda* (a "circle" of hymns). The *Ṛg-veda* is made up of ten *maṇḍala*.

mantra (Sanskrit): prayer, sacred formula (from the root *man-*, to think), sacred word, a Vedic text or verse. Usually only the part of the *Veda* consisting of the *Samhitā* is called a *mantra*. As it is a word of power it may also take the meaning of magic formula or spell.

Manu (Sanskrit): the father of humanity, the man par exellence; also the first priest to establish sacrifices.

mārga (Sanskrit): road, path, way.

martys (Greek): martyr; one who gives testimony for his own life, even through death.

maṭha (Sanskrit): monastery.

mauna (Sanskrit): silence, practiced by the silent itinerant monk; cf. *muni*.

māyā (Sanskrit): the mysterious power, wisdom, or ability of the Gods, hence the power of deceit, of illusion. In the Vedānta it is used as a synonym of ignorance and also to indicate the cosmic "illusion" that shrouds the absolute Brahman.

mederi (Latin): to heal, to treat.

metanoia (Greek): transformation, change of mentality or heart, conversion; going beyond (*meta*) the mental or rational (*nous*).

metron (Greek): measure, meter.

mikrokosmos (Greek): the entire reality reflected or concentrated in the individual; "man as *mikrokosmos*" refers to man as compendium of the cosmos.

pars in toto (Latin): the part in the whole.

pars pro toto (Latin): the part that represents the whole.

pati divina (Latin): passive attitude of man toward the "touches" of the divine; synonym of mystic experience.

penthos (Greek): repentance, sadness.

perichōresis (Greek): notion of the early Church Trinitarian doctrine describing the interpenetration of divine persons. Corresponds to the Latin *circumincessio.*

phainomenon (Greek): phenomenon, that which appears, that which shows itself.

phaneros (Greek): bright, from *phanos*, light. *plerōma* (Greek): fullness, the full, complete. *pluralism*: cf. *exclusivism*.

polis (Greek): the city-state of ancient Greece.

politeuma (Greek): belonging to the social body, political unit. Cf. *conversatio*.

polysemic: having several meanings.

Prajāpati (Sanskrit): "Lord of creatures," the primordial God, Father of the Gods and all beings. His position is central in the *Brāhmaṇa*.

prajñā (Sanskrit): understanding and awareness, consciousness, wisdom. Cf. *gnōsis*, *jñāna*.

pramāṇa (Sanskrit): means for attaining valid knowledge.

prāṇa (Sanskrit): vital breath, life, the breath of life, the vital force that holds the body together. In the *Upaniṣad* one of the three constitutive principles of the human being (cf. *vāc*, *manas*). It is made up of five types of breath (*prāṇa*, *apāna*, *vyā*na, *samāna*, *udā*na). The cosmic equivalent of *prāṇa* is *Vāyu*, air, wind.

prasthānatraya (Sanskrit): term referring to the three principle texts of the Vedānta (*Upaniṣad*, *Bhagavad-gītā*, and *Brahma-sūtra*).

pratiṣṭhā (Sanskrit): foundation, support, base.

pratītyasamutpāda (Sanskrit): Buddhist doctrine of the "conditioned genesis" or "dependent origination," which claims that nothing exists for itself but carries within itself the conditions for its own existence, and that everything is mutually conditioned in the cycle of existence.

primum analogatum (Latin): the point of reference for every analogy.

pro-fanum (Latin): pro-fane; outside the temple (*fanum*).

psychê (Greek): soul, psyche, heart, animated being.

pūjā (Sanskrit): worship, reverence, adoration. The concept is more closely related to the *bhakti* cult than the Vedic cult.

purohita (Sanskrit): priest, liturgy.

Puruṣa (Sanskrit): the Person, the spirit, man. Both the primordial man of the cosmic dimension (*Ṛg-veda*) and the "inner man," the spiritual person existing within man (*Upaniṣad*). In the Sāṃkhya it is the spiritual principle of reality (cf. *prakṛti*).

quaternitas perfecta (Latin): the perfect quaternity.

qui/quid pro quo (Latin): substitution of one thing for another; error consisting in the mistaking of one person (*qui*) or thing (*quid*) for another.

rāhib (Arabic): instructor, teacher, monk. *Rāmāyaṇa* (Sanskrit): Indian epic poem. *ratio* (Latin): reason.

res cogitans / res extensa (Latin): thinking thing / extended thing, division of reality, according to Descartes.

res significata (Latin): signified thing.

Ṛg-veda (Sanskrit): the most ancient and important of the *Veda* texts.

ṛṣi (Sanskrit): seer, sage, wise man; the poet-sages to whom the *Veda* were revealed. Regarded as a special class of beings, superior to men and inferior to the Gods. According to one tradition there were seven *ṛṣi*, probably the seven priests with whom Manu performed the first sacrifice and the seven poet judges in the assembly. Their identification with the names of ancient seers and with the stars of the Ursa Major occurred later (*Brāhmaṇa*).

ṛta (Sanskrit): cosmic and sacred order, sacrifice as a universal law, also truth; the ultimate, dynamic, and harmonious structure of reality.

Saccidānanda (Sanskrit): Brahman as Being (*sat*), Consciousness (*cit*), and Bliss (*ānanda*).

sadguru o *satguru* (Sanskrit): eternal teacher, teacher archetype, universal *guru*.

sādhaka (Sanskrit): one who practices a spiritual, yoga discipline.

sādhana (Sanskrit): spiritual practice or discipline.

sādhu (Sanskrit): straight, leading straight to the goal, good, just. A good person, renunciant, monk, or ascetic.

sādhvī (Sanskrit): female ascetics in Hinduism and especially Jainism; feminine form of *sādhu*.

saeculum (Latin): the human age, era, century; also spirit of the day.

saguṇa-brahman (Sanskrit): Brahman with quality, corresponding in the Vedānta to *Īśvara*, the Lord.

śaivasiddhānta (Sanskrit): religion, philosophical/religious school pertaining to Hinduism; dominant Śivaism in Tamil Nadu.

śakti (Sanskrit): energy, potency, divine power, the creative energy of God. The active, dynamic—feminine—aspect of reality or of a God (generally of Śiva). Personified as the goddess Śakti, consort of Śiva with a creative function.

salus (Latin): health, salvation.

śama (Sanskrit): calm, tranquility, method of mental appeasement.

samādhi (Sanskrit): state of deep concentration, compenetration, immersion, perfection (enstasy); the last of the yoga stages; also the tomb of a saint.

saṃgha (Sanskrit): the (monastic) community of those who follow the path of the Buddha.

saṃnyāsa (Sanskrit): renunciation, the fourth stage of life spent as an errant monk (from *samnyas-*, to suppress, to renounce, to abandon).

saṃnyāsin (Sanskrit): renunciant, ascetic; pertaining to the fourth stage or period of life (*āśrama*), to some the superior stage.

sampradāya (Sanskrit): tradition, religious system and community that follows a tradition.

saṃsāra (Sanskrit): the impermanent phenomenic world and the condition of identification with it, the temporal existence, the cycle of births and deaths, of conditioned existences; state of dependence and slavery.

saṃskāra (Sanskrit): "sacrament," rites that sanctify the various important stages and events in human life. Also karmic residues, physical impressions left over from previous lives, which in some way influence the individual existence of a person.

samudaya (Sanskrit): origin.

Śaṅkara (Sanskrit): eighth-century Hindu philosopher and teacher; one of the most famous exponents of nondualist Vedānta.

śānti (Sanskrit): peace, tranquility, quiescence. The closing *mantra* of many prayers and oblations.

śānti-mantra (Sanskrit): introductory invocation or prayer of an *Upaniṣad*, which is generally common to all the *Upaniṣad* of the same *Veda*. Recited at the beginning and usually also the end of an Upaniṣadic reading, although not actually part of the text.

sarvam duḥkham (Sanskrit): "all is suffering," a classic Buddhist statement.

śāstra (Sanskrit): precepts, orders, rules, authoritative teachings; body of traditionally authorised texts.

sat (Sanskrit): essence (present participle of *as-*, to be), existence, reality. Ultimately, only the Brahman is *sat*, as pure Being is the Basis of every existence. In the Vedānta one of the three "qualifications" of the Brahman (cf. *cit*, *ā*nan*da*).

Śatapatha-brāhmaṇa (Sanskrit): "*Brāhmaṇa* of one hundred paths," the most complete and systematic of the *Brāhmaṇa*.

satori (Japanese): experience of enlightenment in *Zen*.

satyāgraha (Sanskrit): active nonviolence of those who live for the truth. *satyasya satyam* (Sanskrit): true truth, true reality, the being of the existent. *schola Domini* (Latin): school of the Lord.

secularity, secular: of this world, being-in-time, being-in-the-world (from Latin *saeculum*).

semper maior (Latin): always greater.

septuaginta (Latin): "the Seventy" (translators); translation of the Hebrew Bible into Greek, carried out in the third to first centuries BC in Alexandria.

simplicitas cordis (Latin): simplicity of heart.

śiṣya (Sanskrit): disciple (cf. *guru*).

Sitz im Leben (German): vital setting, context.

Śiva (Sanskrit): propitious, gracious, pleasant, benevolent. He who is of good omen; in the *Veda* it is Rudra who is known to the *Śvetāśvatara-upaniṣad* as Śiva, one of the most important Gods of Hindu tradition. He is the destroyer of the universe (cf. also *Brahmā*, *Viṣṇu*), and also the great *yogin* and model of ascetics. His consort is Pārvatī or Umā.

Śivaism, *Śivaita* (Sanskrit): one of the two great families of the Hindu religion, whose God is Śiva.

sobrietas (Latin): sobriety, moderation.

sola fides (Latin): "the one faith," the response of Scholasticism to philosophically unsolvable theological questions; the central doctrine of Luther.

soma (Sanskrit): the sacrificial plant from which the juice of the *soma* is extracted through elaborate rituals, hence the sap or drink of immortality (*amṛta* is another name for *soma*); a divinity ("Soma the king"). *Soma* was used ritually for entering a higher state of consciousness. Later it also took on the meaning of "moon."

sōma (Greek): body.

sophia (Greek): wisdom.

sōteria (Greek): salvation, liberation, redemption.

śraddhā (Sanskrit): "faith," the active trust (in Gods or in the rite itself) required in every act of worship; confidence (in the teachings of the *Veda*). In the *Íg-veda* (X.151), *śraddhā* is invoked almost as a divinity.

śrāddha (Sanskrit): rite of homage to deceased relatives; offering to ancestors generally made by the son of the deceased and repeated on certain occasions. Consists in oblations of food to the ancestors and a meal for relatives and priests.

stūpa (Sanskrit): sacred place or sacred mountain in Buddhism.

sui generis (Latin): "of its own kind."

sukha (Sanskrit): happiness, pleasure, joy, bliss.

śūnya, śū*nyatā* (Sanskrit): void, vacuity, nothingness, the structural condition of reality and all things; represents the ultimate reality in Buddhism (cf. *nirvāṇa*).

suṣupti (Sanskrit): deep, dreamless sleep; one of the four states of consciousness, along with wakefulness, dreaming, and the state of conscious enlightenment.

sūtra (Sanskrit): lit. "yarn, thread of a fabric." Short aphorism in a sacred text that generally cannot be understood without a comment (*bhāṣya*). The literature of the *sūtra* is part of the *smṛti* and is conceived to be easily memorized.

Ś*vetaketu* (Sanskrit): son of Gautama; in the *Chāndogya-upaniṣad* a famous disciple of Uddalaka, to whom is imparted the highest teaching on the *ātman* and the *brahman*, which ends with: *tat tvam asi* ("that is you").

Ś*vetāśvatara-upaniṣad* (Sanskrit): one of the principles of the last *Upaniṣad*, frequently cited in the Vedānta, which tends to personify the supreme principle (Brahman) and identify it with the God Śiva or Rudra.

symbolon (Greek): symbol.

syneches (Greek): continuous, uninterrupted, persevering, solid: that which keeps something in cohesion.

Taboric light: the light that illuminated Jesus in the transfiguration; this light may be regarded as the visible character of divinity, the energy or grace by which God allows himself to be known; Man may receive this light.

taṇhā (Pāli): thirst; thirst for existence; origin of all suffering, according to Buddhism. Cf. *tṛṣṇā*.

Tantra (Sanskrit): lit. weave, weaving, loom; religious system not based on the *Veda*, consisting in secret doctrines and practices that give access to hidden powers; accentuates the interrelation between body and soul, matter and spirit; the development of special powers. The Tantric tradition has practically permeated the entire spiritual tradition of Asia. The basic assumption of all Tantric practices is the interrelation between body and spirit, matter and soul, *bhukti* (pleasure) and *mukti* (liberation).

tao (Chinese): "way," a central concept in Chinese philosophy, especially Taoism.

Tao-te Ching (Chinese): "the book of the way and its power," a fundamental work of philosophical Taoism in China, attributed to Laotzi (sixth century BC), historically demonstrable from third century BC.

ta panta mataiotes (Greek): all (is) vanity.

tapas (Sanskrit): lit. heat; hence inner energy, spiritual fervor or ardor, austerity, ascesis, penitence. One of the forms of primordial energy, along with *kāma*.

tat (Sanskrit): demonstrative pronoun: "that." Opposite of *idam* (this), refers to Brahman. When isolated, it refers to the ultimate reality without naming it.

tat tvam asi (Sanskrit): "that is you," an Upaniṣadic expression meaning that *ātman* is ultimately Brahman. One of the four Great Sayings (*mahāvākyāni*) of the *Upaniṣad*, as taught to Śvetaketu.

theandric: "divine-human" (from Greek *theos* and *aner*).

theanthropocosmic: "divine-human-cosmic" (from Greek *theos*, *anthrípos*, and *kosmos*). *techne* (Greek): art, ability, handicraft.

theōreia (Greek): theory; originally in the sense of "contemplation."

ṭīkā (Sanskrit): commentary, generally of the *sūtra*.

tīrtha|kara (Sanskrit): line of great sages/saints in Jainism.

tonsura: preparatory religious rank for receiving the minor orders in Christianity; special haircut as a distinctive mark of the clerical status that distinguishes it from the secular and signifies separation from the world.

triloka (Sanskrit): the "triple world," totality of the universe, consisting in three realms: earth, atmosphere, and sky, or earth, sky, and the nether regions (later called hell); the inhabitants of the three worlds are Gods, men, and demons.

tṛṣṇā (Sanskrit): thirst; cf. *taṇhā*.

tvam (Sanskrit): you (personal pronoun, second-person singular).

tyāga (Sanskrit): renunciation, abandonment of possessions and attachments.

umma (Arabic): the community of believers; church.

Ungrund (German): bottomless, without foundations, abyss.

Upaniṣad (Sanskrit): fundamental sacred teaching in the form of texts constituting the end of the *Veda*; part of the revelation (*śruti*) and basis of posterior Hindu thought.

upekṣā (Sanskrit): equanimity, detachment, benevolence.

utrumque (Latin): the one and the other.

vāc (Sanskrit): word; the sacred, primordial, and creative Word; sound, also discourse, language, the organ of speech, voice. Sometimes only the Ṛg-*veda* and other times all the *Veda* are referred to as *vāc*.

vairāgya (Sanskrit): estrangement, renunciation, indifference; one of the requisites of the spiritual path.

vānaprastha (Sanskrit): inhabitant of the forest, hermit; the third stage of life or *āśrama*, when the head of family withdraws into solitude, with or without his wife, after having fulfilled his earthly duties.

Varuṇa (Sanskrit): one of the main Gods of the *Veda*; Varuṇa is king, commander, and supervisor of the moral conduct of men. He is Lord of *ṛta*, cosmic and moral order. He is often invoked together with Mitra. Due to his close association with water he later became known simply as a God of water, the Lord of the ocean.

vāyu (Sanskrit): air, wind, personified as a God in the *Veda*.

Veda (Sanskrit): lit. knowledge (from the root *vid-*, to know); the sacred knowledge incorporated in the *Veda* as the entire body of "Sacred Scriptures" (although originally they were only passed on orally). Strictly speaking, "*Veda*" refers only to the *Saṃhitā* (*Ṛg-veda*, *Yajur-veda*, *Sāma*-veda, *Atharva-veda*); generally, however, *Brāhmaṇa* and *Upaniṣad* are also included. In the plural it refers to the four *Veda*.

vedanā (Sanskrit): sensation, feeling.

Vedānta (Sanskrit): lit. end of the *Veda*, i.e., the *Upaniṣad* as the climax of Vedic wisdom. In the sense of Uttaramī *mā*ṃsā or Vedāntavāda, a system of Indian philosophy (Advaita-ved*ā*nta, Dvaita-ved*ā*nta, etc.) based on the *Upaniṣad*, which teaches a spiritual interpretation of the *Veda*; one of the last schools of Hindu philosophical thought, of which the most renowned representatives include Śaṅkara, R*ā*m*ā*nuja, and Madhva.

viator (Latin): traveller, novice, aspirant, disciple.

vidyā (Sanskrit): knowledge, wisdom, also branch of knowledge; a section of a text in the *Upaniṣad*.

vihāra (Sanskrit): monastery, generally in Buddhism; Buddhist or Jain temple.

vinaya (Sanskrit): collection of moral rules and practices in Buddhism.

viveka (Sanskrit): discernment, discrimination.

*Vivekacūfā*maṇi (Sanskrit): "jewel/diadem of discernment," an important work of the Advaita-ved*ā*nta, written by Ša|kara, which deals with the distinction between true reality and the phenomenic world.

vrata (Sanskrit): vow, religious observance.

vyāvahārika (Sanskrit): "relating to earthly matters, to mundane life," i.e., the earthly way of seeing, the practical perspective; the relative level.

wu wei (Chinese): "nonaction" in Taoist philosophy.

xeniteia (Greek): the state of being a stranger.

yakṣa (Sanskrit): spiritual, semidivine, supernatural being; beings belonging to a higher level than the physical.

Yama (Sanskrit): the "twin" of Yamī, the first man and the first to pass through death and obtain immortality; hence the predecessor of men on the path of death and he who commands in the realm of the dead. Later became the personification of Death and the Lord of the nether regions.

Yamī (Sanskrit): the sister of Yama, with whom she forms the first couple of humans on the earth. Although her brother attempts to commit incest with her, she (according to some texts) does not yield.

yang (Chinese): the solar, celestial, masculine aspect in the yin-yang polarity.

yin (Chinese): the lunar, earthly, feminine aspect; complement of *yang*.

yoga (Sanskrit): from the root *yuj-*, to yoke, to join, to unite, to prepare, to fix, to concentrate; union; method of mental, physical, and spiritual union; concentration and contemplation, which also uses bodily posture (*āsana*), breathing control (*prāṇāyāma*) and spiritual techniques. Yoga appears to be an extremely ancient Indian practice that was developed into a system by Patañjali (*Yoga-sūtra*) and made to correspond to the philosophical system Sāṃkhya. Yoga as a method has become a fundamental factor in practically all religions of Indian origin.

yogin (Sanskrit): the ascetic, one who practices self-control, a follower of the path of yoga.

zen (Japanese): from the Sanskrit *dhyāna* (deep meditation); school of Buddhism that claims to be the purest and most direct path to enlightenment (*satori*, *nirvāṇa*).

Index of Original Texts in this Volume

"Icons of Mystery." *The Experience of God: Icons of the Mystery* (Fortress Press: Minneapolis 2006). The original text is *Les icons del misteri: la experiència de Deu*, Ed. 62, Barcelona 1998.

"The Christian Spiritual Journey" includes three short texts, *Paschal Joy, The Presence of God, and Mary*, first published separately as *La gioia pasquale* (La Locusta: Vicenza, 1968); *La presenza di Dio* (La Locusta: Vicenza, 1970); and *"La Virgen Maria,"* Preface to J. Guitton, *La Virgin Maria* (Rialp: Madrid, 1952), all then published in one volume by Jaca Book (Milano, 2007). Translated from Italian by Daniella Engel.

"Blessed Simplicity: The Challenge of Being a Monk." *Blessed Simplicity. The Monk as Universal Archetype* (Seabury: New York, 1982).

"Letter to a Young Monk." In *Living Prayer*, Barre, XIX, 4 pp. 11–14.

"The Monk According to Hindū Scriptures." *Le moine selon les écritures saintes de l'hindouisme*, in *Les Moines chrétiens face aux religions d'Asie* (AMC: Bangalore, 1973), 80–91.

"*Parivājaka*: The Tradition of the Monk in India." *At the Source of the Ganges: A Spiritual Pilgrimage* (CENS: Milano, 1994), 155-167. Translation from French by Milena Carrara Pavan of an unpublished work, *Parivrajåka: la tradition du moine aux Indes.*

"Letter to Abhi@iktānanda on Eastern and Western Monasticism." In *Studies in Formative Spirituality*, vol. III, n. 3 (Nov. 1982).

"The Dwelling Place of Wisdom." *Der Weisheit eine Wohnung bereiten* (Kösel: München, 1991); *A Dwelling Place for Wisdom* (Westminster/John Knox: Louisville, 1993), reprinted by Motilal Banarsidass, Delhi 1995. Originally from a conference delivered in the church of St. Ursula, Munich, on March 14, 1990, and *Quaternitas perfecta* (a series of conferences during a spiritual retreat in the Domicilium House, in Weyarn, Upper Bavaria, March 16–18, 1990).

Index of Names

E

F

G

H

I

J

K

L

M

Y

Z

About the Author

An international authority on spirituality, the study of religions, and intercultural dialogue, Raimon Panikkar has made intercultural and dialogical pluralism one of the hallmarks of his research, becoming a master "bridge builder," tireless in the promotion of dialogue between Western culture and the great Oriental Hindū and Buddhist traditions.

Born in 1918 in Barcelona of a Spanish Catholic mother and an Indian Hindū father, he is part of a plurality of traditions: Indian and European, Hindū and Christian, scientific and humanistic.

Panikkar holds degrees in chemistry, philosophy, and theology, and was ordained a Catholic priest in 1946. He has delivered courses and lectures in major European, Indian, and American universities.

A member of the International Institute of Philosophy (Paris), of the permanent Tribunal of the Peoples (Rome), and of the UNESCO Commission for intercultural dialogue, he has also founded various philosophical journals and intercultural study centers. He has held conferences in each of the five continents (including the renowned Gifford Lectures in 1988–1989 on "Trinity and Atheism").

Panikkar has received international recognitions including honorary doctorates from the University of the Balearic Islands in 1997, the University of Tübingen in 2004, Urbino in 2005, and Girona in 2008, as well as prizes ranging from the "Premio Menéndez Pelayo de Humanidades" for his book *El concepto de naturaleza* in Madrid in 1946 to the "Premio Nonino 2001 a un maestro del nostro tempo" in Italy.

Since 1982 he has lived in Tavertet in the Catalonian mountains, where he continues his contemplative experience and cultural activities. There he founded and presides over the intercultural study center Vivarium. Panikkar has published more than fifty books in various languages and hundreds of articles on the philosophy of religion, theology, the philosophy of science, metaphysics, and indology.

From the dialogue between religions to the peaceful cohabitation of peoples; from reflections on the future of the technological society to major work on political and social intelligence; from the recognition that all interreligious dialogue is based on an intrareligious dialogue to the promotion of open knowledge of other religions, of which he is a mediator; from his penetrating analysis of the crisis in spirituality to the practice of meditation and the rediscovery of his monastic identity; from the invitation of *colligite fragmenta* as a path toward the integration of reality to the proposal of a new innocence, Panikkar embodies a personal journey of fulfillment.

Among his most important publications with Orbis are: *velo della realtà* (2000); *L'incontro indispensabile: dialogo delle religioni* (2001); *Pace e interculturalità. Una riflessione filosofica* (2002, 2006); *La realtà cosmoteandrica. Dio-Uomo-Mondo* (2004); *L'esperienza della vita. La mistica* (2005); *La gioia pasquale, La presenza di Dio and Maria* (2007); *Il Cristo sconosciuto dell'induismo* (2008).